Reading in the Postgenomic Age

NEW SUNS:

RACE, GENDER, AND SEXUALITY

IN THE SPECULATIVE

Susana M. Morris and Kinitra D. Brooks, Series Editors

Reading in the Postgenomic Age

Race, Discipline, and Bionarrativity in Contemporary North American Literature

Lesley Larkin

THE OHIO STATE UNIVERSITY PRESS
COLUMBUS

Copyright © 2025 by The Ohio State University.
All rights reserved.

Library of Congress Cataloging-in-Publication Data
Names: Larkin, Lesley, author.
Title: Reading in the postgenomic age : race, discipline, and bionarrativity in contemporary North American literature / Lesley Larkin.
Other titles: New suns: race, gender, and sexuality in the speculative.
Description: Columbus : The Ohio State University Press, [2025] | Series: New suns: race, gender, and sexuality in the speculative | Includes bibliographical references and index. | Summary: "Examines how 'postgenomic literature' written around the turn of the millennium (1991–2016) engages in genomic discourse, with particular attention paid to interdisciplinarity and the rearticulation of racial ideology. Covers US and Canadian writers such as Margaret Atwood, Octavia Butler, Ruth Ozeki, Richard Powers, Rebecca Skloot, Alina Troyano, and Gerald Vizenor"—Provided by publisher.
Identifiers: LCCN 2024056042 | ISBN 9780814215852 (hardback) | ISBN 0814215858 (hardback) | ISBN 9780814284124 (ebook) | ISBN 0814284124 (ebook)
Subjects: LCSH: Mukherjee, Siddhartha. Gene. | Skloot, Rebecca, 1972– Immortal life of Henrietta Lacks. | Powers, Richard, 1957– Generosity. | Vizenor, Gerald Robert, 1934– Heirs of Columbus. | Butler, Octavia E. Fledgling. | Troyano, Alina. Chicas 2000. | Atwood, Margaret, 1939– MaddAddam trilogy. | Race in literature. | Genetic engineering in literature. | Genomics. | Literature—History and criticism.
Classification: LCC PN56.R16 L37 2025 | DDC 813/.54093529—dc23/eng/20250202
LC record available at https://lccn.loc.gov/2024056042

Other identifiers: ISBN 9780814259436 (paperback) | ISBN 081425943X (paperback)

Cover image by Black Kirby
Cover design by Laurence J. Nozik
Text composition by Stuart Rodriguez
Type set in Palatino Linotype

*This book is dedicated to Thomas Barrington Frank,
the true scholar of the family*

CONTENTS

Acknowledgments ix

Introduction   Reading in the Postgenomic Age   1

PART 1 • THE BOOK OF LIFE

Chapter 1   To Split or to Lump: Tracing Textual Metaphors in
            Siddhartha Mukherjee's *The Gene: An Intimate History*   37
Chapter 2   From HeLa Cells to Happiness Genes: Reading and
            Writing Life in Rebecca Skloot's *The Immortal Life of
            Henrietta Lacks* and Richard Powers's *Generosity: An
            Enhancement*   68

PART 2 • VAMPIRE PROJECTS

Chapter 3   Stories in the Blood and Bone: Therapeutic
            Bionarrative Signatures in Gerald Vizenor's *The
            Heirs of Columbus*   101
Chapter 4   Reading the Flesh and Fleshy Reading in Octavia
            Butler's *Fledgling*   132

PART 3 • USABLE FUTURES

Chapter 5	Usable Futures and Trans-Corporeal Reading in Alina Troyano's *Chicas 2000*	165
Chapter 6	The Humanities and the Inhumanities: Rereading Discipline and Species in Margaret Atwood's *MaddAddam* Trilogy	192

Works Cited   223

Index   243

ACKNOWLEDGMENTS

The completion of this book has depended unambiguously on the personal and professional support of numerous individuals and institutions. I am indebted to a host of mentors and would like to thank, in particular, Alys Eve Weinbaum, whose intellectual influence is everywhere in this book and not at all limited to the specific references I've made to her essential work on "the afterlife of reproductive slavery," and Paula M. L. Moya, whose generous guidance and collaboration have had a marked impact on this project and my approach to literary study as a whole. My students at Northern Michigan University have also been a consistent source of intellectual stimulation and have shaped the direction of my research in important and unexpected ways. Moreover, NMU has offered material support for the development of this book through a sabbatical, the Peter White Scholar Award, a Faculty Research Grant, travel funding, and a publishing subvention, as well as index costs covered by the College of Arts and Sciences (thank you, Robert Winn!). In an era of diminishing institutional support for humanities scholars, I am deeply grateful for these opportunities.

I am also grateful to have shared my research in different venues organized by the following associations: the American Literature Association, the Center for ELSI Resources and Analysis (CERA), the Hastings Center, the International Health Humanities Consortium, the Shandong University

School of Translation Studies, the Society for Literature, Science, and the Arts (SLSA), the Modern Language Association (MLA), the Reception Study Society (RSS), the Society for the Study of the Multiethnic Literature of the United States (MELUS), the Stanford Humanities Center Interdisciplinary Working Group in Critical Theory, and the Western Michigan University Medical Humanities program. Each event was an opportunity to learn from brilliant scholars across the disciplines and to solicit feedback that advanced my work. I am particularly grateful for the invitation to participate in "The Gift and Weight of Genomic Knowledge: In Search of the Good Biocitizen," organized by the Hastings Center in 2018, and in "Dialogue between ELSI and Literary Studies," organized by CERA in 2022; both events put me in contact with scholars at the cutting edge of research on the ethical, social, and political implications of genome research. The former also led to an article that has been reproduced, with significant revision and expansion, as chapter 2 of this book: "Reading in the Postgenomic Age: On Contemporary Literature and the Good Bionarrative Citizen," published in a special issue of the *Hastings Center Report* (50.S1 [2020], pp. S37–S43). I am deeply grateful to the editors, Joel Michael Reynolds and Erik Parens, for their generosity and critique. Chapter 2 also draws from an earlier and related piece, "Narrative and Medical Exploitation in *The Immortal Life of Henrietta Lacks*," published in *Reader: Essays in Reader-Oriented Theory, Criticism, and Pedagogy* (68 [2016], pp. 164–88), and I am equally grateful to editors Patricia Donahue and Bianca Falbo for the opportunity to share the earliest stages of this project.

Additionally, I have been fortunate to receive feedback on chapters-in-progress from a series of brilliant colleagues and friends, including Lisa Eckert, Amy Hamilton, Caroline Krzakowski, April Lindala, Lyndsey Lynch, Paula M. L. Moya, Amy Reddinger, and Mark Romanski; the value of their input is almost impossible to express. The manuscript reviewers for The Ohio State University Press also provided detailed comments that made a significant impact on the final product. Reading and responding to a book-length manuscript is a substantial undertaking; I am deeply grateful for the readers' willingness to give freely of their time and expertise. Finally, I'd like to thank acquisitions editor Ana Maria Jimenez-Moreno for her exceptional patience and grace and all the staff at OSU Press for their assistance during the publication process. All this said, any errors or faults in this book are mine and mine alone.

Finally, writing a book over the course of several years demands the patience and help of friends and family. I would like to thank my partner, Mark Romanski, for his steadfast and cheerful support even during long periods spent apart: you are the definition of a good human. To my father, Thomas Frank, and my sisters, Lyndsey Lynch and Whitney Frank: thank you for seeing me through a difficult time in my life that coincided with the early stages of this project; I couldn't have made it here without you. And to my brilliant and singular children, Killian and Alexander: thank you for putting up with late nights and weekends spent working. You've made being a single parent easier than it has any right to be, and I am in awe of you.

INTRODUCTION

Reading in the Postgenomic Age

Ruth Ozeki's novel *All Over Creation* (2003) follows several stories that intersect on an Idaho potato farm: Yumi Fuller is a real estate agent and adjunct English professor who has returned to Idaho, three children in tow, after running away twenty-five years earlier in the wake of an "affair" with her teacher, an abortion, and the accumulated challenges of being a mixed-race girl in an overwhelmingly white community. Yumi's parents, Lloyd and Momoko, are former potato farmers who run a mail-order seed business; Lloyd's health is declining, Momoko is beginning to exhibit the signs of dementia, and their farm has been taken over by Cass and Will Quinn, who plant transgenic potatoes against Lloyd's wishes. "The Seeds," an itinerant group of anti–genetically modified organism (GMO) activists, show up at the farm, hoping that Lloyd, whose seed catalogue includes tirades against genetic engineering, will be their guru. Meanwhile, Elliot Rhodes, a public relations representative for an agricultural corporation and Yumi's former teacher, arrives, bringing with him memories of the trauma that sent Yumi packing in the first place and ratcheting up the multisided conflict over proper potato practices.[1]

---

1. My alliterative phrasing is a nod to the novel's recurring references to "too many P's" (145, 165, 168), which I read as a subtle allusion to genetic manipulation or mutation (in the form of repeated letters in a string of DNA) that also calls up potatoes (of which, under corporate monoculture, there are too many exact copies) and Gregor Mendel's famous pea plants.

1

Although the novel critiques corporate monoculture and the genetic innovations designed to maintain it, Ozeki also insists that ethics on the ground are muddy. In *All Over Creation,* potatoes make strange bedfellows, as anarcho-feminist hippies join forces with conservative Christian farmers and war veterans, and as Lloyd rails passionately against abortion, nativism, and transgenics.

This ideological "promiscuity," to borrow a favored term of Ozeki's, echoes in the linguistic promiscuity that permeates the text. Ozeki's frequent language games, by which words recombine semantically and syntactically, are linked to genetic recombination and mutation. Take, for example, the labels Lloyd affixes to everyday objects for the benefit of his dementia-stricken wife: Lloyd's grandson rearranges the labels, externalizing the severed link between signifier and signified in Momoko's mind (what Yumi calls a "demented logic" [117]) but also exposing linguistic contingency and recalling the "spelling mistakes" that result in genetic mutations. Just after describing the mixed-up cards as "demented," Yumi appears with an armful of unidentifiable squashes—the result of uncontrolled admixture—which Momoko promptly compares to Yumi's children, each of whom has a different father and a different skin tone: "Like them. All mixed up," she says (118). The chaos implied by linguistic and biological diversity is countered by the devastating foreclosure of meaning that monolingualism—like monoculture—ensures. The frequent mispronunciation of Yumi's Japanese name as "Yummy," for example, contributes to the Orientalist objectification that fuels Elliot's sexual predation. Even when Elliot approaches a correct pronunciation, he erodes Yumi's autonomy by inserting himself into her name: "You. Me," he intones (386).

Linguistic ambivalence in the form of misnaming reaches absurdist heights in the case of Melvin, an anti-GMO activist who goes by the letter "Y." Here's what happens when Y introduces himself to a new recruit called Frankie:

> "I'm Y," he offered.
> But Frankie heard "I'm why?" and he couldn't answer that.
> "Y," the guy repeated. "Y's my name."
> Frankie shoved his hands in his pockets. Why's his name what?
> "You know," the guy persisted. "Y. Like the letter. Like the chromosome. What's your name?" (48)

In this updated "Who's on first?" routine, Ozeki implies that identity is semantically unstable—even in the case of the supposedly sex-determining

Y chromosome, to which Melvin appeals as a means of foreclosing ambiguity.[2] When Frankie answers with his own name, the potential for double-meanings recurs, this time in relation to species difference and capitalist hierarchy:

> "Frank Perdue." He heard the words of his name come out of his mouth.
> "Frank Perdue! You mean like the chicken dude?"
> Here we go, Frank thought, gritting his teeth. . . .
> But the creep wasn't laughing. "Way cool. You his kid or something?"
> "No way," Frank said. "My parents are dead. No relation to the chickens." (48)

Y, contrary to his anticorporate politics, is impressed by the idea that Frank might be related to the chicken magnate who shares "the words of his name," phrasing that subtly inserts a distinction between language and identity/meaning. Frank replies with two non sequiturs, the latter of which ("No relation to the chickens") conflates the company's founder with the product his company sells and comically asserts the possibility of transspecies genealogy. Frank's "misreading" of Y's question suggests a textual insertion that alters the meaning of the sentence: instead of "You mean like the chicken dude?" the question Frank *seems* to answer is "You mean like the chicken, dude," as if a comma has been placed between "chicken" and "dude" (conjuring the "commas save lives" t-shirts made for grammar lovers as well as epigenetic notations in the genome). Alternatively, Frank's answer alters the relationship between "chicken" and "dude," suggesting a fusing of species, instead of an economic relationship. In either case, Frank has "heard" something different from what was scripted, revealing instability in the relation between text and speech and within language itself—a revelation that also subtly destabilizes the notion of genetic "text."

In these metatextual moments, *All Over Creation* exhibits a tendency that runs through the archive of what I am calling *postgenomic literature*, texts from the turn of the millennium that take genetics as a prominent theme. Many such works draw attention to the instability of language—the gap between text and meaning—that complicates communication *and* enables semantic recombinations and mutations. This metatextual tendency extends from the textual metaphors that suffuse genomic discourse: the presentation of DNA as a language that is read, edited, and translated and the

---

2. See Richardson on the rise of "sex chromosomes" and the idea that sex is fundamentally a genetic attribute.

understanding of the genome as an instruction manual, a map, or, most grandly, as the "Book of Life."[3] A scene in *All Over Creation*, in which Geek, one of the "Seeds," explains (and critiques) genetic engineering, exemplifies these metaphors:

> Genetic engineering is changing the semantics, the meaning of life itself. We're trying to usurp the plant's choice. To force alien words into the plant's poem, but we got a problem. We barely know the root language. Genetic grammar's a mystery, and our engineers are just one click up on the evolutionary ladder from a roomful of monkeys, typing random sonnets on a bank of typewriters. We've learned a lot about letters—maybe our ability to read and spell words now sits halfway between accident and design—but our syntax is still haphazard. Scrambled. It's a semiotic nightmare. (124–25)

In Geek's colorful but ultimately conventional explication, genetics is a matter of "semantics," "poe[try]," "language," "grammar," "letters," "read[ing]," "spell[ing]," "syntax," and "semiotic[s]." Indeed, these textual metaphors are so legion, in Geek's lexicon and genomic discourse at large, that Frank ironically "mistakes" the subject of Geek's lecture: "You lost me, Geek," he laments. "I was never any good at English" (125).

Many scholars have described how textual metaphors have contributed to perceptions of the genome as an abstract code that directly scripts the expression of traits, thus shoring up a faith in genetic determinism aligned with "mechanistic ideals of language as transparent signification" and at odds with the complicated dynamics of gene-environment interaction and organismic development (Kay 35). The "gene fetishism" (Haraway, *Modest* 141–48) that continues to dominate popular discourse on genetics—the idea that genes are a fundamental biological truth that explains all manner of complex physical and social phenomena—has wide-reaching cultural and political implications, including the reinforcement of race and gender essentialism and the displacement of resources away from social and political solutions for social and political problems.[4] By undermining genomics' textual metaphors, postgenomic literature challenges genetic determinism, in part by revealing language and textuality to be wildly unstable figures for the authority of genes. As historian of science Lily Kay explains, "Since the

---

3. See Kay; Kruger 1–25.

4. Health disparities are a striking illustration of both phenomena: attempts to improve outcomes that focus on race-linked genetic differences risk reifying race and distracting policymakers from the effects of structural racism on health. See Bliss, "Defining" 187; Phelan et al. 183–86.

idea of the Book of Life first came into being as universal and absolute writings, the polysemic aspect of its so-called writing undermines the possibility of its absolute reading" (35).

Furthermore, the matrix of shared metaphor linking literary studies and genomics also draws attention to ethical issues that straddle science and the humanities, biology and books. It is not just metaphors that travel back and forth between these two fields; it is also issues of privacy, appropriation, essentialism, discrimination, and exploitation. Making plain this ethical overlap, many postgenomic literary works challenge the perceived chasm dividing the sciences and the humanities; rather than approaching these disciplines as "opposites," a formulation that tends to dismiss the humanities as a secondary field or overestimate its "humanizing" potential, these texts offer complicated representations of the relation between the sciences and the humanities and, in turn, of narrative and material worlds.

Reading in the Postgenomic Age: Race, Discipline, and Bionarrativity in Contemporary North American Literature explores a variety of North American, English-language literary works within a period that ranges from the early 1990s, when the Human Genome Project (HGP)—and other efforts to sequence a composite human genome—launched, through the first two decades of the twenty-first century, a "postgenomic age" that begins with the conclusion of the HGP and encompasses dramatic developments in genomic technologies and notable contradictions between (and within) popular and scientific understandings of the role of genes in our lives. During this period, a significant number of texts, across multiple genres, have addressed the life sciences and genomics, in particular, as thematic points of interest. Many such works illuminate the ramifications—ethical, cultural, social, political—of genomic research. However, a central contention of this book is that literature's engagement of genomics exceeds this critical function, commenting self-reflexively on the practices and value of literary studies and offering critical perspectives on interdisciplinarity itself. The elements I have identified as key to postgenomic literature include: (1) adoption and destabilization of genomics' textual metaphors, (2) illumination of ethical issues overlapping biology and literature, (3) complex treatment of the relationship between the sciences and the humanities, and (4) a materialist approach to literary studies that acknowledges the mutual embeddedness of story and the natural world.

I've begun my exploration of postgenomic literature with *All Over Creation* because it illustrates so many of these threads, starting with its engagement of genomic discourse's textual metaphors. Playing in semantic seedbeds, Ozeki explicitly adopts such figures only to undermine their connection to gene fetishism. Opening with an origin story (titled "in the beginning") and introducing each section with scriptural epigraphs taken from the Bible, as well as sermons, essays, and works of life writing by or about Luther (father-of-the-eponymous-potato) Burbank, *All Over Creation* takes the "Book of Life" as a structural principle. However, the novel refuses genetic and religious reductionism alike, presenting both as practices that involve context-free reading. When the novel elucidates genetics, it expands the textual metaphor to describe not a straightforward process of decoding but an "interactive" bioculture. All plants are "programs," explains an anti-GMO activist, and people are "by-products" of those programs. But this process is a complex "unfolding" embedded in the migrations and adaptations of species in a shared and changing environment: "Vegetables are like a genetic map, unfolding through time, tracing the paths that human appetites and desires have taken throughout our evolution" (124). Here the "map" is a dynamic document that *follows* human paths of migration and longing, rather than a static transcription or instruction manual. Even the Burbank potato, exemplar of monoculture, has resulted from "centuries of cross-pollination, human migration, [and] plant mutation" (4). "Every seed has a story" intimately bound up with the movements, memories, and desires of human beings, a formulation that tellingly transfers the textual metaphor from DNA to seeds: "And if you trace that story, . . . you might find yourself tucked into an immigrant's hatband or sewn into the hem of a young wife's dress as she smuggles you from the old country into the New World. . . . Seeds tell the story of migrations and drifts, so if you learn to read them, they are very much like books" (171). This narrative explication of genetic "migrations and drifts" is distinguished from Lloyd's monocultural cloning of potatoes *and* Momoko's careful hand pollination of diverse plants, both of which fix the unpredictable results of admixture in striking resemblance to the fixing of "geographical populations" at a particular point in the history of human migration for the purposes of genetic ancestry testing or the diversification of gene banks.[5]

All Over Creation thus points toward a reading practice that recognizes not only the contingency of meaning—genetic and literary—but also the responsibility of readers in a diverse bionarrative world in which we are "intimately connected" and "liable for it all" (410). In so doing, it picks up another thread of postgenomic literature: concern for ethical issues that

---

5. Ozeki alludes to genetic drift: "the change in frequency of an existing gene variant in the population due to random chance" (Rotimi).

straddle literature and the life sciences, from privacy and informed consent to medical disparities and genetic reinscriptions of racism and sexism. *All Over Creation* is specifically concerned with ethical debates in the context of agribusiness, over issues such as seed patenting, GMOs, and bioprospecting. From the start, Ozeki does not present these issues as cut-and-dried; for example, Cass and Will debate whether to continue using pesticides or to switch to the new "Cynaco NuLife®" potato, which does not require pesticides because it has been engineered to produce its own toxins, but therefore might not be safe. And the advent of so-called "Terminator" technology, which prevents crops from producing viable seeds (and thus requires farmers to purchase new seeds each year), is opposed by various characters but for vastly different reasons: to some it is a moral abomination analogous to abortion, to others it is a violation of the natural order, and to still others it is a technology of capitalist extraction (98).[6]

Moreover, the ethical issues in the novel escape their original fields and furrows—like seeds (or pesticides) are wont to do. Ozeki draws a direct line between the ecological effects of monoculture farming and the social effects of ethnocentrism, racism, and nativism; indeed, Yumi uses the metaphor of monoculture farming to describe her experience as a mixed-race child in rural Idaho: "I was a random fruit in a field of genetically identical potatoes" (4). The pressure to conform, legible in the uniform rows of Burbank potatoes in Lloyd's fields, is complicated by his culturally mixed family (he is white, Momoko is Japanese, Yumi and her children are mixed), which is also bound up with histories of war, imperialism, and migration (Lloyd is a World War II veteran and Momoko a "war bride"). When Lloyd is no longer able to farm, his perspective shifts closer to that of his wife, whose seed cultivation business involves the preservation of diverse species, rather than the cloning of a single type, and he finds himself ranting against the concept of invasive species, aligning it with racism: "Our plants are as immigrant as we are! . . . I do not intend to promote Third Reich eugenics in our family garden" (67). Meanwhile, Elliot, who represents the interests of Big Farming, embodies the fetishization of difference; his shilling for a company that produces genetically modified potatoes is overseen by a white male boss even more cartoonishly obsessed with Asian culture than he is—a boss who talks feng shui and qi and, in striking repetition of an imperialist directive Elliot has earlier given teenaged Yumi in bed, tells Elliot to "stay open" to

---

6. On "Terminator" seeds and other controversial CRISPR-related technologies, see Contreras 355.

the needs of the company (84). Ozeki thus aligns corporate agriculture and its extraction, commodification, and contamination of natural resources with cultural appropriation and race- and gender-based exploitation.

In addition to interlacing genetic engineering with racism, imperialism, ethnocentrism, and patriarchy, *All Over Creation* also aligns its critique of corporate monoculture with a subtle commentary on literary studies, illustrating another notable tendency in postgenomic literature. During her bumpy early adulthood, Yumi puts herself through school, eventually earning undergraduate and graduate degrees in English and Asian studies. She does not, however, enter the professoriate, instead becoming an adjunct instructor, forced to supplement her income through other kinds of work. *All Over Creation* thus illuminates a parallel between corporate agriculture and the corporate university—and the vulnerability of adjunct humanities faculty within the latter. In a letter to her mother, Yumi relates her former husband's commentary on precarious academic labor: "Paul used to say that adjunct teaching was like any economy of scale, and you just have to treat it like farming potatoes—standardize your product, increase your volume, work the margins, and make sure your courses are cosmetically flawless" (43). The impossibility of this charge is revealed by the economic pressures faced by small potato farmers, like Cass and Will, throughout the book; eventually, Yumi decides that adjunct faculty are less like potato farmers and more like the temporary workers they hire: "Adjunct teachers are the professorial equivalent of the migrant Mexican farm laborers hired during harvest. . . . Neither job gives you health insurance or benefits. . . . The nontenured faculty form a downtrodden, transient underclass, inferior in every way to the landed professorial gentry" (172). Although Yumi's analysis does not extend to the issues of race and class that complicate this analogy, she does perceive that corporate education and corporate agriculture are alike part of an overarching capitalist system of exploitation. In drawing our attention to this overlap, Ozeki is in line with other works of postgenomic literature that highlight the vulnerability of humanities laborers—and the humanities themselves—within profit-driven institutions.

Finally, Yumi's academic career points to another trend in postgenomic literature: an embrace of the materiality of narrative and the narrativity of the material world. Yumi's master's thesis addresses "the way images of nature are used as metaphors for cultural dissolution" in Asian American literature—a topic that explicitly brings together the natural world, cultural identity, migration, and literary study. However, Yumi admits that her "love of plants is purely poetic," suggesting that literary scholars have a tendency to approach the natural world as an abstraction, or as metaphor (42). Yumi's return to Idaho involves, in part, a physical reconnection to the land of her youth, which she comes to see as narrative in its own right, rather than as an object of narration: she describes "planting," for example, as a kind of writing that "tease[s] forth . . . stories from the earth," and she begins to suspect that the stories found in nature are of greater significance than those found in books:

> The planet can do quite well without books. However, the information contained in a seed is a different story, entirely vital, pertaining to life itself. Why? Because seeds contain the information necessary to perform the most essential of all alchemies, something that we cannot do: They know how to transform sunlight into food and oxygen so the rest of us can survive. (171)

The bionarrative perspective articulated here is systemic: the biological story isn't just the genetic code; it's the seed, the plant, the process of photosynthesis. And literary studies is reframed as one of many human activities made possible by photosynthesis—as part of a living, breathing system. *All Over Creation* and other works of postgenomic literature thus point toward new, systemic ways of thinking about literature in relation to material reality; it is in this way that its metatextual flourishes are brought down to earth.

The Postgenomic Age

Throughout this book, I explore the trends illuminated in Ozeki's *All Over Creation* through an archive of literary works from the United States and Canada, in conversation with science studies, health humanities, material ecocriticism, Indigenous studies, Black studies, and other interdisciplinary fields. My focal point is molecular biology as it is imagined by literary works published between 1990 and the present, with most of my attention falling on the last two decades, a period described by some scientists and social scientists as *the postgenomic age*. The simplest definition of *the postgenomic age* is *the period after the advent of whole-genome sequencing technologies*, which we might timestamp to June 26, 2000, when the International Human Genome Sequencing Consortium announced that it had successfully completed the first draft of a human genome sequence. However, the complications attendant to that moment, chief among them the illusion of a singular, universal human genome, hint at the complications that attend any effort at straightforward chronology.[7] As it does for other terms that share this nettlesome if necessary prefix (*postmodern, postcolonial*), the *post* in *postgenomic* points to incomplete transcendence, a shift that carries with it the baggage of the past. In this case, it is genetic determinism—faith in *the genome* as the ultimate Book of Life—that persists, alongside more nuanced understandings of *genomes* in dynamic and reciprocal relationship with somatic, environmental, and social contexts. The disjunctures only partially papered over by *post* apply to both scientific and cultural applications of *postgenomic*. Postgenomic research involves significant contestation over the role genes play in our lives and the promise (still only partially fulfilled) of "personalized medicine." Outside the laboratory, the casual fetishizing of genes is evident everywhere from the corporate lingo of advertising and the boardroom ("it's in our genes," intone Celgene and Starbucks and even the United Methodist Church) to everyday conversations about disease (*why does she have breast cancer if she doesn't have the BRCA gene?*), ancestry (*I thought I was Irish but this DNA test proves I'm Scandinavian*), gender (*she shouldn't compete as a woman if she doesn't have XX chromosomes*), and even personality (*my bad temper is* in my genes!), reanimating longstanding nature-versus-nurture debates whose binary terms are belied by advances in postgenomic research.[8] Furthermore, the metaphorical shift from *blood* to *genes* in private and public discourse does not escape the former term's implication in regimes of racial exclusion, even if it masquerades as "objective" and purified of problematic references to the body. Despite being a material, chemical substance, the genome continues to be primarily understood as *information*, a secret code that, now unlocked, either enunciates our fate or is available for manipulation in the service of a technotranscendent utopia / technocoercive nightmare. The *postgenomic age*, then, is characterized by contradiction and complexity, and

---

7. Not only does such a universal genome not exist, but the completed sequence was based on a "patchwork" of genetic material derived from twenty anonymous individuals ("Human").

8. Pharmaceutical company Celgene's promotional materials include a pamphlet titled "Passion, Innovation, Courage: It's in Our Genes" that offers an extended metaphor of corporate uniqueness based on the genome as the repository of individual uniqueness. Such metaphors are not exclusive to biomedical contexts: "It's in our genes—in our family's genes and in our company's genes—to help others," says Elsa Ali, a Starbucks store manager quoted in a company newsletter ("What Makes"), and the United Methodist Church's *Discipleship Ministries* website includes a page titled "It's in Our Genes," which attributes a need for Christian fellowship to genetics ("It's"). Also see AncestryDNA advertisements that promise genealogical "truth" (e.g., "Introducing") and contemporary debates about transgender athletes and chromosomal sex (Ghorayashi).

postgenomic literature is an equally dynamic field whose boundaries (temporal or otherwise) are not self-evident, even if certain trends are identifiable.[9]

As Sarah S. Richardson and Hallam Stevens discuss in their introduction to *Postgenomics: Perspectives on Biology after the Genome* (2015), postgenomic has both "temporal" and "technical" significations and encompasses a period characterized by dramatic developments in genomic research and technology as well scientific and cultural debates prompted by these developments. *Postgenomic*, they explain, marks the era that follows the advent of whole-genome sequencing and that is characterized by the rapid development of technologies for genome sequencing and analysis (including genome-wide association studies [GWAS]), the commodification of such technologies for patients and genealogy enthusiasts, a progressively complex scientific understanding of how genes work, a redoubling of public interest in genomics, and a continued—even heightened—popular belief in genetic determinism (3). This last point is paradoxical inasmuch as *the postgenomic turn* marks a "break from the gene-centrism and genetic reductionism of the genomic age," with more attention being paid to gene-environment interactions—what is captured under the rubric of "epigenetics"—and to the noncoding DNA that makes up the bulk of our genomes (Richardson and Stevens 3).[10] Recent work in genomics challenges genetics' "Central Dogma" (the idea that "genetic information flows only in one direction, from DNA, to RNA, to protein" [Ostrander]) and prompts a reconceptualization of the genome as responsive and dynamic, rather than "a mere collection of genes" (Keller, "Postgenomic" 9).[11] As physicist and philosopher Evelyn Fox Keller explains, although the sequencing of the human genome was initially directed toward the discovery and study of genes (i.e., stretches of DNA that code for specific proteins that are, in turn, expressed in specific traits), the relatively small number of protein-coding DNA units discovered has prompted researchers

---

9. "Postgenomic" can thus describe texts published prior to the completion of the Human Genome Project and/or that do not make genomics a major theme, based on the presence of characteristics I identify throughout this book.

10. Other areas of study that challenge the singular genome are "proteomics," "the study of the interactions, function, composition, and structures of proteins and their cellular activities" (Al-Amrani et al. 58); genetic "mosaicism," "the presence of two or more cell lineages with different genotypes arising from a single zygote in a single individual" (Queremel Milani and Chauhan); and pleiotropy, "the phenomenon in which a single locus affects two or more apparently unrelated phenotypic traits" (Stearns 767). See Hamner 35–37.

11. "Whether we identify this shift as postgenomics, metabolomics, proteomics, epigenomics, or stem cell biology, the linearity of the central dogma—DNA makes RNA makes protein—is being corrected by the elaboration of other complex temporal and spatial relationships between biological molecules that are ordered by the structure and function of the living cell" (Landecker 4).

to look to what was formerly understood as "junk DNA" as potentially functional ("Postgenomic" 14–21).[12] Furthermore, postgenomic research has demonstrated that environmental stimuli—including stimuli normally understood as "cultural"—can lead to changes in the genome, some of which might even be heritable (24).[13] And systemic approaches to biology have complicated our understanding of an organism's relationship to overlapping environments—and of the definition of "organism" itself.[14] John Dupré, for example, contests the "one genome–one organism doctrine," arguing that "the most fundamental way to think of living things is as the intersection of lineages and metabolism" (69). And Hallam Stevens has shown how network studies can enable "holistic" approaches that emphasize the genome's multidimensional, dynamic, and interactive character (122).

It is important to point out that these trends in postgenomic research are not uniformly accepted; postgenomic science is characterized by "transition and contestation," Richardson and Stevens explain, rather than consensus (7). Furthermore, although the promise of genomics to deliver a "disease-free" and egalitarian future has not been realized—due to "the limitations of genetic approximations" failing to align with "the grandiosity of genomic utopianism" (Choksey 8)—the "pressure to identify specific causal mechanisms at the molecular level" remains present in the biomedical research context (Hanson 5). There is significant debate among scientists regarding the validity of postgenomic approaches, and outside the laboratory, the "gene-talk" that began to saturate popular discourse in the early 1990s has not waned (Rose and Rose 22); "popular media . . . have suggested that DNA's insights are far reaching," purportedly explaining "religiosity," infidelity, intelligence, sexual orientation, and so on (Wailoo 13). Furthermore, genomic research, often pursued in explicit service of "inclusion" (Bliss, "Defining" 175), has reinscribed racial essentialism in a process

---

12. The representation of noncoding DNA as functional is controversial. The ENCODE project's claim that "over 80 percent of human DNA had some function," led to "scathing" critiques (Richardson and Stevens 5).

13. The effects of environmental stimuli on methylation, "a chemical modification of DNA and other molecules that may be retained as cells divide" (Segre), is a key site for epigenetic research. At the same time, these effects are likely "limited to short stretches of time or the lifetime of individuals," are "not highly uniform," and do not affect all offspring (Lock, "Comprehending" 162). Lock cautions against epigenetic "neoreductionism" (163).

14. "Systems biology" emphasizes "the larger picture—be it at the level of the organism, tissue, or cell," as opposed to "reductionist biology, which involves taking the pieces apart" (Wanjek). A systems approach to evolution counters the "Modern Synthesis" view that "individual genes" were "both the underlying cause of biological variation/innovation and . . . the best measure of change over time in the history of life on Earth," proposing instead that "genes have evolved in the service of living organisms" (Corning).

that sociologist Troy Duster has memorably described as a "backdoor to eugenics."[15]

This last development is, from a certain vantage, ironic, given the faith many observers had in the potential for genomics to hammer the final nail in racism's coffin. President Bill Clinton famously declared, upon the (preliminary) completion of the Human Genome Project, that "one of the great truths to emerge from this triumphant expedition . . . is that in genetic terms, all human beings, regardless of race, are more than 99.9 percent the same" ("Remarks"). And yet the HGP led almost immediately to genomic rearticulations of race, through research into the genetic origins of contemporary "racial" categories, the development of race-specific medicines (such as the high profile case of BiDil),[16] and the marketing of DNA ancestry testing to members of specific racial groups. In other words, the postgenomic era is decidedly not postracial, as preexisting racial formations have adopted the language of molecular genetics and influenced its undertakings. Rather than the demise of racism, postgenomic redefinitions of race, distributed through textbooks, newspaper and magazine articles, medical marketing, and recreational genealogy, herald a resurgence in racial thinking. Furthermore, mainstream genomic research on ancestry and "personalized medicine" often employs preexisting racial categories or directly pursues genomic rationales for these categories, even if, as Josie Gill points out, it does so within an explicitly antiracist framework (3).[17] In her ethnographic study of genomics

---

15. On the relationship between the promise of genetics to relieve human suffering and the promise to "improve" the human race, see Comfort ix. Although it is beyond the scope of this book, the genomic rearticulation of sex and gender is also of significant interest. In *Sex Itself: The Search for Male and Female in the Human Genome* (2013), Sarah S. Richardson explains that, at the turn of the twentieth century—before the eclipse of developmental biology by molecular genetics—life scientists viewed sex as a plastic characteristic that existed on a continuum and that resulted from a complex set of biological processes, including interactions between organism and environment. By the middle of the century, the ascendance of genetics edged out these theories in favor of a deterministic binary condensed into the gendered figures of X and Y chromosomes. Biologists continue to look for sexual essence in the genome, resulting in claims of species-like differences between men and women and distinct male and female "sexomes" (21).

16. On the heart medication BiDil, the first medication to be approved by the FDA for use in a specific racial group, see Bliss, "Marketization" 1015–18; Gannett 364–65; Gill 28; Washington 319–24; Weinbaum, "Racial" 209–10.

17. In 2014, science writer Nicholas Wade's *A Troublesome Inheritance: Genes, Race, and Human History* (2014), which argued that social and political inequalities result from genetic differences among "races," prompted an open letter from 143 prominent scientists denouncing the book. A similar phenomenon occurred four years later in response to an article in the *New York Times* by geneticist David Reich, which argued against the "orthodoxy" that race is not biologically real and claimed that recognizing genetic racial differences was necessary to bridge health disparities (Gill 2).

research communities, sociologist Catherine Bliss has demonstrated the contradiction at the heart of the field: "Contrary to the overwhelmingly race-critical tone of the field's mainstream debate, researchers have been reinvestigating the likelihood of a biological basis for race with each new advance" ("Racial" 1022), leading to a "resurgence of racial biomedicine" (1019). Often, this tendency stems from a desire among researchers to respond to very real health disparities and to redress the historical exclusion of people of color and Indigenous people from the benefits of medical advances. At the same time, these approaches risk "imposing a racial perspective, consciously or otherwise" on the genome (Schubert 705).[18]

Dorothy Roberts has written extensively of how molecular biology is "redefining race in genetic terms," explaining that scientists have attempted to evade the "fraught" language of "race" by employing instead the categories of "population" and "ancestry" (*Fatal* 57).[19] Using sophisticated computer technologies to analyze large data sets in search of shared strings of DNA (e.g., single-nucleotide polymorphisms [SNPs] and ancestry informative markers [AIMs]), geneticists have sought new ways of grouping human beings that do not rely on external signifiers of race (e.g., skin color, hair texture, facial features); this shift from phenotype to genotype, as Jenny Reardon describes it, is believed to be more "objective" than previous techniques of racialization (Reardon, *Race* 55). However, in Roberts's view, such efforts "tend to merely repackage race as a genetic category rather than replace it" (*Fatal* 57). Discussing, for example, the 2002 study led by Noah Rosenberg that used a software program known as Structure to "discover" five population groups that map onto longstanding racial categories, Roberts explains that the results depended on human inputs already shaped by racial ideology, including the scientists' preference for the five-group finding (over other equally valid groupings) and a data set composed of genetic samples from isolated populations made to stand in for broad racial categories. In fact, "closer inspection of the Rosenberg team's findings reveals that they do not verify five classic racial groups at all. Instead, the study's overall results confirmed the basic rule of human genetic unity: within-group genetic

---

18. These are the words of Charles Rotimi, Scientific Director of the National Human Genome Research Institute. Rotimi cautiously supports genomic research on racial health disparities.

19. On the genomic rearticulation of race, also see Bliss, "Marketization"; Abu El-Haj; Gannett; Gill 58–60; Koenig et al.; Morning; Reardon, *Race*; Rose and Rose; TallBear.

variation is much greater than between-group variation" (59–60).[20] Efforts to replace "race" with "geographical ancestry" transmute *"social* categories" into *"biological* ones" (64) and rely on sampling methods that "do not represent humankind's genetic diversity," diminishing the significance of "migrations and intermixing" in the constitution of human populations (65). More representative sampling would demonstrate that differences among human populations are actually clinal, gradually changing as one moves across the globe, according to historical patterns of migration and geographical proximity (61).[21]

Despite the shortcomings of genetic ancestry research, popular interest in the field has only grown in the last two decades. Consumer ancestry testing is big business, as individuals seek to confirm or discover the "truth" of their ethnic and racial backgrounds, replacing family histories with genetic calculations of relatedness. As sociologist Kim TallBear (Sisseton-Wahpeton Oyate) explains, such reformulations of identity have potentially catastrophic implications for Indigenous communities, whose claims to self-determination have already been compromised by externally imposed mechanisms of tribal belonging.[22] At the same time, some individuals and communities have sought to use genetic technologies to assert tribal membership or sovereignty—or to fill in genealogical blanks left behind by colonialism and imperialism (Benjamin 139). Alondra Nelson, sociologist and former director of the White House Office of Science and Technology, has delved into the complicated meanings of genetic ancestry testing in the context of African American "root-seekers," for example, whose family histories have been violently disrupted by the dislocations of slavery (*Social* 73). In search of a "usable past" and a "sense of autonomy and empowerment" (Nelson, "Bio Science" 776), Black people have engaged in "affiliative self-fashioning" through a diverse repertoire of practices that include genetic ancestry testing (771). Although she acknowledges that these endeavors "may come at the cost of acquiescence to a classificatory logic of human

---

20. The genetic data used in the Rosenberg study was derived from cell lines created by the Human Genome Diversity Project, which, as I discuss in chapter 3, focused on isolated populations (Roberts, *Fatal* 65). The HapMap project, which sought to describe "patterns of human genetic variation" in service of future medical research (Tate and Goldstein S39), employed similarly problematic approaches to ancestry (Wade et al. 6). On Structure and the Rosenberg study, also see Bolnick 73–80. On genetic variation within and between populations, also see Feldman and Lewontin 95.

21. Also see Bolnick 72.

22. Gill argues that genetic ancestry testing encourages an individualized approach to race that undermines collective antiracist action (15–16).

types that compounds, rather than challenges, social inequality" (776), Nelson also recognizes genetic ancestry testing as a technique of "reconciliation" that can ameliorate "genealogical disorientation" (*Social* 91).[23]

The genomic rearticulation of race illustrates historian Barbara Fields's description of how racial ideology persists across changing historical contexts, as updated vocabulary conceals the perpetuation of oppressive structures and the contradictory beliefs that circulate within those structures. It will, as Reardon has argued, take far more than scientific "proof" to dispense with racial ideology; after all, scientific consensus regarding the invalidity of race was supposedly achieved well before the advent of genomics, yet race continues to hang on in research contexts and the popular imagination.[24] Furthermore, Josie Gill makes the important point that "race (in science) has never been wholly deterministic, essentialized, or biologized" (18). Scientific approaches to race are varied, dynamic, and deeply inflected by culture. Arguing that the social constructionist paradigm problematically maintains a binary opposition between science and culture, Gill explains that "racial forms emerge from the entanglement of literature and science in ways which highlight both historical precedents for contemporary racial formations and continuing racist realities" (19). Neither science nor culture is the natural or exclusive domain of race's deconstruction or perpetuation; rather, science and culture are inextricably entangled with each other and with processes of racial formation and rearticulation, and debates over the place of race in postgenomic science or culture do not have a simple resolution.

The postgenomic period has also been characterized by intense debates over bioprospecting, patenting, informed consent, bodily autonomy, genetic discrimination, privacy, and ownership of genetic information—debates that extend from longstanding histories of the scientific and medical exploitation (and exclusion) of racialized, colonized, imprisoned, and enslaved populations. As Harriet Washington explains, in her study of the "medical apartheid" experienced by African Americans: "Dangerous, involuntary, and nontherapeutic experimentation . . . has been practiced widely and documented extensively at least since the eighteenth century," extending from slavery, through segregation, to mass incarceration (7). The "afterlife of slavery," to borrow Saidiya Hartman's apt phrase, is also legible in the line drawn from the enslaved research subjects of Dr. Marion Sims (the "father" of modern gynecology), through Henrietta Lacks (the "mother" of the first

---

23. On genetic ancestry testing as a tool of "self-fashioning," see Wade et al. 9.

24. Debates among midcentury scientists regarding the definition and validity of "race" bely the progressive narrative that a scientific consensus was achieved after the Second World War; rather than disappearing, race was rearticulated (Reardon, *Race* 26–44).

immortal human cell line), to the contemporary use of HeLa cells in genetic research and to contemporary reproductive technologies and discourses—all of which disproportionately benefit privileged white people (Hartman 6).[25]

Postgenomic bioprospecting is also an extension of the exploitation of the bodies, knowledge, and land of colonized people. At the turn of the millennium, as genomic technologies promised the development of highly profitable pharmaceutical and agricultural technologies, conflicts emerged over ownership of body parts and genetic information, leading to several high-profile legal cases, bookended by *Diamond v. Chakrabarty* (1980), which legalized the patenting of biological material, and *Association for Molecular Pathology v. Myriad* (2013), which prohibited the patenting of isolated human genes. In neocolonial contexts, anxieties about bodily autonomy are distributed asymmetrically: while some individuals are transformed into "biological citizens" (Rose and Novas 439–59) and "patients-in-waiting" (Timmermans and Buchbinder) responsible for managing their health within a corporate biomedical system, others are transformed into bio*resources*—the very stuff of genetic innovation.[26] The hunt for new medicines in the "exotic" flora of the global South has been paralleled by the hunt for "exotic" genomes among the world's Indigenous populations (Lock, "Alienation" 580). And international trade agreements, such as the General Agreement on Tariffs and Trade (which became the World Trade Organization), have protected the ownership rights of corporate entities over the expressed objections of Indigenous leaders and activists concerned about the extraction of resources, the suppression of biodiversity, and the patenting of both genes and seeds (568). Within this context, the Human Genome Diversity Project (HGDP), which sought to collect and preserve genetic samples from isolated populations, was a flashpoint in debates over research on Indigenous people—criticized for reinforcing essentializing myths, threatening Indigenous sovereignty, and cutting Indigenous people out of the research process and its potential profits. In the wake of the HGDP, more attention has been paid by researchers to developing community-based and collaborative research procedures, and Indigenous-led organizations devoted to genomics, such as the Native BioData Consortium (NBDC), have arisen. But there is no easy resolution to the issues raised by Indigenous activists, not least because the neocolonial conditions in which the HGDP was developed still remain.

---

25. On the reverberations of a "slave episteme" in contemporary practices of technology-mediated reproduction, with special attention paid to surrogacy, see Weinbaum, *Afterlife* 1–28.

26. See Choksey on the "corporate instrumentalization of genomics into an ideology of ostensibly private decision making" (11).

Postgenomic Literature

In this book, I explore the social, scientific, and ethical complications of the postgenomic age as they are represented in a diverse archive of *postgenomic literature*. Postgenomic literature, in the broadest sense, is literature published during the postgenomic age, though, as I discuss above, *postgenomic* is far more than a simple temporal marker, in that it names an era dominated by complex and contradictory ideas about genomics—in fact, we might say that it names those complexities and contradictions themselves. Any contemporary literary work could, theoretically, be analyzed through a postgenomic lens, with attention paid to how it addresses issues such as health and illness, ancestry, agriculture, criminal justice, bodily autonomy, privacy, sex and gender, race, and what it means to be human.[27] (Indeed, even earlier works could be analyzed through this lens, with attention paid to questions of contemporary reception and circulation.) However, works that foreground genomics as a theme are of special interest to this project, particularly those that offer meditations on the intransigent presence of gene fetishism alongside competing understandings of the genome as a dynamic and responsive agent within complex biological and social systems. A more specific definition of postgenomic literature, then, is literature that is both *of* and *about* the postgenomic age and its contradictions. Many contemporary literary works fall into this category, as genomics has become a subject of popular fascination and, increasingly, a feature of everyday life.

My exploration of postgenomic literature began, perhaps ironically, with a book about cells, rather than DNA. In 2013 Rebecca Skloot's *The Immortal Life of Henrietta Lacks* (2010), a popular work of narrative nonfiction (addressed in chapter 2), was chosen for a common reader program on my campus. *Immortal Life* intertwines the story of the first "immortal" human cell line (known as HeLa) with the story of Henrietta Lacks, the woman whose cancer cells were transformed into HeLa, and the story of Skloot's effort to track down Lacks's story. I was fascinated by Skloot's desire to write a "biography" of the HeLa cell line (Skloot 6) and of "the woman behind the cells" (175)—a phrase that seemed to reverse the natural order of things (isn't it more natural to think of "cells" as preceding a "woman"?), to imply a feminist project of recovery (behind every great cell line there's a great woman?), and to revise what is meant by "life writing." I was especially

---

27. Choksey begins her illuminating study, *Narrative in the Age of the Genome* (2022), with the startling statement that "the genome has destroyed humanity." The genome age, she argues, "contains the ingredients for the destruction of its primary reference subject: the modern concept of the human" (1).

interested in how the text's effort to bring into view a Black woman erased from public consciousness paralleled Black feminist projects of literary and historical recovery, such as those focused on Zora Neale Hurston or Sally Hemings—the latter, of course, also intersecting with genetic research, as DNA testing has confirmed the family histories preserved by Hemings's descendants. Skloot's book is at once a collaborative biography, a memoir, and a social history that raises important questions about the ethics of both medical and literary practice within a context of ongoing oppression.

It was this last overlap that fascinated me most. At the time, I was writing a monograph on modern and contemporary African American literature and ideas about "responsible reading," and it seemed that Skloot's book modeled and solicited various reading practices, some problematic, some promising. I recognized the effectiveness of Skloot's storytelling and was also haunted by the words of David Lacks, Henrietta's son, whom I interviewed in 2013; referring to a passage in *Immortal Life* in which Skloot describes Henrietta Lacks examining her cervix in the bathroom, he asked, "How could Rebecca know what my mother was doing behind closed doors?" (Lacks). Prompted by David Lacks's discomfort over his family's loss of privacy, I started to wonder how the medical ethics question that Skloot's book brings to the fore—who can study whose body parts for whose benefit?—might also relate to a question at the heart of narrative ethics—who can tell whose story to whom? I started looking for other contemporary narratives that might engage similar ethical overlaps, and it turns out that there are many, especially among texts that engage molecular biology, perhaps because of the metaphorical overlap that links these fields. Since my initial encounter with *Immortal Life*, other questions have emerged: How does the concept of DNA as a genetic script alter our understanding of "life writing"? How does contemporary biomedicine make demands on patients-as-consumers to manage genetic and other forms of risk, and how do these demands shape the literary marketplace? How do challenges to biocolonialism, medical disparity, exploitation, and abuse circulate in specific literary tropes and forms? How do genomic and postgenomic rearticulations of race influence literary representations of race? How do the health humanities offer insights to literary scholars about their own discipline? And how do practices of literary speculation inspired by genomic research imagine futures and comment on present and ongoing dystopias?

One primary argument of this book is that many contemporary literary works take genomics not only as an object of critique but also as an occasion for addressing questions in the fields of creative writing and literary criticism regarding the politics and practices of reading. In these works, reader agency, authorial responsibility, editorial influence, and the commodification of literature are intertwined thematically with the agency of patients and research subjects, researcher and doctor responsibility, corporate influence on politics and personal lives, and the commodification of DNA. Through this intertwining, such works offer strategies for reading the social language of DNA, modeling critical practices that resist commodification, exploitation, appropriation, and the problematic reinscription of race and gender on genomic terms. These are works that find in the ethical conundrums and crises of the postgenomic era opportunities for staging the conundrums and crises of postmodern storytelling, for attending to the multivalent meaning of textual metaphors "after the genome" (a richly ambivalent phrase), and for resisting reductive modes of reading that focus on "codes" and the "text itself" at the expense of context.[28]

Stories can be powerful tools of biopower.[29] This is why both the coercion and prohibition of literacy have been crucial weapons in the management of Black and Indigenous populations in North America, as in the distinct cases of residential "Indian" schools and chattel slavery. In addition to training their audiences to be critical readers of popular narratives about genomics, many postgenomic literary works ask readers to consider how power circulates in the circulation (or restriction) of literature—and to reflect on their own role in the creation and reception of stories. Through this dual intervention, postgenomic literature shapes readers into critical bionarrative citizens, acutely aware of how both biology and story shape our lives. Postgenomic texts employ a variety of techniques that encourage a reading practice attentive to ethical questions across disciplines. Such a practice is necessarily sensitive to how context shapes meaning, whether the "text" at hand is literary or biological; as Lily Kay asserts, DNA is just as "polysemic" and context-dependent as poetry (35). Postgenomic texts thus emphasize the multiple meanings of stories and DNA, and they present reading and writing as deeply entangled with accountability and agency. These are texts that take reading—a term that resonates in both molecular biology and literary criticism—as a site for sustained ethical inquiry.

The interdisciplinary impulse of postgenomic literature also illuminates important issues regarding interdisciplinarity itself. It is now widely acknowledged that humanists and social scientists are crucial actors in the pursuit of responsible genomic research. Since the incorporation of the

---

28. "After the genome" could mean after the advent of genome sequencing *and* after the end of genome fetishism.

29. Michel Foucault defines "biopower" as the "numerous and diverse techniques for achieving the subjugation of bodies and the control of populations" (140).

Ethical, Legal, and Social Implications (ELSI) program within the HGP in 1990, ethicists have been routinely hired to advise research teams, and sociologists have embedded themselves everywhere from biotech labs to informal genealogical communities. The contributions of literary scholars to such interdisciplinary endeavors are modest but growing. Trained to identify how information circulates and meaning is constructed through language, images, and stories, literary critics are well suited to describe and analyze narratives and rhetorical vocabularies that inflect the public understanding of science.[30] In his recent book *Literature, Science, and Public Policy* (2023), Jay Clayton has made a strong argument for the role literary scholars should play in the development of science policy: "Thinking about narrative can be of special value to policy work because of the power stories possess to immerse readers in richly imagined worlds, worlds in which the complexity of issues can be explored on multiple levels" (xv). Literary scholars can "bring the techniques of literary analysis to bear on the language of science," helping researchers and medical practitioners to develop "a nuanced understanding of how the language they use affects their audience" (16). Although they have yet to participate in the development of public policy in large numbers, scholars of literature are well represented in the growing fields of health humanities and narrative medicine. Researchers in these fields have focused on storytelling as integral to medical practice and have called for empathy and narrative competency (Charon, "Narrative"), "joint" storytelling and shared power (Brody), and "narrative humility" (DasGupta) at medical encounters. If hyper-specialization and corporatization have transformed medicine into a dehumanizing assembly line, the techniques of narrative theory and literary criticism are called upon to restore what has been lost.[31]

These developments are, on the whole, highly salutary, and this book is aligned with the project of highlighting what literary studies can contribute to the public understanding of and response to genome science, as well as its application in medical and consumer contexts. However, the central motivation of *Reading in the Postgenomic Age* is also distinct, proceeding from the observation that relatively less attention has been paid to the value of

---

30. Hamner writes, "Some of the most penetrating reflections on the significance of genetics have needed to arrive via fiction simply because of the greater imaginative openness with which Western cultures usually approach fictional narratives as opposed to more traditionally pedagogical genres" (4). On the relevance of literary study to the ethical and social implications of genomics, also see Clayton, *Literature*; Wald and Clayton.

31. For a rich discussion of interdisciplinary exchange between the sciences and the humanities, with a focus on genetics, ethics, and public policy, see Clayton, *Literature*, 6–13, 41–45.

interdisciplinary exchange for the humanities themselves. Like G. Thomas Couser, Josie Gill, Everett Hamner, and Susan Squier, I argue that interdisciplinary encounters should be, in Hamner's words, a "two-way street"—a position also implied by many postgenomic literary works themselves (5).[32] The self-reflexive insights expressed by these works extend from a complex view toward genome science and literary studies alike. These are texts that reject both genetic determinism and "genetic dismissivism" (i.e., "the readiness of some to ignore or downplay this field's expanding value" [Hamner 16]); that resist the uncritical celebration of literary studies as naturally empathizing, humanizing fields; and that undermine the disciplinary opposition of the sciences and the humanities, instead viewing both disciplines as mutually constitutive and equally embedded in complex ethical and social contexts.[33]

Implicit in my argument that the humanities cannot go it alone is the idea that the humanities, like the sciences, are not always "humane." As humanities scholarship over the last several decades—from postcolonial, feminist, antiracist, queer, poststructuralist, and posthuman perspectives—has made clear, by centering the figure of the "human," the humanities are explicitly premised on historical and ongoing practices of othering. And yet, when we talk about the relationship between the sciences and the humanities, we sometimes lose sight of this self-reflexive critique.[34] This oversight

---

32. Hamner argues that narratives about genetics shape scientific horizons and that advances in genetics "chang[e] the very structures and purposes of fiction" (2). Gill posits that science and literature comprise both fact and fiction and that investigations of science and literature must not reinforce their binary opposition. She models a "biofictional" approach that "recognizes the complex imbrication of biology and culture, scientific fact and fiction" and "situates contemporary fiction as key to comprehending how the current racial formations . . . are the product of entanglements of scientific fact and fiction (18–19).

33. See Hamner's discussion of "technotranscendence" and "technophobia" (42), as well as Clayton's discussion of literary and cultural representations of genetics (*Literature* 20–25).

34. Gill articulates a distinct interdisciplinary concern, arguing that critical race theorists, particularly those trained in literary studies, have deferred to biology as the ultimate authority on the reality of race by reiterating the claim that "genetic science has proved that race is fiction" without engaging scientific debates about "race" or the mixture of fact and fiction that characterizes science and literary study (9). She is concerned with scholarship that overvalues the authority of science, while I am concerned with scholarship that overvalues the authority of the humanities; however, we share an interest in approaching interdisciplinarity in a way that avoids binary opposition. Gill offers recent work on the "biohumanities" (Stotz and Griffiths), the "biosocial" (Meloni et al.), and the "biocultural" (Keller, "Thinking") as examples of contemporary scholarship aligned with her "biofictional" approach (20).

is perhaps due to the weak structural position the humanities find themselves in within the contemporary academy. Humanities enrollment has declined precipitously in recent years, thanks to a combination of structural and ideological issues (including declining state support for public universities, skyrocketing out-of-pocket costs for students, the corporatization of higher education, and cultural messages regarding the supposed uselessness of humanities degrees). Funding for humanities programs has contracted accordingly, leading to an overreliance on adjunct labor and significant pressure to defend the value of literature, languages, philosophy, history, and the arts. It is no wonder that many English departments have, as I discuss in chapter 6, asserted the practical value of skills learned in writing and literature classes and attached themselves to more financially stable STEM programs, while also proclaiming the intrinsic value of the humanities—their ability to teach, as philosopher Martha Nussbaum argues, critical, empathetic, and global thinking.

These contradictory gambits risk an evasion of the humanities' own complicated legacies. Even Nussbaum, in her eloquent defense of humanities education as essential to the preservation of democratic institutions, acknowledges that the humanities can be marshalled toward inhumane ends when they activate empathy only for an in-group or are used to manipulate the masses in support of undemocratic regimes. The role humanities fields have played in transforming human beings into objects of knowledge, and in aiding and abetting colonial, capitalist, and racist forces, has been illustrated by scholars as diverse as Toni Morrison, Donna Haraway, Edward Said, Gayatri Spivak, Gerald Vizenor, and Cary Wolfe (to name only a few). In her 1993 Nobel Lecture, Morrison alludes to "academic" and "literary" discourses as "policing languages of mastery" when they "do not permit new knowledge or encourage the mutual exchange of ideas": "Whether it is *the proud but calcified language of the academy* or the commodity driven language of science; whether it is the malign language of law-without-ethics, or *language designed for the estrangement of minorities, hiding its racist plunder in its literary cheek*—it must be rejected, altered and exposed" (emphasis added). In *Nothing Ever Dies: Vietnam and the Memory of War* (2016), literary scholar and novelist Viet Thanh Nguyen is equally attentive to the cruel potential that the humanities—like human beings themselves—carry, what he calls "the heart of darkness [that] beats within."[35] Nguyen argues that the term "inhumanities" is a more accurate and responsible name for the unwieldy domain

---

35. Nguyen's allusion to Joseph Conrad's *Heart of Darkness* (1899) calls up the colonial dynamics of racializing projection.

usually described by "the humanities," in that it recognizes the "inhuman" that is always inside the "human" (19). The *inhumanities* are premised not on an ever-expanding notion of the human (which requires the continual production of "others" against whom the human is measured) but, rather, on the recognition of humanism's contradictions and disavowals. Many postgenomic literary works are projects of the inhumanities, in Nguyen's sense, in that they take neither "the human" nor "the humanities" as self-evidently good. Instead, they illuminate the role the humanities have played in shoring up colonial and racist regimes, while also maintaining that literary works can intervene in contexts of inequity.

I would suggest that the postgenomic age inspires—even requires—self-reflexive critical approaches like Nguyen's "inhumanities," given the prominent place genomics has achieved in our culture and the role ideas about genes play in our understanding of what it means to be human. In making this claim, I am inspired by a similar move taken by Tobias Menely and Jesse Oak Taylor in their introduction to *Anthropocene Reading: Literary History in Geologic Times* (2017). Like genetics, geology has also been characterized by "metaphorical traffic" with literary studies and a notable "incorporation of literary modes," despite its "disavowal" of these borrowings. "The literary dimensions of geology . . . become even more pronounced in the Anthropocene," write Menely and Taylor, referring to the "proposed geological epoch" in which humans have literally left their mark on the earth (Menely and Taylor 2). This material inscription in the geological record necessitates interdisciplinary inquiry because "any definition of the Anthropocene identifies a point of entanglement between the Earth system and social systems" (4). The authors specifically call upon literary scholars to apply their skills to the Anthropocene "as a literary object" and to reflect upon the practices of literary scholarship in light of this major "geohistorical event": "The Anthropocene provides an opportunity for literary studies to test and transform its methods by examining how the symbolic domain might, or might not, index a historicity that exceeds the human social relation and encompasses planetary flows of energy and matter" (5). It seems to me that the postgenomic age offers a similar opportunity to reconsider literary critical methods in light of genomics' literal and metaphorical formulations of reading and the implications of these formulations for questions of selfhood, agency, humanity, and belonging. To read a (literary) text about the (scientific) reading of a (biological) text that is metaphorized as a (literary) text is heady business indeed, and the material and metaphorical exchanges and overlaps involved in this process invite reflection on the business of reading in both literary and scientific contexts.

The critical investments of postgenomic reading also align with the recent "material turn" in literary studies, which has rejected the "linguistic turn" associated with poststructuralism in favor of methods that acknowledge the physicality of readers and texts and the interrelatedness of living beings, the material world, and stories (Iovino and Opperman 2). Throughout this book, I use the term *bionarrativity* to capture these important insights, particularly the notion that narrative agency encompasses living and nonliving entities within sophisticated matrices that human beings are part of but not centered within. In developing this approach, I have drawn from the work of material ecocritics, who not only illuminate the ecological perspectives present in literary works but also investigate the inextricability of stories, land, matter, and organisms, understanding all matter as "storied matter" (1). Importantly, these practices are not the exclusive innovation of ecocritics; they echo longstanding beliefs among Indigenous peoples, even if the ecocritical debt to Indigenous thought has not been consistently recognized (Hamilton 13–17).[36] Indigenous writers and scholars, such as Gregory Cajete (Tewa), Robin Wall Kimmerer (Potawatomi), N. Scott Momaday (Kiowa), Gerald Vizenor (White Earth Chippewa), Kyle Whyte (Potawatomi)—and many others—have written extensively about the mutual relationships linking life, matter, and narrative. I elaborate the notion of *bionarrativity* through Vizenor's work in chapter 3, but this concept also underlies my explication of *fleshy reading* (chapter 4) and *trans-corporeal reading* (chapter 5), in relation to the works of Octavia Butler and Alina Troyano, respectively. Rather than simply rejecting inapt applications of textual metaphors to the *matter* of the genome, these concepts (and the texts from which I derive them) apply the *bionarrativity* legible in the genome (its simultaneous biological and textual status) to narrative itself, emphasizing reading as an embodied act in material relation with the world. Although it is addressed most directly in these chapters, *bionarrativity* underlies all the chapters in this book, inasmuch as postgenomic literature draws our attention to how stories (like genes) materialize in dynamic physical, interpersonal, social, political, economic, and historical contexts. The texts in my archive emphasize the material dimensions of narrative and the narrative dimensions of matter, perhaps because of the way both dimensions are called upon in postgenomic discourse.[37] In

---

36. On connections between Indigenous studies and ecocriticism, also see Adamson; Monani and Adamson.

37. As Choksey explains, calling upon the work of philosopher Eugene Thacker, "Genomics is . . . based on a contradiction": it is both material and immaterial, both biological and informational (3).

parallel fashion, they represent genetics through a systemic lens that emphasizes dynamic relationships among environments and living beings.

A turn to the material, it should be said, need not come at the expense of poststructuralist insights about the contingency of language. Indeed, many of the literary works in my archive—including several that illustrate the embeddedness of matter and story—engage prolifically in language games and metafictional devices. Such works, what Hamner calls "genetic metafiction," emphasize uncertainty and chance as intrinsic characteristics of genome and story alike (10).[38] Postgenomic literature thus invites both materialist and poststructuralist techniques, rejecting text-centric critical approaches that underplay contingency and context. Lily Kay has explained that the understanding of language as direct and unambiguous that accompanied the rise of molecular biology was already outmoded in linguistics and literary studies, given the structuralist insight that "the sign derived its meaning only through differences with other signs" (35).[39] Moreover, the proliferation of textual metaphors in genomic discourse practically demands a deconstructionist critique, as they function to undermine the very model of genetic transcription they were first adopted to reinforce. Reading these figures from a postgenomic perspective not only contributes to a critique of gene fetishism but also enables, upon their "return" to the field of literary study, contemplation of the traces they bring with them from the field of

---

38. Hamner identifies three forms of "genetic fiction": "genetic fantasies," produced when "popular speculation . . . surged ahead" of the actual science; "genetic realism," which takes more "nuanced" approaches to developments in genome science; and "genetic metafiction," which "describes an increasing self-awareness in fiction about cloning, genome testing, and gene editing, one that blurs fantasy and realism and that reinvigorates discussions of ultimate questions about what it means to create and to be a person" (10). Building on Hamner's insights, I suggest that the metafictional impulse in postgenomic fiction reinvigorates discussions of what it means to create and read literature.

39. Hanson describes the misalignment between *genomics* and *poststructuralism* in this way: "When [Richard] Dawkins represented human beings as 'lumbering robots' created for the benefit of self-replicating genes, he was striking a blow at human self-understanding which in some respects resembled the anti-humanism of poststructuralism and postmodernism. . . . However, here the parallels with poststructuralism and postmodernism end, as in place of a world of shifting signifiers and mobile identities, neo-Darwinism offers a decisive picture of human nature and history, a Lyotardian 'grand narrative' backed by the epistemological authority of science" (8–9). Also see her discussion of the "multiple and contradictory meanings of the metaphors most often associated with genetics" (10).

molecular biology, including traces of the biological itself.[40] In other words, rather than reinforcing abstract and deterministic models of the genome, textual metaphors undermine abstract and deterministic models of literary works, drawing attention at once to the ambivalence and materiality of metaphor.

In addition to the varied critical approaches postgenomic literature invites, I am also interested in how this archive challenges genre boundaries. I agree with Lara Choksey that reading in the postgenomic age "involves a certain promiscuity when it comes to genre" (12). The genre-bending potential of postgenomic literature, like its interdisciplinary potential, extends in part from the textual metaphors that suffuse genomic discourse. Drawing attention to textuality, such metaphors—even in nonfiction and realist fiction—create metatextual moments and invite self-reflexive interpretations, supporting Richard Powers's position that all texts, regardless of genre, should be read metatextually (Burn 167). Throughout this study, I take a metatextual and materialist approach to various textual forms, including memoir, biography, science writing, realist fiction, vampire fiction, slipstream, performance art, and Black, Indigenous, and Latine futurisms. In so doing I do not intend to disregard concerns particular to those genres; rather, the textual juxtapositions that punctuate this book are meant to illuminate, rather than suppress, such concerns alongside questions that might not arise in a project focused on a single genre.

Genomics, as a theme, is well represented in speculative fiction, where writers consider its implications through alternative present and future worlds. Indeed, Peter R. Bergethon has argued that contemporary molecular biology requires a new term in the periodization of science fiction: "Just as Isaac Asimov considered the atomic age of science fiction to have begun because the atomic bomb changed the general view of the seriousness of science fiction, the deep implications of biology on life, liberty, destruction, and survival and the philosophical questions of epistemology and purpose make it likely that we will soon need to have a new era of science fiction, perhaps named the 'post-genomic era'" (12). Many scholars have argued that science fiction is a genre specially suited to exploring the impact of science on human societies; as Bergethon explains, "Science fiction is a modeling exercise in which a model of scientific knowledge is internalized and used to simulate change in a society of human interest. This allows an

---

40. Hamner describes the metaphorical traffic between literature and genetics as a "doub[ling] back" (4).

exploration of what is possible and speculative analysis of how those possibilities might play out in a human context" (11). And Choksey argues, along similar lines, that the advent of genomics requires speculative modes that can account for its rearticulation of the human being and the legal and ethical questions it raises (5).[41] A few well-known examples of contemporary speculative fictions that explore the specific ethical, political, and personal implications of genome science include Atwood's *MaddAddam* trilogy, discussed in chapter 6; Paolo Bacigalupi's *The Windup Girl* (2009); Octavia Butler's *Fledgling* (2005), the subject of chapter 4, and *Xenogenesis* trilogy (1987, 1988, 1989); Louise Erdrich's *Future Home of the Living God* (2017); Kazuo Ishiguro's *Never Let Me Go* (2005) and *Klara and the Sun* (2021); and David Mitchell's *Cloud Atlas* (2004). Many such works imagine dystopian futures in which genetic engineering has exacerbated social inequality or environmental destruction, though Butler's work is an interesting exception; presenting genetic engineering as neither dystopian nor utopian, she explores instead the negotiations and compromises required in diverse communities where technological innovations meet competing interests.

Molecular biology is not, however, the exclusive purview of speculative or dystopian fiction. There are several notable works of "realist" and "literary" fiction that also take up this theme, works that fall under Hamner's rubric of "genetic realism" (17–22).[42] In addition to Ozeki's *All Over Creation*, examples include Jeffrey Eugenides's *Middlesex* (2002); Ann Patchett's *State of Wonder* (2011); Richard Powers's *Generosity: An Enhancement* (addressed in chapter 2), *The Gold Bug Variations* (1991), and *Orfeo* (2014); and Zadie Smith's *White Teeth* (2000). Though their techniques differ, these works explore the same ethical, social, and political issues as their "speculative" or "genre" counterparts, asking "informed, penetrating questions about present and near-future testing and intervention capacities" and addressing "questions about sex, gender, race, and religion" with attention to real scientific advances and the moral ambiguities they raise (Hamner 22). Genetic realism is at times difficult to distinguish from its more overtly speculative counterparts; one could easily imagine shifting Butler's or Atwood's work to this category, and as the *New York Times* reviewer observed of Powers's *The Gold*

---

41. Also see Clayton's discussion of science fiction's capacity to "deconstruct the claims of scenario thinking [by prominent bioethicists] to the status of nonfiction" and to "help us see the policy value of some . . . imaginary futures" (*Literature* xvii). On the intersection of financial and narrative speculation in the genomic and postgenomic ages, see Choksey 8–9; on the "promissory" (113) vision of genomics in an era of "speculative capitalism," see Rajan 14.

42. Also see Roxburgh and Clayton.

Bug Variations in 1991, "It's a 'science' novel, but closer to science fiction" (Jones).[43] Drawing from the work of Seo-Young Chu and Paula M. L. Moya (and my own collaborations with Moya), I would venture that all literary forms can enable the kind of speculative work Bergethon attributes to science fiction. As Moya explains, literature as a social-aesthetic practice makes possible ethical inquiry into questions of deep social, political, material, and personal significance: "Thinking through literature is one of the best ways to confront social issues such as race, ethnicity, gender, and sexuality because literature allows writer and reader alike to explore them in all their particularity and embeddedness in the social world" (10). Directly challenging a hard-and-fast distinction between science fiction and realist fiction, Chu has argued that all literature exists on a realism/science fiction spectrum, with realist fiction at the "low-intensity" end of that spectrum and science fiction (in its most explicit forms) at the "high-intensity" end; the more "cognitively estranging" the subject a writer is attempting to represent, the more explicitly speculative techniques are required (9). Topics such as transgenic agriculture, seed patents, genetic testing, tissue rights, cloning, bioterrorism, and biocolonialism are, arguably, highly cognitively estranging, explaining why so many authors turn to speculative forms to address them—including some who are not writing science fiction per se. The fact that science has deeply permeated every aspect of daily life only serves to weaken the distinction between "science" and "fiction." We do not need a special genre when it comes to literary explorations of the impact of science on society, and it is wrongheaded to formulate the relationship between science and society as one of "impact on," in the first place. Sociologist Jenny Reardon's model of "co-production" (*Race* 6) and physicist and philosopher Karen Barad's "intra-action" ("Posthumanist" 133) are terms that more accurately describe the mutual constitution of science, society, culture, and the material world. Literary and realist fiction draw attention to the mutual imbrication of story and world just as surely as speculative fiction, especially when focused on the material-discursive object of the genome.

The same can be said of nonfiction genres. Like speculative fiction, life writing, which I discuss in part 1, constitutes, according to Choksey, a kind of literary "laboratory" where narratives and ideologies can be produced and tested (87). And the pervasiveness of the "book of life" metaphor in genomic discourse invites a reading of contemporary life writing through a postgenomic lens—particularly in the case of life writing focused on the

---

43. "'Realist' accounts of science often rely on the more radical temporalities and topographies of sf to set out their programmes and to institute their legacy" (Choksey 12).

life sciences. The recent boom in life writing about illness, medicine, and disability includes many works that focus on biology and genetics. In addition to Mukherjee's *The Gene* and Rebecca Skloot's *Immortal Life* (2010), both discussed in part 1, examples include Michael Bérubé's *Life as We Know It: A Father, a Family, and an Exceptional Child* (1998) and *Life as Jamie Knows It: An Exceptional Child Grows Up* (2016); Taylor Harris's *This Boy We Made: A Memoir of Motherhood, Genetics, and Facing the Unknown* (2022); Margaret Nowacyk's *Chasing Zebras: A Memoir of Genetics, Mental Health and Writing* (2021); and Alice Wexler's *Mapping Fate: A Memoir of Family, Risk, and Genetic Research* (1995), discussed briefly in chapter 1, and *The Woman Who Walked into the Sea: Huntington's and the Making of a Genetic Disease* (2007). Like their fictional counterparts, these works investigate the personal and sociopolitical implications of genetic testing, research, and disease, often in relation to other intersecting structural issues. As they do so, such works also call our attention to how structural inequality shapes the genre of life writing itself. The dual meaning of "life writing" in the postgenomic context also lends a metatextual cast to these works; indeed, their deployment of textual metaphors introduces semantic instability, even when they appear to describe genetic operations as stable and determinative. Postgenomic life writing, like other postgenomic literary forms, thus offers a terrain for rethinking genre divisions.

•

Throughout the chapters that follow, the postgenomic literary trends I describe above recur with startling regularity, though not always within a single text and certainly not in the same way across all texts. Their confluence has revealed itself through a gradual unfolding, emerging in rereadings, novel juxtapositions, and recontextualizations—a process not unlike the genetic "unfoldings" described by many of the texts themselves. I have limited my attention to North American (mostly US) literature primarily because this is my area of specialization. There are numerous literary works from other national (and transnational) contexts that invite analysis through a postgenomic lens; indeed, rich readings of such texts have been provided by Jay Clayton, Josie Gill, and Clare Hanson, among others. That said, the scope of my project allows me to zero in on political, historical, and cultural contexts specific to the United States and Canada, including the historical and ongoing oppression of Indigenous people and people of color, which is rearticulated in significant ways in the postgenomic era. I have deliberately chosen works from a range of cultural, artistic, and intellectual perspectives, but these selections are not meant to be comprehensive or representative; they are merely a sampling drawn from a diverse, significant, and growing archive.

Part 1 of this volume, "Life Writing," centers on one of genomic discourse's signal metaphors: "the book of life." Here, I explore both the operations of that figure, alongside other textual metaphors, as well as its implications for the genre of life writing. In chapter 1, "Tracing Textual Metaphors in Siddhartha Mukherjee's *The Gene: An Intimate History*," I explore how a work of (literary) life writing about (biological) life writing employs and destabilizes textual metaphors. Intertwining the history of genetics with Mukherjee's own family history, and explaining key genetic concepts along the way, *The Gene* is at once history, memoir, and science communication (a confluence that is not unusual in postgenomic life writing). *The Gene* also evinces a decidedly metatextual, even metafictional, character, drawing attention to the instability of texts even when textual figures are used to present DNA as a powerful form of life writing. Working through several examples of textual metaphor and literary allusion, I pay special attention to Mukherjee's representation of his title subject as an *indivisible* unit of biological information, a formulation that is juxtaposed with discussions of the Partition of India and Pakistan—a catastrophic instance of *division* that, in Mukherjee's family, is irrevocably tied to the "splitting" that accompanies hereditary mental illness. Ultimately, I argue that *The Gene* presents its title subject, like the textual figures so often used to describe it, as indivisible from history.

Chapter 2, "From HeLa Cells to Happiness Genes: Reading and Writing Life in Rebecca Skloot's *The Immortal Life of Henrietta Lacks* and Richard Powers's *Generosity: An Enhancement*," also takes up "life writing" as a potent genetic metaphor. Here, the focus is on how this term, shared by biology and literature, points to shared ethical concerns, with particular attention paid to the expropriation of cells, DNA, and stories. Though one is an example of life writing and one is a novel about life writing, both texts discussed in this chapter tell a story of medical exploitation that raises questions about narrative exploitation. In *Immortal Life*, these questions are mostly raised implicitly, as the narrative exchange that makes the text possible resembles the biological exchange being narrated. The book thus risks reiterating the exploitation it critiques; however, its structure also invites an alternative reading that unearths "insurgent" voices and trains readers to look for such voices in postgenomic literature at large. In *Generosity*, the parallel between questions of narrative and medical/scientific ethics is raised explicitly, and the novel employs metatextual devices that challenge both literary and biological methods of "close reading" that ignore sociopolitical context and encourage readers to examine their own complicity in exploitative systems.

Drawing upon Powers's call for metatextual reading practices to be applied to all texts, I argue that *Generosity* might help train readers in interpretive techniques that make possible alternative readings like the one I offer of *Immortal Life*.

Part 2 of this book, "Vampire Projects," is organized around a specific metaphor coined by Indigenous critics of genomic research. In 1993, the World Congress of Indigenous Peoples used the phrase "vampire project" to describe the Human Genome Diversity Project (HGDP), the scientific effort, discussed above, that ran afoul of Indigenous activists for its reiteration of longstanding colonial approaches to research. Both of the novels explored in part 2 engage vampiric relations in the context of genetic research, though, notably, neither makes genetic engineering the direct object of its critique. The subject of chapter 3, Gerald Vizenor's *The Heirs of Columbus*, was published shortly after the launch of the Human Genome Project and on the eve of the Columbus Quincentenary. *Heirs* reimagines Columbus as a "crossblood" ancestor to the title characters, whose shared "signature of survivance" becomes the basis of a therapeutic genetic technology. Octavia Butler's *Fledgling*, the subject of chapter 4, is a literal vampire story that also involves a therapeutic genetic signature: in this case, a bit of DNA extracted from a Black woman and used to engineer transspecies vampires who can tolerate the sun. Exhibiting a feature that runs through the postgenomic archive, neither Vizenor nor Butler presents genetic engineering as an unavoidably vampiric technology; indeed, in both texts, it appears to be largely beneficial. The focus, rather, is on creating livable communities that do not reproduce colonial and racist structures of power.

Notably, both *Heirs* and *Fledgling* are explicitly *bionarrative* works that emphasize the material dimensions of story and the narrative dimensions of the material world, another important postgenomic literary thread. In chapter 3, I explore this characteristic through an explication of the novel's insistence on the narrative agency of material objects, the material effects of stories, and the indistinguishability of biological, material, and narrative appropriation. In chapter 4, I draw upon the field of embodied cognition, as well as Black feminist theories of the flesh, to identify in *Fledgling* a practice of "fleshy reading" that is attentive to the way stories are "enfleshed" in bodily and environmental systems—and to the way some subjects are narratively and physically disembodied. The insistence, in both Vizenor and Butler's work, on the inextricability of body, world, and story is the ground from which they make their interventions; the efficacy of specific narrative techniques employed in these novels depends on the idea that stories have a material impact on readers and their world.

The final section of *Reading in the Postgenomic Age*, "Usable Futures," explores two works of near-future speculation: Alina Troyano's farcical play/performance art piece *Chicas 2000* (1997) and Margaret Atwood's *MaddAddam* trilogy. Although working in different genres and different tonal registers, both works imagine dystopian surveillance states characterized by extreme inequality and in which genetic engineering has led to a proliferation of transgenic species. Like Vizenor and Butler, neither Troyano nor Atwood makes genomics the target of their critical efforts, despite the eye-catching inventions—*oso-women, humani,* and clones made from the buttocks of a *chusma* (Troyano); *chickie-nobs, pigoons,* and *Crakers* made from splicing human and nonhuman genomes (Atwood)—that populate their works. Rather, *Chicas* and *MaddAddam* are primarily concerned with elucidating the continuity between their imagined dystopias and the real one in which their audience already lives. In so doing, they exemplify what I am calling the "usable future," a technique of future speculation aimed not just at preventing an apocalypse to come but, more immediately, at illuminating apocalypses both historical and ongoing. If the "usable past" is a technique through which writers—particularly Indigenous writers and writers of color—draw upon repressed and marginalized histories in order to navigate an inhospitable present and chart a more just future, then the usable future is a parallel technique that illuminates injustice in the present.

In chapter 5, "Usable Futures and Trans-Corporeal Reading in Alina Troyano's *Chicas 2000*," I elaborate the notion of a usable future, drawing upon the temporal experiments undertaken by "ethnofuturist writers" as well as Jay Clayton's influential theorization of "genome time." I argue that Troyano's employment of the usable future decenters late twentieth-century white anxieties about a growing Latine population and the vague specter of genetic engineering, drawing attention instead to the specific intersection of racism, sexism, and homophobia facing queer Latinas in the present. The "peculiar temporality" (Bould 221) of *Chicas 2000*, materialized through the techniques of performance art, also draws attention to synchronic and diachronic bonds of relation among species, encouraging a *bionarrative* practice I describe, in reference to the work of material ecocritic Stacy Alaimo, as *trans-corporeal reading*.

In chapter 6, "The Humanities and the Inhumanities: Rereading Discipline and Species in Margaret Atwood's *MaddAddam* Trilogy," my focus is on Atwood's illumination of the degradation of the humanities as a key feature of the present dystopia. However, rather than offering a simple defense of the humanities as a bulwark against a coming world in which science and technology run amok, Atwood reveals how the sciences and humanities alike are subject to capitalist rationalization and deployed in service of colonial, racist, and sexist endeavors. I argue that the *MaddAddam* trilogy is what Viet Thanh Nguyen refers to as "a project of the inhumanities": a work that emphasizes the intimacy of the human and the inhuman and that serves what Nguyen calls "just memory," the ethical "re-membering" of both selves and others as complex human beings (19). Ultimately, I argue that Atwood's illustration of these concepts cuts through the simple opposition of the sciences and the humanities, suggesting that interdisciplinary exchange should be more complex than the instrumentalization of the latter as a humanizing "add-on" to scientific endeavor (Reardon, "On" 192).

•

As I hope this introduction makes clear, my primary interests lie at the intersection of science, literature, and ongoing practices of racialization and colonization. I come to this topic as a structurally privileged subject: a white settler academic, based in the United States, with reliable access to food, shelter, and health care. Although I am subject to some forms of gender discrimination, including those that plague the US medical system, as well as the pressures of biocitizenship, these are moderated by race and class privilege. Not only am I unlikely to be subjected to medical or scientific exploitation; I *am* also likely to receive the benefits of research derived from such exploitation. And although questions of privacy, bodily autonomy, and risk management potentially affect all of us, they do so asymmetrically; I am likely to experience these phenomena as a personal challenge rather than as part of a broader system of oppression. I am not subject to postgenomic racism and am unlikely to have my identity, citizenship, or property rights challenged on genomic terms. In other words, I come to this study as someone whose direct experience of the social, political, and moral issues raised by postgenomic literature is relatively minimal, with a sense of both humility and responsibility to the subject at hand and to the many scholars, writers, and activists who are affected directly by these issues. In developing this project, I have attempted to foreground a wide range of cultural and critical perspectives without suggesting that any given author speaks for an entire community and while recognizing both the impossibility and inadvisability of comprehensiveness. If I argue, in this project, that the human genome should not be approached in a totalizing manner that suppresses its diversity and dynamism, I hope that my approach to literary perspectives on genomics remains attentive to fluidity, contradiction, and change.

PART 1

The Book of Life

CHAPTER 1

To Split or to Lump

Tracing Textual Metaphors in Siddhartha Mukherjee's
The Gene: An Intimate History

About a third of the way into his substantial history of genetics, *The Gene: An Intimate History* (2016), physician, scientist, and writer Siddhartha Mukherjee recounts an instance of family conflict seared into his memory. Mukherjee's uncle Jagu, one of three paternal uncles affected by hereditary mental illness, has angered members of their community in Kolkata with his erratic behavior, breaching the family's carefully tended social façade. When Mukherjee's father erupts in humiliation and rage, his grandmother steps in to defend Jagu, and the exchange that follows illuminates the complicated nexus of family, history, culture, and biology from which *The Gene* explores its title subject:

> I have never seen her more formidable. Her Bengali furls backward, like a fuse, toward its village origins. I can make out some words, thick with accent and idiom, sent out like airborne missiles: womb, wash, taint. When I piece the sentence together, its poison is remarkable: *If you hit him, I will wash my womb with water to clean your taint. I will wash my womb,* she says.
>
> My father is also frothing with tears now. His head hangs heavily. He seems infinitely tired. *Wash it,* he says under his breath, pleadingly. *Wash it, clean it, wash it.* (200)

The implication of Mukherjee's grandmother's words is that her son, should he strike his brother, will leave *her* body tainted—that *she* will carry *his* disgrace, a charge that reverses the typical direction of inheritance.[1] In contrast, Mukherjee's father's "pleading" repetition ("*Wash it, clean it, wash it*") emphasizes retroactive genetic *cleansing*, the washing away of a genetic "taint" that plagues their family. Both seize upon the womb as the site of disgrace and shame, as an origin and end point for the family conflagration. But the passage itself takes us back beyond Mukherjee's grandmother's body. "Her Bengali furls backward, like a fuse, toward its village origins," Mukherjee tells us, using a verb, "furl," whose opposite, "unfurl," is one of his favored terms for describing genetic operations. Speaking accented and idiomatic Bengali, Mukherjee's grandmother seems to transcend the temporal and geographical boundaries of the moment, reversing the timeline and path of migration just as she reverses the timeline and path of moral and genetic "corruption."

In this passage, notions of origin and inheritance that have to do with language, culture, and geography, as well as genetics, gestation, and organismic development, crash into one another—indeed, the passage is replete with violent metaphors: "missiles," "poison," and the unnamed bomb whose fuse leads back to Mukherjee's grandmother's village. The tension of the moment is heightened by the lag in translation effected by Mukherjee's relative distance from his grandmother's native tongue. And the meaning of his grandmother's statement is multiplied by the synonymy that characterizes his father's reply: "wash" and "clean" being both "same" and "not same." In other words, the linguistic translations, repetitions, and recombinations of this passage echo the genetic translations, repetitions, and recombinations that have traversed the Mukherjee family genealogy, conspiring with environmental, cultural, political, and social forces in leading to this moment.

Although it does so less directly than the illustrative sample sentences offered elsewhere in *The Gene* to explain the book's title subject, the sentence at the heart of this scene functions as a metatextual illustration of the structure and operations of DNA and of the textual metaphors (e.g., sentence, text, transcription, translation) used to describe them. The adoption of textual metaphors by molecular biology is by now a familiar topic; indeed, some of the central metaphors of the field are so familiar as to be completely naturalized. The notion, in particular, of DNA as the "Book of Life"—the fundament from which all organisms spring—has shaped the direction of

---

1. This scene calls to mind the phenomenon of fetomaternal microchimerism, in which a small number of fetal cells remain detectable in a mother's blood or organs after childbirth (Bianchi et al.).

genomic research and continues to contribute, in the public imagination, to overestimation and oversimplification of the role genes play in the complex stuff of life, even if biology has moved on from such hyperbole. This state of metaphorical affairs is relatively ironic, given the ambivalence and context-dependency of language; if you're looking for a metaphor to express genetic determinism or agency, textuality is relatively inapt. The messy and inexact deployment of textual metaphors in genetic discourse has led some scholars and scientists to propose alternative metaphors, derived from music, architecture, geography, gastronomy—even airplane mechanics—in an effort to more accurately represent the complicated interactions among genome, epigenome, and environment, though, as Judith Roof points out, many such figures (e.g., "score," "recipe," "blueprint," "parts list") do not escape the realm of textuality (Roof 109–13).[2]

But I don't wish to abandon textual metaphors too quickly. As figures of textuality travel back and forth between scientific and literary discourse, they pick up marks and traces (diacritical? epigenetic?) along the way and, in so doing, illuminate and inform both fields. *The Gene: An Intimate History* is a rich text for exploring such metaphorical journeys. Not only does it, like Rebecca Skloot's *The Immortal Life of Henrietta Lacks* (discussed in chapter 2), attempt two kinds of life writing—interweaving a "biography" of the gene with Mukherjee's own family history—but it also abounds in literary allusions and metaphors that signify on the notion of DNA as the "Book of Life." At times, *The Gene* exemplifies the typical deployment of genetics' textual metaphors, reinforcing the idea that genes are a script to be read in linear, decoding fashion, for example, or presenting the genome as the ur-text of the human species. At other times, Mukherjee stretches, undermines, or alters textual metaphors, bringing to light their limitations and possibilities. If one of the shortcomings of such figures is that they have tended to present the genome as a sui generis manuscript divorced from context, *The Gene* makes such severing difficult, drawing attention to historical contexts of colonialism, war, racism, and migration. In *The Gene,* the 1947 Partition of India and Pakistan reverberates through Mukherjee's family history as surely as allelic variations correlated with mental illness. Mukherjee's rearticulation of textual figures and allusions draws our attention again and again not only to the supposed (and, ultimately, fragile) "indivisibility" of the gene itself but, more significantly, to its indivisibility from history—including the various ways it has been "lumped" and "split" to serve specific political or cultural

---

2. On alternatives to textual metaphors, also see Avise; Condit et al.; López; Noble 17; Porta; Van der Weele.

purposes, in ways that echo the lumping and splitting of literary works themselves. The overwhelming effect of Mukherjee's deployment of textual metaphors in *The Gene* is not the reinforcement of genetic authority but the illumination of the title subject's semantic instability and inextricable embeddedness in historical and material context. In the course of this illumination, Mukherjee also subtly encourages a reading practice attentive, at once, to the metatextual and material aspects of both literary and biological texts.

Rereading Textual Metaphors

Textual figures (e.g., "translation," "transcription," "vocabulary," "code," "punctuation," "editing," "reading," etc.) have been used to describe genetic functions and processes since the 1950s. These terms made their way to biology through structural linguistics (particularly the work of Roman Jakobson) and informatics, whose rise to prominence coincided with that of molecular genetics. The ascension of the gene—and, later, the genome—depended upon metaphorical appeals to a textual authority figured as both quasi-religious and computational, as both the "Book of Life" and the "Code of Codes." Such figures have often relied on a notion of "information" that, historian Lily Kay argues, is both potent and "catachres[tic]" (24), departing from the technical definition developed by informatics (i.e., a system of differentiation, rather than meaningful content) and relatively inapt to the concerns of molecular biology, which involve "table[s] of correlations" (2), rather than codes, and "biological and chemical specificity," rather than "information" (42). A metaphor whose referent is also a metaphor, "information" is a potent but ambiguous figure upon which scientists can project a variety of "scriptural" meanings (Kay 22). According to physicist and philosopher Evelyn Fox Keller, imbuing DNA with the authority of informatics and, contradictorily, the folk understanding of information "vastly fortified the concept of gene action" (*Refiguring* 19), which is to say the "attribution of agency, autonomy, and causal primacy to genes" (8). Through textual and informatic metaphors, DNA came to be understood as linear, meaningful, imperative, agential, and "mastering," and studying DNA became a "mission of 'reading' and 'editing'": "Beyond the material control of life, there is now a quest for controlling information—the DNA sequence, the 'word'—frequently perceived as life's logos" (Kay xv).[3]

---

3. The metaphor of the "book" is "a brutally coercive device—a 'binding'" (Rosner and Johnson 109).

This quest can even take on metaphysical dimensions, a development Kay contextualizes within the ideological conflicts of the Cold War period, in that the theological resonance of the "Book of Life" countered Communist godlessness. "The attempt to sequence the human genome" has often been "articulated as a quest for the 'Holy Grail' of life itself" (Rajan 124), and "the human genome is often referred to in terms more appropriate for texts, even sacred texts, than for the chemical code of which it actually consists" (Couser 165).[4] Seeing the genome as a book—perhaps, even, *the* Book—necessarily raises questions of authorship, which can be answered, Kay explains, by objectivism (nature wrote the Book of Life), constructivism (scientists wrote the Book of Life), and deconstruction/poststructuralism ("it is the writing itself that writes"; xviii).[5] Drawing from Derrida and Foucault, Kay leans toward the third explanation, arguing that, even if the textual metaphor is taken at face value, it cannot underwrite a one-to-one relationship between genotype and phenotype. Genes, like words, are deeply context-specific, such that "genetic messages might read less like an instruction manual and more like poetry, in all their exquisite polysemy, ambiguity, and biological nuances" (xviii–xix). If the genome is a book, it is open to interpretation.

Molecular genetics' adoption of textual metaphors is both problematic and productive, informed by "anxiet[ies]" about reproduction, property, and individualism, and influencing both the direction of scientific inquiry and the popular understanding of life itself (Roof 101).[6] Textual metaphors, Judith Roof argues, have been used to reinforce gendered assumptions regarding biological reproduction and capitalist and patriarchal notions of property, as well as to "[displace] causality" from social, political, and economic contexts to the individual genome (97). These effects have implications within and beyond scientific contexts, as conflicts arise over the transformation of genetic technologies and biological products into property; as scientists compete for public and private funding for genomic research; and as "everyday gene-talk, with its genes for this and genes for that" sends claims for the determinative power of the gene and genetic technologies "into orbit" (Rose and Rose 22–23). The metaphorical force of "the gene" as the ultimate source of complex somatic, behavioral, and cultural phenomena, and as a privileged site of medical and sociopolitical intervention, is underwritten (as it were) by textual metaphors.

---

4. See Hamner 4, 43–45; Van Dijck 45–49. Critics of genetic research have also reached for religious language, arguing that scientists are "playing God" (Nelkin 556).

5. Rosner and Johnson argue that textual metaphors obscure the role researchers play in determining what is included in the genetic "book" (109).

6. Avise explores how the "Book of Life" metaphor motivated funding for the Human Genome Project (86).

Rather than understanding textual metaphors—or figurative language, in general—as a kind of infection from which scientific objectivity must be cured, some scholars see metaphor as an inescapable, even necessary, element of the scientific endeavor. Roof explains that scientists "are not entirely responsible" for the power of their "analogies," in that they are drawing from "available models attached to contemporaneous assumptions about how the world works" (10). Further, because language itself operates through metaphor,[7] stripping scientific discourse of figurative language is impossible—though some figures may have more deleterious (or salutary) effects than others. Keller takes the position that metaphor allows inquiry to continue despite gaps in knowledge; the many metaphors employed to describe the gene help scientists grapple with a concept that is difficult, if not impossible, to define. From the "discourse of gene action" to the "discourse of gene activation," from the Central Dogma to epigenetics, from "information" to "feedback" to "systems," the language used to describe genetic concepts and processes has contributed to the emergence and transformation of the field of genetics, distinguishing it from embryology/developmental biology, directing researchers to specific problems and questions, and resulting in some of the most dazzling scientific discoveries of the twentieth and twenty-first centuries.

In 1993, when Keller delivered the lectures that became *Refiguring Life: Metaphors of Twentieth-Century Biology* (1996), she saw the limitations of textual metaphors giving way to more nuanced and complex understandings of genetic processes made possible by the very technologies developed via research prompted by the formulation of genes as deterministic.[8] Similarly, on the heels of the Human Genome Project, Roof noted a metaphorical shift away from textuality—and, implicitly, structuralism—and toward "a systems understanding of phenomena" (112). Indeed, new models for genetic mechanisms are today in circulation. Emily Herrington and Eva Jablonka, for example, offer several metaphors linked to the "Extended Evolutionary Synthesis" (EES), which seeks to move past the so-called "Modern Synthesis" and its explication of evolution in genomic terms at the expense of organismic development. Herrington and Jablonka argue that EES metaphors, many drawn from music, do a better job of expressing the complex relationship between genotype and phenotype than textual figures. Other

---

7. Unlike DNA, whose reproductive mechanism is metonymic—another reason that language is an inapt genetic figure (Roof 26).

8. Also see Keller's discussion of the "humility" that followed the completion of the Human Genome Project, as scientists recognized the excess of some genomic claims (*Century* 7).

scholars have shifted focus from finding the "right" metaphors to a more robust analysis of how context shapes the meanings and effects of metaphor in scientific contexts.[9]

Despite these developments, textual metaphors remain a powerful aspect of postgenomic discourse, especially in popular science writing and everyday "gene talk," underwriting the image of genes as "clear and distinct causal agents, constituting the basis of all aspects of organismic life" (Keller, *Century* 136). And yet, this outcome, though persistent, is not a fait accompli, given the metatextual potential of textual metaphors to draw attention to the semantic ambivalence of genomes. Furthermore, having traveled through genomic discourse, perhaps textual metaphors carry with them some trace of material experience, even as they threaten to abstract all life to bloodless cyberspace; already drawing attention to the textual status of genes and bodies, textual metaphors also potentially highlight the material status of language itself. In *Dear Science and Other Stories* (2020), Katherine McKittrick makes a strong case, in the context of interdisciplinary Black studies, for recognizing the material valence and effects of metaphors used in scientific discourse, for metaphors can both "[fix] social identities in place" (10) and "offer an (entwined material and imagined) future" (11): "Metaphors function to radically map existing useable (entwined material and imagined) sites of struggle and liberation and joy! Metaphors move us. Metaphors are not just metaphoric, though. They are concretized" (12). To reread the textual metaphors that circulate in postgenomic discourse and literature, then, is to grapple with the real world as it is constructed and reconstructed through metaphor. In *The Gene*, this grappling involves reading the gene not as indivisible in and of itself but as indivisible from the material experience of history. Further, approaching the gene as a figure that is bidirectional—that illuminates genetics with reference to textuality *and* textuality with reference to genetics—militates against determinism and abstraction in either field and helps us trace the connotational accretions textual figures take on and the material traces they leave behind.

Although textual metaphors have contributed their share of mischief to genomic discourse, reinforcing determinist understandings of genetic operations, they do not necessitate such understandings all on their own; indeed, to suggest as much is to succumb to a deterministic reading of its own kind. Rather, textual metaphors rely on contextualization, accreted cultural meanings, and the interpretive operations of readers—including the expectation that texts have stable meanings that can be divorced from

---

9. See, for example, López.

contexts of circulation and reception. Illumination of the ambivalence and context-dependency of texts themselves, achieved, for example, through a deconstructive reading of textual metaphors of the sort I attempt throughout this book, renders them unstable at the very moment they are called upon to signal the stability of DNA.

The Book of Man: Metaphors and Allusions in *The Gene*

In his prologue to *The Gene* (*after* discussing his family history, it should be noted), Mukherjee introduces his title subject as "the fundamental unit of heredity," "the basic unit of all biological information," and "one of the most powerful and dangerous ideas in the history of science" (9). From the very start, it is clear that "the gene," as Mukherjee describes it, is both scientific and cultural, both material and conceptual—and that, as he explains the basics of how genes work, Mukherjee will also explain the social impact of this revolutionary *idea,* the ethical questions surrounding it, and its impact on his own life and the life of his family. In other words, this ambitious work interweaves science, history, and memoir as it addresses the complexity of genetics—its near paradoxical imperative to balance sameness (the inheritance of traits) and difference (the changing of traits through recombination and mutation)—as well as its inseparability from environment, culture, politics, and language.

Given this complex approach to his subject, it should not surprise readers that Mukherjee's employment of genomics' textual metaphors is equally complex. Textual metaphors abound in *The Gene,* from passing references to "codes," "translation," "editing," and "instructions"—terms so enshrined within genomic discourse to have practically lost their metaphorical resonance—to extended illustrations of genetic processes that rely on viewing DNA sequences as "sentences" and the genome as the "Book of Life." Although often presented in a seemingly straightforward manner, textual metaphors in *The Gene* just as often draw attention to their ambivalence and multiplicity. Mukherjee's many literary allusions—references to specific literary works as well as genres and movements—further complicate textual metaphors by attaching to abstractions (such as "sentence" or "book") the concrete elements of content and context suggested by particular texts or genres. Literary allusion draws attention to *The Gene*'s place within a web of texts and suggests that the gene, a kind of biological text-within-a-text, is similarly contingent. Even when he explicitly endorses the gene as an irreducible unit of biological information, Mukherjee's allusions to literature and textuality undermine deterministic readings of its operations, working against the reification of the gene as ur-text.[10]

The Gene begins with several familiar textual metaphors. Mukherjee describes the genome as "the entire set of genetic instructions carried by an organism," offering this clarifying parenthetical: "Think of the genome as the encyclopedia of all genes, with footnotes, annotations, instructions, and references." Despite its breadth, "genetic code, it turns out, is astoundingly simple," Mukherjee tells us; "there's just one molecule that carries our hereditary information and just one code" (11). Emphasizing the rapid development of genetic engineering, he explains that "we can now 'read' human genomes, and we can 'write' human genomes in a manner inconceivable just three or four years ago" (12). Throughout the book, Mukherjee regularly offers the view that genetics is primarily a structure of information exchange: "The flow of information is the closest thing that we might have to a biological law. When the technology to manipulate this law is mastered, . . . we will learn to read and write our selves, ourselves" (410). Mukherjee's relatively direct presentation of genetics as information exchange relies on a similar understanding of language. In ordinary language (what Mukherjee calls "natural language," in distinction from "scientific language"), "a word is used to convey an idea," he explains (71).

Mukherjee associates the gene's role as a unit of information (to be read and translated) with its fundamental indivisibility. The gene can be divided from the genome but no further, and this fact imbues it with indisputable primacy in the study of life. Mukherjee places the gene in the context of three other revolutionary scientific and technological developments, each of which "represents the irreducible unit—the building block, the basic organizational unit—of a larger whole: the atom, of matter; the byte (or 'bit'), of digitized information; the gene, of heredity and biological information" (9–10). Mukherjee is addressing here the conceptual power of the gene, its ability to impact "culture, society, politics, and language"; it is the *idea* of indivisibility that gives the gene its cultural force (9). But Mukherjee locates this quality in a fundamental biological reality, the hierarchical structure of life:

> Why does this property—being the least divisible unit of a larger form—imbue these particular ideas with such potency and force? The simple answer is that matter, information, and biology are inherently hierarchically

---

10. Mukherjee's repeated turn to the textual and the literary undermines what Choksey calls "unit-thinking": "narrative is both a strategy of containment and a way of dancing with complexity" (4).

> organized: understanding that smallest part is crucial to understanding the whole. When the poet Wallace Stevens writes, "In the sum of the parts, there are only the parts," he is referring to the deep structural mystery that runs through language: you can only decipher the meaning of a sentence by deciphering every individual word—yet a sentence carries more meaning than any of the individual words. And so it is with genes. An organism is much more than its genes, of course, *but to understand an organism, you must first understand its genes.* (10; emphasis added)

Although he acknowledges that in biology, as in language, the whole always exceeds the sum of its parts, the type of reading Mukherjee describes here is hierarchical and teleological: a reader starts with "the irreducible unit—the building block, the basic organizational unit—of a larger whole" and makes their way up a ladder of complexity to a sentence (or, even, a poem). In parallel fashion, genes, according to this analogy, have primacy in the interpretation of an organism; one *must* start with genes, before one can understand a living being, even if that living being cannot actually be reduced to its genetic code.[11]

Setting aside whether this is an accurate way to understand genetics, Mukherjee's analogy—itself embedded with a literary allusion—strains a bit under close examination. Individual words are only one unit of language that can be identified within the whole of a poem (we might also identify phonemes or morphemes), and there is significant ambiguity, in the field of linguistics, regarding what counts as a word and how to divide words from one another (how "to split or lump," to use language that appears later in *The Gene*; 350).[12] In other words, it is not obvious that words are the natural or necessary starting place for reading a poem. Furthermore, the poem Mukherjee chooses to illustrate the irreducibility and primacy of genes, Wallace Stevens's "On the Road Home" (1938), seems to resist this repurposing. Indeed, it can be read as a *rejection* of a hierarchical or teleological relationship between word and (ideal) referent—or between word and world. "Words are not forms of a single word," writes Stevens, and "the world must be measured by eye" (Stevens 204); these lines, preceding and

---

11. See Rose and Rose on "molecular reductionism," which "conceives the overall project of the life sciences as one of disaggregation—breaking down nature into ever smaller parts, explaining higher level phenomena . . . in terms of lower level sciences" (52).

12. In this respect, the analogy might actually suit genetics well, given the fact that genes, too, are not self-evidently definable, though their fluid borders within the genome are not addressed in this passage. On the changing definition of "the gene" and recent "cracks in the concept," see Portin and Wilkins 1357.

following the line quoted by Mukherjee, contest attempts to understand the world by systematically reading its constituent parts. Rather, Stevens suggests that the only way to approach the world in its fullness (represented by terms like "largest," "longest," and "roundest" [203]) is to let go of such methodologies, embracing instead a vision of multiple truths that are not, according to the poem, "parts" of a single or universal truth (204). Emphasizing a holistic vision of a dynamic world and rejecting foundational truth, "On the Road Home" does not align neatly with the presentation of the gene as an irreducible unit of biological information.

This is less a criticism of Mukherjee's deployment of the poem (or the specific textual metaphor Mukherjee links it to) than an illustration of how textual metaphors and literary allusions can undermine their intended meanings. Something similar occurs when Mukherjee writes about the human desire to control—and even "reverse"—our fates through genetic engineering. Here, he repeats a common textual metaphor ("instruction manual") while also making a literary allusion (to the Faust story) that is itself contained in a direct quotation (from Jeff Lyon and Peter Corner's *Altered Fates: Gene Therapy and the Retooling of Human Life* [1996]): "Embedded in the history of the gene is 'the quest for eternal youth, the Faustian myth of abrupt reversal of fortune, and our own century's flirtation with the perfectibility of man.' Embedded, equally, is the desire to decipher our manual of instructions. *That* is what is at the center of this story" (12). The ambiguous antecedent that ends this passage—to which of the preceding phenomena does "that" refer?—subtly captures *The Gene*'s complicated subject matter, belying the apparent simplicity of DNA. And the doubled textual citation—Faust via a secondary text—gestures toward a complex web of citation that exceeds the figure of "instruction manual." Indeed, one wonders if the "desire" Mukherjee refers to encompasses the desire to reduce the genome to just such a utilitarian text, making it available for straightforward deciphering.

Throughout the text, Mukherjee's use of textual metaphors and literary allusions create ambiguity and complication at the very moment they are called upon to offer clarification. These turns to the textual or the literary are often surprisingly complex, particularly when Mukherjee discusses the intricacies of the genome, rather than focusing on its role in information transfer. For example, the final chapter of part 4 of *The Gene* is built entirely upon the "Book of Life" metaphor, and yet, very quickly, Mukherjee complicates simplistic interpretations of that figure, unsettling the supposed coherence of this living book. Titled "The Book of Man (in Twenty-Three Volumes)," this section includes twenty-three bullet points—one for each chromosome in a human genome—highlighting key facts; the first two points extend the metaphor by counting the "letters of DNA" and the number of pages it would fill ("over 1.5 million"), were it to be published (322). The order of the bullet points is not hierarchical or linear, and they vary in length, specificity, and significance—just as human chromosomes do. Further, several oddities of the human genome are mentioned: it contains fewer genes than wheat and fewer chromosomes than apes, a significant portion of it is "not particularly human," and a great deal is not "genes" (324). In other words, Mukherjee's Book of Man challenges received ideas about what it means to be human and undermines the idea that the genome is the "essence" of the species.[13] Rather than "it *is* us," Mukherjee writes, "it *resembles* us," subtly centering the organism by making it the model to which the genome is compared, rather than the other way around. The genome, in this depiction, is not a hallowed text. Like us, it is "adaptable" and "poised to evolve" (326).

A nuanced approach to textual metaphors is also evident in Mukherjee's discussion of gene regulation, a process that involves the activation and inactivation of genes in response to various chemical tags and markers appended to the genome "in response to cues from a cell or from its environment." It is through such mechanisms that the same genome can produce different body parts, functions, and traits in a single organism or, in the case of identical twins, in different organisms who share a genome but encounter different physiological and environmental variables. Mukherjee explains that such epigenetic marks

> may function like notes written above a sentence, or like marginalia recorded in a book—pencil lines, underlined words, scratch marks, crossed-out letters, subscripts, and endnotes—that modify the context of the genome without changing the actual words. Every cell in an organism inherits the same book, but by scratching out particular sentences and appending others, by "silencing" and "activating" particular words, by emphasizing certain phrases, each cell can write a unique novel from the same basic script. (401)

Importantly, these notations are not easily erased. Once the DNA within a cell nucleus has been marked so that, say, skin rather than liver cells are produced, the marking cannot be reversed—at least not without difficulty. Mukherjee explains the irreversibility of this type of gene regulation with a metaphoric reference to literary genre: "An embryonic cell might be able to write a thousand novels from the same script. But Young Adult Fiction, once

---

13. See Nelkin on DNA as the "essence" of life (556).

scripted, cannot easily be reformatted into Victorian Romance" (402). In this figuration, literary genres are the variable but irreversible expressions of the genetic ur-text. Of course, within literary studies, genre boundaries are hotly contested and regularly revised. Young adult fiction is an especially slippery (and relatively new) category, one that can encompass a wide variety of genres (e.g., dystopian fiction, thrillers, romance) and is defined primarily based on audience, rather than literary features. In other words, this turn to textual metaphor ironically opens, rather than eliminates, ambiguity just as it is called on to illustrate a limit in cell development.

Mukherjee's explanation of gene regulation through appeals to annotation and literary genre is followed by a series of literary allusions that align epigenetics—the study of how a genome interacts with its environment—with modernist fiction and, eventually, postmodern notions of inter- and metatextuality. The first allusion appears when Mukherjee explains that even identical twins acquire epigenetic differences and develop differently as their lives unfold: "Chance events—injuries, infections, infatuations; *the haunting trill of that particular nocturne; the smell of that particular madeleine in Paris*—impinge on one twin and not the other. Regulatory proteins turn genes 'on' and 'off' in response to these events, and epigenetic marks are gradually layered above genes" (403; emphasis added). The suggestion here is that even passing or trivial phenomena—an injury, an illness, a sensory experience—can have long-term effects on how a genome is expressed. Included in the list of such "chance events" are allusions to Marcel Proust's modernist masterpiece À la recherche du temps perdu (1913–27), in which the narrator experiences memories brought on by sensory experiences, as when a few musical notes bring to mind a woman he loved or the taste of a pastry carries childhood experience into the present moment. The reference to Proust is apt, given the existence of two equally well-known English translations: *In Search of Lost Time* and *Remembrance of Things Past*; one could say that the original text is the shared genome, and the two English versions are twins that have diverged from the same source material. But turning to Proust also allows us to see that genetic development is not a matter of unidirectional temporality, however complex. As Mukherjee deploys the allusion, the storied madeleine leaves behind an inscription that is carried forward in the development of the organism, but it also activates (or suppresses) a potential already carried in the genome, allowing the past, as it were, to be "remembered" (or "forgotten") in the present.

In this same passage, Mukherjee turns to another modernist master, Jorge Luis Borges, underscoring the necessity of "forgetting" in gene regulation through a discussion of Borges's story "Funes the Memorious" (1942), in which a man is tormented by his inability to forget. Borges is an especially apt interlocutor, given that his favored metaphors include both libraries and labyrinths—figures that could be used to describe the nearly infinite recombinative possibilities of the genome. Although Mukherjee does not make the point himself, one might consider his description of epigenetics to be a literalization of Borges's famous assertion, in "Kafka and His Precursors" (1951), that "each writer *creates* his precursors. His work modifies our conception of the past, as it will modify the future" (365). Borges explains that new works reframe the works of the past, reorganizing them according to a lineage projected backward and then forward again. This notion resonates with the history of biology in a literal way, as scientific discoveries lead to the reframing of earlier discoveries (as in the dramatic case of Gregor Mendel),[14] but also metaphorically, as new advances in genomics, including epigenetics, "modify our conception" of the genome as a record of the human past—a literal "tissue of quotations," to borrow Roland Barthes's description of literature's inescapable intertextuality (146). It is through a contemporary lens that we determine which genetic "quotations" (i.e., regions of the genome) are relevant to inquiries into human migration and ancestry, for example, and how to interpret and categorize them in relation to preexisting population categories, such as race (i.e., whether "to split or lump"). The allusions to Borges and Proust draw our attention to the fact that our understanding of the genome (like the genome itself) requires editing to be viable, and that such editing is always shaped by contemporary biases and concerns. In other words, Mukherjee's modernist allusions lead eventually to a postmodern perspective on the genome, one that eschews singular, ahistorical readings of its "truth."

What we might describe as a postmodern treatment of textual metaphors frequently appears in the "analogy to an English sentence," which Mukherjee returns to throughout *The Gene*, using illustrative sentences to explain genetic functions or structures. These sentences, like the sentence I highlight in the introduction to this chapter, are inescapably metatextual, drawing attention to their fundamental ambivalence and therefore introducing ambivalence into the explanations they are meant to serve. Take this passage, in which Mukherjee explains, again, the regulatory sequences that govern gene activation:

---

14. Mendel's revolutionary research on pea plants, which laid the groundwork for the modern understanding of biological inheritance, was forgotten for decades, only to be rediscovered well after his death, retroactively reframing Mendel as a powerful scientific "precursor."

We might return to our analogy to an English sentence. . . . Specific sequences of DNA [are] appended to a gene that provide[ ] context for its activity—its "work." These sequences, meant to turn genes on and off, might be likened to punctuation marks and annotations—inverted quotes, a comma, a capitalized letter—in a sentence: they provide context, emphasis, and meaning, informing a reader what parts are to be read together, and when to pause for the next sentence:

> *"This is the structure of your genome. It contains, among other things, independently regulated modules. Some words are gathered into sentences; others are separated by semicolons, commas, and dashes."* (176–77)

Here Mukherjee uses a textual metaphor to elucidate an important aspect of genomic complexity: that some genetic sequences are "expressed" in traits, while others play a role in determining whether and how such expression happens. Similarly, "an English sentence," he explains, contains markings that can be expressed (e.g., words and phrases) and markings that govern whether and how the former will be expressed (e.g., commas and dashes).

Although Mukherjee names his metaphor a "sentence," what he means is a *written* sentence. This may be obvious—we're talking about a *textual* metaphor, after all. But the slippage matters. Mukherjee's textual metaphors often elide the distinction between writing and language, as when he writes, later in the book, that "genetics, like any language, is built out of basic structural elements—alphabet, vocabulary, syntax, and grammar" (215). Although languages can exist very well without a writing system, Mukherjee chooses "alphabet" instead of "phoneme" here, elevating writing to a building block of language. If we understand DNA, metaphorically, as "writing" and the organism as its "expression"—in other words, its speech—we might say that textual metaphors reverse the traditional hierarchy of speech and writing, presenting a written text (the genome) as the ultimate origin of a life form. This move recalls the deconstructionist critique of the primacy of speech over writing, but rather than destabilizing the hierarchical dualism of speech/writing (organism/DNA), the textual metaphor as deployed in genetics seems simply to reverse it.[15] In other words, it figuratively endows written language with authority over speech: genetic writing is a script that governs expression, rather than a transcription of such.

At the same time, the passage above subtly resists this claim. The italicized sentence at the end of the excerpt underscores the natural logic and

---

15. For the classic deconstructionist take on speech and writing, see Derrida.

straightforwardness of DNA by implying that (written) language also possesses these traits.[16] The ease with which we read and understand the sentence is the ease with which DNA is read and understood. However, Mukherjee's turn to metatextuality here—his use of a sentence that describes the elements of a sentence while also deploying them—draws attention to the multivalence, arbitrariness, and incompleteness of any utterance. There isn't a one-to-one correspondence between what is described and what is deployed (e.g., italics are used but not mentioned; dashes are mentioned but not used), and the referent for the sentence ("the structure of your genome") is an absent presence that cannot manifest through textual representation, whether it is written in English or in a sequence of As, Cs, Gs, and Ts. The very move meant to capture the genome in text (*"This is the structure of your genome"*) reveals the impossibility of the task. If DNA is like language, then it, too, is defined by supplementarity and undecidability.

Mukherjee's distinction between ordinary language (what he calls "natural language") and "scientific language" is relevant here: "In natural language," Mukherjee explains, "a word is used to convey an idea. But in scientific language, a word conveys more than an idea—a mechanism, a consequence, a prediction. A scientific noun can launch a thousand questions—and the idea of the 'gene' did exactly that" (71). In linguistics, the phrase "natural language" is used to distinguish human languages from artificial languages (like Klingon or JavaScript). But here Mukherjee uses it to distinguish everyday language from the specialized language developed by scientists. He understands the former to arise naturally for the purpose of communicating ideas (and therefore as analogous to the gene itself), while the latter is performative, leading to changes in scientific discourse and practice (and therefore applicable to the *concept* of the gene, rather than the gene itself). Addressing Wilhelm Johannsen's coinage of "gene" as a term intended to be "free of any hypothesis," and therefore appropriate for a concept that was still in flux, Mukherjee counters that "in science, a word *is* a hypothesis," detailing the effects the new term had on the development of genetics (71).

Setting aside the question of exactly where one might draw the line between "natural" and "scientific" language, it is worth pointing out that all language "conveys more than an idea" and "launch[es] . . . questions." That ordinary—or "natural"—language is always performative, that it is always *doing* something as well as *saying* something, poses a challenge to the

---

16. Also see Mukherjee's discussion of intergenic DNA and introns—"spacers between genes and stuffers within genes"—in which he uses extended ellipses to illustrate the structural elements he describes (307).

special distinction Mukherjee affords scientific language.[17] It is important to clarify that the performativity of what Mukherjee calls "natural language" is, like that of scientific language, often *perlocutionary*, setting in motion various actions and effects, rather than doing what it says in the moment of the utterance. In contrast, the gene is often seen as performative in an *illocutionary* sense, as if there were no distinction between its saying and its doing.[18] To suggest, however, that the gene, like "natural language," might be performative in a perlocutionary sense—that there is a gap between the "code" and its meaning—allows room for the vagaries of gene development in relation to environment.[19]

Understanding the gene as a text whose meanings and effects are open-ended and context-dependent, as many of the textual metaphors and allusions in *The Gene* encourage us to do, also draws our attention to the modes of reading employed to make sense of this figure. If there is not a one-to-one relationship between the (postmodern, performative) gene and its expression in the organism, neither is there a one-to-one relationship between the gene and its interpretation in scientific and cultural contexts. Despite assertions to the contrary, the many meanings of DNA are not self-evident in its structure. To make sense of the "chapters" or "sentences" of the genome requires context; it is only in relation to family histories, medical databases, or racial categories, for example, that regions of the genome can be linked to diseases or populations, and these associations can change with changes to material, social, or ideological context. Throughout *The Gene*, Mukherjee emphasizes the fact that the gene is "irreducible" and "individual," but he also acknowledges that how to divide the genome into genes is a subject of debate. Differences in genomic interpretation have notable ramifications in scientific and medical contexts, but it is the relationship between "splitting and lumping" the genome and "splitting and lumping" human beings into categories of race, ethnicity, and nationality that is most relevant to this project.

The Gene: An Indivisible History

Mukherjee is clear from the start that the history of genetics is inextricably intertwined with other histories, public and private. His family's experience of hereditary mental illness and the Partition of India and Pakistan

---

17. On the performativity of ordinary speech, see Austin 246–52.
18. On illocutionary and perlocutionary speech acts, see J. Butler 3.
19. On the relationship between performativity and ideas about gene agency, see Roof 3.

are offered as *The Gene*'s framing narrative and woven throughout the text, and the scientific story of discovery that is arguably the book's main narrative is regularly contextualized, including explorations of genetics' (mis)use in service of oppressive political agendas. The structure of the book itself suggests that there is no addressing genetics outside of these contexts, and much of its content challenges a facile understanding of the field that sidesteps sociopolitical context. In the sections most directly related to histories of oppression and trauma—specifically racism, colonialism, and their aftermaths—Mukherjee's use of textual metaphor and literary allusion complicate the relationship between the genome and identity, sometimes in unexpected ways. Additionally, Mukherjee's discussion of these histories introduces new figures into the discursive mix, figures that bump up against typical textual metaphors and destabilize their accreted meanings. In particular, the notion of the genome as an indivisible and irreducible unit of biological inheritance is juxtaposed with figures of division and scarring—metaphors drawn from the trauma of Partition—that result in a redefinition of the gene as indivisible not from itself but from history.

In the section of *The Gene* devoted to the complicated relationship among genetics, race, and racism, Mukherjee argues that genomics can tell us a great deal about ancestry while also affirming that all humans are very closely related—unlike "older" ape species within which there is more significant variation. Mukherjee critiques the racist "misuse" of genetics, as in texts like Richard Herrnstein and Charles Murray's *The Bell Curve* (1994), as well as efforts to define races genetically or identify genetic explanations for intelligence (Mukherjee 349). "If we go hunting for discriminatory features and clusters," he explains, "then we will, indeed, find features and clusters to discriminate" (341). We must, therefore, resist "slips between biology and culture," turning to the latter when we want to understand human variation: "Genes cannot tell us how to categorize or comprehend human diversity; environments can, cultures can, geographies can, histories can. Our language sputters in its attempt to capture this slip." Terms such as "normal," "mutant," "illness," and "enhancement" imbue biological variation with "moral" meanings, enacting a form of "linguistic discrimination" that "mix[es] biology and desire" (349): "The synthesis of evolutionary biology and genetics reminds us that these judgments are meaningless: *enhancement* or *illness* are words that measure the fitness of a particular genotype to a particular environment; if you alter the environment, the words can even reverse their meanings" (350). For Mukherjee, DNA cannot speak directly to us; instead, meaning is "interpos[ed] on" genetic variation, not expressed by it (349). Words, like genes, are not stable; their meaning is dependent on context, and just as context changes the "meaning" (i.e., "fitness") of the genome, it also changes the meaning of the words used to describe genetic fitness, going so far as to reverse them. It's apt that the first example following this explication of genetic undecidability is dyslexia, a variation that may have conferred an advantage in nonliterate societies but is considered a disorder in our own; dyslexia is both a phenomenon of textual reversals and an illustration of the kind of semantic reversal a trait can undergo in a new environmental context.

Perhaps tellingly, literary allusions abound in the chapter of *The Gene* devoted to race, as if the historical and political stakes of the subject matter call the literary to mind, even as Mukherjee asserts a boundary between culture and biology. These allusions, as expected, complicate genomics' textual metaphors and are, therefore, apt as metatextual illustrations of the semantic manipulations required to read race or other forms of human division into the genome. The title of the chapter, "So We's the Same"—a line from Kathryn Stockett's 2009 novel *The Help*—frames Mukherjee's assertion that genomics has incontrovertibly demonstrated our shared humanity: "Genetics unleashed the specter of scientific racism," Mukherjee writes, but "genomics, thankfully, has stuffed it back into its bottle. Or, as Aibee, the African-American maid, tells Mae Mobley [a white child she cares for] plainly in *The Help*, 'So, we's the same. Just a different color'" (343). As I discuss in the introduction to this book, the promise of genomics to transcend racism—captured most famously in Bill Clinton's optimistic citation of the fact that humans are "99% the same"—has been repeatedly undermined by the persistence of racial categories in both the popular imagination and genomic research. In light of the failure of genomics to render racism defunct, the reference to *The Help*, a novel that has been accused of reinforcing the idea that racism is a thing of the past, seems naïve.[20] Furthermore, the sentiment expressed in the quote presents skin color as the primary determinant of racial classification, which it has never been in the United States (despite holding a central place in the vocabulary of racism) and which it is certainly not today, when genomic research makes possible the identification of ever more specific genetic markers linked to racial or ethnic categories.[21] My point here is not that Mukherjee holds this naïve view (although he does express more optimism about the antiracist effects of genomics than some other observers), but that literary allusion is an unwieldy vehicle for communicating straightforward messages about genomics and race.

---

20. For critiques of *The Help*, see Gay; V. Smith, "Black."
21. On the illusion that skin color determines racial categorization, see Fields 145–46.

This unwieldiness is again evident in Mukherjee's explication of genetics and racial categorization, where he offers "the English novel" as a figure for the human genome:

> The desire to categorize humans along racial lines, and the impulse to superpose attributes such as intelligence (or criminality, creativity, or violence) on those lines, illustrates a general theme concerning genetics and categorization. *Like the English novel, or the face, say, the human genome can be lumped or split in a million different ways. But whether to split or lump, to categorize or synthesize, is a choice.* (350; emphasis added)

"Like the English novel, or the face," writes Mukherjee, the doubled simile startling with its dissimilar terms: one cultural, one biological—one specific to a particular time and place, one universal. And yet both are called upon to stand for the genome's status as a "whole" that "can be lumped or split in a million different ways," a surprising rhetorical purpose, given the fact that both figures are *already* the product of lumping and splitting: "English novel" is a subcategory of literature dependent on a subcategory of nationality, while also serving as a (disputed) umbrella term for disparate textual forms; "face," too, is a subcategory of the body that lumps together dissimilar elements (some of which could be contested—does it include the ears?). With this juxtaposition of analogies, Mukherjee describes the genome's multivalence and its status as part of a larger whole, rather than presenting it as the foundational unity upon which the body depends. Additionally, his linking of the genome, the English novel, and the face alludes to the embeddedness of literary and physiological categorization in capitalist and colonial structures. The face has substituted metonymically for race or nationality, and it can be divided according to those categories, as features are identified as "English," "African," "Japanese," and so on. Furthermore, the English novel has been used to define Englishness against cultural "others." Within this semantic network, the genome is an entity always already shaped by social and political categories, rather than a neutral object upon which social meanings are imposed.

The use of the *English* novel as a metaphor for the *human* genome also draws our attention back to the "English sentence" that Mukherjee calls upon as a figure for the gene. Surely these references are partly an effect of writing a book for an English-reading audience, but given the attention Mukherjee pays to the native language of his grandmother and to the Partition of India and Pakistan, his references to "an English sentence" and "the English novel" call up colonial and postcolonial histories. Reading Mukherjee's metaphors "backwards"—that is, reading DNA as a metaphor for an English sentence, and the genome as a metaphor for the English novel, rather than the other way around—risks reifying English as a kind of ur-language, with operations as "logical" and "natural" as those attributed to the genome. At the same time, reading these metaphors in a less deterministic way suggests the parallel fashion in which histories of migration, colonialism, and war are written into both genome and language—and the role scientific, bureaucratic, and literary writing, much of it in English, played in producing India and Pakistan as concepts as well as political and geographical entities.[22] Yasmin Khan's description of a bureaucrat busying himself with the minutiae of Partition symbolically captures the role played by texts and discourse in the splitting and lumping that made two nations out of one:

> A photograph published in *Life* magazine in 1947 shows a frowning young official with his head in one hand, a pen in the other and a balance sheet spread open on the desk before him. All around him, piles of leather-bound books tower in great heaps. One pile of the books is labelled with a large white sign that says INDIA, while the tottering stack on the other side of the table is marked PAKISTAN. The official is dividing up a library between the two nations. (118)

These "tottering" stacks stand in for the nations themselves, suggesting the role discourse plays in producing national identities and boundaries as well as the precariousness and arbitrariness of this process. Surely the books could be stacked in different ways, but once separation is complete, each nation's archive will seem essential, natural. With genomics' textual metaphor in mind, it's nearly impossible not to see the library in this photo as a figure for the genome, an instance of the splitting and lumping Mukherjee refers to in his critique of "slips" between science and culture.

Even when Mukherjee asserts a boundary between science and culture, his references to English novels and English sentences suggest the impossibility of splitting the gene from colonial and postcolonial history. This impossibility is further illustrated by Mukherjee's meditation on Bengali, as in the scene that opens this chapter and, later, when his father offers a

---

22. The conceptual and political production of India and Pakistan has also influenced interpretations of the genome. Until recently, ancestry testing results for South Asians were extremely broad, due to limited representation of South Asian populations in genetic databanks. As the tests begin to yield more detailed results, they still rely on self-referential systems of categorization that fuse political, cultural, and biological traits (Dore).

Bengali translation for *gene*. This latter passage not only erodes Mukherjee's distinction between "natural" and "scientific" language; it also irrevocably links the gene with histories intimate and public. "Is there a Bengali word [for gene]?" Mukherjee asks his father:

> "*Abhed*," he offered. I had never heard him use the term. It means "indivisible" or "impenetrable," but it is also used loosely to denote "identity." I marveled at the choice; it was an echo chamber of a word. Mendel or Bateson might have relished its many resonances: indivisible; impenetrable; inseparable; identity.
>
> I asked my father what he thought about [his mentally ill brothers] Moni, Rajesh, and Jagu.
>
> "*Abheder dosh*," he said.
>
> A flaw in identity; a genetic illness; a blemish that cannot be separated from the self—the same phrase served all meanings. He had made peace with its indivisibility. (91)

Citing fathers of genetics Gregor Mendel and William Bateson, Mukherjee explicitly draws a parallel between his father's selection of *abhed* to denote "gene" and the quest among scientists to name the smallest unit of inheritance. While seeming to arise from what Mukherjee would call "natural language," his father's linguistic innovation illuminates our understanding of the gene and, therefore, functions as "scientific language," as Mukherjee defines it. *Abhed* also draws attention to the cultural and linguistic specificity of *gene*, which, like most scientific terms, passes as contextless and cultureless, while reinforcing European/Western epistemological hegemony. Multivalent and straddling multiple discourses, *abhed* captures the indivisibility *of* the gene itself and its indivisibility *from* personal, cultural, and historical contexts.

The immediate context for this conversation is what Mukherjee describes as a familiar "refugee" scene: he and his father return to the latter's childhood home in Kolkata, which Mukherjee's grandmother rented decades earlier, on the eve of Partition. This context further complicates the implications of *abhed*: it means *indivisible* and *inseparable* but is enunciated at a site associated with division and separation. And its other meanings—"impenetrable" and "identity"—resonate dissonantly with a family history scarred by British colonialism and Partition. What is colonialism if not a penetration of what is meant to be impenetrable? What is partition but a division of what was thought to be indivisible? Are not both in the business of shaping and reshaping identities in service of powerful social and political forces?

The term *partition* is as slippery and inadequate as *gene*: the degree of upheaval and trauma caused by the Partition of India and Pakistan—including hundreds of thousands (possibly millions) dead from violence, starvation, disease; the abduction and rape of tens of thousands of women; the migration of twelve million people across a newly drawn border; the incalculable psychic wounds—are difficult to capture in words (Butalia 3). As Urvashi Butalia writes,

> *Partition*: the word itself is so inadequate. Partition is a simple division, a separation, but surely what happened in 1947 was much more than that. . . . How could a simple word, a word invested with the literalness of geographical division, even approximate the many levels of experience that people had lived through? Where would you find the words that located, that identified the violence not only "out there" but inside you? (285)

Butalia's final line is instructive in that it describes the Partition of India and Pakistan not just as a geographical and sociopolitical phenomenon but also as a physical and psychological one. Partition has left its scar on land and maps as well as inside bodies and minds. Indeed, recent research has found evidence of trauma not only in survivors of Partition but also in their children, suggesting that its scars are passed down intergenerationally (Kaur and Jaggi). Further, the cross-community kidnapping of women resulted in children who carried evidence of Partition in their bodies: "Inside the bodies of children the blood that flowed was intimately mixed. No separation could be made here, no clear lines drawn about where these children should go" (Butalia 222). Partition, in addition to being a complex personal and political trauma, is an apt figure for the impossibility of dividing human beings into irreducible categories of difference. Like the (synonymous) verb *cleave*, *partition* might even be said to be a contronym; it names an ineffable, irreducible experience of separation that cannot be separated from the self.

Referring to the gene's indivisibility alongside the traumatic divisions caused by the Partition of India and Pakistan is a move that Mukherjee makes in the very first pages of *The Gene*, when he discusses the title term as an "irreducible unit" which, like the atom and the byte, has completely altered the world and our understanding of it. This assertion of the gene's "irreducibility" is immediately linked to the Mukherjee family's experience of Partition as inextricable from the upheavals caused by hereditary mental illness. Mukherjee's grandmother and father "believed that Jagu's and Rajesh's mental illnesses had been precipitated—even caused, perhaps—by the apocalypse of Partition, its political trauma sublimated into their psychic trauma. Partition, they knew, had split apart not just nations but also minds."[23] The parallel Mukherjee draws between the splitting of the nation and the splitting of the mind allows for a notable swapping of metaphors, as when Mukherjee describes Kolkata, where his grandmother and uncles arrived in 1946 to escape upheaval in East Bengal, as subject to mental splitting: "The city was itself losing sanity—its nerves fraying" (4). It is in the context of mass violence—including over four thousand deaths and ten thousand injuries in Kolkata that August—that Rajesh's mental decline accelerates and Jagu "confined himself voluntarily at home" (5).

Mukherjee acknowledges that any suspicion that Partition *caused* the mental breakdown of his uncles loses coherence in the face of a third uncle's mental decline: "Moni, of course, was not a 'Partition child.' . . . Yet, uncannily, the trajectory of his psyche had begun to recapitulate Jagu's" (5). Moni's descent into madness draws attention, finally, to the possibility "that a hereditary component lurked behind this family history" (7). This apprehension, however, does not override the perception that history has a role to play in this story of inheritance. Indeed, the term "history," as Mukherjee uses it, refers at once to the social/political and the biological/genetic. The book's subtitle, "an intimate history," can apply alike to the history of genetics and to family histories, including those carried in our genomes. Such semantic doubling also appears in Mukherjee's use of the phrase "scar of history":

> Had Moni inherited a gene, or a set of genes, that had made him susceptible—the same genes that had affected our uncles? Had others been affected with different variants of mental illness? My father had had at least two psychotic fugues in his life—both precipitated by the consumption of *bhang* (mashed-up cannabis buds, melted in ghee, and churned into a frothing drink for religious festivals). Were these related to the same scar of history? (7–8)

In this context, "scar of history" refers not to sociopolitical context but to genetic inheritance. However, on the heels of several pages about the Partition of India and Pakistan, "scar of history" also calls up this powerful historical referent, the parenthetical explanation of bhang further underscoring the role (precipitating role, even) of culture in the expression of genetic inheritance. Later, we learn from Mukherjee that "scar of history" might

---

23. Hamann-Rose argues that Mukherjee illustrates the journey from a localized sociopolitical and cultural explanation of illness to a Western geneticized explanation without leaving the former completely behind (168).

have an even more literal meaning, as environmental events (e.g., famine, war) can leave heritable marks on one's genetic code, epigenetic notations that themselves challenge the idea that the relationship between DNA and environment is unidirectional (401–2). "The gene," therefore, cannot be divided from—or understood to supersede—its context, literally or figuratively. There can be no partition of gene and history.

The metaphorical layering of partition and genetic indivisibility appears again when Mukherjee's father is diagnosed with normal pressure hydrocephalus (NPH), an illness with a not-yet-understood heritable component. Mukherjee's mother finds her husband facedown and in pain, and when she cuts his shirt to remove it from his body, he complains about this waste, activating an "ancient quarrel" that Mukherjee interprets through the lens of Partition: "*His* mother, who had never had five shirts for all five boys at a time, would have found a way to rescue it. You could take a man out of Partition, but you could not take Partition out of the man" (255). Mukherjee implies that his father carries Partition in his body, the violent division of land recapitulated in the splitting of flesh and bone (the "gash" on his forehead, his broken shoulder). Partition is a split that cannot be split from him, even as his body threatens to lose coherence (and even species distinction—his hand "tucked under his body unnaturally, like a snapped wing"). Simultaneously, he seems to straddle time, at first answering Mukherjee's query about what year it is with "nineteen forty-six": "It was a fugitive memory," Mukherjee explains; the incident/illness has called up "another season of catastrophe—the year that Rajesh had died," the year before Partition (255–56).[24]

The textual intimacy of Partition and genetic inheritance in *The Gene* leads to another key figure in genomic discourse: the map. Dorothy Nelkin has explained that maps, like other textual metaphors, have contributed to decontextualizing and ahistoricizing approaches to the genome: "indicat[ing] that once a gene is located, its interpretation will be objective and independent of context" (558). Maps are not "impersonal reflections of nature but . . . distortions, . . . value-laden constructions that reinforce cultural myths," and their use in genomics calls up the long history of scientific exploration as a constitutive element of European imperialism, a tool used in the taming of people and land (Rosner and Johnson 116). Mary Rosner and T. R. Johnson have argued that, in the early days of gene mapping, DNA was presented "as mysterious lands to be conquered and controlled," with some

---

24. Butalia notes temporal incongruence as a common element in stories told by survivors of the Partition of India and Pakistan (18).

scientists even citing European exploration and imperialism in describing the Human Genome Project. "Like imperialist maps," Rosner and Johnson maintain, "genome maps are claims to ownership, not only of the specific sites of genes that scientists have identified (with the fortunes that can come from patents) but also of the power and status associated with making sense of what has been unknown, with imposing order on chaos, with telling a plausible story, with . . . structuring the world" (117).[25] More recently, as gene mapping has become more sophisticated, Ruha Benjamin has offered vivid examples of this structuring, as in the use of genetic ancestry testing to "diagnose" national origin (and thereby regulate refugee migration) or, in contrast, to support Indigenous sovereignty claims (134–39).

In *The Gene*, the race to map the human genome—between Celera, a private company led by Craig Venter, and the publicly funded Human Genome Project, led by Francis Collins—is presented as parallel to the race, centuries earlier, to map the globe. Perhaps unsurprisingly, this parallel is helped along by yet another literary allusion, one that aligns mapmaking and poetry. A chapter about the genome mapping competition, aptly titled "The Geographers," offers as its epigraph an oft-cited quatrain from Jonathan Swift's "On Poetry: A Rhapsody" (1733):

> *So Geographers in Afric-maps,*
> *With Savage-Pictures fill their Gaps;*
> *And o'er uninhabitable Downs*
> *Place Elephants for want of Towns.* (qtd. in Mukherjee 306)

The poem, a satirical takedown of the poetic enterprise, advises writers to gain patronage by imitating the cartographers who brazenly obscure the empty spaces on their maps with exotic creatures drawn from imagination. Mukherjee's citation of the poem aligns the competition to fill gaps in genographic knowledge with the competition to gain geographic knowledge during the long period of European imperialism—and the histories of conquest and genocide whose rough edges are smoothed over by clean cartographic lines. Given *The Gene*'s backdrop of Partition, the hastily drawn map dividing India and Pakistan in 1947—whose "complex boundaries" ran inexplicably "through villages, deserts, shrines"—immediately comes to mind (Butalia 67). The Partition map, quite literally the result of a poorly informed

---

25. Rosner and Johnson recommend "map as collage" or "palimpsest" as alternatives to map as "picture" (121).

colonial imagination, shadows Mukherjee's citation of the map as a genomic metaphor. Furthermore, as I discuss in chapter 3, genetic mapping projects—especially those having to do with genetic ancestry (thus intertwining two types of mapping)—have been accused of being neocolonial in their own right, thus materializing the map's semantic shadow.

This shadow also hovers over Mukherjee's discussion of Nancy Wexler's desperate effort to locate the genes that cause Huntington's disease, a devastating neurological disorder that plagued her family. Mukherjee describes how Wexler became obsessed, in the late 1970s, with the (then new) technology of gene mapping—an obsession that soon found her traversing the globe:

> Nancy Wexler could not shake the image of gene maps from her mind. A few years earlier, [her psychoanalyst father] Milton Wexler had heard from a Venezuelan neurologist of two neighboring villages, Barranquitas and Lagunetas, on the shores of Lake Maracaibo in Venezuela, with a striking prevalence of Huntington's disease. In a fuzzy, black-and-white home movie filmed by the neurologist, Milton Wexler had seen more than a dozen villagers wandering on the streets, their limbs shaking uncontrollably. . . . It was in Barranquitas, several thousand miles from Los Angeles, that the gene for her family's illness would most likely be found. (284)

This passage is fascinating in its paradoxical descriptions of Barranquitas and Lagunetas as, at once, distant and close, foreign and familiar. Wexler must travel to the most remote corner of this remote location, the *"pueblo de agua"* or "village on stilts," where the disease is concentrated. However, upon arrival she is faced with Huntington's "achingly recognizable dance: 'It was a clash of total bizarreness and total familiarity,' she recalled. 'I felt connected and alienated'" (Mukherjee 286–87). The film taken of the villagers is described as a "home video," and their affliction as *"her* family's illness," Mukherjee's language grafting the villagers' story onto the Wexler family's story (emphasis added). In the months that follow, Wexler and her team collect the family histories and the blood—"vial upon vial" of it—that will be used to map the Huntington's gene. When the location of the gene is finally "discovered," after years of "hunting," it is described, like Barranquitas and Lagunetas, as "remote": "It was a strange region of the genome, largely barren, with a few unknown genes within it. . . . It was like the sudden landing of a boat on a derelict beachhead, with no known landmarks in sight" (286). Echoes of exploration, discovery, and expropriation reverberate throughout this passage.

Nancy's sister Alice Wexler writes about the family's effort to map the Huntington's gene in her memoir *Mapping Fate* (1996), another work that, like *The Gene*, intertwines family and scientific histories.[26] In telling these entangled stories, Wexler, like Mukherjee, employs a notable literary sensibility; her book overflows with literary references, from *One Hundred Years of Solitude* to *The Wizard of Oz*.[27] Moreover, Wexler describes Huntington's itself in narrative terms: it is a story with a beginning ("First there is the grandfather who has died of 'nervous trouble'"), a middle ("There is always a moment of discovery when the protagonists finally learn the truth"), and an (unsettled) end ("In the end, the characters all come to resemble one another, and the action winds down to a predictably gruesome close, with no resolution or release and always the promise of more performances to come"; xi). Predictable but unsatisfying, the story refuses "resolution" in favor of "endless replication," echoing the pathogenic genetic repetition that causes Huntington's (a trinucleotide repeat on the fourth chromosome) and is repeated generationally (xxv). The shame and stigma surrounding Huntington's are presented as narrative flaws—obfuscating silences that get in the way of the story that needs to be told.

Like *The Gene*, *Mapping Fate* is shadowed by colonial history. Although Wexler has an advanced degree in Latin American studies and elsewhere contextualizes Huntington's in relation to European colonialism, she does not substantively address politics, economics, or history in the section of the book devoted to the Venezuelan villages that would prove crucial to the gene-mapping efforts.[28] Here, her historical knowledge slips into romanticism; as she describes "eager, barefoot, brown-skinned children, sometimes with the fair hair and blue or grey eyes that recall their European ancestry," the facts of European colonialism, and its relationship to the etiology of Huntington's, is transmuted into exotic genealogy (192). Although the remainder of the book focuses on the ethical problem posed by the development of a genetic test without an accompanying therapy, Wexler does not ask how this problem affects the Venezuelan research subjects or how they might benefit from a breakthrough dependent on their bodies, preemptively

---

26. The third strand of the braid—the telling of the telling of the story—Wexler narrates separately, in her essay "Mapping Lives: 'Truth,' Life Writing, and DNA."

27. Wexler also makes an interdisciplinary argument, attributing scientific breakthroughs to collaboration among artists, scientists, and psychoanalysts.

28. This oversight is doubly surprising given Wexler's contextualization of both scientific and family stories. She historicizes the arrival of Huntington's in the US (through migration and colonialism), the medical discovery of the disease (associated with the rise of eugenics), and her mother's diagnosis (coincident with the assassinations of Martin Luther King Jr. and Robert Kennedy and with the Soviet invasion of Prague).

dismissing such questions with a generalization: that Venezuelans, unlike US Americans, "tolerate ambiguity" (199). The counterpoint to this generalization is found in the local oral history of the disease. Attributing the arrival of Huntington's to the arrival a Spanish sailor (i.e., aligning it with the impacts of colonialism), the villagers are as eager for an origin story for Huntington's as Wexler is for a denouement. As differently positioned readers of the same "scar of history," Wexler and the Venezuelan families make different choices in constructing the story of that scar.

My detour through Wexler's accounting of the discovery of the Huntington's gene—and Mukherjee's accounting of Wexler's sister's accounting—is meant to suggest how the lessons of genomic (re)contextualization and (re)signification, as they are accomplished in *The Gene*, can travel beyond their respective textual origins to inform the reading of metaphors in other postgenomic works and, perhaps, beyond. Reading *The Gene* with attention to the instability of metaphors, their embeddedness in intertextual webs of meaning, and their inextricability from historical contexts is salutary training for navigating the postgenomic discursive context, in which nuanced research on genetics and epigenetics proceeds alongside stubborn reiterations of gene fetishism and rearticulations of racism in genomic terms. Mukherjee himself offers nuanced deployments of metaphor and allusion that challenge simplistic thinking about genetics. But even when he employs more typical uses of textual metaphors, these figures are vulnerable to destabilization and resignification, given the semantic ambivalence the figures themselves carry. *The Gene*'s own metatextual elements encourage such readings in relation to other works of postgenomic literature, a great many of which, as we shall see throughout the remainder of this book, explicitly train readers in metatextual and materialist approaches to the subject of genomics that mirror Mukherjee's approach.

The Road Home

I close this chapter by returning to Wallace Stevens's poem "On the Road Home," which Mukherjee cites in his discussion of the conceptual power of indivisibility. Mukherjee cites Stevens's line "In the sum of the parts, there are only the parts" in order to assert genes as fundamental units of biological meaning and to recommend a hierarchical reading practice that acknowledges the organism as "greater than the sum of its parts," while also insisting that the starting point for any good reading of the organism is the gene. Having already argued that the poem resists Mukherjee's citation of it,

I now suggest that Mukherjee's citation ultimately transcends the very tension it introduces. One cannot help but notice that Stevens's poem resembles the scene, described above, in which Mukherjee's father offers the term *abhed* as a Bengali translation for *gene*. In the poem, two persons stand among the trees while night falls, discussing the relationship between parts and wholes and experiencing a sense of awe as they approach (without reaching) the fullness of the world. Although the setting is urban, rather than arboreal, and the tone darker than Stevens's, Mukherjee's scene is strikingly similar, as he and his father stand on the roof of a house in Kolkata in the early evening, discussing language, genetics, and identity: "We climbed up to the balcony on the roof. The sky dilated at last. Dusk was falling so quickly that it seemed you could almost sense the curvature of the earth arching away from the sun. My father looked out toward the lights of the station. A train whistled in the distance like a desolate bird" (91). Mukherjee and his father, like Stevens's figures, apprehend the "roundness" of the night, and the trappings of city life seem to drop away in favor of nature (the train whistle transforming into the call of a "desolate bird"). Although Mukherjee does not echo the warmth and amplitude with which Stevens ends his poem, he does end on a note of acceptance made possible, it seems, by the multiple meanings implied by *abhed*: "A flaw in identity; a genetic illness; a blemish that cannot be separated from the self—the same phrase served all meanings. [My father] had made peace with its indivisibility" (91). Here, "indivisibility" refers at once to the gene as an "irreducible unit of heredity" and the gene—translated as *abhed*—as irreducibly multiple in meaning. *Abhed*, in dialogue with Stevens's poem, allows us to see the gene not just as an irreducible part of a larger whole but also as a term that shuttles between semantic levels, eluding semantic hierarchy. The resemblance between the two scenes also reveals history to be present even in those passages, like the one in which Mukherjee cites "On the Road Home," where it is not explicitly called up. Indeed, the turn to literary allusion might be said to always call up history—if not the specific context of the literary work, certainly the understanding that a literary work only *means* in relation to context.

The modest suggestion of this chapter is that this is also the case when textual metaphors—sentences, books, instruction manuals—circulate in genomic discourse. To read such metaphors as communicating the authority or fixity or ahistoricity of the genome is to read with flagrant disregard for the inextricability of language from context. Furthermore, when these same figures and allusions circulate in literary discourse—in the self-conscious moves of postmodern inter- and metatextuality—they do not signal the dematerialization of language (heightened by the genomic reduction of text to bloodless code); rather, they carry some trace of the biological, of the body in which DNA is a physical and active part. In the chapters that follow, postgenomic literature's tendency, even in its most postmodern forms, to point back to material reality and embodied experience, is a recurring theme. If I have found, in Mukherjee's discussion of the gene, a persistent turn to both metatextuality and historicity, in the work of Gerald Vizenor and Octavia Butler, the subjects of part 2, "Vampire Projects," I have found a persistent turn to the embodied, the *fleshy*—even when these writers employ explicitly metatextual techniques. Furthermore, in approaching the exploration of life writing undertaken by Rebecca Skloot and Richard Powers, the subjects of chapter 2, I recommend a metatextual reading practice that makes space for characters to exceed their narrative roles and that draws attention to the material responsibility of readers in the citation, circulation, and interpretation of biography in its literary and genomic forms.

CHAPTER 2

From HeLa Cells to Happiness Genes

Reading and Writing Life in Rebecca Skloot's
The Immortal Life of Henrietta Lacks and
Richard Powers's *Generosity: An Enhancement*

Near the end of *The Immortal Life of Henrietta Lacks* (2010), Rebecca Skloot's nonfiction narrative about the first "immortal" human cell line and the woman behind it, the author recounts an emotional encounter between Henrietta Lacks's daughter, Deborah Lacks-Pullum, and Deborah's cousin Gary.[1] Deborah is in a physically and emotionally strained state, having recently visited the institution where her sister died as a child and, separately, having

---

1. It may seem odd to include *The Immortal Life of Henrietta Lacks* in this study, inasmuch as it focuses on cells, not DNA. However, important developments in cell biology, such as the creation of hybrid cells—in which HeLa played a key role—prefigured those in genomics and were met with similar public fascination, fear, and disgust (Landecker 180–218). Furthermore, postgenomic science evinces a renewed concern with DNA's overlaying environments, beginning with cells themselves, and ethical debates regarding the collection, (re)production, and commercialization of biological material apply to cell lines and genetic codes alike. As Lock points out, immortal cell lines and genetic databases are intertwined technologies ("Alienation" 573–74). From a postgenomic vantage, HeLa is imbued with some of the significance of DNA, and the "social life of DNA," to borrow Nelson's phrase, is inflected by the story of HeLa. Not incidentally, in 2017 a family rift regarding who can speak for the Lackses—and who can be paid for such speech—resulted in DNA tests to confirm parentage (Hendrix). That competing definitions of family, and conflicts over the commodification of the Lacks story, should be resolved by genetic testing techniques that might not exist without the cultivation of HeLa cells neatly captures the thoroughgoing interimplication of flesh, story, and capital in the postgenomic age.

seen her mother's cells for the first time. Breaking out in hives, pacing the floor, talking compulsively about her mother, her sister, and HeLa cells, and convulsing in laughter and tears, Deborah seems to be losing control. Gary intervenes by clutching her to his chest and calling out to God to lift the "burden" of her mother's cells. Deborah responds with prayers and petitions of her own, as Rebecca watches—speechless, but taking notes: "I'd been watching all this from a recliner a few feet away, dumbfounded, terrified to move or make noise, frantically scribbling notes.... As I watched, all I could think was, *Oh my god . . . I did this to her*" (292).

The narrative that has led to this moment intertwines three stories: a tale of scientific discovery (what Skloot calls a "biography" of the HeLa cell line); an actual biography (of Henrietta Lacks, the Black woman whose cancer cells were used to develop HeLa without her knowledge or consent); and what we might call the biography of the book itself, as Skloot recounts her writing journey—from the first time she heard of Henrietta Lacks, as a young white college student, through years of research and roadblocks, including many erected by the Lacks family (6). By this point in the narrative, Rebecca has mostly overcome the Lacks family's resistance and has worked closely with Deborah to reconstruct her family history. But now she is faced with evidence that her efforts might have harmed one of the subjects of her narrative-in-progress.

The possibility that Rebecca is responsible for what is happening to Deborah is underscored by Gary, who, Skloot recounts, "stared into my eyes as he hugged Deborah's sobbing body and whispered to her, 'You're not alone'" (292). Although his words are meant for Deborah, he is looking at Rebecca, reminding her, perhaps, that she is not a singular author in pursuit of a story but a human being in complex relation to the human beings whose story she is constructing. Gary continues to look at Rebecca while praying for God to transfer Deborah's burden to the scribbling witness in the recliner: "LORD, I KNOW you sent Miss Rebecca to help LIFT THE BURDEN of them CELLS!" he exclaims. "LET HER CARRY THEM" (292–93). Invoking HeLa cells as a metonym for the impact their discovery has had on the Lacks family, Gary calls upon Rebecca to carry the weight of the story she is writing in all of its emotional, ethical, and scientific complexity. Although Rebecca, just moments earlier, has contemplated the possibility that she is answerable for what is happening to Deborah, Gary's words still surprise her: "*Wait a minute, that wasn't supposed to happen!*" (293).

This scene highlights one of postgenomic literature's key interventions: to illuminate ethical issues that overlap the fields of science, medicine, and literature, particularly as they relate to ownership of stories and bodies, questions of the "public good," and constructions of racial and ethnic difference. Indeed, throughout *Immortal Life*, the book's central question—who can study whose body parts for whose benefit?—is inextricably intertwined with the question of who can tell whose story to whom. "Life writing," in both its literary and biological valence, is at once the form and the subject of the book. If, as I discuss in the previous chapter, DNA is widely seen as the ultimate "Book of Life," a biological ur-text that determines our lives on an individual and species level, postgenomic life writing is, by definition, a commentary on this figure and on the field of life writing itself. Indeed, works like *Immortal Life*, despite being "biographical" or "nonfictional," invite metatextual forms of engagement that can exceed their apparent limitations. And works of fiction that engage life writing (as genre and/or gene) similarly invite methods of reading that blur generic and disciplinary lines.

In this chapter, I *look closely*[2] at how life writing, as both figure and genre, is engaged by two very different works of postgenomic narrative: Skloot's *Immortal Life* (an example of life writing) and Richard Powers's 2009 novel *Generosity: An Enhancement* (an example of metafiction *about* life writing). Despite their many differences—one is nonfiction, the other fiction; one is focused on cells, the other on DNA; one addresses anti-Black racism, the other colonialism and ethnocentrism—*Immortal Life* and *Generosity* alike engage parallel ethical issues in the fields of science and literature. Skloot, I argue, robustly addresses questions of medical ethics but only partly acknowledges the corresponding questions of narrative ethics that shape her project, risking a reiteration of the biological violation being narrated. However, she also includes insurgent counternarratives that can be highlighted through reading practices attentive to the instability and multivocality of life writing and to contexts of medical and literary racism. Unlike *Immortal Life*, *Generosity* makes the ethical overlap between life writing and life science a narrative centerpiece, while critiquing reading practices (literary or biological) that ignore context and polysemy in the pursuit of "truth." Highlighting the narrative demands that shape *both* life writing and life science, Powers uses "creative nonfiction" as an oxymoronic fulcrum for examining—and, ultimately, eroding—the opposition between fact and fiction that informs the "two cultures" divide.[3] The metafictional reading practice *Generosity* models, I argue, is transferable to other postgenomic texts (literary or otherwise) and helpful for reading against dominant formulations of the textual metaphor and context-free reading practices. Reading *Immortal Life* and *Generosity*

---

2. As will become clear, I borrow this phrase from Powers's *Generosity: An Enhancement* (2009).

3. See Snow for a classic critique of the science/humanities binary.

together casts light on the significance of life writing—and strategies for "life reading"—in the postgenomic age.

Critical Life Reading in the Postgenomic Age

The capacious category of "life writing," comprising biography, autobiography, memoir, testimony, personal essay, diary, confessional poetry, and other forms focused on individual lived experience, has long raised ethical questions. The right of an author to tell the story of another person's life—to subordinate the privacy of the subject to the (narrative, social, political, economic, or scientific) value of their story—is at the forefront of biography, "collaborative" life writing,[4] and even autobiography, inasmuch as "all *auto*biography is necessarily *hetero*biography" involving the author's reconstruction of the experiences, words, and actions of others (Couser x). The reverse is also true: even in the case of straightforward biography, decisions about what to include or exclude, what questions and themes to pursue, and how to order the narrative can reveal as much about the author as the subject. Life writing also raises questions about compensation and harm. Should authors who profit from the stories of others remunerate them in some way? When does the public good outweigh potential harm to an individual or community? Narratives about human rights abuses can, for example, lead to positive change, but they can also contribute to a "global trade in represented suffering" and perpetuate "cultures of rescue" when they do not robustly address systems of oppression (S. Smith 569).

The issues of privacy, consent, and compensation raised by life writing are also accompanied by questions of authenticity. Life writing is often valued according to measures of factuality not normally applied to other genres, even though auto/biography is not always easily distinguishable from fiction. Controversies arise when a memoirist, for example, is found to have dramatically embellished their life story, and the stakes are raised when the text is focused on a marginalized identity or tale of oppression. Although expectations of authenticity are generally higher for life writing than for fiction, fictional stories of suffering can also be subjected to the kind

---

4. Collaborative life writing encompasses "those narratives that emerge from the joint project of an informant lacking literacy and an interlocutor or editor interested in bringing the informant's story to a broad audience"; in such texts, the question of whether a "colonized subject" can "speak in or through cultural formations other than those of the colonial master" is "particularly vexed" (Smith and Watson, Introduction 28). Also see Couser 48. *Immortal Life* is, arguably, an example of both biography (of Henrietta Lacks) and collaborative life writing.

of scrutiny usually reserved for life writing.[5] Take, for example, the allegations that Jeanine Cummins's recent novel *American Dirt* (2020) appropriates and distorts the stories of Mexican immigrants or, on the coin's reverse side, the pressures put on writers of color to satisfy the expectations of white readers who mistake stereotypes for authenticity or hunger for tales of sorrow, as satirized in Cord Jefferson's 2023 film *American Fiction*.[6] These phenomena suggest that life writing is both a genre and a way of reading, and that "life reading" is enacted upon texts differentially according to regimes of race, ethnicity, gender, class, and sexuality—categories that exist in uneasy relation to genetics.

The figurative alignment of literary and biological "life writing" in the postgenomic age draws our attention to how ethical questions that apply in literary contexts also apply in scientific and medical contexts. G. Thomas Couser, whose work has focused on life writing's "vulnerable subjects" (i.e., subjects structurally disadvantaged in relation to the authors who write their stories), has argued that DNA is an especially "powerful form of life writing, one with the potential to render all of us vulnerable" (xiv). It is "not the degree to which our genes may write our lives directly" that makes this the case, "but the degree to which 'knowledge' of our genes may write our lives" (169). Indeed, to have one's genetic story told without one's knowledge or consent can have far-reaching personal, political, and social implications, including health stigma, government surveillance, criminal prosecution, and public and private forms of discrimination. Genetic research also leads to the development of valuable medical technologies, pitting privacy and bodily autonomy against collective and corporate well-being and raising questions about who benefits from genetic research.

Like life writing vis-à-vis other literary forms, DNA is also understood as "true" in a way that other biological attributes are not. Genetic testing can be used to verify individual identities, family relationships, and group membership—sometimes in conflict with other ways (somatic, familial, cultural, narrative) of authenticating all of the above. Genetic ancestry testing, for example, is marketed as the "true story" of one's ethnic or racial heritage—truer, even, than family histories; chromosomal review has been asserted, wrongly, as a means of assigning biological sex and thus resolving

---

5. See Smith and Watson on the "fluid boundary" between autobiography and the novel, especially for writers from marginalized and/or colonized communities (*Reading* 10).

6. On the controversy around Cummins's novel, see Grady. For my discussion of Percival Everett's *Erasure* (2001), the novel on which *American Fiction* is based, see Larkin 148–63.

controversies over transgender athletes (Ghorayshi); and efforts to identify genetic bases for violence, criminality, or intelligence recur with unfortunate regularity (Washington 244–70; Roberts, "Can"). Like earlier means of tracing "bloodlines," genetic genealogies, infused with the self-verifying force of DNA, can be mobilized in service of nationalism, racism, and "filiopietism" (S. Smith 566).

The postgenomic age also coincides with growing interest, among both lay readers and scholars, in illness and disability narratives, many touching on the personal implications of genetic testing or heritable disease, as in the case of Siddhartha Mukherjee's *The Gene: An Intimate History* and Alice Wexler's *Mapping Fate,* both discussed in chapter 1. Such narratives bring even closer into view the ethical concerns that overlap literary and biological life writing.[7] However, while genetic research is subject to bioethical review, there are no formal or informal ethical principles governing life writing. Narrative ethics plays a smaller role in literary studies than bioethics does in the life sciences, even though literary studies is sometimes mobilized to assist science and medicine in developing ethical practices. Though he warns against mistaking ethical "ideals" for "obligations," and thus becoming "hypercritical" of authors, Couser argues that life writing should look to bioethics as a model for developing voluntary ethical principles, not least "because life writing partnerships sometimes resemble the sorts of confidential fiduciary relationships that exist between physicians and patients, and also because in some cases the narratives themselves recount scenarios in which . . . biomedical issues are the subject" (30). Couser calls for authors to respect the right of individuals to their own stories, recommending that they give subjects opportunities to grant and withdraw consent, to take an active role in shaping their stories, and to be fully aware of the economic terms under which the story is being produced. Indeed, he urges authors to include in their texts "accounts of the transactions and negotiations that produced them" (25).

Despite its ethical complications, life writing may also be well suited to respond to bioethical issues, particularly those raised by genomics. Couser, for example, argues that a "robust" life writing that proceeds with an awareness of its own ethical complications could "help to contextualize and resolve some of the complex ethical questions raised by DNA research" (xiv). Scholars of narrative medicine, a field positioned as a corrective to the "biomedicalization" of health care, also contend that narrative—and,

---

7. On the illness and disability narrative "boom," see Conway 4.

particularly, life writing—can have a salutary effect on the practice of medicine.[8] Physicians must learn to "[enter] into the suffering of another" like a "novelist" or a "careful reader" (DasGupta 980), and to "think *with* stories," in order to provide care that is both humane and effective (Frank 23). By engaging in "joint" storytelling with patients, they can also begin to share power with those who have been disempowered by the institutions of medicine (Brody 79).

At the same time, narrative medicine, like any other clinical practice, carries "iatrogenic risk"—the risk of harm caused by medical treatment (Peterkin 397). A number of scholars have noted that physicians often approach illness narratives as if they are "unmediated reality" (Chambers xiii), making readers vulnerable to taking "scripts and stock representations" (Garden, "Telling" 122)—such as the popular narrative of triumph over adversity—at face value and ignoring potential "fault lines and counterstories" (124).[9] Some have also argued that clinical empathy, one of narrative medicine's key competencies, is "potentially dangerous" if it leads doctors to believe that they can "gain direct access to what is going on in [a] patient's head" (MacNaughton 1941) or if it is not paired with an understanding of sociocultural context (Garden, "Expanding" 124).[10] Physicians also risk causing harm when telling patient stories—though there may be important reasons to take that risk: "We cannot speak for another . . . except in flawed and potentially dangerous ways," writes Rebecca Garden, "while at the same time accepting the risk of ethical pitfalls to open up channels for understanding and agency" ("Who" 79–80).[11]

Because we live in a society structured by inequity, our enactment of narrative agency is never pure. Awareness of this fact might discourage us from taking on the responsibilities of narrative agency altogether; indeed, this is how the main character in *Generosity* responds to the sudden realization that he has caused harm through his writing, as I discuss below. But, as Powers makes clear, we are narrative creatures, and our narrative desires—whether we are professional readers and writers or not—will continue to shape the world we live in. If we don't reflect on those desires and their

---

8. "Biomedicalization" is "the process by which all of life has come to be under the governance of biomedical technologies" (Squier 335).

9. Also see Solomon 200.

10. For a more positive assessment of clinical empathy, see Engel 3. See Liatsos for a discussion of "entanglement," "a type of attentiveness whose empathic quality is founded on the reader's capacity to remain attentive without any expectation of integration or comprehension," as an alternative to typical formulations of empathy (19).

11. Peterkin has raised ethical questions regarding the motivation of physicians who publish patient histories (403–4).

embeddedness in regimes of power, we are not well positioned to intervene in them. Readers and writers alike have a responsibility to keep power structures in view; indeed, if life writing is a genre defined in part by the expectations of its audience, then the ethical issues raised by life writing can be reframed as issues of life reading—as questions of how to approach narratives about the lives of others, especially when those narratives are also about the kind of life writing ascribed to DNA. Critical intervention should not be limited to critiques of authors and texts; it should also encompass reflection on how we read.

I would suggest that *critical life reading* for the postgenomic age might productively draw from physician and narrative medicine scholar Sayantani DasGupta's concept of "narrative humility,"[12] a welcome corrective to "narrative competency":

> Narrative humility acknowledges that our patients' stories are not objects that we can comprehend or master, but rather dynamic entities that we can approach and engage with, while simultaneously remaining open to their ambiguity and contradiction, and engaging in constant self-evaluation and self-critique about issues such as our own role in the story, our expectations of the story, our responsibilities to the story, and our identifications with the story. (981)

DasGupta's definition of narrative humility requires readers to give up expectations of mastery and authenticity (critical approaches that align reading with diagnosis), instead embracing plurality, uncertainty, and open-endedness. It also demands self-reflexivity, making the reading subject a text to be read in its own right, as readers take stock of their psychological, emotional, structural, and ethical relation to stories. Importantly, self-reflexive reading should be paired with socially conscious reading; "There are larger forces that enable the telling of certain sorts of stories and silence other stories," DasGupta reminds physicians, drawing attention to power imbalances beyond the clinic (981).

Narrative humility also requires attentiveness to counternarratives that have been muted in a text—or that have been muted by dominant readings of a text. Life writing scholar Leigh Gilmore has argued that such "interruptions and eruptions," often found in the "interstices" and "margins" of texts—including those "that have not been seen as autobiographies"—constitute

---

12. This concept is aligned with Sheila Jasanoff's "technologies of humility," which Benjamin offers as a corrective to the "allure of objectivity" attached to genetic ancestry testing (132).

"strategies of self-representation" and "resistance" for marginalized subjects (184). These voices demand ways of reading that are resistant to "fantasies of the real," including those, I would add, that apply to life writing in its narrative and biological formulations (189). This kind of reading against the grain is aligned with poststructuralist critical trends, which undermine hegemonic narratives in favor of undecidability, performativity, and dialogism (Smith and Watson, *Reading* 137–46). However, narrative humility also requires readers to keep in view the embodied, lived experience of narrative subjects, authors, and readers. Einat Avrahami argues that illness narratives demand this kind of attentiveness, "insist[ing] on the concretely situated body not only as an undeniable reality that should be reckoned with but also as an indispensable source of knowledge" (11).

Critical life reading, then, involves several intertwined elements: acknowledging the limits of what one can know or understand of another's story; resisting the urge to mastery and the expectation of "authenticity"; recognizing a story's social, political, and material contexts; and remaining attentive to counternarratives. These elements are especially crucial in the postgenomic era, when the idea of the genome as the "Book of Life" persists in the public imagination. Practices of critical life reading that are developed in relation to works of life writing about the life sciences (or, more dizzily, that are developed in relation to writing about life writing about the life sciences) might be especially helpful in training readers to read dominant representations of the genome with a critical eye, especially as genomic science alters what constitutes a life story as well as how life stories are told and circulated.[13] The texts discussed below illustrate the risks and responsibilities of life writing while also modeling or soliciting distinct practices of critical life reading for the postgenomic age.

Insurgent Readers in *The Immortal Life of Henrietta Lacks*

The family of Henrietta Lacks, the working-class Black woman whose cervical cancer cells were used to develop the first immortal human cell line, did not learn of her contribution to medicine until decades after her death, and, until very recently, the benefits of this contribution were mostly out of reach for them. The HeLa story evokes the violent alienation of Black persons from their bodies under slavery, what Hortense Spillers refers to as the "seared,

---

13. "In the future, surgically, genetically, or digitally altered modes of embodiment will surely inform the tropes, narrative arcs, subject positions, and affective charges of life writing" (Smith, "Presidential" 571).

divided, ripped-apartness" of African "flesh" (67), and the long history of medical exploitation and abuse of Black people, what Harriet Washington calls "medical apartheid." Lacks's genetic material was—and continues to be—grown, harvested, bought, and sold in the material interest of others. Her "precious babies" (Skloot 58), as the doctor who developed the HeLa line called Lacks's cells, chillingly recall the reproductive politics of slavery and its "afterlife" in ongoing health disparities and medical inequities.[14]

For a long while, the official HeLa story not only muted this history but also trafficked in race and gender stereotypes. Initially, as Hannah Landecker has shown, media and medical representations of HeLa conformed to a narrative of maternal sacrifice.[15] In these accounts, Lacks, sometimes mistakenly referred to as "Helen Lane" (a renaming that recalls another dehumanizing aspect of slavery), was a devoted housewife and mother who, struck down too soon, lives on in her cell line and the medical treatments indebted to it, giving life to countless others. Such accounts fit an inspirational story of medical progress that ignores not only the absence of informed consent and patient rights (virtually nonexistent in Lacks's time) but also the racial inequity that structured Lacks's life and death. When race does enter the storyline, it follows the earth-shattering discovery that HeLa has "contaminated" cell lines around the world—a discovery that hinges on race, as HeLa becomes recognizable via a cellular marker associated with African heritage. Lacks's Blackness, supposedly legible in her cells, shifts the narrative from maternal altruism to racial pollution, as HeLa is described in threatening terms: "aggressive," "surreptitious," "renegade," "catastrophic" (Landecker 171). *Black* HeLa is viewed as "promiscuous" and unnatural, a contagion, a cancer, and recurring fascination with the total mass of HeLa cells kept in laboratories around the world corresponds not only to an obsession with the technological alienation of life from bodies but also to an obsession with transforming Black women's bodies into radically available flesh (171).[16]

Rebecca Skloot's *The Immortal Life of Henrietta Lacks* is a welcome corrective to dehumanizing HeLa stories, returning a name, body, and history to a

---

14. See Weinbaum's discussion of the "afterlife of reproductive slavery" for the way a "slave episteme" continues to inform reproductive biotechnologies today (*Afterlife* 1–28), as well as Clayton and King's discussion of the reverberating, transgenerational impact of medical violation in Black communities. Also see chapter 4 for further discussion.

15. This narrative also serves a biocommercial system that demands sacrifice in the service of corporate profit: "The concept of sacrifice has been central to the consolidation of an intellectual property regime that supports contemporary biocommerce" (R. Mitchell 127).

16. My reference to "flesh" as undifferentiated human tissue, vulnerable to violence, exploitation, and disposal, is influenced by Spillers's differentiation between "bodies" and "flesh"; see my discussion in chapter 4.

woman who had been abstracted to a string of letters in textbooks and medical journals, reduced to a collection of cells in test tubes and under microscopes (or, more recently, to genetic code), and burdened with an assortment of race and gender stereotypes. Skloot's work has not only brought mainstream attention to the Lacks story and to medical racism in general; it has also led to some positive impacts for the Lacks family. Although no members of the family were compensated for sharing their stories (a point of contention in the narrative), Skloot has set up a Lacks family scholarship fund, and Lacks family members have been remunerated for public lectures and other events in the wake of the book's publication. More broadly, the visibility *Immortal Life* brought to the Lacks story has resulted in significant policy changes, most notably the agreement reached with the National Institutes of Health in 2013 giving the Lacks family partial control over the release of the HeLa genome to researchers ("NIH"). The family has also sought legal action, in the wake of the book's publication, against biotech companies that have profited from the HeLa cell line; in 2023, a settlement was reached with Thermo Fisher Scientific, and additional lawsuits are likely to follow (Holpuch).

In its commitment to redressing Lacks's erasure from the historical record and acknowledging the contribution made by African American women to medicine—as well as the suffering caused by medical exploitation and neglect—Skloot's work is aligned with Black feminist projects of recovery and revision, such as Washington's and Roberts's. *Immortal Life* is distinct from other works in this archive, however, in that the race and class differences between Skloot and Lacks echo those between Lacks and (most of) the doctors, scientists, and biomedical executives who have treated, studied, and profited from her body. Skloot acknowledges the differences separating her from her subject in an autobiographical gloss that emphasizes her whiteness, secularism, and bourgeois status (7). And she makes visible, as Couser recommends, the "transactions and negotiations" that characterized her collaboration with "vulnerable subjects" (25). At the same time, *Immortal Life* mirrors the story it tells: both are instances of appropriation that alter the life of a Black family in service of unevenly distributed public goods, corporate profits, and personal and professional gains. Like her cancer cells, Lacks's story has been collected by an outsider, transformed into a marketable product, and sold to great profit.[17] In other words, *Immortal Life*—in content, form, and circulation—reveals extensive

---

17. Note: the doctor who first developed the HeLa cell line did not attempt to patent it and did not profit from it.

overlap between medical and narrative expropriation. Burdened with the ethical complications of collaborative life writing, Skloot's book specifically recalls the fraught publication histories of slave narratives and abolitionist texts, which involve white experts authenticating the experiences of Black people for largely white audiences.[18] Once again, a white-authored text has brought widespread attention to issues that receive less attention when written about by Black writers.

The impact of white reader demands is evident not only in the reception of *Immortal Life* but also within the narrative itself, as Skloot recounts her effort to write a story that would satisfy her own narrative desire. As Skloot recounts, her drive to authorship is preceded by a drive to readership and repeated demands for narrative access. Rebecca—Skloot's narrative persona—overcomes numerous obstacles to construct the story she wants to read, a story to replace the inadequate version she encountered in school.[19] Here is Rebecca learning about Henrietta Lacks for the first time:

> "HeLa cells were one of the most important things that happened to medicine in the last hundred years," [Professor] Defler said.
> Then, matter-of-factly, almost as an afterthought, he said, "She was a black woman." He erased her name in one fast swipe and blew the chalk from his hands. Class was over.

Erased from the historical record, Lacks's unique identity is atomized, multiplied, and cast to the wind like the bits of chalk Rebecca's professor blows from his hands. Left behind is the chalkboard, a symbolic blank space that Rebecca seeks to fill. She wants to know the rest of Lacks's story, but "no one knows anything" about Henrietta, a formulation that subtly negates the family knowledge that does exist (4). Rebecca is a persistent researcher whose academic and professional career stems from her curiosity about Lacks: she studies biology because she wants to understand the impact of HeLa cells on medicine; she studies writing because she wants to write a biography of Lacks. Readers follow along as Rebecca stares obsessively at a picture of Lacks's daughter, reads magazine articles and biology textbooks, combs through medical and legal records, watches documentaries.

Rather than "narrative humility," Rebecca at times evinces what Doris Sommer calls "cannibalistic" reading, whereby "majority" readers approach

---

18. On slave narrative and abolitionist writing, see Morrison, "Site" 70; V. Smith, *Self-Discovery* 35–43.

19. When referring to character, I use first name ("Rebecca"); when referring to author, I use last name ("Skloot"). However, slippage between the terms is unavoidable.

"minority" texts with the expectation that authenticity will be proffered and secrets divulged, satisfying a hunger for knowledge and mastery. Imperialist readers take roadblocks as invitations to push forward, conquering texts that seek to keep outsiders at bay. The text says "no" but means "yes," and the persistent reader presses on (Sommer 10–15). Skloot's zeal for the Lacks story demands full disclosure. Although she is warned that Deborah might suffer emotionally or physically from talking with her, Rebecca pursues her indomitably and is, early on, cut off by the family. Undeterred, she begins a campaign of harassment, "calling Deborah, her brothers, and her father daily" (54). Over the course of a year, Rebecca uses her growing knowledge to tempt Deborah into conversation: "I imagined Deborah leaning over her answering machine listening, dying to know what I'd found" (232). This manipulation, particularly the vision of Deborah *"dying* to know" about Rebecca's discoveries, should give readers pause. Skloot also narrates the Lacks story with limited caveats, source citations, and quotation marks, passing on reconstructions as fact, suggesting an intimacy between author and subject that readers are invited to share, a repeated intrusion that recapitulates the intrusion performed by Lacks's doctors. This narrative tendency is most uncomfortable when Skloot recounts Henrietta locking herself in the bathroom to inspect the tumor growing on her cervix (Skloot 15). As David Lacks has asked, how could Skloot know what his mother did behind a closed door? (Lacks). Skloot escorts readers behind this door and into the recesses of Henrietta's body, staging closeness at the cost of privacy.

This demand for narrative intimacy is accompanied by an altruistic claim: Skloot and her (fellow) readers demand a sacrifice—a "donation"—from the Lackses for a "greater good": a public discussion of medical racism and patient rights. However, *Immortal Life* is not exclusively concerned with issues that disproportionately affect vulnerable subjects. This fact is clearest in the afterword, which Skloot begins by reporting frequently asked questions: "Wasn't it illegal for doctors to take Henrietta's cells without her knowledge" and "Don't doctors have to tell you when they use your cells in research?" The universalizing trajectory of these questions is signaled by the move from the singular third-person ("her") to the universal second-person ("you"): "When *you* go to the doctor for a routine blood test or to have a mole removed, when *you* have an appendectomy, tonsillectomy, or any other kind of *ectomy*, the stuff *you* leave behind doesn't always get thrown out. Doctors, hospitals, and laboratories keep it" (315; emphasis added). Skloot's implied audience has access to regular health care and "cultural health capital" (Shim), and the plight of the under- and uninsured, as well as the racially marginalized, is largely dropped.[20] This elision is repeated in the remarks of David Korn, former vice provost of research at Harvard: "Since everybody benefits, everybody can accept the small risks of having their tissue scraps used in research" (qtd. in Skloot, 321). The glaring issue left unremarked upon is that everybody does not benefit (or does not benefit equally) from medical research. As Priscilla Wald explains, the injustice at the heart of the HeLa story is not the failure to compensate Lacks; it is the failure to create an equitable health care system and to eradicate a long-standing racial ideology that insists on Black people's biological inferiority while endorsing the use of their bodies for the benefit of white people: "The properties of their cells should not entitle individuals to what should be basic expectations. . . . [Lacks's] family should receive state-of-the-art health care because such care should be a basic entitlement" ("American" 187–88).

Immortal Life effectively introduces medical ethics to a broad audience, including those who have little knowledge of the medical exploitation of African Americans. However, it risks recentering a white middle-class point of view and encouraging a reading practice that seeks narrative satisfaction at the expense of both privacy and antiracist action. In the spirit of narrative humility, and its call for self-reflexivity, it is important to say that I am a white, middle-class reader whose race, class, gender, educational, and geographical backgrounds hew closely to Skloot's. I am the reader that Skloot's narrative persona chaperones through unfamiliar territory, whose personal medical concerns, regarding privacy and property, are highlighted alongside the distinct concerns of the Lacks family and of poor and working-class Black people. I am also a reader who devoured the text, staying up late into the night to satisfy my curiosity about the Lacks family's trajectory and crying over Deborah's death. Like the nurse who, upon examining Henrietta Lacks's corpse, recognizes her humanity upon seeing her painted toenails, I am the reader who is invited to identify with the title character based on shared femininity—on the representation of Lacks as a woman and a mother. Given my alignment with the narrative perspective of *Immortal Life*, it is imperative that my reading go beyond mere critique of the text, instead decentering a white perspective, centering Black perspectives, remaining attentive to contexts of oppression, and seeking out counternarratives in the text's margins and interstices. This alternative reading is enabled, I should point out, by the collaborative process and braided

---

20. As Henrietta Lacks's son Zakariyya says, "Only people that can get any good from my mother cells is the people that got money, and whoever sellin them cells—they get rich off our mother and we got nothing" (Skloot 247).

structure that characterize *Immortal Life*. By including the story of the writing of the story—by drawing attention to its own constructedness—Skloot leaves the text open to critique, while also making space for "interruptions and eruptions" that "resist" dominant narratives and allow opportunities for insurgent "self-representations" (Gilmore 184).[21]

Deborah's cousin Gary, discussed in the introduction to this chapter, is one such insurgent voice, in that his interjections have the potential to shift reader perspective on the relationship between the text's author and its subjects in an ethically significant way. Another such figure is Cootie, a Lacks cousin who resembles the bluesman Jim Trueblood in Ralph Ellison's *Invisible Man* and raises the possibility that narrative strategies of misdirection and double-voicedness, what African American vernacular culture calls "signifying," are in play. Such techniques, along with silence, deferral, and withholding of information (as in Deborah's sporadic refusal to speak to Rebecca or to hand over medical records), constitute narrative "roadblocks" that, Sommer argues, lead to interpretive and ethical error when ignored (Sommer 17). As in the Trueblood episode, the Cootie episode begins when a white benefactor (here, Rebecca) travels away from civilization and (it seems) backward in time to encounter a Black storyteller. "Past Difficult Creek and on the banks of the River of Death," Clover, Virginia, gets "darker than dark" (Skloot 77). Main Street is mostly boarded up, clocks have stopped, and a strange man known as "the Greeter" silently directs Rebecca to Lacks Town, where "Slave-era cabins . . . sat next to cinder-block homes and trailers" (78). Into this liminal no-man's land walks Cootie, an exemplary country bumpkin who repeatedly refers to his own ignorance in ways that strain credulity: he asks Rebecca, for example, to read a 1970s *Rolling Stone* article on his cousin Henrietta that he has kept under his mattress for years because he doesn't "know what it say" (81) and explains that he was given his nickname after contracting polio but "was never sure why" (79). Cootie's description of the building and rebuilding of his home—a story whose repetitions with a difference recall the structure of a folktale—similarly emphasizes his innocence and ignorance. And, in whispering to Rebecca that Henrietta's illness was the result of voodoo, Cootie makes good on Skloot's eerie introduction to Clover.

Why Cootie should volunteer these self-deprecating and folkloric anecdotes is unclear, not least because we do not read Rebecca's interlocution. While cannibalistic reading might encourage readers to receive Cootie's

---

21. Choksey reads Deborah and Zakariyya as insurgent figures in their resistance to Skloot's erasure of the "horror" at the heart of the Lacks story: "white experimentation on Black bodies" (129).

stories through the lens of authenticity (shaped by stereotype), narrative humility might encourage readers to pause—to wonder if there is something more to the story. Indeed, we might ask whether Cootie is entertaining a white audience with the depictions of Black rural life they expect, "hitting a straight lick with a crooked stick," to use Zora Neale Hurston's phrase (Hurston 141).[22] Introducing this ambiguity into Cootie's narration destabilizes other portions of the narrative as well, including Skloot's bucolic description of Henrietta Lacks's childhood in Clover, which underplays the effects of poverty, racism, and an early pregnancy on Henrietta's life. With Cootie's performance in mind, Skloot's statement that the Lacks family makes Clover sound "idyllic as a fairy tale" suggests that Cootie might not be alone in shaping a particular version of the Lacks family story for public consumption (24). To be clear, I am not suggesting that Skloot is unaware of such possibilities; rather, I am suggesting that there are opportunities—built into the structure of the text—for readers to acknowledge alternative accounts, ambiguities, and occlusions stemming from the racial politics of the collaborative narrative.

Another—and perhaps the most significant—insurgent voice in *Immortal Life* is that of Deborah Lacks-Pullum, Henrietta's daughter and, arguably, Rebecca's "significant other," an essential figure in the story Skloot tells about her own narrative journey (Smith and Watson, *Reading* 65–67).[23] A case can be made for Lacks-Pullum as coauthor of the text, not only because much of the book is given over to her story but also because she worked closely with Skloot to bring the book to fruition.[24] As the narrative develops, Deborah is revealed to be an enthusiastic reader and researcher in her own right, and it is by depicting her (often unruly) reading practices that the text complicates its own narrative point of view. Lois Brown has written of the way Black women's private practices of reading and writing, recorded in a variety of unpublished, quotidian documents, undermine "official" narratives about Black women; Deborah's reading practices, recorded by Skloot, function similarly to complicate the "official" narrative. Accompanying Rebecca on information-gathering missions and operating much like an assistant, Deborah also develops independent research and

---

22. See Meisenhelder 1–13 for a discussion of Hurston's incisive phrase and the signifying strategies it captures.

23. Henrietta is, in turn, the "idealized absent Other," despite Deborah and Rebecca's attempts to bring her back to life (Smith and Watson, *Reading* 87).

24. Notably, the recent film adaptation of *Immortal Life* focuses primarily on the story of Deborah and Rebecca's journey of narrative discovery, subordinating the biographies of HeLa and Henrietta Lacks to the relationship and joint research that produced the book.

academic agendas. Like Rebecca, Deborah tracks down and decodes documents and learns to navigate multiple discourses. Readers watch as Deborah enrolls in college courses, studies textbooks, performs internet searches, carries a dictionary to Johns Hopkins, and prints out reams of paper on HeLa cells, genetics, and medical ethics—as well as apparently extraneous topics captured by the wide net she casts. In other words, Deborah steps into the long African American tradition of pursuing literacy as a crucial step toward self-realization.

Deborah's early attempts at research are haphazard. In a chapter focused on her declining mental and physical health, her unorganized studies seem to be the result of an unorganized mind: "Deborah often woke up with her face on the desk, surrounded by a mountain of pages that spilled from her printer onto the floor: scientific articles, patent applications, random newspaper articles and blog posts, including many that had no connection to her mother but used the words *Henrietta* or *lacks* or *Hela*" (254). Unconscious and surrounded by "random" papers, Deborah appears ill-prepared to perform research as well as literally ill. Playing the role of teacher, Rebecca corrects Deborah's early efforts, even when she herself is ailing: "One day, . . . my phone rang as I slept, feverish with flu. Deborah yelled on the other end, 'I told you London cloned my mother!' . . . 'They didn't clone her,' I said. 'They just made copies of her cells'" (255). Eventually, and thanks, it seems, to Rebecca's tutelage, Deborah becomes more organized and knowledgeable: "She made lists of questions for me and printed articles about research done on people without their knowledge or consent," reports Skloot, and she "started organizing information into carefully labeled folders" (256). In other words, Deborah becomes a good student because Rebecca is a good teacher, as *Immortal Life* risks veering toward a familiar "white savior" narrative.

However, embedded in this literacy narrative are alternative ways of reading HeLa that only appear because of Deborah's early, scattered efforts, suggesting that Rebecca's "organized" way into the story might not be the only way. Rebecca notes the many referents for *hela* that Deborah discovers during her nocturnal web-surfing sessions:

> Hela is the native name for the country of Sri Lanka, where activists carry signs demanding "Justice for the Hela Nation." It's the name of a defunct German tractor company and an award-winning shih-tzu dog; it's a seaside resort in Poland, an advertising firm in Switzerland, a Danish boat where people gather to drink vodka and watch films, and a Marvel comic book character who appears in several online games.

Without Deborah's influence, exploring alternate meanings of *hela* would be a fanciful undertaking for Skloot. As it stands, Skloot uses the list to characterize Deborah as her irrational, if beloved, foil and does not pursue its implications. Deborah, however, approaches her "random" discoveries more openly. Skloot reports that "when Deborah found pages describing Hela the Marvel character, she thought they were describing her mother, since each of Hela's traits in some way matched what Deborah had heard about her mother's cells." Hela is

> a seven-foot-tall, half-black, half-white goddess who's part dead and part alive, with "immeasurable" intelligence, "superhuman" strength, "godlike" stamina and durability, and five hundred pounds of solid muscle. She's responsible for plagues, sickness, and catastrophes; she's immune to fire, radiation, toxins, corrosives, disease, and aging. She can also levitate and control people's minds. (254)

Skloot responds, naturally, with a correction: "It turned out the sci-fi Hela was inspired by the ancient Norse goddess of death" (254–55). But Deborah is difficult to correct: "Deborah figured that goddess was based on her mother too" (255). It would be easy to view this exchange as evidence of Deborah's insufficient education and deteriorating mind—or of Skloot's presentation of Deborah as foolish.[25] But this passage also shows Deborah using reading as a source of agency. Through Hela, Deborah discovers a powerful figure—Black and female—who can control or repel many of the forces that have shaped the Lacks story: "sickness," "catastrophe," "fire," "radiation," "toxins," "disease," "aging," and, perhaps most poignantly, "people's minds" (254). A narrative figure herself—distributed in comic books—Hela represents Black women telling their own stories in their own words.[26]

Recentering Deborah (and Cootie and Gary) and destabilizing *hela* makes possible a feminist, deconstructive, and Black-centered counter-reading of *Immortal Life*. Deborah's inventive and interruptive reading practices, a refreshing contrast to Rebecca's efforts to tame the Lacks story, symbolically challenge the effort to shoe-horn dynamic biological data into "stable" racial categories—and the popular belief that the most fundamental truths

---

25. Choksey also notes that Skloot interprets "Deborah's reading [as] paranoid or even pathological, a neurotic symptom" (129).

26. By signifying on the term "hela," Deborah approaches "the name as a potential site of experimentation rather than a contractual sign of identity," a technique of self-representation that Gilmore identifies in a text's "autobiographics" (184).

about human identity are inscribed in cells or DNA. Drawing attention to the unequal social, political, medical, and narrative systems that shape the Lacks story, these insurgent voices also draw attention to the intransigent contradictions of these systems, to their false certainties. Consuming a version of the story that "makes sense" risks sacrificing these contradictions to narrative coherence, allowing readers to sympathize with the Lackses and object to particular medical or research practices without fundamentally questioning the race, gender, and class hierarchies that structure them. In contrast, a reading of *Immortal Life* that emphasizes Deborah's narrative agency demands, particularly from the text's implied (white, middle-class, female) readers, reorientation toward these systems and lays the groundwork for reading other biomedical narratives with an eye toward marginalized perspectives, muted critiques, and constitutive contradictions. Deborah Lacks may not succeed as an author, hindered by numerous biosocial roadblocks. However, she leaves her mark as a model for how to read lives in the postgenomic age.

Looking Again in *Generosity: An Enhancement*

Like *Immortal Life,* Richard Powers's *Generosity: An Enhancement* centers on a white nonfiction writer whose pursuit of narrative satisfaction leads to the emotional and physical breakdown of a character marked by both ethnic difference and biological exceptionality. *Generosity* is focused on Russell Stone, once a rising literary star known for his ironic retellings of other people's stories. After being challenged by readers personally connected to the subjects of his stories, including a Tohono O'odham man who attempts suicide after Stone's story about him is published, Stone abandons writing and becomes a teacher and magazine editor. Despite this career change, he finds himself responsible for another instance of narrative exploitation. Thassadit Amzwar, one of Stone's writing students, is a Tamazight[27] woman who writes about her experiences of war and loss in Algeria for Stone's creative nonfiction class. Despite her trauma, Thassa exhibits preternatural cheerfulness, or, in psychiatric jargon, "hyperthymia." Stone becomes obsessed with Thassa, viewing her as an antidote to his stubborn depression and admiring

---

27. *Tamazight* is the feminine term (and *Amazigh* the masculine term) for the North African people still widely referred to as *Berber,* a word Thassa counsels Stone to avoid: "Careful saying Berber. . . . Berber means barbarian. Say *Amazigh*. That means free people" (Powers, *Generosity* 37). For a succinct discussion of the names used for the Amazigh people, see Said 4–5.

her essays as the kind of writing he wishes he could produce. His obsession inadvertently sets in motion a series of events, including invasive attention from geneticists and the media, that eventually leads Thassa to attempt suicide, her breakdown revealing that her genetic profile might not be as valuable as it has been assumed to be by the biotech speculators, fertility clinic representatives, and journalists circling her like vultures.

Stone feels vaguely guilty about his role in Thassa's downfall, but he does not fully recognize its similarity to the event that jettisoned his writing career in the first place. In a breathtaking display of self-centeredness, it is Stone who feels betrayed by Thassa, after she reveals, while they are driving to Canada to escape a media maelstrom, that the stories she wrote for his class were more "creative" than "nonfiction." Although he can see that Thassa is in the throes of depression, Stone can't stop thinking about this narrative deception: "He wants to knock on the door to makes [sic] sure she's all right. He's thinking: *Her beautiful essays for me were lies.*" Ruminating on how to recategorize her writing ("Performance, in place of the real. Devices, in place of facts"), Stone suddenly recognizes a second narrative betrayal, this one related to the story supposedly written in her genes:

> Then, a thought that sits him up in bed. Those essays are not her only fiction. She has been authoring something else. How high is her real emotional set point, by nature? How happy is she, *really*? All of that testing, out in Boston, the psychological measurements so carefully correlated with the rigorous gene sequencing: nothing but self-reportage. Even science asked her to tell them a story. (307)

In other words, both the stories Thassa wrote and the story written in her genes were "enhanced" to satisfy the narrative demands of others. This revelation subtly shifts Stone's—and our—attention from author to audience: what stories have been demanded from her by him, by her classmates, by the viewers of daytime talk shows, and by the scientists and speculators desperate to correlate her self-reported bliss to a genetic sequence transformable into a marketable product? What stories have been projected onto Thassa's body, read into her genes? And what damage have those demands and projections wrought?

Though its plot is largely plausible, *Generosity* is not a "true story." Rather, it is a work of fiction that makes truth one of its primary objects of critique. Emphasizing parallel ethical questions in science and literature, and employing techniques that draw attention to the reader's role in the production of meaning, Powers questions both reading and research as paths to objective reality.[28] According to Powers, no matter how close you look (at story or cell or gene), you cannot look past race, gender, or social context—or one's own narrative investments. While *Immortal Life* illustrates a reading practice at odds with its own impulse toward consuming other people's stories, *Generosity* elicits such a practice by drawing attention to the actors who contribute, often in conflicting ways, to the construction of narrative and scientific "truth."

Powers has long been interested in genetics, and, in both fiction and essay, his approach to this theme has served to complicate textual metaphors as well as the lines between fiction and nonfiction, art and science. In *The Gold Bug Variations* (1991) and *Orfeo* (2014), for example, Powers engages DNA as a material language that is both life itself ("at its smallest functional level") and a representation of life—in other words, DNA as both text and metatext (Frye 108). Like music, which Powers foregrounds in these novels, DNA is also a performative form of expression that does what it says and only makes sense within a structure defined by intervals; this intertwining of language, music, and genetics deliberately "erode[s] the barrier between science and the liberal arts" (101): "There truly are no independent disciplines that operate exclusively of any other," Powers has said (qtd. in Burn 171).[29] And, speaking on "developments in reproductive technology and genetic manipulation," he has insisted that "fiction can provide a way of thinking about the revolution in life that other disciplines are bringing about but are not yet equipped or permitted to evaluate" (178). What Powers does not say here, but what the novel that resulted from his deep thinking on "germ-line modification" implies, is that thinking about genetic engineering through fiction can also provide an opportunity to think about fiction through genetic engineering.[30]

In addition to challenging the art/science divide, Powers's writing on genetics also blurs the boundary between fiction and nonfiction. This blurring is evident in his 2008 piece for *GQ*, "The Book of Me," an actual piece of life writing in which Powers recounts his experience as one of the first

---

28. Höpker also draws a parallel between the novel's foregrounded ethical concerns (pertaining to biomedicine) and questions of narrative ethics, but she is more concerned with how biomedicine affects narration of the self, rather than narration of others.

29. Herman and Lenout approach *The Gold Bug Variations* as an encyclopedic "two cultures" novel that attempts to bridge the gap between science and the arts.

30. Hamner emphasizes *Generosity*'s complex rejection of both genetic determinism and "genetic dismissivism," arguing that texts like Powers's will prove necessary as we navigate a world in which genomics plays a more significant role (16). Although Hamner notes the analogy Powers draws between literature and biology, the thrust of his reading is directed toward ethical issues in the sciences, which fiction can helpfully illuminate.

people in the world to undergo whole-genome sequencing. An engaging exploration of the wide-ranging implications of personalized genomic technologies, the essay overflows with literary allusions, figurative language, and references to reading. Powers immediately complicates genomics' textual metaphors by describing the human genome not as a book but, rather, as twelve thousand 250-page books, and a genome sequencing machine as having a "cartridge the size of a small paperback book," leading one to wonder whether the machine is the book or the genome is the book—or whether a book is being used to read a book. Powers describes the difference between sequencing the genome and actually making sense of it as "something like the difference between sounding out the word *w-a-t-e-r* and knowing what the word means," the latter requiring knowledge of other books and a rich, cascading context. Walking through Boston, where he has traveled to provide his genetic sample, Powers thinks of the books he read while he lived there—all of which "wrestle with the limits of the human," often in relation to scientific technologies. And, contemplating the interactions of research and capital, he decides that he has "wandered into a Pynchon novel for the post-Bayh-Dole biocapitalist age: *The Crying of Lot Six Billion*."[31] It is through the lens of literature that Powers reads his medico-scientific experience and, at least temporarily, rereads his own life: "For two days, my old life is beyond strange," he recalls.

In this essay, Powers takes familiar textual metaphors and metatextualizes them, commenting on their deployment in postgenomic discourse and redeploying them toward the kind of critical consciousness he aims for in his fiction. He blurs the line between fact and fiction just as he blurs the line between literature and science—not by playing with the facts but by drawing attention to the narrative structure in which he is presenting them. Powers's encounter with whole-genome sequencing is presented as a story, complete with carefully rendered setting, dialogue, and characters (including a scientist who "could go up against any scientist in fiction"), as well as section markers identifying "complication," "climax," and "denouement." The story of the genome, in this rendering, is not the individual (whose body realizes the genetic script) but the ongoing human effort to move "from scripted characters to co-authors of our own lives." By "authorship," Powers does not mean anything as instrumentalist or narrow as gene editing. Rather, reading and writing, as Powers uses them in this essay, extend to questions of economics, culture, and ethics: "privacy and public good, research and entrepreneurship, risk and susceptibility—all the dangers of

---

31. On economics as a significant theme across Powers's oeuvre, see Grgas.

knowing the full story." By the end of the essay, Powers directly calls for a heightened, self-aware, anticipatory, and promiscuous reading practice for the postgenomic age: "Get literate. Read wider. Read deeper. Read more variously, more critically, more suspiciously, more vicariously. Read in anticipation of retrospection. Page one is already being changed by all the pages still to come."

That Powers does not advise us on what to read is notable. No need to make a list of genres, if the boundaries between them are porous and what matters is the acquisition of critical, self-reflexive literacy. Powers's metatextual gesture (we are living on "page one") reminds us that the text to be read is everywhere around us. The reading error Powers warns against is the error of reading narrowly, without attention to context and self-reflection. It is reading as escape or self-help—reading aimed toward individual "happiness" (the subject of *Generosity*) at the expense of collective well-being.[32] Signifying on the argument made by some theorists of life writing, that all texts are autobiographical, Powers suggests that all texts are metafictional: "I am on a long quest," he has said, "to show that even the most conventional 'realist' fiction depends on invoking a kind of metafictional awareness in the reader for its full effects" (qtd. in Burn 167). "Metafictional awareness" resists being "lost" in the world of the text, instead encouraging awareness of context and thus running parallel with critiques of genomic "readings" that are aimed at "personalized medicine" without sustained attention to socioeconomic context. Powers challenges readers (of genres and genomes) to resist the sort of close reading that seems to disappear everything but the text, while actually layering the desires of readers on top of it.

In *Generosity*, Powers offers several illustrations of how reading can go wrong in the postgenomic age, starting with his hapless main character, Russell Stone. Although Russell has given up telling other people's stories, he has not given up reading them and specifically seeks the dubious satisfaction to be found in stories of suffering. Mired in white, middle-class, middle-America malaise, Stone finds inspiration in Thassa's triumph over an adversity he will never face. Thassa's class nickname, "Miss Generosity," evokes the problematic logic of "donation" that characterizes the discourse on tissue sampling; like Lacks, Thassa is viewed as a resource whose "gift," whether genetic or narrative, should be shared for the public good. When Thassa's stories turn out not to be "true," Stone betrays his sense of narrative entitlement, recalling literary scandals involving the accuracy of

---

32. On *Generosity* and postwar theories and critiques of happiness, see Esteve.

narratives about war and resistance.[33] In such situations, the demand for "truth" (as determined by a privileged outsider) outweighs the significance of the story that is told. Thassa's stories about Algeria, which involve complex histories of settler colonialism and ethnic and religious conflict, are not well understood by Stone, who reads them through an inaccurate "Arab" lens and in service of his own desire for inspiration.

Generosity consistently raises questions about both the ethics and the definition of nonfiction, from blogs and social media posts to the kinds of essays Stone himself used to write and the crowdsourced self-help magazine articles he edits now. Stone's students discuss whether it's ethical to publish online what you overhear people saying in public, and Stone and his girlfriend debate the implications of a literary "hoax": "It turns out that a troubled teenager's searing memoir . . . is really the work of a seasoned, middle-aged feature writer. Candace calls the whole episode fascinating contemporary ethnography. Stone wants the fraud to serve time" (177). These issues also play out in the context of science entertainment, as Tonia Schiff, host of a popular television series, is forced to shape complicated research into digestible stories. Tonia is especially frustrated by the edited version of an episode on happiness and genetics, in which the ambiguities of the research—and the "rockier" elements of Thassa's story (279)—are eliminated, resulting in a final product that Thassa dismisses as "science fiction" (208).

At the heart of these conflicts is the question of where to draw the line between fiction and nonfiction. Is there a way to be, in Tonia's words, a "blameless observer" (282)? Does storytelling always involve fictionalizing and, as such, constitute appropriation, violation, or dishonesty? Early on, one of the students in Stone's creative nonfiction writing class asks a question that haunts the novel: "There's something I don't get about this class. I mean, are we supposed to be making up stories, with a plot and everything? Or are we just supposed to put down what actually happens?" (40). Even the narrator seems to grapple with this conundrum, vacillating between observation and invention (Höpker 306). Often, it is suggested that the narrator is writing a biography of Russell, requiring detailed research: "I search for Russell Stone all over. I read the almanac for that year. I read his class textbook, of course. I read back issues of his magazine." But the biographical impulse immediately veers toward fiction—specifically, metafiction—as

---

33. The most prominent example of such a controversy is *I, Rigoberta Menchú* (1983), by the titular K'iche' activist, transcribed by Elizabeth Burgos. See Beverley 79–94; Sommer 115–37.

the narrator tries to understand Russell through the books he likes to read: "I even loot those hall-of-mirrors avant-garde novels whose characters try to escape their authors, the kind he once loved, the kind he thought he'd write one day, before he gave up fiction" (40). The postmodern novels Stone used to like represent the possibility of fiction becoming nonfiction, of characters escaping into the "real world," a fanciful notion that, nevertheless, Stone has actually experienced when the "characters" in his "nonfiction" essays appear in *his* real life to take issue with his rendering of *their* real lives. The narrator also struggles with the sense that their responsibility to the story is in competition with their responsibility to the characters—and the simultaneous sense that narrative shapes reality: "All I want is for my friends to survive the story intact. All the story wants is to wreck anything solid in them. No one would write a word, if he remembered how much fiction eventually comes true" (246). The metafictional intimacy Powers draws between fiction and nonfiction suggests that an author does not escape ethical concerns simply by choosing to write fiction. Indeed, Candace's prescription for Russell's writer's block—to "slightly" fictionalize what he observes so that "no one gets hurt"—is a decided failure: "I just kept thinking, *We're overrun with this stuff. It's out of control. Kill yours before it multiplies*" (164–65).

In addition to blurring the lines between fiction and nonfiction, metafiction and life writing, *Generosity* blurs the line between science and literature, suggesting that the former is just as governed by narrative desire as the latter. Indeed, the narrator suggests that genomics itself is a form of creative nonfiction. Stone's hunger for Thassa's story, which recalls Skloot's obsession with Lacks's story, quickly goes molecular, culminating in a close look at her DNA by way of a study led by geneticist Thomas Kurton, a champion of transgenics who regularly debates ethicists and novelists on the ethics of transgenic science. Kurton even rants against fiction for what he sees as its narrow, biased perspective, longing instead for a "post-genomic fiction" that "shakes free of the prejudices of any individual maker" through "precise molecular fine-tuning" (249–50). At the same time, we learn that his scientific interests were born from passionate reading—everything from "cheap science-fiction paperbacks" to Darwin (44)—and that he is prone to describing his work in narrative terms: "We're . . . stuck in a bad plot. We want to become something else. It's what we've wanted since the story started" (64). By editing DNA, Kurton is determined to write a new chapter in the human story, and Thassa seems to offer him the opportunity to do so. When he meets her, Kurton has been waiting to fill in a single point on a graph tracing the distribution of allelic variations influencing emotional well-being. Thassa's genetic profile fills in that point, fulfilling both scientific and narrative desire: "You know what the lab will have to discover," the narrator insists (160). Rather than revealing the truth, Kurton (whose name suggests obfuscation) creates it. Like Stone, Kurton feels betrayed by Thassa at the end of the book, when his research is called into question by her suicide attempt. He also sues for patent infringement when a reproductive clinic contracts with Thassa for her eggs, belying his altruistic arguments about the public good.

Although they are foils for each other—representatives of the sciences and the humanities, respectively—Kurton and Stone share a hunger for Thassa that Powers presents in narrative terms: they are both bad readers of her life story.[34] Stone and Kurton alike ignore Thassa's human complexity, including the cultural background and history that have shaped her life. During his first conference with her, Stone is "baffled" by the fact that Thassa has artistic interests beyond trauma and sees her optimism as unbelievable—as if she is a poorly written character: "A child of death who's thrilled about the future. An Algerian who shuns politics" (53). Thassa does not fit the story of suffering that he associates with the part of the world she is from, and, as Karin Höpker points out, when Thassa does descend into depression, Russell experiences a disturbing "elation" (299). After Russell tells the police about Thassa's suspected hyperthymia (when questioned about a rape attempt she experiences at the hands of a fellow student), she becomes "an instant creative-nonfiction commodity," plugged into a preexisting narrative that Stone is certain she can't read: "Everyone knows this story but her. The Berber wouldn't know how to read this story for the life of her" (118–19). Although his reasoning is based on her preternatural optimism about human nature, his seemingly irrelevant reference to her ethnicity here—using a term, not incidentally, imposed by colonial outsiders and considered by many to be pejorative—underscores the poverty of his interpretation. He does not see the fullness of her humanity.

Kurton's contemplation of Thassa's background is similarly impoverished. Listening to an audiobook of Camus's *The Plague*, Kurton recalls a conversation he had with Thassa about the author, during which "she filled him in on all the context he missed when reading the work in his twenties." Considering Camus's "notorious declaration, at the height of the savage war [in Algeria]: *If I have to choose between justice and my mother, I would choose my mother*," Kurton immediately evacuates the statement of its original context and substitutes content that matters to him: "Kurton's justice is

---

34. That Kurton is something of a vampire—the postgenomic figure I take up in part 2 of this book—is suggested by his uncanny agelessness and demands for Thassa's blood.

the freedom of research, rapidly decamping to the western Pacific Rim. His mother has been in a home in Westchester County for the last four years. . . . The choice would still not be easy, but it would be clear" (248).[35] Kurton then shifts his attention to literature: "The problem is with the craft of fiction," he decides, insisting that Camus is guilty of "an environmental determinism more reductive than anything that has ever come out of Kurton's labs. *My upbringing made me do it.*" Kurton believes that science can evade the biases of literature by focusing on "facts": "The double-blind study frees human history from the trap of bias and sets it loose in a place beyond personality" (249). But he has blinded himself to the way that narrative desire and political and social context shape his own work—to the ways that "upbringing" might matter. Scientific ethnocentrism is subtly suggested by Thassa being renamed "Jen" in the scientific literature (echoes of Henrietta Lacks's renaming in scientific and journalistic texts) and in the shock on the part of a television audience when they recognize that Thassa is "foreign" (238). Thassa's background does not fit Kurton's postgenomic story, in its academic or popular formulations.[36]

Stone and Kurton are not the only figures implicated in the practice of self-fulfilling reading, in *Generosity*. The narrator's frequent use of the second person (e.g., "*You* know what the lab will have to discover") implicates readers too. Powers uses this and other metafictional devices to alert readers to their own ethical enmeshment, offering revision as a principle that runs counter to narrative reduction, whether literary or scientific. Recalling the braided structure of *Immortal Life*, *Generosity*'s narrator tells Stone's and Kurton's stories while also telling the story of the crafting of the story. Revising as the novel goes on, the narrator recognizes both the limits of their knowledge and the presence of their readers. A second meaning of revision appears in the narrator's frequent admonishments to "look again." This imperative phrase is self-reflexive, but it also addresses the readers who are collaborators in imagining Stone and his milieu. Take, for example, the novel's dizzying opening passage, which follows Stone's train ride to his first day as a writing instructor. Here, Powers writes a narrator who is writing a character who is rewriting a lesson plan that he has largely copied from a book on writing and from which the narrator is now copying. The narrator admits that they "can't see [Stone] well, at first" (3), but eventually they fill in the details, claiming both that "*I* know this story like I wrote it myself" (5;

---

35. Also notable here is Kurton's ethnocentric concern that Western science is losing out to the East.

36. Powers's treatment of Kurton, as well as the science program Tonia Schiff hosts, aligns with Hanson's description of the "inflated and potentially misleading rhetoric" of popular science (9).

emphasis added) and "*you* know this story" (16; emphasis added), thus suggesting that writers and readers alike play a provisional authorship role.[37] It is fall, "the season of revision" (3), and throughout the scene, the narrator repeats the phrases "look again" and "look harder." Stone's lesson plan, balanced precariously on his lap as he rides backward on a train, underscores the textual instability that readers attempt to manage.

The ambivalence of *revision* captures the ethical complications of life writing in both its literary and biological sense. If *revise* means *look again*, then it signals an effort to see more clearly the reality in front of one's face, to record what's there as faithfully as possible. This is life writing—and science—at their most naïve, ignoring the fact that observation always has an effect on the observed, unselfconsciously accepting "the priority of vision" and "the historical scientific fantasies of its disinterested neutrality" (Höpker 306). If *revise*, alternatively, means to edit a text, then it signals an effort to make meaning out of the random facts of life, genetic or otherwise—to put them in the right order to create a satisfying story. The writer and the geneticist alike are in the business of editing, a fact driven home when Russell, desperate in the face of Thassa's overdose, turns to the revisions possible in both fields: "He bargains, ready to accept anything in science's arsenal. Cloning. Genetic editing. Yes to it all. . . . He can do nothing for her but revise" (315). Russell imagines a new story, in which he and all the "principal" characters agree to pursue "posthumous reproduction," reducing Thassa to a biological and narrative incubator. At this moment, he and Kurton, who goes on to pursue a privately funded study of children genetically related to Thassa, are one in their desires.

In *Generosity*, *revision* is a creative and scientific practice that can never actually reach its target. Powers suggests that every attempt at close observation and interpretation—what literary critics call "close reading" and genomicists call "mapping"—is in fact self-reflexive rather than objective, revealing as much about the person doing the reading as it reveals about the text being read. This point is aimed at methods that would emphasize the text (aesthetic or genetic) as authoritative, authentic, autonomous. Presenting literature as an important site for negotiating what sociologist Jenny Reardon calls the "co-production" of science and culture (*Race* 6–7), *Generosity* opposes the naïve belief that stories *or* DNA can be read out of context. For Thassa, such readings—of her stories and her DNA—instrumentalize her, reducing her to a genetic or narrative profile that ignores the complexity of her life and puts the needs of others above her own. Near the end of the

---

37. Höpker notes that "the reader becomes oddly complicit in the knowledge and narrative production" (306).

novel, Thassa, meeting with the filmmaker Tonia Schiff (now working on a film about the ethical and technical complications of genetic engineering), speaks against this reduction by making reference to the impact that political conflict in Algeria has had on her life: "Tell them my genes had no cure that this place couldn't break," she says, a message meant for the novel's characters and its readers (320). And yet, in *Generosity*'s final scene, the context that Thassa has brought into view disappears:

> [Thassa] slips the [writing textbook] back across the space between them. But just as Schiff takes it, the text disappears. . . . The next to vanish off the table will be the camera, then the poems. . . .
>
> As the two look on, the menu's French fades. The Arabic follows it into white. So, too, do the sounds from the air around the café, until the only language running through the nearby streets is the one that existed in these parts long before the arrival of writing.
>
> Then the menus and the tea and the condiments dematerialize. Then the filmmaker's bag. Then the filmmaker herself vanishes back into documentary, banished to nonfiction.

The narrator is left alone with Thassa, who "always knew it would end like this" (321). Narrative desire wins out in the end, as Thassa, stripped of context and particularity, reverts to her essential role in the story, and the narrator slips into "delight" (322). Powers leaves his readers with a moment of deceptive purity that threatens to wipe away all that has come before, and the question is whether they will reflect on how the preceding narrative has drawn attention to their own longing for such purity—if they will be left with a productive unease, unable to bask in the "happy ending" that makes their own pleasure the point of the story / the point on the graph.[38]

•

Life writing, as both genre and narrative subject, is an especially fruitful site for illuminating ethical questions that straddle the sciences and the humanities. Postgenomic life writing, in particular, is well poised to critique misrepresentations, misunderstandings, and misapplications of the life sciences

---

38. Alternatively, Höpker argues that, in the novel's final scene, "narrative creation and supposedly passive objective observation finally come to a strange state of balance," and readers are invited "to not force the narrative into a discrete state of an either/or, but to simply give to the story the full attention of our imagination, suspending the ending as an open-ended experiment" (308).

and to return an ethical lens to the study of literature itself. Such works do not repeat the truism that the value of the arts and humanities vis-à-vis the sciences is the introduction of ethical sense to—or the injection of humanism in—fields construed as objective or, worse, inhumane. As I discuss further in chapter 6, the arts and humanities do not have a monopoly on "the ethical" or "the human"; indeed, they are freighted with their own histories of exclusion and oppression, their own complicity with systems of power, as *Immortal Life* and *Generosity* alike illustrate. That no discipline can fully extricate itself from this complicity is an important lesson of both texts, and one that also applies to authors and readers, however critical or well-meaning—including the author of this book.

Postgenomic life writing engages the ethical challenges that face readers and writers, who must always act within particular social and political contexts. *Immortal Life* and *Generosity* specifically challenge modes of reading that privilege text over context, whether the text at hand is literary or chemical, instead insisting on the complex interrelationship of both terms. And they insist upon multiple meanings for both stories and DNA. HeLa cells, and the mutating stories about them, are a powerful metaphor for the kind of reading postgenomic literature encourages. Like any eukaryotic cell, HeLa contains a genetic script in its nucleus. This script—the cell's DNA—is understood to determine morphology, what we might call the "meaning" of DNA. However, the development of an organism involves the complex interaction of genes and their environments. The same genetic script can produce different "meanings" depending on complex environmental factors and transcription processes that turn "on" and "off" various genes in order to produce different kinds of cells or respond to varying environmental pressures. The literary works I have discussed above echo this biological fact in their understanding that meaning results from complex and unpredictable exchanges among a script, its environments, and diverse actors. Through multifaceted representations of this insight, and solicitation of reading practices attentive to it, postgenomic life writing invites and models ethical modes of reading for the postgenomic age. Together, Powers and Skloot offer lessons in narrative humility and metafictional reading that apply not only in literary contexts but also broadly, as we learn to read one another in ways that allow life stories to unfold in rich complexity and to read our own narrative investments alongside the lives we encounter in literature and in the world.

PART 2

Vampire Projects

CHAPTER 3

Stories in the Blood and Bone

Therapeutic Bionarrative Signatures in
Gerald Vizenor's *The Heirs of Columbus*

The Heirs of Columbus, a 1991 novel by writer and theorist Gerald Vizenor (White Earth Chippewa), follows the adventures of a group of "crossbloods" descended from Christopher Columbus and Samana, an Indigenous "hand talker" who has been erased, according to the Heirs, from official records of Columbus's voyage to the Americas (4). Claiming that Columbus has both Mayan and Jewish ancestry, these title characters make it their mission to repatriate his remains to America and to isolate the "genetic signature of survivance" they share with him (135).[1] By the end of the book, the Heirs have developed a gene therapy that they make widely available, via a newly constructed "Genome Pavilion" (130) in the utopian community of Point Assinika, as part of their plan to "make the world tribal" (162). There's much more to the story, including a moccasin game with the cannibal spirit Wiindigoo,[2] the creation and destruction of the Santa Maria floating casino,

---

 1. The isolated genes are mitochondrial and therefore passed down from mother to child. In other words, the Heirs did not inherit this signature *from* Columbus.
 2. The wiindigoo "is a monster with a heart of ice, the unseen ghost who trails behind and appears in order to eat the human soul," who, "transfigured" in Vizenor's oeuvre, "feeds off claims of cultural dominance" and is aligned with "violent monoculturalism" (Lockard 209).

a heist involving stolen medicine pouches, a shaman with a degree in gay studies, the discovery of a death herb capable of destroying the world, and the regular appearance of blue puppets, panic holes, rare books, and laser light shows. This gloss should suggest the mix of critical play and playful critique that upends both the mainstream Columbus story and the story of Indigenous people's relationship to genetics and biotechnology. In *Heirs*, Indigenous communities do not watch their biological property transformed into marketable molecules for the medical benefit of others, nor do they resist biotechnology altogether; rather, they pursue the radical healing of individuals, communities, and the world through the ironic and unpredictable admixture of narrative and medical intervention.

Heirs was published just as the Human Genome Project (HGP) was getting under way, just before the 500th anniversary of Columbus's arrival in the Americas,[3] and just after the passage (in 1990) of two federal laws that quickly became sites of conflict over identity and authenticity, rather than simple means of their resolution: the Native American Graves Protection and Repatriation Act (NAGPRA), which created a legal process for the return of human remains and sacred objects from museums and federal institutions to tribal authorities, and the Indian Arts and Crafts Act (IACA), which prohibited the sale of goods falsely attributed to Native artisans.[4] At this fraught intersection, the celebration of the so-called "discovery" of the New World also coincided with tremendous enthusiasm for "discovering" the secrets of human DNA, suggesting that the world was entering a new "Age of Exploration" in which geneticists would map every corner of the genomic frontier. Simultaneously, Indigenous activists organized protests and summits across

---

3. *Heirs* was one of several Indigenous works published around the Columbus quincentenary; others include Jeannette Armstrong's "History Lesson" (1991), Michael Dorris and Louise Erdrich's *The Crown of Columbus* (1991), Joy Harjo's "The Real Revolution Is Love" (1990), Thomas King's "A Coyote Columbus Story" (1992) and *Green Grass Running Water* (1993), and Leslie Marmon Silko's *Almanac of the Dead* (1991). See Sarkowsky 357–70; J. Smith.

4. Neither law has been easily enforced or had straightforward effects. Repatriation under NAGPRA "has been slowed by a variety of factors, including institutional reliance on archaeological and biological lines of evidence, even in the face of compelling oral history evidence or expert opinion supplied by Indigenous nations," leaving tens of thousands of remains "with little or no path to repatriation" (Wheeler et al. 9). Similarly, IACA "adds up to a law of good intentions and unintended consequences.... Ethnological ... and racial definitions ... do not necessarily map onto legal ones, thereby making some persons 'Indian' ethnically or racially but not politically or legally" (Hapiuk 1011–12). On NAGPRA, also see Lonetree; Nash and Colwell; Riding In. On IACA, also see Sheffield.

the Americas (including the first Indigenous People's Day, held in Berkeley, California, in 1992), demanding that governments reckon with the legacies of European exploration instead of celebrating one of its heroes, and critics of genomic research fought to protect Indigenous communities against new forms of "bioprospecting."[5] The Human Genome Diversity Project (HGDP), launched in 1991 as an alternative to the HGP, was singled out as a "Vampire Project," a vivid reiteration of the plunder that characterized the first Age of Exploration and its aftermath. Although there has been no singular Indigenous response to genomic research, Indigenous populations remain underrepresented in the gene banks that have developed since the early 1990s in part because of on-going resistance to the imposition of genetic research on Indigenous communities by outside interests. As a result, "Native American DNA" remains a highly sought-after object of study and "discovery."[6]

It is within this complex context that *The Heirs of Columbus* highlights the vampiric impulses of Western research and draws attention to several vectors of biocolonialism, including the disturbance of Indigenous burial grounds, the appropriation of Indigenous knowledge, and the capture, distortion, and erasure of Indigenous stories in favor of colonial and neocolonial narratives, both scientific and literary. One of the key claims of this book is that postgenomic literature challenges the disciplinary boundary between the sciences and the humanities—by, for example, playing with the textual metaphors that redound within literary and scientific discourses (as I discuss in chapter 1), drawing attention to how ethical concerns on one "side" of the line inform those on the other (as I discuss in chapter 2), or revealing how the sciences and humanities are both vulnerable to instrumentalization within capitalist systems (as I discuss in chapter 6). Vizenor adds another strategy to this list, demonstrating how the sciences, social sciences, humanities, and fine arts are part of the same dead-end "monologue" when they approach Native peoples as static objects, displayed in both literal and literary museums. Histories, exhibits, translations, criticisms, ethnographies, novels, and genetic studies can all be instances of colonial culture talking to itself, using stereotyped and false images of Native people as props in their academic "dioramas" (Vizenor, "Socioacupuncture" 412). Such misrepresentations are grounded in the material exploitations of colonialism—the

---

5. On representations of Indigeneity that accompanied quincentenary celebrations, see Gillan 242.

6. See Lock, "Alienation" 572.

intertwined theft of bodies, stories, and land.[7] It is within this broad critique of Western research that Vizenor has articulated specific critiques of genomic discourse, particularly of the idea that genetic science would reveal the fundamental truths of human identity and history. In a global capitalist and neocolonial context, the ecstatic pursuit of genetic knowledge has marginalized Indigenous ways of knowing and made possible innovative ways of exploiting the bodies and land of Indigenous peoples, figured as repositories of exotic genetic signatures with potentially profitable biotechnological applications—from new medications to ancestry testing kits available to consumers. While the specifics of these bioprospecting adventures might be new, the story they are part of is as old as Christopher Columbus.

In *Heirs* and elsewhere in his oeuvre, Vizenor asserts that genomic projects are fundamentally narrative and are, therefore, vulnerable to narrative intervention. At the heart of such intervention is what Vizenor calls "genome survivance": the fluid, adaptive practice of bionarrative agency in the face of biotechnological threats to Indigenous self-definition and sovereignty. Responding to the cultural ascendance of the gene and the hegemony of Western biotechnology, Vizenor narrates an alternative genomics that undercuts gene fetishism, centers Indigenous people, supports the sovereignty of Indigenous communities, and sets out to heal the wounds of colonialism.

---

7. As a white settler scholar of US American literature, I enter discussions of Vizenor's work cautiously, acutely aware of the complicity of white settler scholarship in the racialization, exploitation, marginalization, and attempted genocide of Indigenous people—and aware of the privilege (social, economic, political, and academic) my identity affords me. Drawing upon Sayantani DasGupta's concept of "narrative humility," discussed in the previous chapter, as well as Vizenor's own robust critique of colonial research, I acknowledge that my knowledge is limited—and that "knowledge" itself is a contested term, one that has been used to justify the objectification of Indigenous cultures while, simultaneously, devaluing Indigenous ways of knowing. In this chapter, I do not seek "mastery" of Vizenor's (deliberately) unwieldy text, nor do I approach his work as representative of an "authentic" or universal Indigenous or Anishinaabe perspective. I attempt to provide critical and cultural contextualization where possible, but I encourage readers interested in interpretations of Vizenor's work that are informed by Anishinaabe traditions, and/or in Anishinaabe oral and literary traditions themselves, to seek out the work of Anishinaabe scholars, such as Kimberly Blaeser, Benjamin V. Burgess, Jill Doerfler, Lawrence W. Gross, Molly McGlennen, Margaret Noori, and Niigaanwewidam (formerly Niigonwedom) James Sinclair. (This list includes scholars with acknowledged Anishinaabe heritage; their tribal enrollment status may vary. Readings of specifically Anishinaabe cultural references and contexts in *Heirs* are also provided by Lush and Madsen ["On Subjectivity"].) Meanwhile, I offer this chapter as a necessary but necessarily partial component of my exploration of how North American writers from a variety of literary, intellectual, and cultural perspectives approach genome science, a field that has had significant impact on—and has been significantly engaged by—Indigenous communities and artists.

Crucially, Vizenor's vision has implications not only for genomics but also for literary studies and, specifically, for critical debates regarding narrative appropriation and "authenticity" in the field of Native American literature—debates that were prominent at the time of *Heirs*'s publication and that continue today. Remixing both genomic and colonial discourse, and inscribed with an ironic, trickster signature, *The Heirs of Columbus* is a recombinative masterpiece that challenges readers to read against the grain of dominant scientific, social scientific, and literary discourse.

Central to Vizenor's intervention is a technique I call *therapeutic bionarrative signatures*: strings of text repeated in the novel, often with key revisions, that are analogous to a kind of gene therapy. If the larger purpose of *Heirs* is to interrupt and redirect the Columbus narrative, then these bionarrative signatures recapitulate that larger purpose on the novel's "molecular" level, interrupting and resignifying the surrounding text and setting off a cascade of semantic change that has the potential to reverberate through the grand colonial narrative of which the Columbus story is but one unique expression. I describe this technique as *bionarrative* because, for Vizenor, a narrative intervention is always also a living material intervention; indeed, one of the fundamental premises of the novel (and of much of Vizenor's work), is the inextricability of story, matter, and life. To distinguish narrative from the living, breathing world—to separate stories from blood and bone—is, for Vizenor, impossible. Even readers fully steeped in Western binary thinking must recognize that the Columbus story has organized the physical world in ways that can be seen and touched. If the Columbus story is a kind of bionarrative plague, then a bionarrative therapy is required.

There is a second layer of therapeutic purpose in Vizenor's bionarrative signatures, one that engages readers directly. Throughout the novel, Vizenor draws a connection between literary and genomic archives and highlights the practice of identifying *associations* and *signatures* that can be brought to bear on both. In so doing, Vizenor might appear to invite a reading practice analogous to gene sequencing and genome-wide association studies. Indeed, the *difficulty* of the novel—the way it overflows with terms that have no obvious referents, terms that depend upon internal structures of meaning whose grounds are constantly shifting—might appear to be a reading challenge not unlike sequencing a genome or identifying shared polymorphisms across several genomes. It would be tempting indeed to put *Heirs* through computer-assisted analysis, in an attempt to make sense of an onslaught of unfamiliar data and discover the meaning secreted within. But such an approach would seem to miss the point of the novel's therapeutic intent. Rather than training readers in a literary form of "gene hunting" that could slip into academic "vampirism," Vizenor's bionarrative signatures challenge readers to resist the impulse toward atomization as analysis and, instead, to give oneself over to the play of meaning. It is important to emphasize that this technique is not part of a wholesale rejection of genome science; like the other authors in this collection, Vizenor does not reject genomics out of hand and, in fact, revels in imagining a genome therapy developed and controlled by Indigenous scientists. Rather, Vizenor's therapeutic bionarrative signatures interrupt understandings of the genome that emphasize determinism and fixity, at the expense of chance and play, and challenge colonial and extractive ways of reading Native American stories and Native American DNA.

Vampire Projects, Native American DNA, and Genome Survivance

Although the term "vampire project" is applicable across the disciplines, it was first coined in response to the HGDP, an undertaking that, despite the intentions of its organizers, came to be seen as emblematic of the potential for genomics to harm Indigenous peoples. The HGDP was a response to the HGP, which, focusing on a single (composite) human genome, was limited in scope, even if the discourse surrounding it suggested universality.[8] In contrast to the remit of the HGP, eminent geneticist Luigi Luca Cavalli-Sforza and his colleagues, including Mary-Claire King and Robert Cook-Deegan (all known for their antiracist, progressive politics), sought to gather genetic information from underrepresented and isolated populations around the globe. The scale of the proposed project was huge: it aimed to collect biological samples from 10,000–100,000 individuals from 400–500 populations, with an emphasis on remote communities presumed to be genetically distinct. The study of these "isolates of historical interest" (Harry) would, according to Cavalli-Sforza, "deepen our understanding of [the human species'] genetic richness and show both humanity's diversity and its deep and underlying unity." In his 1994 report to UNESCO about the project, Cavalli-Sforza stated his belief that the initiative would "help combat the scourge of racism" ("Human" 1).

At the same time, the primary goal of the HGDP was not to serve the interests of marginalized populations but to advance the research agenda of

---

8. "Although the trope constructs the composite as a definitive master text against which to match individual genomes, the composite genome is itself a fictive text—and a pastiche, at that" (Couser 182). Also see Reardon, "On the Emergence" 188.

evolutionary biology: "Social changes that facilitated the mixing of populations, [HGDP scientists] warned, threatened the identity of groups of greatest importance for understanding human evolutionary history" (Reardon, *Race* 1).[9] This focus on "endangered" genomes immediately raised concerns among observers who saw it as, in sociologist Jenny Reardon's words, "turning [Indigenous people] into entities that existed only in the past" (qtd. in "Vampire"). By 1993, before it could even begin widespread sampling, the HGDP was accused of "using twenty-first-century technology to propagate the concepts of nineteenth-century racist biology," and various Indigenous groups, alarmed by the biocolonial implications of the program—as well as the exclusion of Indigenous perspectives from the planning process—called for its suspension.[10] The World Congress of Indigenous Peoples, which had declared 1993 the "Year of the World's Indigenous People," is also the group that declared the HGDP a "Vampire Project," linking it to a long history of exploitative research conducted on Indigenous peoples (Reardon, *Race* 2).

Indigenous studies scholar Debra Harry (Northern Paiute) summarized apprehensions about the HGDP in a 1995 report for the Indigenous People's Council on Biocolonialism, citing, among other concerns, the project's "assumption that indigenous peoples are inevitably going to disappear" and raising questions regarding access to genetic databanks, informed consent, the violation of Indigenous belief systems, and the potential for "misuse of the genetic materials or data for racist purposes." Despite the fact that the HGDP was not a commercial project, many Indigenous leaders worried about bioprospecting (citing the case of a Guaymi woman from Panama whose cell line had been patented without her knowledge [Lock, "Alienation" 567–68]) and challenges to Indigenous sovereignty, "should culturally defined groups be found not to be genetically 'pure'" (580).

---

9. As scientist and activist Judy Gobert (Biterroot Salish) has said, "We know who we are. We know where we come from. We know who we're related to. We know where our traditional lands are. We know where we originated from. We know where we moved to. We know all of our histories, you know. . . . So, we don't have any need for that science" ("Vampire").

10. The Rural Advancement Foundation International (RAFI) accused the HGDP of "threatening the livelihood and autonomy of indigenous groups" and, in 1993, shared the "hit list" of Indigenous communities the project planned to study with Indigenous organizations ("Vampire"). Soon after, the Third World Network accused the project of human rights violations and the *Mataatua Declaration on Cultural and Intellectual Property Rights of Indigenous Peoples* called for "an immediate halt" to the project "until its moral, ethical, socio-economic, physical and political implications have been thoroughly discussed, understood and approved by indigenous peoples" (*Mataatua* 5). Opposition was also articulated at the Maori Congress Indigenous Peoples Roundtable, the Guaymi General Congress, and the Ukupseni Declaration on the HGDP (Wasserloos 74n25).

The organizers of the HGDP reacted to such criticisms with surprise and no small degree of defensiveness. "I am not surprised when I am attacked by racists because of my ideas," Cavalli-Sforza stated, but

> the confusion made by some others between our study and eugenics is less easy to understand or to forgive. . . . It has even been asserted that the knowledge we generate can be used for the genocide of indigenous people. . . . These kinds of baseless allegations stem largely from a general lack of understanding of human genetics. ("Human" 10)

Although motivated by a desire to confound racist principles, Cavalli-Sforza remained firmly grounded in a Western scientistic perspective, maintaining that "science, per se, done in the interest of intellectual curiosity and in respect of life of humans and other species, is morally clean" (10).[11] This naïve position underestimated the effect of historical and contemporary scientific racism on the willingness of Indigenous communities to participate in the HGDP and justified a stubborn refusal to recognize the validity of Indigenous concerns (Lock, "Alienation" 575).[12] The controversy sparked by the HGDP did advance ethical discussions regarding research relationships between Indigenous peoples and non-Indigenous institutions, leading to groundbreaking redefinitions of informed consent that included both individuals and communities. However, the HGDP was unable to fully pivot away from a posture of colonial condescension (what Vizenor might describe as "manifest manners"),[13] and the project ultimately lost its National Institutes of Health funding.[14]

---

11. On Cavalli-Sforza's contradictory positions on race, see Roberts, *Fatal* 67. Hamner defines "scientism" as "militant, exclusive forms of *metaphysical* naturalism" that "reject[ ] out of hand any knowledge claim or way of being that exceeds scientific verifiability" (42).

12. "Organizers assumed that critics would become supporters if they participated in a rational and informed dialogue about the Project's intentions and goals. They had difficulty recognizing how specific histories of colonialism and racism, and legacies of Western domination, might interfere with the possibility of such a dialogue" (Reardon, *Race* 124).

13. "Manifest manners" is "a cultural legacy of Manifest Destiny—representations or simulations produced by both Natives and non-Natives" (Stanciu 1370). Also see Vizenor, *Manifest* vii.

14. Some samples were collected, mostly from subjects in Asia, and a more modest, privately funded, research project took the place of the HGDP. The cell lines created from this research have been used in human population research, including the 2002 Rosenberg study that purported to discover a genomic basis for five "continental" races (Roberts, *Fatal* 65). On the HGDP also see Rose and Rose 45–48.

The HGDP failed in its explicit aims, but it succeeded, anthropologist Margaret Lock has argued, in setting the terms of genomic-era bioprospecting: "In effect, the HGDP conceptualize[d] 'exotic' bodies as a scarce resource, the essence of which"—i.e., blood, cells, and DNA—"can be extracted to . . . join the never-ending circulation of commodities integral to late modernity" ("Alienation" 580).[15] The increasing urgency to pursue genetic discovery in Indigenous communities led to legal and political disputes, throughout the 1990s and beyond, regarding ownership of and access to bodies, body parts, and human remains. For example, two agreements pertaining to the General Agreement on Tariffs and Trade (GATT), ratified in 1993 and 1994 against the objections of Indigenous leaders, "ensured that virtually all signatories to GATT (now the World Trade Organization) . . . must agree to intellectual property provisions," stipulating that research subjects give up property rights when "donating" body parts (568).[16] Patents related to human genetics "surged" throughout the decade, and policies expanded to allow for the patenting of tiny units of genetic variability known as single nucleotide polymorphisms (SNPs; Liddicoat et al. 997). Although the US Supreme Court ruled in 2013 that human genes cannot be patented, invalidating over four thousand patents previously granted, "relatively broad protection for gene-related patents" exists in Europe and elsewhere, and debates regarding how to negotiate bodily autonomy, property rights, and scientific innovation continue apace (998).[17]

Despite the passage of NAGPRA in 1990, disputes over the possession and repatriation of human remains also continued, with genetic analysis serving as both a catalyst of conflict and an ambivalent means of its resolution. For example, the 1996 disinterment of Paleolithic human remains in Kennewick, Washington, led to a protracted battle between scientists, who claimed that "Kennewick Man" was not related to contemporary Native Americans and therefore not subject to NAGPRA, and representatives of the Umatilla and Colville peoples, who claimed the "Ancient One" as an ancestor. Although the dispute was ultimately decided in favor of the tribes, this decision was based on DNA evidence, leaving in place the rationale that genetic analysis, rather than Indigenous formulations of genealogy, is

---

15. Also see L. Smith 26.

16. In 1993 the Guaymi General Congress unsuccessfully petitioned for the exclusion of human genetic material from the GATT patenting agreement. "By 1997 the U.S. patenting office had received more than 4,000 applications to patent human genes, over 1,500 of which had been ratified" (Lock, "Alienation" 567).

17. For a detailed discussion of *Association for Molecular Pathology v. Myriad* (2013), the US Supreme Court case that made the patenting human genes illegal, see Contreras.

paramount in determining ancestry—a rationale that, as critics of the HGDP argued, has problematic implications for Native sovereignty. If genetic testing can scientifically "disprove" Indigenous genealogies, origin stories, or migration histories, it might also be used to invalidate land claims and further undermine traditional tribal membership practices already undermined by existing federal policy. Furthermore, unlike lineal descent and other means of identifying community belonging practiced in Indigenous communities, genetic ancestry testing articulates relatedness via genetic markers that are probabilistic, rather than deterministic; that represent a miniscule portion of one's genetic inheritance (and thus one's ancestors); and that are analyzed according to problematic understandings of race and population (TallBear 5–6). As Kim TallBear (Sisseton-Wahpeton Oyate) explains, in her groundbreaking book *Native American DNA* (2013), "Native American DNA as an object could not exist without, and yet functions as a scientific data point to support the idea of, once pure, original populations" (6). Moreover, it is a concept that depends entirely upon colonial conceptions of Indigeneity:

> Native American DNA could not have emerged as an object of scientific research and genealogical desire until individuals and groups emerged as "Native American" in the course of colonial history. Without "settlers," we could not have "Indians" or "Native Americans." . . . It is the arrival of the settler in 1492 and many subsequent settlements that frame the search for Native American DNA before it is "too late," before the genetic signatures of the "founding populations" in the Americas are lost forever in a sea of genetic admixture. (5)

This assessment reveals that the HGDP's project of genetic preservation is the flip side of the US project of assimilation via the mechanism of blood quantum. Although they differ in the particulars, both rely on the subordination of Indigenous practices of identification and belonging to a biological standard that undermines Indigenous sovereignty.[18]

---

18. Notably, TallBear sees blood quantum as having some utility as a proxy for genealogical relationships. In contrast, Jill Doerfler (White Earth Chippewa), who, alongside Vizenor, played a leading role in rewriting the White Earth Constitution, critiques blood quantum as a system designed to dissolve Native nations: "Defining identity via blood ensured that once enough 'mixing' took place, American Indians would disappear into the melting pot of social and political life," allowing the US government to "limit the number of people they have political and financial obligations to, and to gain control of American Indian resources" (xvi–xxvii).

In his essay "Genome Survivance" (2012), Vizenor comments directly on the implications of using genetics to authenticate Indigenous identities and relationships, citing both TallBear's work and the HGDP along the way. Assigning blood quantum and genetic ancestry testing alike to a continuum of "scientific modernism" governed by a logic of separation, rather than connection, he explains that "genetic ancestry is not a family":

> We are animals, but there are no genomes of visionary totemic associations. The chance unions of humans, animals, and native families are connections by creation and trickster stories, by transmotion, or by the visionary sense of natural motion, sacred and secular imagination, but not by the genetic science of haplotypes or the abstract counts and codes of ancestry. (223)[19]

Vizenor describes genetic ancestry testing as a practice of categorization linked, ideologically, to precursor scientific theories, such as polygenesis and phrenology, which supported the spurious notion of racial hierarchy. Identity, family, and genealogy are enacted not in genetic code, he argues, but in narrative, imagination, vision, movement, and the complex union of human and more-than-human life. These are the principles of "survivance," a well-known Vizenorian concept that describes not the "instinct[ual]" continuation of life (i.e., "survival" or "subsistence" [Vizenor, "Aesthetics" 11]) but an active and collective "presence of natural reason and resistance to absence and victimry" (19).[20] Unlike Western political categories, "survivance" is not grounded in static biological or geographical indices of belonging or inheritance; it emerges, rather, in dynamic relationships of community, narrative, and place: "Native sovereignty is the right of motion, and transmotion is personal, reciprocal, the source of survivance, but not territorial" (Vizenor, *Fugitive* 182).[21] These concepts are not abstractions for Vizenor; he has applied them to political concerns facing the White Earth Nation, as it "rethinks tribal membership away from an antiquated,

---

19. "Transmotion . . . is the practice of transmitting tribal cultural practices across time as well as spaces of travel and trade" (Madsen, "Sovereignty" 24).

20. For Vizenor, "victimry," associated with absence and stasis, is a product of domination that must be repudiated (Vizenor, "Aesthetics" 11). Also see Lee, Introduction 4; Kroeber 31. On "survivance," see Vizenor, "Aesthetics"; Kroeber 25; Lockard 209–12; Madsen, "On Subjectivity" 61.

21. Contra Vizenor, Christie argues that trickster discourse threatens to fall into meaningless language play unless it weds itself to a robust politics of place. He faults Vizenor for imposing Anishinaabe cultural terms and a pan-Indian vision on the land of the Lummi People (Point Roberts, refigured as Point Assinika in the novel), reproducing the violation of Lummi sovereignty undertaken by land developers.

colonial blood quantum system, and toward a traditional tribal membership based on adoption, kinship, and family ties." Vizenor led the rewriting of the White Earth Constitution, resulting in a document (ratified in 2009) that "offers a Native perspective on Indigenous sovereignty" and protects the rights of "mixed-blood family members," like Vizenor himself (Stanciu 1369). Genetic testing was deliberately excluded from the articles governing tribal membership.[22]

Although Vizenor takes special aim at genomics, the problems he identifies in the field are of a piece with the academic study of Indigenous people across the disciplines. Vizenor has written extensively in opposition to the "simulations" propagated by social science, in particular, which reinforce a counterfeit representation of Native people as stuck in the past and defined by stereotype masquerading as authenticity:

> Jingoists, historians, anthropologists, mythologists, and various culture cultists, have hatched and possessed distorted images of tribal cultures. Conference programs and the rich gossip at dinner parties continue to focus on the most recent adventures in tribal commodities. This obsession with the tribal past is . . . a statement of academic power and control over tribal images, an excess of facts, data, narrative interviews, template discoveries. Academic evidence is a euphemism for linguistic colonization of oral traditions and popular memories. ("Socioacupuncture" 413)

Vizenor undermines claims to academic objectivity and authority, linking research to prurience, commodification, and naked power—and illuminating the material and discursive effects of scholarly hegemony over Indigenous stories, artifacts, and people. Research, he makes clear, has literally extended the violence of colonialism.[23] Vizenor also describes academic simulations of Indianness as a failure of *interpretation*—a monologue, rather than a discourse, through which scholars produce "absolute fakes" for their own "consumption" ("Postmodern" 5). Built on debased stereotypes or nostalgic ideals, simulated "Indians," such as those captured in works by Henry Rowe Schoolcraft or Henry Wadsworth Longfellow (both addressed

---

22. These articles were written to "satisf[y] the serious interests of those delegates who favoured the blood-quantum concession, and those delegates who insisted that genealogy or direct family descent and identity determine the actual meaning of citizenship" (Vizenor, "Genome" 222). Also see Doerfler 61–90.

23. As Indigenous studies scholar Linda Tuhiwai Smith (Maori) writes, "The term 'research' is inextricably linked to European imperialism and colonialism" (1).

in *Heirs*), are tragic, not comic; static, not dynamic; transparent, not ironic.[24] The problem Vizenor identifies in genetic ancestry testing, which elaborates a Native identity from tiny sequences of genetic code, is not dissimilar from the interpretive errors of social science, which amass "an excess of facts" while ignoring complexity and change. "There are no genetic codes or trickster haplotypes of irony," Vizenor writes, implying that the genomic project of "decoding" and "discovery" is an interpretive practice that fails by way of a fatal literalism ("Genome" 228).

Vizenor links academic misreadings of Native peoples to academic misreadings of Native literature, which are influenced by logics of objectivity, discovery, acquisition, categorization, separation, and tragedy (Preface x–xiii). In contrast to these "semantic dioramas," Vizenor calls for a critical approach inspired by the motion and play of Native stories ("Trickster" 192): "There can never be 'correct' or 'objective' readings of the text or the tropes in tribal literatures, only more energetic, interesting and 'pleasurable misreadings'" ("Postmodern" 5).[25] This approach takes seriously the "chance" and "humor" in Native storytelling, rejecting the "tragic modes" imposed on it by social scientific methodologies (11). And it proposes narrative as an "event" and a "discourse" in which listeners and readers are active and creative participants—"interlocutors" ("Trickster" 189–91). In his essay on "Trickster Discourse," Vizenor even goes so far as to claim that readers/listeners both "imagine" and "become" tricksters, if they engage Native stories in the spirit of dialogism (193).[26]

At the risk of attempting to summarize what should, perhaps, remain "a loose seam in consciousness" ("Trickster" 196), I would identify the following principles in Vizenor's articulation of a reading practice that honors the trickster spirit of Indigenous narratives in opposition to academic misreadings and misappropriations, genomic or otherwise: such reading *is not* decoding, discovery, collecting, or categorizing; it *is* dialogical, active, nonlinear, and attentive to surprise, pleasure, chance, and humor; and it has the potential to heal readers and communities. For Vizenor, these principles apply not only to the reception of oral or written narratives but also to the engagement of artifacts, bodies, body parts, DNA, "natural objects," and human remains, all of which he presents as narrative entities in *Heirs*.

---

24. "The Indian was an occidental invention that became a bankable simulation; the word has no referent in tribal languages or cultures" (Vizenor, *Manifest* 11). Vizenor has proposed "postindian" as an alternative; see Lee, Introduction 5; Doerfler xxiv–xxv.

25. Vizenor borrows the term "pleasurable misreadings" from Vincent Leitch's *Deconstructive Criticism*.

26. Also see Hogue 171.

Furthermore, the novel makes good on this faith in narrative agency—and narrative healing—as Vizenor employs bionarrative signatures as critical techniques of genome survivance.

Bionarrativity: Stories in the Blood and Bone

It may seem at first that *The Heirs of Columbus* replicates the hunt for "Native American DNA" that motivated the HGDP and other "vampire projects." After all, the plot hinges on the discovery of an Indigenous genetic signature that is transformed into an in-demand (and potentially profitable) medical treatment, fulfilling the therapeutic promise of "exotic" Native genes for non-Native people. Furthermore, the "signature of survivance" is also a unique genealogical marker used to trace Native ancestry; in other words, it appears to fulfill the anthropological promise of "isolates of historical interest" and to authenticate the Indigenous heritage of the Heirs, who are not recognized members of any tribe. However, Vizenor complicates this narrative template. Although the plot hinges on the theft of Indigenous remains and artifacts, the theft of *genes* is, surprisingly, not a plot point. The isolation of the genetic signature is led by the Heirs themselves, and it is made available to whoever seeks its healing powers, rather than hoarded for profit. Moreover, it is not discovered within a remote population of the sort the HGDP focused on; instead, it is isolated in the DNA of the "crossblood" Heirs, emphasizing mixture and connection, as opposed to isolation and stasis. Rather than simply authenticating the Heirs' tribal identity, the "signature of survivance" is used to "make the *world* tribal," a project of decolonial rehabilitation that involves far more than gene therapy.

At the heart of the novel's healing project is storytelling, from which the "signature of survivance" is inextricable. By using the term "signature" to describe a genetic variation, Vizenor draws from genomics' font of textual metaphors. Indeed, the signature of survivance is directly linked to a literal text: a now-lost tome, the "Bear Codex," which the Heirs believe to be a translation of "the picture codex of the Maya House of Cocom"—in other words, a foundational text from a foundational civilization (25).[27] However, Vizenor's narrativization of genetics' textual metaphor—his insistence that DNA is at once story, storyteller, and part of a larger story—resists both the reductive and aggrandizing effects that sometimes accompany metaphors

---

27. Like nineteenth-century archeologist Augustus Le Plongeon, cited in relation to the "Bear Codex," the Heirs believe that the Maya were the first civilization and that their cultural contributions have been forgotten and repaid with violence.

like "sentence" and "code," on the one hand, and "book of life," on the other. Vizenor uses a variety of narrative techniques designed to alter his readers' relationship to the story of Native American DNA and to offer healing from the wounds and ongoing violence of colonialism, including in its academic and scientific registers. Underlying these techniques is the conceptual linking of biology and narrative. Rather than presenting biological entities, like blood, bone, or DNA, as metaphors for story—or stories as metaphors for body parts—Vizenor presents biology and story as thoroughly intertwined. It is through the lens of *bionarrativity* that Vizenor addresses the appropriation of Native stories, artifacts, and remains, and it is through this lens that he offers chance, humor, and narrative signatures as healing practices.[28]

Throughout *Heirs*, Vizenor understands narrative as a property of the body, as the presence of stories in blood, flesh, bone, and DNA. Critic Arnold Krupat has pointed out that the phrase "stories in the blood" appears at least fifty-three times in *Heirs*; it is a favored expression among the title characters, who preserve and affirm their heritage by telling stories (Krupat, "Stories" 168). Krupat is troubled by "stories in the blood" because it appears to posit a biological basis for Native identity (though he ultimately argues that Vizenor deconstructs the concept), and he has criticized allied concepts in Kiowa writer N. Scott Momaday's work, such as "racial memory" and "memory in the blood," as essentializing "mystification[s]" (Krupat, *Voice* 13).[29] Like Sarah Eden Schiff, however, I see such deployments of "racial memory" as refusing the material/metaphorical binary on which Krupat's criticism (and others' defense) rests—or, to take up Vizenor's language, as exemplary of a creative union of supposed opposites.[30] "Stories in the blood," as the concept is used in *Heirs*, at once accedes to the idea that DNA makes us who we are and insists that DNA is neither proprietary nor static, evacuating genetics of its determinative power and rendering it resistant to the appropriation of racial essentialists.[31] Stories in the blood are not

---

28. For a rich accounting of Vizenor's use of narrative strategies drawn from genetics, see Koepke and Nelson.

29. Krupat's dismissal of Momaday's use of such terms has received heat from critics who defend Momaday's language as metaphorical; see Schiff 96–98; C. Allen 93–96.

30. In his discussion of animals in American literature, Vizenor distinguishes between metaphor and simile, arguing that the latter tends toward anthropomorphism, aligning the animal with the human imagination, whereas the former enacts a complex relation of animal and the rest of the natural world (*Fugitive* 123). Anishinaabe totems, for example, are metaphors, but never *mere* metaphors.

31. The novel "holds in balance . . . the ideas of 'stories in the blood,' the inherited power of tribal identity . . . and . . . the trickster desire . . . to 'make the world tribal, a universal identity'" (Madsen, "On Subjectivity" 79). Also see Burgess 32–33.

deterministic or inert, and they cannot be reduced to DNA. They constitute a genetic signature of survivance, but their therapeutic enactment requires the ongoing agency of those who tell, dream, imagine, and remember them.

From the very beginning, the novel's references to DNA are linked to storytelling. The signature of survivance is introduced as part of the Heirs' retelling of the Columbus story, embedded, that is, in the novel's signature narrative revision. And the remembering of tribal stories is presented as inextricable from the remembering of "tribal genes" (9): the Heirs meet at the Stone Tavern to "remember the best stories about their strain and estate, and the genetic signature that would heal the obvious blunders in the natural world" (4). The therapeutic aims of the Heirs are narrative *and* genetic, the unusual phrase "strain and estate" suggesting both inheritance (in multiple senses) and the ongoing effort required to enact it. To move from the conditional "would heal" to the future-tense "will heal"—a move realized in the novel's final chapters—requires the telling and retelling of stories in the blood.

Contending that there is no way to understand genetics outside of storytelling, the novel offers contradiction and irony (often articulated as "opposition") as (anti-)foundational principles that apply to both narrative and genetic inheritance. Pir Cantrip, director of research at the Genome Pavilion, explains that "genetic signatures do not exist in isolation" (135) and that the "four letters" that make up DNA "are held together in a signature by their opposites"; moreover, "those who can imagine their antinomies and mutations are able to heal with humor" (134). In this account, the strength of DNA—its literal ability to stay whole—is located in the union of opposing forces, as if DNA were a physical expression of irony and juxtaposition, or irony and juxtaposition literary expressions of biology. The genome's antinomic bonds are expressed in "communal imagination, ironies, and memories, the very energies and agonistic humor of tricksters and shamans" (135), and the human capacity for creativity and healing extends from a "primal" union of opposites (134).

Even when DNA is associated with written, rather than oral, texts, Vizenor emphasizes instability and multiplicity, rather than fixity. A little over halfway through the novel we are introduced to Pellegrine Treves, whose extensive rare book collection includes several signed first editions by major authors of the so-called Native American Renaissance.[32] The value of this collection is measured, Treves explains, through the principle of

---

32. The term "Native American Renaissance" has been criticized for applying a European conceptual category to Indigenous literatures and for diminishing earlier oral and literary traditions (Nelson 377–79).

"association": the content of each work is less relevant than its connection to specific authors, owners, or readers, as evidenced by signatures and marginalia. The emphasis on "association" and "signatures" recalls the association studies used to isolate meaningful genetic sequences, including, presumably, the Heirs' "signature of survivance," and evokes epigenetic notations inscribed in DNA. If such notations inform which genes are "turned on" and "off," signatures and marginalia function similarly, drawing readers' attention to (and thus "turning on") certain passages, silencing (or "turning off") others, and shaping the meaning of specific elements of the text. In other words, the texts in Pellegrine's collection are literally marked as polysemic.

The clearest example of this polysemy is Pellegrine's copy of *The Voice in the Margin: Native American Literature and the Canon* (1989), by Krupat himself. The text includes marginal notes, written by a "notable novelist" posing as Momaday, that critique Krupat's critique of Momaday (110). In a monograph about literary canons and margins—which, not incidentally, includes "substantive" footnotes "where a number of other voices speak" (Krupat, *Voices* 18)—the contested marginalia constitute a literal voice in the margin that results in a contradictory "double association" (Vizenor, *Heirs* 110). One character, after learning of the book's unusual provenance, describes Krupat as "the trickster on the margins," further unsettling the relationships between text and margin, canon and margin, and author and reader, and injecting Krupat's critique of "blood memory" with the possibility of mischief and play via a term not typically applied to non-Native people (111). Pellegrine's marked-up copy of *The Voice in the Margin* thus subtly undermines Krupat's charge of essentialism, not by reducing the concept of "memory in the blood" to metaphor, but by suggesting that texts, like DNA, are subject to significant variation based on differences in annotation, expression, and context. If DNA is a variable, unstable text, then to say that Indigenous memory or story is present in DNA is not to say that it is fixed or isolated—quite the opposite. Indeed, research on the epigenetic changes brought about by environmental factors, including the traumas of attempted genocide, seems to confirm Momaday's assertion that tribal stories are, at least in one sense, physically inherited. But the larger point is that the concept of stories in the blood does not have to be read as *either* metaphorical *or* essentializing, inasmuch as Vizenor represents both stories and DNA as material *and* metaphorical, as dynamic, rather than deterministic.

For Vizenor, DNA is both body and story, but it is not the only—or even the most important—body part or material object that can be described in this way. Throughout *Heirs*, stories inhere in blood, skin, hair, fingernails, and bones, body parts that can be subjected to genetic testing (and are so subjected in the novel) but that also carry their own meanings and associations.[33] Even inorganic objects are presented as, at the very least, narrative "containers." Binn Columbus, for example, can hear stories in "even the abandoned bodies of automobiles" and "common trash" (19). And stones, perhaps because they can be so easily (mis)read as inert, are repeatedly aligned with stories in the blood: Vizenor describes the genetic signature claimed by the Heirs as a "secret in the stone" (128), the Stone Tavern is "warm[ed]" by stories in the blood (5), the "stones once told stories" and "listen at the mount" (13), and the character who introduces the Heirs' alternate genealogy is *Stone* Columbus. Vizenor's presentation of stones as sentient narrative agents is aligned with the animate status of the Anishinaabemowin word for stone and with the widespread recognition of stones, across Indigenous cultures, as relatives and ancestors.[34] Appearing on talk radio to spread the word about Christopher Columbus's "crossblood" heritage and the signature of survivance, Stone articulates a link among stones, genes, and stories and reveals none of these to be fixed in meaning: "The stone is my totem, my stories are stones, there are tribal stones, and the brother of the first trickster who created the earth was a stone, stone, stone." The interviewer cannot follow Stone's references and dismisses him with a bit of wordplay that falls flat in comparison to the "serious" language games Stone is playing: "You must be stoned," she says. "My stories are evermore serious, serious, serious," Stone replies, "teas[ing] the sounds of the words" (9). The echo of "stone, stone, stone" in "serious, serious, serious" imbues the latter with a playful irony that, along with Stone's "teasing" of the *sound* of the word, highlights the linguistic "play" in both "stone" and "teasing."[35] The point here is the possibility—the necessity—of reinterpretation and resignification, the linguistic openness that allows Stone and the Heirs to "overturn" (185) the official Columbus narrative in favor of a new story, engaging in what LeAnne Howe (Choctaw) calls "tribalography": the "rhetorical space" cleared by Native stories that have "the power to transform"

---

33. Juana María Rodríguez has pointed out that bones appear as "silent witnesses" (250) and metaphors for "untold stories" throughout Vizenor's oeuvre (249).

34. In "The Stones Shall Cry Out: Consciousness, Rocks, and Indians," George "Tink" Tinker (Osage) describes the "ubiquitous Indian notion of interrelationship and the respect that Indian people maintain for all life forms in our world, including rocks and trees," as well as the specific Osage view "that rock is *tsage*, the oldest living being—for which reason some call the *tsage* 'grandparents' or 'beloved old ones'" (122). On the status of "stone" as an animate term in Anishinaabemowin, see Valentine.

35. On Vizenor's comic repetition of specific words "to glean multiple uses and meanings," see Lush 5.

("Tribalography" 118).[36] By choosing stones as a figure of narrative agency and revision, Vizenor drives home the point that no narrative is written in stone, even the most hegemonic. Native storytelling is a bionarrative inheritance, in *Heirs*; material, embodied, and replete with irony and humor, it has the power to create and recreate the world.

Bionarrative Appropriation

Although *Heirs* does not make the appropriation of Native American DNA a plot point, it does center on the theft of sacred objects and remains: the bones of Pocahontas and Columbus, held by acquisitive collectors; stones stolen from the Stone Tavern by a missionary, an anthropologist, and a "blond shaman" (Vizenor, *Heirs* 14)—a trio of "culture cultists," if ever there were one (Vizenor, "Socioacupuncture" 412); and bear paw and otter medicine pouches stolen by Henry Rowe Schoolcraft, the nineteenth-century geographer, ethnographer, and Indian agent famous for his study of Native American cultures, which depended on the uncredited contributions of Anishinaabe people, including his wife's family. Because the objects in question are presented as bionarrative entities—living objects that hold stories of survivance—their theft is a form of bioprospecting: for Vizenor, to steal bones and artifacts is to steal stories; to subject them to social scientific methodologies is to misread and silence stories; and to misread and silence stories is to commit an offense not unlike those governed by legislation like NAGPRA and IACA or undertaken by projects like the HGDP.

Schoolcraft's legacy is key to Vizenor's critique of bionarrative appropriation. "The mission ethnographer," the narrator explains, "seldom cited his sources, and he demonstrated no gratitude to the tribe for his reputation as an expert on the language and culture of the Anishinaabe" (48). The theft of the medicine pouches, which are "tribal stories, not capital assets," are an extension of this violation, not a separate transgression (46). Further, the conflict over them plays out between characters who tell very different *stories* about colonialism. Doric Michéd, in possession of stolen tribal artifacts, embodies the neocolonial motto of the "Brotherhood of American Explorers," which closely links linguistic and geographical imperialism: "Explore new worlds, discover with impunities, represent with manners, but never

---

36. Vizenor's centering of Indigenous people in the colonial narrative echoes Howe's assertion that "America is a tribal creation story" ("Tribalography" 118). Also see Howe's discussion of earth mounds, songs, and ball games as embodied stories that enact Native "continuance" ("Embodied" 76).

retreat from *the ownership of land and language*" (50; emphasis added). In contrast, Felipa Flowers, the "trickster poacher" who heads the repatriation mission, counters Doric's language of "discovery" ("*Stolen* is the right word," she says [50]) and describes colonialism as ongoing bionarrative consumption: "The shamans, the bear and beaver, and now the earth must survive the diseases of the fur trade. . . . Not so the new fur traders can consume our blood, shadows, and sacred stories." Notably, Felipa and Doric are both "crossblood heirs" to Schoolcraft, though they also tell starkly different stories about their shared ancestry: Felipa identifies herself as a descendant of Jane Johnston Schoolcraft, also known as Bamewawagezhikaquay, an important Ojibwe literary forebear who was married to Henry Schoolcraft and whose translations of Anishinaabe oral traditions were included in his work without citation.[37] Meanwhile, Doric claims Henry Schoolcraft as a remote ancestor and "pretend[s] to be tribal" when it "serve[s] his . . . interests" (47). In other words, Felipa centers her tribal and female ancestry, while Doric centers his European and male ancestry and mimics its appropriative posture. Like Felipa, the narrator also centers Bamewawagezhikaquay within literary and literal genealogies ("what *her husband* learned about the language and stories of the tribe he learned from her relatives" [48; emphasis added]), suggesting that, by privileging Henry Schoolcraft, academic genealogies reproduce and obscure his acts of appropriation.

The conflict over Pocahontas's remains raises a similar set of issues regarding genealogy, appropriation, and misreading. The book collector Pellegrine Treves hopes to return the remains to the House of Life where one day he—believing his family and Pocahontas's are "of the same tribe"—might be "united" with her (109).[38] However well-meaning, Pellegrine is guilty of "romantic revisions of tribal cultures and women," viewing both through the lens of the "noble savage" (108).[39] Speaking of his own genealogical connection to "marranos and refugees," Pellegrine states that "the adversities of the past are measures of honor and compassion," glibly revising historical trauma into a status marker in the way only a person already in possession of status can do. "Marvelous, the turns of language," Felipa

---

37. On Jane Johnston Schoolcraft's uncredited contributions to Henry Schoolcraft's work, see Cavalier 100. For a thorough discussion of her life, work, and legacy, see Parker.

38. Pellegrine believes that his Sephardic Jewish heritage links him to the hand talkers and, thus, to Pocahontas. For an in-depth discussion of references to Sephardism in *Heirs*, see Casteel.

39. Notably, Pellegrine has "never collected books about exploration or ships," suggesting that a distaste for narratives of conquest can coincide with problematic ways of reading Indigeneity (Vizenor, *Heirs* 113).

dryly replies, noting the obfuscating power of language that can transform—in Pellegrine's words—"rubbish tips into civic amenities" (109). The discussion of "association" as a measure of his book collection's value takes on a new cast in light of this conversation: Pellegrine is as much in the business of collecting "associations" to Nativeness as he is in the business of collecting Native books with valuable associations. Case in point: the "twenty volume set of *The North American Indian*, by Edward Curtis, with association signatures of the author and President Theodore Roosevelt," a text that underscores Pellegrine's association with curated "Indianness" (112).[40] Pellegrine's refusal to touch Pocahontas's bones is further evidence of his preference for romance over reality; although he attempts to remediate the appropriation of Native remains, he is guilty of an allied error: misreading them through Native "simulations."

Vizenor's solution to such misreading is to let bones speak for themselves. In the essay "Bone Courts: The Natural Rights of Tribal Bones" (1986), published just a few years before NAGPRA, Vizenor proposes a special court for the adjudication of conflicts over Indigenous remains. Noting that legal representation is already accorded to nonpersons (such as corporations) and drawing upon environmentalist claims that "natural objects" should also have legal standing (324), Vizenor argues that human remains have a right to legal defense—and a right "to be their own *narrators*" (319; emphasis added). In *Heirs*, Vizenor elaborates on this argument in a chapter (also called "Bone Courts") about a hearing to determine legal standing with respect to tribal artifacts and remains. Citing *Should Trees Have Standing?* (1972), by Christopher Stone—whose name, by (wonderfully Vizenorian) chance, seems to link him to the Heirs so closely that the judge is compelled to note that he "is no relation"—one of the witnesses explains that "the heirs nurture the view that stories are in bones, stones, trees, water, bears, air, everywhere, and stories have natural rights." The judge initially understands this argument as "metaphor[ical]" (78), but over the course of the hearing, the boundary between metaphor and reality is repeatedly destabilized, as when one of the Heirs produces physical manifestations of the judge's "silent thought[s]" (73), when another appears as a panther to those who "imagine[] animals in their blood" (71), and when a third stages a virtual reality experience.[41]

---

40. For Vizenor's critique of Curtis's photographic simulations, see "Socioacupuncture" 412.

41. On Vizenor's use of virtual reality simulations to challenge dominant "simulations" of Indigeneity, see Arnold; Gillan.

The bionarrative strategies of these witnesses challenge the appropriation of Native stories and sacred objects by making visible, audible, and tactile that which would otherwise remain in the realm of imagination. Their testimony releases stories contained in (presumably inert) matter and transforms (presumably imaginary) stories into material realities. At the Bone Court, bones are neither inert objects on which value (cultural, economic) is projected, nor symbols of a meaningful story. They are themselves story and storyteller. The arrogation of bones, stones, and stories is not only coincident, in *Heirs*, with stealing, misreading, or overwriting Native stories; it *is* stealing, misreading, and overwriting Native stories. And the reverse of this claim is implied as well: the stealing, misreading, and overwriting of Native stories is not strictly a violation of the imagination; it, too, has a material register and impact. One need only look to the physical suffering justified by the overwriting of Indigenous experiences of colonialism with the official Columbus narrative to see brutal illustration of this fact.

But the Heirs' testimony at the Bone Court also suggests the possibility of intervening in and upending official narratives. Although the hearing does not result in a firm decision on the legal standing of human remains, Doric Michéd is censured by the Court and the possibility of future hearings remains open. The bionarrative techniques used by the Heirs in this scene also draw attention to strategies employed by Vizenor over the course of the novel. Their deployment of humor and language play, in particular, are indicative of the novel's strategies for altering readers' relationship to hegemonic colonial narratives. If the Genome Pavilion the Heirs build at the end of the novel offers bionarrative therapy to all who seek it, so does *The Heirs of Columbus*.

Therapeutic Narrative Signatures

Contrary to Vizenor's assertion in "Genome Survivance" that "there are no trickster haplotypes of irony," I would playfully contend that not only do they exist but they are the outstanding narrative feature of *The Heirs of Columbus*. In the field of genetics, "haplotype" describes a set of alleles (genetic variations) inherited together because of their physical proximity; haplotypes are used in ancestry testing, because certain genetic variations are inherited together at higher frequencies in specific populations. The "signature of survivance" that the Heirs, like Columbus, have inherited from Indigenous hand talkers—and that is transformed into a genetic therapy at the Genome Pavilion—is just such a haplotype. But it is also a "haplotype of irony," given Vizenor's association of irony with survivance *and* his critique of genetic definitions of identity, which suggests that any reference to genetic signatures in Vizenor's work *must* be ironic. Indeed, irony, humor, and chance are always in narrative proximity for Vizenor, as if they themselves were genes on a shared chromosome—a kind of narrative haplotype. By passing on to readers the trickster haplotype of irony, through the recombinations that take place at scenes of reading, Vizenor offers a form of bionarrative therapy whereby readers can share in his trickster inheritance.

Vizenor has made clear that he sees healing as a primary goal for *Heirs*.[42] Rather than reciting the litany of horrors that followed Columbus's arrival in the Americas, an exercise he associates with perpetuation of harm against Indigenous people, Vizenor fundamentally alters the terms of the colonial narrative, telling a comic story that is both *about* healing and intended to heal: "I have turned around the Columbus story to serve healing rather than victimization" (qtd. in Coltelli 103). Vizenor thus articulates what Lawrence W. Gross (White Earth Chippewa) identifies as an Anishinaabe "comic vision" that promotes healing from "Post Apocalypse Stress Syndrome" (437).[43] It is important to add that the healing the novel offers is distinct for colonized and settler readers: while the former are offered the relief that accompanies the comic takedown of a discourse that has oppressed them directly, the latter are offered the opportunity to disidentify from a harmful discourse clearly rendered absurd. Further, when Vizenor says that his story does not serve victimization, he refers not only to the experience of Indigenous readers, who risk being revictimized by static repetitions of colonial violation, but also to the *action* of victimizing that non-Indigenous readers participate in by demanding narrative "simulations."

Given Vizenor's investment in humor as a way of countering damaging stories, it makes sense that the novel's story-within-a-story—the alternate genealogy passed down by the Heirs—centers on an act both comic and therapeutic. The Heirs claim that Samana, their Indigenous hand talker ancestor, straightened Columbus's crooked penis, a suggestive (in both senses) metaphor for the novel's reorienting of the official narrative of European discovery. That the story of survivance in *Heirs* issues metaphorically from a "crossblood" penis set right by an Indigenous female healer is comic in both the ordinary sense (Columbus's wayward penis is a recurring bawdy

---

42. For a reading of *Heirs* based on the narrative practice of the Midewiwin, traditional Anishinaabe healers, see Burgess. On Vizenor's "socioacupuncture" technique, see Gillan.

43. Also see Blaeser, "New" 39; Kroeber 37. On the link between Native humor and activism, as well as Columbus jokes, specifically, see Deloria 147.

joke) and in the dramatic sense (Columbus's return is associated with life, not death—continuity, not annihilation). Vizenor does not "turn the tables" on European colonialism by reversing the historical direction of colonial violence and domination; after all, healing is offered to Columbus at the story's beginning and to all people at its end. Instead, Vizenor disassembles "the tables" of colonial history, a figure of speech that, by (Vizenorian) chance, brings to mind both the shared meal at the center of the mythic Thanksgiving story and the tabulation of blood quantum and genetic ancestry. In the process, he reorients readers to these stale stories, opening up "new landscapes of narrative possibility" (Rodríguez 249).

Closely linked to humor, chance—whether in the form of literal games (such as the therapeutic bingo played at Point Assinika) or language games (the puns that permeate the narrative)—is also associated with healing and survivance in *Heirs*. In a world governed by constant change, chance is a fact of existence that requires narrative play: "The wild world [is] a deal with chance and survivors [tell] the best stories," explains a witness at the Bone Court, reimagining "survival of the fittest" by recasting adaptation as a narrative practice that responds to the unpredictable conditions of survival (83). As this passage suggests, the principle of chance has implications for both DNA and narrative, emphasizing the probabilistic (rather than deterministic) character of genetic inheritance and presenting storytelling, like the reproduction of life itself, as a game that must never end. This principle is illustrated in the moccasin game the Heirs play near the novel's conclusion. Rather than win the game but lose his antagonists (who would be destroyed by his victory), the wiindigoo spirit walks away, announcing that "the game never ends" (183). In so doing, he articulates a core principle of the novel: stories do not, cannot, end. They are told, retold, and modified for new circumstances in a process that parallels genetic recombination. Associating DNA with the oral tradition, Vizenor emphasizes adaptation and change, rather than decoding and translation, as practices of genome survivance.

Vizenor also illustrates these principles in a specific narrative strategy—what I am calling *therapeutic narrative signatures*—that involves the comic repetition and novel recombination of words and phrases in ways that both invite and confound totalizing interpretations, undermining the reproduction of colonial discourse and making space for new discursive possibilities and material realities. Like the moccasin game, Vizenor's language games are not win-or-lose, and the healing they promote is not once-and-for-all. Rather, they invite a way of reading that can meet the ongoing challenges of postcolonial and postgenomic life, by sidestepping dead-end monologues and embracing adaptation. The structural principle behind Vizenor's use of narrative signatures is not teleology (a principle used to consign Native people to a "primitive" biological or mythical past) but open-endedness. Although his narrative signatures do not determine a specific outcome (or meaning), they do inform interpretation of the surrounding text, inviting readers to join in a postmodern and postgenomic game of interpretation that does not end in triumph or defeat.

This play-to-play, rather than play-to-win, principle is legible in how certain motifs, such as the color blue, the number nine, and specific names, contribute to the novel's unique semantic web. Many such signatures are given minimal—if any—explanation; their meanings tease and shimmer, through repetition, accretion, and contextualization, but are never finally determined. The color blue, for example—connected to puppets, healers, and the light of creation—gradually becomes intelligible as a sign of life and health. And the repetition of names links characters across time and space, without making their connection fully clear. (Is Treves Brink, a US police officer who assists the Heirs, confirmation of Pellegrine Treves's hope that the geographical pilgrimage implied by his first name has been realized by a genealogical connection in the Americas? Or are we to stay perched on the "brink" of connection?) Overflowing with ambiguous motifs, *Heirs* seems to invite a reading practice that anticipates the massive association studies that, following the mapping of the human genome, promised to revolutionize medicine. Following leads and identifying patterns, readers are rewarded with moments of insight and pleasure and participate in the novel's critical revision of colonial and neocolonial narratives. However, any attempt to map the novel is necessarily partial and unstable. Healing is to be found, it seems, not in the values of collection, categorization, or mastery, but in willingness to continue playing the game. It is important to emphasize that continuing to play the game means continuing the effort of tracing and following while, simultaneously, recognizing that this effort will never be "complete." I do not see in *Heirs* a wholesale rejection of *association* and *sequencing* as reading practices, whether applied to literary or scientific archives. Rather, I see an emphasis on open-endedness, multiplicity, and chance as necessary conditions of interpretation in both contexts.

Sometimes "the game," as Vizenor sets it up, involves bionarrative signatures that extend from the novel's comic revision of the standard Columbus tale; by identifying translations, edits, and recontextualizations of Columbian motifs, readers participate in the novel's therapeutic work. For example, they might notice that Columbus is transformed from "admiral of the ocean sea" (title of a well-known Columbus biography) to "tribal mariner of chance" (7) and a figure "ever on the move in [the Heirs'] stories"

(11). Or they might notice the repurposing of the names of Columbus's ships for Stone Columbus's floating casinos, a repetition that unmoors the names from their original context, making them available for Vizenor's vision of Native sovereignty in motion. Vizenor even enables playful rereadings of quotations from Columbus's diaries, instances of colonial misapprehension that have been faithfully repeated, with devastating consequences, for centuries. For example, the narrator first recounts Columbus's arrival in the Americas in this way:

> He landed at dawn with no missionaries or naturalists and heard the thunder of shamans in the coral and the stone. "No sooner had we concluded the formalities of taking possession of the island than people began to come to the beach," he wrote in his journal on October 12, 1492, at Samana Cay.
>
> Columbus unfurled the royal banner, and the green cross of the crown shivered on the wind over the island the tribe had named *Guanahaní*....
>
> "They ought to make good and skilled servants, for they repeat very quickly whatever we say to them," but he misconstrued a tribal pose and later traced his soul to the stories in their blood. "They all go naked as their mothers bore them, including the women, although I saw only one very young girl." (3–4)

Already this citation is structured in ambivalence, Columbus's colonial misreading juxtaposed with critical commentary, the Indigenous name of the colonized space, and the Heirs' alternative genealogy. Later, the passage is rearticulated from an Indigenous perspective when Point Assinika is "declared a sovereign nation" five hundred years after Columbus wrote in his diary:

> "At dawn we saw pale naked people, and we went ashore in the ship's boat.... Miigis [the "luminous child" of Stone and Felipa Flores] unfurled the royal banner, and the heirs brought the flags which displayed a large blue bear paw.
>
> "The Heirs of Columbus bear faith and witness that we have taken possession of this point in the name of our genes and the wild tricksters of liberties, and we made all the necessary declarations and had these testimonies recorded by a blond anthropologist.
>
> "No sooner had we concluded the formalities of taking possession of the point than people began to come to the beach, all as pale as their mothers bore them, and the women also, although we did not see more than one very young girl," said Stone Columbus.... (119)

This comic adaptation of the previous passage potentially defuses a key citation of colonial discourse, appropriating and revising its language and symbolism in service of the Heirs' decolonial project, all the while maintaining a trickster posture. Importantly, this effect relies upon readers taking Vizenor up on his invitation to enact a trickster reading—to "adopt" a trickster "state of mind" by recognizing (and taking pleasure in) the revisions in play (Hogue 171).

Offering up scholarly citations as narrative game pieces, Vizenor also gives readers the chance to assist in interrupting the repetition of scholarly simulations without replacing them with equally fixed images of Native "authenticity." The chapter "Miigis Crowns," which explores textual ambivalence through Pellegrine Treves's rare book collection, also includes abundant references to scholarly works on Pocahontas, Sephardism, and English maritime history. These citations encourage readers to wonder what buried "associations" link these topics, thus opening them up to cross-pollinating, nonstandard interpretations. And in "Storm Puppets," which relates the standard Columbus story alongside the Heirs' alternative version, multitudinous academic citations are undermined by their derivation from texts that are based on colonial misapprehensions derived, in turn, from fragments and copies of Columbus's journals.[44] The proliferating scholarly citations in *Heirs*, rather than creating a sense of narrative wholeness—as if, the more references cited, the more complete the story—challenge academic faith in citation, the "excess of facts, data, narrative interviews, template discoveries" Vizenor aligns with colonial research ("Socioacupuncture" 413). Scholarly discourse is a game that only appears to end with each new "definitive" text. As the narrator explains at the start of "Miigis Crowns," offering a critical frame within which to read the chapter's citations, "The New World is heard, the tribal world is dreamed and imagined. The Old World is seen, names and stories are stolen, construed, and published. The trickster would be the seasons, neither mortal nor possessed in a cold sentence, neither delivered nor consumed, but heard and created in the crowns of miigis" (93).[45] Scholars produce "simulations" through appropriation and

---

44. The various spellings of Columbus's name used across these texts ("Christopher Columbus," "Cristoforo Colombo" [29], "Cristóbal Colón" [34]) further underscore narrative instability by drawing attention to the vagaries of translation. And an extended comic discussion, in *Heirs*, of Realdo Columbo, the sixteenth-century anatomist credited with "discovering" the clitoris—and Thomas Laquer's comparison of the two Columbuses as "conquistadors"—further undermines the standard Columbus narrative's academic authority (31–32).

45. "Miigis" is Anishinaabemowin for cowrie, "a source of visionary presence in the northern woodland lakes" (Vizenor, *Bear* 3).

misreading; in contrast, the trickster tradition is alive and changing, like the seasons, rather than "possessed in a cold sentence" for the consumption of others. To read within this tradition is to seek connection and meaning, while eschewing semantic stasis.

One of the most notable narrative signatures in *Heirs* is a repeated reference to Antonín Dvořák's *New World Symphony* (Symphony No. 9, "From the New World"), an especially illuminating citation, in that the symphony itself is a work brimming with motifs that allude to colonialism and enslavement. The first reference to the symphony appears in the opening chapter, when Stone Columbus is being interviewed on talk radio about his recent triumph in court, which has granted sovereignty to the Santa Maria casino. Admire, the "mongrel" Heir with a "blue tongue" (8), whistles a melody "from a familiar symphony based on tribal themes," and then Felipa broadcasts a recording of the piece over loudspeakers, along with Admire's excited barking (9–10). "What are you playing?" asks the interviewer:

> "The *Santa María Overture*," said Stone.
> "No, that's Dvořák," said Luckie White.
> "Dvořák was at the headwaters," said Stone.
> "Please, tell our listeners why."
> "Dvořák heard tribal music in the stones," said Stone.
> "What about Columbus?"
> "He sought gold and tribal women," said Stone.
> "So, what did he find?"
> "He found his homeland at the headwaters."
> "Really, so what's the real story?"
> "Samana, the golden healer," said Stone. (10)

Stone first renames the symphony according to his newly recognized casino/tribal nation, reclaiming it alongside the Columbus story. He also reimagines the symphony as an "overture"—a musical "headwaters" played at the headwaters of the Mississippi River. This reclaiming is apt, given both the context and content of Dvořák's famous work. The *New World Symphony* was completed in 1893—just over four hundred years after Columbus's arrival in the Americas (and three years after the official closing of the US frontier); that same year, Dvořák participated in the Columbian quadricentennial celebrations held at the Chicago World's Fair. Although the *New World Symphony* was drafted in New York, it was likely edited during a summer spent in Spillville, Iowa, about fifty miles from the Mississippi River and four hundred miles from its headwaters (Beckerman, "Henry" 466) and where Dvořák may have encountered a group of traveling Native performers.[46] Dvořák, inspired by the Mississippi River, the open plains of the West, and the musical traditions of America's Black and Indigenous communities, included motifs derived from spirituals as well as "original themes" informed by, in his words, "the peculiarities of Indian music" (qtd. in Clapham, "Evolution" 169). He also identified Henry Wadsworth Longfellow's *The Song of Hiawatha* as a source of inspiration, further adding to the symphony's layers of citation (168).[47]

Vizenor's citation of Dvořák's citation of Indigenous and African American motifs (partially filtered through Longfellow's citation) calls up, at once, the composer's championing of "American" art forms, their filtration through European and Euro-American "simulations" of Indigeneity, and their co-optation by a narrative frame of "discovery" that extends from 1492 through 1892 to 1992—and beyond.[48] At the same time, Vizenor resists this colonial frame. In his telling, Dvořák did not *discover* "tribal music"; he *"heard"* it "in the stones"—just as Columbus did not *discover* America but *"found* his homeland at the headwaters" (emphasis added). The genes that call Columbus back to the (old) land (proleptically named "New") have reverberated—like a musical motif—throughout Europe, their source material forgotten but not lost. Every time Vizenor cites the *New World Symphony*, he calls up a complex set of citations and reversals that undermine the colonial value of "discovery." The deletions, insertions, and alterations—failures, perhaps, in "transcription"—that characterize each repetition of this signature also suggest variations in its efficacy.

The second appearance of the *New World Symphony* occurs after the Bone Court hearing, and, expectedly, it differs slightly but significantly from the first citation: "Admire . . . licked her blue lips and whistled a tribal tune from the *New World* Symphony, by Antonín Dvořák" (90). Within the text's symbolic matrix, the addition of the color blue might indicate the qualified legal success of the Heirs. But the insertion of Dvořák's name, in place of the previous "familiar symphony based on tribal themes," subtly alludes to the problem of appropriation the hearing fails to fully address. If the previous wording presents tribal themes as the symphony's cultural foundation, the new wording attributes creative authority to the composer; the "tribal tune" is now *from* the symphony, rather than its source.

---

46. The tribal identities of these performers are an unresolved question, one that draws attention to Dvořák's superficial understanding of Indigenous American music and overstatement of their influence on the symphony (Clapham, "Dvořák" 867).

47. See Beckerman, "Dvořák's" on the relationship between the symphony and *The Song of Hiawatha*.

48. Vizenor writes about Dvořák's pursuit of Indigenous "hyperrealities" in his introduction to *Narrative Chance*, "Postmodern" 6–9.

When the motif appears again, it is whistled by Felipa, after she rescues Pocahontas's remains from a church in England and just before she is murdered. This time, however, the word "tribal" is deleted from the quotation: "She whistled a tune from the *New World* Symphony, by Antonín Dvořák" (115). This alteration suggests her vulnerability to European control over the meaning of her tribal inheritance (whether figured as genes, bones, or melodies). Following a discussion of Felipa's murder, Panda, a "biorobot" created at the Genome Pavilion, "*tried* to whistle a tune from the *New World* Symphony, but her mouth was not designed for music" (175; emphasis added). Here, the deletion of "tribal" is exacerbated by the addition of "tried"; now the tune cannot be repeated at all. This misfired motif, which also precedes an accounting of the "disinformation" campaign undertaken by federal agents against the Genome Pavilion, reflects the relatively weak position of the Heirs at this point in the story and implies that Panda has not received—or cannot carry—a correct copy of the signature of survivance (175).[49] At the very end of this (final) chapter, after the Heirs have survived the moccasin game, the motif appears for the last time: "Admire whistled a tune from the *New World* Symphony by Antonín Dvořák. The children danced on the marina, and their wounds were healed once more in a moccasin game with demons" (183). This is a moment of celebration and healing, but the game is not over. The children have been healed "once more," not once and for all. Rather than utopia, Vizenor leaves us with a vision of healed children *and* games with demons, the ambivalent "Indian" themes of the *New World Symphony* playing in the background, an apt score for this moment of ambivalence.

The proliferation of references and motifs in *Heirs*, its suggestive bionarrative signatures, might be understood as an overarching instance of humor—a kind of joke played on the reader. Whether out of a sense of responsibility to the text and its contexts, or out of a desire to play (and win!) at postmodern language games, at least some readers who stick with *The Heirs of Columbus* are likely drawn in by a sense of adventure, as they try to crack the code of this supremely dense, proliferant text. Indeed, much of what has preceded this paragraph illustrates that kind of effort, as I have traced certain bits of text as they are repeated, recombined, and recontextualized across the novel. The staggering number of such narrative signatures, however, makes tracing *all* such signatures, or assigning them *final* meanings, an impossible task. As I state above, *Heirs* could be an appealing text

---

49. The novel does not resolve the question of whether the signature of survivance can or should be shared with "living" machines.

for computer-assisted analysis—the sort of analysis that resembles genomic association studies—that would map the text's vocabulary and grammatical structures and identify patterns within the work and in relation to a larger corpus.[50] However illuminating, this urge to "discovery" would seem to violate the novel's narrative ethic by ending the game, as it were, replacing narrative openness with interpretive fixity. The narrative structure of *Heirs* slyly invites a reading practice that resembles the practices of collection, categorization, decoding, and discovery that it simultaneously cautions against as practices of colonial appropriation. The true therapeutic effect of the novel, then, can be measured in the degree to which readers pursue connection and meaning while resisting final interpretations that reiterate academic simulations, instead embracing ambivalence, surprise, and the meanings-in-motion that arrive by chance.

The Heirs of Columbus is not unlike a form of gene therapy. Inserted into the body of colonial and genomic discourse, it rewrites their codes. Vizenor imagines the undoing of colonial damage in the repatriation, reburial, and regeneration of story. This is not to say that the unfathomable harm set in motion by Columbus can or should be erased with a happier tale. Rather, it is to say that narrative play can provide relief in the aftermath of colonialism. As Vizenor writes in the epilogue to *Heirs*, "Columbus arises in tribal stories that heal with humor the world he wounded; he is loathed, but he is not a separation in tribal consciousness. The Admiral of the Ocean Sea is a trickster overturned in his own stories five centuries later" (185). *The Heirs of Columbus* is a text that resists discovery and decoding. But it does not turn readers away. Rather, its proliferating signs invite proliferating interpretations produced by readers who, like the character in *Heirs* who learns to read from half-burned books, must fill in the narrative margins destroyed by violence—and, from time to time, laugh while doing so.[51]

---

50. "Vizenor's novel subtly undermines the very premise on which the logic of discovery rests: as readers we never have the feeling that we progress in our knowledge of what happens in the novel, either because things we already know are repeated again or, secondly, because new and apparently unrelated narratives develop" (Irmscher 95).

51. "Almost [Browne] learned how to read from books that had been burned in a library fire; he sounded the words on the center of the pages, and imagined the others" (Vizenor, *Heirs* 83).

CHAPTER 4

Reading the Flesh and Fleshy Reading in Octavia Butler's *Fledgling*

Gerald Vizenor's *The Heirs of Columbus* (1991), the subject of the previous chapter, counters the vampiric impulses of Western research/reading practices, demonstrating that "vampire projects" abound in the sciences and the humanities alike and deploying *therapeutic narrative signatures* that confound consumptive approaches to the text itself and to Indigenous narrative in general. It would be misleading to say that vampirism is *just* a metaphor in the novel, given that Vizenor challenges the distinction between metaphor and material reality, but *Heirs* is not a vampire story in the literal sense. In contrast, Octavia Butler's *Fledgling* (2005), the subject of the current chapter, explicitly manifests the figure of the vampire that stalks genomic discourse at the turn of the millennium. *Fledgling is* a literal vampire story, one that adds DNA to the heady brew lapped up by the genre's seductive monsters and the readers seduced by them. Rather than displacing blood, DNA exists within and alongside the genre's essential substance, vying for attention and implying that the structures of genealogy and belonging signaled by its predecessor continue to obtain in the supposedly bloodless postgenomic age. Indeed, the novel's genetic storyline presses readers to notice a series of elisions and absences that structure postgenomic discourses of race and family.

After suffering a brutal attack that wiped out her maternal family and left her with a serious case of amnesia, Shori, *Fledgling*'s narrator, begins to reconnect with her paternal relatives and relearn the history and customs of the Ina people, the vampire-like species among whom she occupies an unusual place. Shori is an "experiment"—the result of genetic engineering designed to help Ina become more resistant to the sun. Unlike most Ina, Shori has dark skin and can stay awake during the daytime, enhancements achieved through the insertion of DNA derived from a Black woman into her genome. Shori learns from her brother Stefan, who is also enhanced, that her Ina mothers were geneticists and that her "black human mother" (76), as Stefan calls her, "donated DNA" for their experiments (77). These innovations in Ina-human admixture have made some Ina so angry that they have attempted, with partial success, to destroy Shori's family.

Most of the novel is taken up with Shori's efforts to reconnect with her Ina kin, build her own interspecies family, and defend that family against enemy Ina. Shori spends relatively little time thinking about or discussing her human mother, whose name, in fact, is only mentioned twice—both times in a single passage. When she does think about Jessica Grant, who was murdered alongside Shori's Ina mothers, she confronts a blank space where a memory should be:

> Jessica Margaret Grant. I shut my eyes and tried to find something of this woman in my memory—something. But there was nothing. All of my life had been erased, and I could not bring it back. Each time I was confronted with the reality of this, it was like turning to go into what should have been a familiar, welcoming place and finding absolutely nothing, emptiness, space.

At the very moment her name is uttered, Jessica becomes a receding figure, always just out of reach. And yet Shori carries Jessica's signature on her very person. She is told by one of her "symbionts"—humans who have entered into a symbiotic relationship with an Ina—that Jessica bestowed on her not only a distinctive skin color but also a distinctive name: "Your human mother claimed the right to name you," Brook tells her; "'Shori' is the name of a kind of bird—an East African crested nightingale." Shori literally carries this name in the form of a necklace—"a gold chain with a crested bird"—retrieved from the ruins of her home. An emblem of her bond with Jessica ("Your human mother gave you this," explains Brook. "I think she loved you as though she had given birth to you herself"), the necklace also signals

Shori's African ancestry (132). And yet, this ancestry, and the woman who connects her to it, go relatively unexplored in the novel, even while Shori tirelessly pursues information about her Ina kin and the Ina diaspora, which reaches from Eastern Europe around the globe.

The lack of narrative attention paid to Shori's Black mother and African ancestry stands out in a novel otherwise explicitly interested in kinship as well as broader categories of collective identity, such as species and race. Shori spends considerable time undertaking genealogical, historical, and cultural research, but this research does not extend to her human lineage. Shori's dark skin is the chief sign of her difference from other Ina, yet little attention is paid to the human being who serves as the origin of that trait. And the symbiotic relationship between Ina and human repeatedly raises ethical questions regarding consent, bodily autonomy, and family, but these questions are not extended to the "donation" of DNA from a human being for the purposes of genetic engineering—even though it is this act that sets the narrative in motion. One might view these gaps in the narrative as missed opportunities—failures to fully explore the questions of race, species, kinship, and agency explicitly and repeatedly raised by the novel. But I would suggest instead that these gaps constitute a Morrisonian "ghost in the machine," an "ornate" absence that draws attention to itself and, in this case, to the abstraction, erasure, and disembodiment of Black people in both literary and scientific contexts (Morrison, "Unspeakable" 11).

In "Unspeakable Things Unspoken" (1988), Toni Morrison describes "the ways in which the presence of Afro-Americans has shaped the choices, the language, the structure—the meaning of so much American literature." It is through this previously unrecognized presence, which Morrison further elaborates in *Playing in the Dark: Whiteness and the Literary Imagination* (1992), that Black characters constitute a "ghost in the machine" of canonical American literature, a crucial and constitutive element made to appear invisible. She goes on to explain that this spectral *presence* often appears in the shape of an *absence*: "We can agree, I think, that invisible things are not necessarily 'not-there'; that a void may be empty, but is not a vacuum. In addition, certain absences are so stressed, so ornate, so planned, they call attention to themselves; arrest us with intentionality and purpose, like neighborhoods that are defined by the population held away from them" (11). Morrison's theorization of the ghost in the machine is developed in reference to works by white writers who undertake "intellectual feats . . . to erase me from a society seething with my presence"; in citing this foundational work, I do not intend to suggest that Butler, a Black writer who thought carefully about how, when, and whether to address race and racism in her works, is attempting parallel fugitive maneuvers (12).¹ Rather, my adoption of Morrison's formulation here is meant to draw attention to a "stressed," "ornate," "planned" absence that mirrors and illuminates the erasure of Black women from narratives of medical and scientific innovation and from genealogies disrupted by slavery. In other words, this absence is a constitutive element of the novel's contemplation of the severing of bodies and blood ties to which Black women have been repeatedly subjected.²

The core narrative absence in *Fledgling* additionally highlights two related phenomena: the cultural commodification and circulation of "Blackness" delinked from living, breathing, human beings and, more subtly, the representation of reading as a disembodied process that takes place in an abstract mental space, rather than a material context. The connection between these issues is helped along by the novel's interest in genomics, a field whose impact on Black people has been contradictory and whose understanding of "reading" as a matter of decoding data heightens the sense that texts—whether genetic or literary—are a matter of the mind, rather than the body. This notion has troubling implications for Black people, whose skin is simultaneously read as a sign of potential violence (an

---

1. On the practice of delayed racialization in Butler's work, see Mehaffy and Keating 48–49.

2. My argument is aligned with recent interventions by Alys Eve Weinbaum and Lara Choksey. In *The Afterlife of Reproductive Slavery* (2019), Weinbaum explores the "sublation" (i.e., "simultaneous *negation and preservation*") of slavery's reproductive economy in the contemporary neoliberal moment (5). Drawing upon a "black feminist philosophy of history" (3), Weinbaum demonstrates how Butler's works expose this sublation, even—and perhaps especially—when they do not make slavery an explicit theme. In her reading of "Bloodchild," which makes no direct references to US chattel slavery, Weinbaum illustrates how Butler engages the "transformation" of reproduction under slavery in contemporary reproductive practices, particularly surrogacy. The story challenges readers to recognize this continuity in its "uncanny" (138) depiction of past and present practices of "reproductive extraction" (146). As in my reading of *Fledgling*, the absence of direct references to slavery heightens the text's commentary by encoding the contemporary disavowal of slavery's continuity with the present. In *Narrative in the Age of the Genome* (2021), Choksey explores techniques for remapping kinship and ancestry, in opposition to technologies of "concealment," in her reading of Saidiya Hartman's *Lose Your Mother* (2006) and Yaa Gyasi's *Homegoing* (2016), two works that, like *Fledgling*, are marked by the disruption and suppression of family lines (119–48). Informed by Black feminist theories of the flesh, geography, and cartography, Choksey argues that Hartman and Gyasi "consider the ongoing crisis of genealogy by subverting its supremacy as a description of human belonging." Genealogy is not replaced by genetic reckoning but is reimagined through "practices of making and remaking pasts for the sake of speculative futures," which draw from the longstanding African American tradition of nonbiological kinship (148). *Fledgling*, I argue, is similarly interested in the speculative work of remaking family.

interpretation that justifies the constant threat of disembodiment under which Black people live) and as a valuable cultural object that can be separated from bodies subject to racist violence. In my discussion of *The Immortal Life of Henrietta Lacks* in chapter 2, I addressed the reduction of Black women to serviceable, undifferentiated flesh; here I am concerned with a related phenomenon: the specter of a Black woman's reduction to code, to information whose exchange and circulation is used to manipulate flesh not her own.[3] Although Shori's human mother is given minimal narrative space in *Fledgling*, the reading encounter should be capacious enough to consider the human being who has been condensed at once to genetic script and narrative device. How does *Fledgling* encourage its audience to read this aperture in the text? To translate code to flesh?

In this chapter, I argue that the elision at the heart of *Fledgling* operates in three distinct but connected ways. First, it highlights questions of consent in medical and familial contexts and mirrors the erasure of Black women—and, specifically, Black mothers—from both genealogical and scientific narratives. Second, it invites a rethinking of race, species, and kinship in line with Black feminist theorizing of "the flesh": to "enflesh" the Black mothers who were excised from historical, scientific, and genealogical narratives at the very moment their flesh was excised from their bodies is, following the work of theorists like Hortense Spillers and Sylvia Wynter, to do no less than reimagine the contours of the human. Finally, the gap at the heart of the novel invites a bionarrative interpretive method that I call *fleshy reading*. Aligned with both Black feminist theorizations of the flesh and the insights of embodied cognition, which emphasize the material dimensions of thinking and learning, fleshy reading is sensory and tactile; it draws attention to reading as an embodied practice that shapes us and our world in material ways, and it illuminates connections between reading the flesh and reading literature. Fleshy reading keeps in view the depredations of the flesh that precede or accompany narrative erasure, while remaining open to the possibility of reorganizing the flesh into different embodied subjectivities and kinship arrangements. Illustrated throughout the novel by Shori, who is in a constant state of information gathering and interpretation necessitated by amnesia, fleshy reading emerges in *Fledgling* as a narrative practice that readers can employ to flesh out the elision at the center of the novel and the elision of Black women from hegemonic medical and cultural narratives.

---

3. These are intertwined phenomena; the reduction to code is always an illusion and is helped along by the reduction to flesh.

Consenting to Kinship

Like Alina Troyano's *Chicas 2000* and Margaret Atwood's *MaddAddam* trilogy, the subjects of part 3 of this book, *Fledgling* addresses anxieties about genetic engineering in circulation at the turn of the twenty-first century, particularly the fear that when scientists "play God," they risk eroding the species distinctions on which human supremacy is founded. Troyano mocks such anxieties as the psychic property of white America and draws attention to racial hierarchies that predate the postgenomic age, while Atwood suggests that the fear of proliferating transgenic "abominations" is a distraction from the capitalist horror that subsumes them. In contrast, Butler dismisses superficial anxieties about genetic engineering by relegating them largely to the novel's background and attaching the anti-genetic-engineering position to its most reprehensible characters, those who are openly racist and speciesist.[4] Genetic engineering might even appear tangential to the novel's most urgent ethical questions, which center on kinship: What kind of family structure allows for a balance of intimacy and autonomy? When do existing power structures impinge on the health of a family and its individual members, and when is the exercise of power necessary for both? How are family bonds formed through biology, physical intimacy, law, memory, story? And how does kinship interact with larger categories of collective identity, such as race and species?

Although the theme of genetic engineering is not in the novel's foreground, the questions above extend from the transgenic innovation on which the entire novel hinges; without this innovation, and the violence it has inspired, Shori would not need to rebuild her family, renegotiating Ina kinship along the way. Furthermore, kinship and genetic engineering directly overlap in *Fledgling*: Shori is twice-begat by her Ina mothers (who are her biological progenitors *and* the scientists responsible for her enhancements), and her human mother is also her gene donor. In other words, her family is a laboratory engaged in both biological and familial experimentation. And so more questions arise: Will genetic donation become an expected part of symbiosis? How might species roles within the family change if Ina can stay awake in the daytime? How will genetic engineering alter the Ina sexual marketplace?[5] How will it alter what it means to be Ina—or human?

---

4. Unlike Atwood and Troyano, Butler locates anxieties about genetic engineering in nonhuman characters, resulting in a vampire novel in which, against the norms of the genre, vampires fear the corrupting influence of humans.

5. As much as Shori is hated by some for the threat she poses to Ina purity, she is also an attractive reproductive partner for those who want their descendants to possess her enhancements. On the reproductive pressures Shori is under, see Brox 404–5; McDevitt 235.

For readers, these questions also prompt reflection on how genetic engineering might affect gender roles, reproductive practices, and interspecies relations in our own world. Despite its apparent decentering, genetic engineering is crucial to the novel's contemplation of consent, power, and intimacy in relation to race, species, and kinship.

Family relationships between Ina and humans follow a symbiotic pattern familiar to readers of Butler's oeuvre: Ina feed on humans and, in return, provide erotic pleasure, as well as improved memory, strength, and longevity. Although Ina can feed from humans not bonded to them, they only thrive when they form lasting emotional and physical connections with a stable group of symbionts. Relying on each other for physical and emotional intimacy, Ina and humans build complex polyamorous, interspecies families that allow for a variety of satisfying romantic, erotic, platonic, and familial relationships. One thing these families do not allow for is an easy exit. Humans can refuse the symbiotic relationship, but this option is only offered after they are already under the (partial) chemical influence of Ina saliva. Once they are fully bonded to an Ina, leaving is next to impossible.[6] Furthermore, even the most enlightened Ina, sensitive to the exploitation of humans, maintain a kinship system in which human beings are structurally subordinate.[7] Humans have agency in this system: most are free to pursue relationships, careers, and even families of their own. But it is their Ina partners who allow (or curtail) this agency. "Whatever agency . . . symbionts have," writes Florian Bast, "they have because [their Ina partner] does not take it away from them." This asymmetry is recorded in the vocabulary of symbiosis: humans become "symbionts" and are renamed according to the Ina to whom they are bound (e.g., "Judith Cho" becomes "Judith Cho sym Ion Andrei"); there are no parallel conventions for Ina partners (202).[8] As in other works by Butler, such as the *Xenogenesis* trilogy and "Bloodchild,"

---

6. Symbionts are unlikely to tolerate the venom of an Ina to whom they are not bonded, and they depend on their Ina's saliva to manage the overproduction of red blood cells stimulated by feedings.

7. As Bast points out (contra Lacey), although Ina and human characters describe their relationships as "mutualistic symbiosis," this phrasing obscures the hierarchical structure of these relationships.

8. One might see parallels to Atwood's *The Handmaid's Tale*, in which fertile women are called "handmaids" and renamed according to the high-status men for whom they are reproductive vessels. However, one need not look that far. After all, although "husband" and "wife" are parallel terms in Western English-speaking societies, they do not have parallel meanings; special titles exist to distinguish married from unmarried women, when no such distinctions are made for men; and changing one's name upon marriage remains common among heterosexual women.

agency and intimacy exist in complex relation with biological imperatives and power imbalances.[9]

The collision of intimacy and hierarchy in Ina-human families raises specific questions about bodily autonomy and consent that evoke parallel questions in the fields of medical and scientific ethics, particularly in relation to the donation of bodily fluids and organs; the use of subordinated populations as research subjects; the extraction of information, knowledge, or biological materials from Black and Indigenous communities for commercial or scientific use; and property and privacy rights over genetic information.[10] The historical (and ongoing) medical and scientific exploitation of Black people, especially Black women (also discussed in chapter 2), is particularly relevant here, given the positioning of a Black woman at the (elided) center of the novel's exploration of bodily expropriation. As Harriet Washington has comprehensively detailed, the staggering history of anti-Black medical racism runs the gamut from withheld treatment to forced experimentation; from exposure to disease to exposure to leering audiences; from coerced reproduction to coerced sterilization; from the desecration of graves to the exploitation of prisoners, soldiers, and children; from the pathologizing of "Black" bodies to the pathologizing of "Black" DNA. "Medical apartheid," to use Washington's phrase, intersects with slavery, mass incarceration, and militarization and is responsible for significant health disparities; for continuing medical bias, misdiagnosis, and mistreatment; and for prompting contemporary discussions of tissue rights and other questions of medical ethics. If, as Dorothy Roberts argues, the commodification of human flesh under slavery haunts the contemporary practices of paid surrogacy and egg and sperm "donation," it also frames the debates on these topics, even if those debates too frequently leave out the material and embodied concerns of Black people (*Killing* 246–93).[11] The medical mistreatment of Black *women* is an especially important thread in the larger history of medical apartheid. Under slavery, Black women's bodies were both productive and

---

9. Bast locates *Fledgling* in an oeuvre defined by "constant ambivalences and critical interrogations of the concept of agency." Also see Fink 418; Lacey; Lundberg.

10. Medical practitioners and ethicists continue to consider how relations of power limit the ability to freely acquiesce to treatment or research. As I discuss in chapter 3, research can become "vampiric" when structurally advantaged scientists acquire information, knowledge, or biological samples from structurally disadvantaged subjects. Efforts, on the part of non-Indigenous researchers, to engage Indigenous people as research partners are perhaps analogous to Shori's efforts to practice an enlightened vampirism: she seeks human advice and insight, but she does not give up her structural authority.

11. See Weinbaum's extensive discussion of this point (*Afterlife* 29–60).

reproductive, rendering them doubly valuable and doubly abused. Enslaved women who were no longer able to work were not infrequently sold or rented to physicians as available bodies for experimentation (Washington 25–51). Major advances in gynecological treatment were developed through surgical experiments that were, effectively, torture (1–2, 61–70). And the vast gulf between the representation and treatment of white and Black femininity, which hinged on conceptions of Black women as, by turn, radically sexually available, oversexed, immune to pain and shame, natural servants, and unnatural mothers, justified their transformation into living tissue for medical experimentation, in anticipation of the transformation of Henrietta Lacks's cancer cells into the first "immortal" cell line. From the enslaved research subjects of Dr. Marion Sims to the "mother" of HeLa cells, Black women have been crucial but forgotten contributors to scientific innovation, not only erased from the narrative of scientific progress but often excluded from its benefits.

This history haunts the vision of symbiosis in *Fledgling*, which can never quite override the specter of vampirism—the material fact of subordinated bodies exploited for the well-being of the dominant population. Despite the tendency among some Ina to criticize the history of racism among humans, the Ina also carry their own history of brutal exploitation of "others," having, in earlier periods, ruthlessly exploited their human symbionts—using them, for example, as cannon fodder in intraspecies conflicts in addition to their everyday use. In the novel's present day, most Ina have moved past flagrant exploitation and have even developed an informed consent process for potential symbionts that underscores the parallel between the ethical questions the novel considers and those raised in contexts of medical and scientific research. Brook, one of Iosif's symbionts, explains:

> Iosif told me what would happen if I accepted him, that I would become addicted and need him. That I would have to obey. That if he died, I might die. . . . Then he asked me to come to him anyway . . . because I could live for maybe two hundred years and be healthy and look and feel young, and because he wanted me and needed me. I wasn't hooked when he asked. . . . I could have walked away—or run like hell. (161)

In this context, informed consent involves describing, in detail, both the risks and benefits of entering into symbiosis and respecting the human's right to refuse. Martin, another symbiont, describes a similar experience, though he notes a vulnerability in the system: "I'd only been bitten three times in all, so I wasn't physically addicted. . . . But psychologically . . . I couldn't forget it.

I wanted it like crazy" (204). Martin initially withholds consent, concerned that the arrangement "sounded more like slavery than symbiosis," an especially poignant statement, given his identity as a Black man. He makes clear that the scientific language used to describe Ina-human kinship ("symbiosis" and "mutualism") obfuscates the power imbalance and physical exploitation that characterize the system. The desire that ultimately overcomes his resistance, rather than belying his insight, reinforces it by suggesting that the effects of Ina venom might render free acquiescence impossible—that the Ina informed consent process is a bit of "consent theater."[12]

Within this fraught situation, Shori is acutely concerned with doing interspecies kinship "right" and seeks advice about the ethics of feeding, choosing symbionts, and building interspecies families. Her Ina father, Iosif, advises her to "treat [her] people well" (73), and Martin similarly counsels her to protect her symbionts' autonomy: "Help them. . . . Only when they need help" (205); in other words, she is encouraged to approach the symbiotic relationship paternalistically. Shori retains authority over "her people," taking responsibility for decision-making and reserving the right to use their bodies when she wishes, but she is more willing than many Ina to engage in interspecies dialogue: "Not everyone treats symbionts as people," Brook observes (131). Shori demands open communication from her human partners and asks for their opinions and insights; she even worries over the ethical treatment of humans who have attempted to harm her family, as in the case of an assassin being interrogated by another Ina family: "It was clear from the Gordons' expressions that they didn't care. . . . But I did care what happened to him" (184). These moments of dissonance between Shori's instincts and Ina norms suggest a productive discomfort out of which different social norms might be created.

Shori's ethical sensibility—the fact that she is, in her symbiont Wright's words, a "weirdly ethical little thing"—does not mean, however, that her actions are without moral complication (162).[13] Indeed, her initial encounters with Wright illustrate this fact. When Shori is well enough to leave the woods where she awakens at the start of the story, but still unaware of who or what she is, she is picked up by a young man who sees her as a vulnerable child and wants to help her. Because Wright smells "interesting," she complies—until she worries that he will take her to the hospital

---

12. The term "consent theater" has been used to describe the privacy agreements social media sites and other online entities use to manipulate users into sharing their data while appearing to offer the freedom to say no (Doctorow).

13. Shori fits into a recent trend in which "vampire and zombie characters . . . repress their monstrous appetites" (Erman 594).

or the police. A physical struggle ensues, and Shori bites him, eliciting confusion, arousal, and rage. Shori "[doesn't] want him afraid or angry," even though she "[doesn't] know why [she] cared about that," suggesting a latent ethical sensibility that also serves her physiological interests (11). She convinces him to let her bite him in a more serious way, "hear[ing] consent in his voice," rather than his words.[14] After this encounter, Wright agrees to keep her with him, and Shori feels that she has done things the "right" way, reading Wright's body for evidence of pleasure and consent: "He had enjoyed it—maybe as much as I had. I felt pleased, felt myself smile. That was right somehow. I'd done it right" (12). Although Wright's name seems to underscore Shori's sense that she has done "right" by her first symbiont, the silent "W" that distinguishes "Wright" from "Right" also raises questions: has Shori, misled by homophony (i.e., the "sound-alikeness" of consent and physical arousal) misread the situation? Has she missed the fact that ethics do not simply exist in nature but must be created—*wrought*—by complex people in complex situations (a possibility underscored by Wright's employment as a construction worker)?[15] After all, later in the book Wright expresses dissatisfaction with how they came together: when Shori tells him, "From the night you found me, we wanted each other," he replies, "I don't know. I never really had a chance to figure that out" (83).

Although thorny ethical questions arise consistently and explicitly in *Fledgling*'s treatment of Ina-human kinship and the expropriation of human blood, they are not raised with respect to the expropriation of human DNA.[16] No one—including Shori, who asks a surfeit of questions and is highly attuned to ethical concerns—asks whether Jessica wanted to donate her DNA, whether she was fully informed on the research her Ina partners were undertaking, or whether serving as something akin to Mitochondrial Eve for the (hoped-for, feared) dark-skinned Ina-to-come was a role she embraced.[17] One might be tempted to see the "donation" of DNA by Shori's human mother as a simple extension of the "donation" of blood that characterizes Ina-human symbiosis, and therefore not in need of special attention. Indeed, the genetic sampling procedure is not described and might be coterminous with a feeding session. Regardless of method, the expropriation of

---

14. This rationale is also prominent in Butler's "Bloodchild" and *Xenogenesis* series.

15. McDevitt reads Wright's name as a gesture toward his privileged identity status (231).

16. "The connection between the speculative genetic engineering in the novel and historical theft is nearly lost because Shori's mother 'consented'" (Ibrahim 96).

17. Mitochondrial Eve is theorized to be "the woman from whom all modern human mitochondria descend" (Cavalli-Sforza, *Genes* 79).

genes and the expropriation of blood take place under the same asymmetrical relations of power, and the provision of genetic material should invite at least as much ethical consideration—even more, given the fact that, while humans derive direct benefits through the act of "feeding" their Ina, there is no automatic compensation for the donation of DNA.[18]

At the same time, because of its (incomplete) erasure, the DNA extraction at the interstitial narrative center of *Fledgling* calls up the history of medical exploitation and abuse of African Americans—and of Black women, in particular—even more cogently than the exchange of fluids upon which the novel's consideration of consent focuses. The most direct narrative corollary of this vampiric history is not found in the literal scenes of vampirism in *Fledgling*'s foreground but in its off-screen scenes of genetic extraction. Although Jessica's situation is not identical to those of her real-world precursors, her ability to consent, like theirs, is limited. Like them, she will not benefit from the medical innovations developed through the use of her body, and her life is nearly erased from the story of genetic innovation. Jessica's absent presence in *Fledgling* reiterates the erasure of Black research subjects and, specifically, Black women from medical history. As Habiba Ibrahim writes, "Since we know almost nothing about Shori's DNA donor/biological mother, aside from the fact that she was black, the question of how historical precedents of obligation in the absence of consent factored into her exchange, donation, or motherhood looms large" (95).

The parallel between *Fledgling* and *The Immortal Life of Henrietta Lacks* is inescapable: a Black woman's body becomes the source of a scientific/medical product that is endlessly reproducible for the direct medical benefit of others, a phenomenon Ibrahim calls "the afterlife of being transformed into flesh" (95).[19] There is another salient, if subtle, connection between these texts: both center on a daughter who has lost her mother—a fact that evokes the family separation and genealogical disruption visited upon African Americans from the Middle Passage to mass incarceration, including the devastatingly common experience of Black women taking care of other people's children while separated from their own. Science and medicine have regularly abetted the separation of families; consider the use of psychiatric evaluation or DNA testing to enable the disproportionate sterilization,

---

18. Humans might benefit indirectly: if Ina are able to stay awake during the daytime, this might create a safer environment for symbionts.

19. Ibrahim also connects Jessica to Henrietta Lacks: "We do know that Jessica's DNA outlived her own mortal life. As Lacks's cancer cells illustrate, the black body can be broken apart, so that the resulting separate parts are granted separate timelines of their own" (95).

institutionalization, or incarceration of people of color, poor people, and disabled people. At the same time, as Alondra Nelson has demonstrated, genetic technologies have been used for the purposes of "reconciliation projects" (*Social* xii).[20] Whether used to reunite families separated in the Argentine Dirty War, to authenticate the oral histories of Black descendants of US Founding Fathers, or to free wrongly incarcerated people, genetic technologies have rearticulated genealogies disarticulated by violence (27–42). Consumer ancestry testing has taken on special significance for Black people who, because of slavery's assault on kinship, often have limited access to genealogical records. Indeed, companies like African Ancestry have been founded for the express purpose of filling in these incomplete family histories. Although she is clear that genes should not outweigh "historical archives and autobiography," Nelson argues that genetic ancestry testing "provid[es] a lexicon with which to continue to speak about the unfinished business of slavery and its lasting shadows. . . . DNA-based techniques allow us to try—or try again—to contemplate, respond to, and resolve enduring social wounds" (6–7). Like many African Americans, Shori's DNA is a tenuous but potent link to a mother who has been violently erased from the world and from memory.

Fledgling alludes to the disruption of African American genealogies in Shori's separation from—and effort to reconnect with—her Ina family.[21] However, in striking parallel to the novel's lopsided engagement of consent (which addresses the extraction of blood but not DNA), Shori pursues significant research regarding her Ina background but does not investigate her human ancestry, which has not only been disrupted in the recent past but may also have been disrupted, further back on Jessica's family tree, by slavery. Extending this parallel is the fact that, while the rupture of Ina kinship evokes the African diaspora (among other diasporas and genocides), the lack of information about Shori's mother evokes it even more acutely, calling up innumerable scenes of Black children ripped away from their mothers, leaving them with little more than a name and other people's memories. Every time Shori's name is uttered, every time she fingers the pendant hanging from her neck, readers are reminded of those histories, though they remain inarticulate in the text.

In addition to a name and a pendant, Shori's human mother has also given her a genetic signature: select DNA sequences that confer higher

---

20. A. Nelson describes "reconciliation projects" as "endeavors in which genetic analysis is placed at the center of social unification efforts" (*Social* xii).

21. This theme is also legible in the gradual separation from their families of origin that symbionts undertake, in order to conceal the existence of the Ina species from humans.

melanin production and other advantageous characteristics. Although these constitute a biological bond, they are not the kind of sequences that are used to identify genetic ancestry: the single-nucleotide polymorphisms (SNPs) that are inherited together at higher frequencies among specific populations—and that are usually *not* expressed in physical characteristics. Nor are they sequences, as far as we know, that carry epigenetic notations related to environmental pressures, migrations, or trauma. No, the sequences inherited by Shori, which literalize the specious notion of "Black DNA," have been severed from the rest of Jessica's genome, cutting Shori off from the histories that might be inscribed there just as surely has she has been cut off from the mother from whom they were extracted. Blackness as a physical trait is thus quite literally separated from the histories that make Blackness a culturally meaningful concept—and from the people who carry the cultural and biological records of those histories.

Among the Ina, Blackness as a complex set of physical, cultural, and historical elements is dismissed in favor of skin color, which, in a second sleight-of-hand, is reduced to a genetic signature that can be adopted without respect to prior somatic or social contexts. In a familiar irony, dark skin is at once a sign of subordination and a sought-after trait, valuable to the degree that it is severable from a human being.[22] And yet this severing is never complete. Dark skin is seen by most Ina as pointing directly to species difference, serving as a marker for "human" (and, therefore, species inferiority), since it is not a "natural" Ina trait.[23] Furthermore, this species meaning is regularly overlain with racial meaning, as when Shori's enemies call her a "black mongrel bitch" (300) or argue that her human ancestry is degraded because of its association with enslaved people (272).[24] Black people's flesh is thus read, among the Ina (as it often is in the world outside the text) as a mark of degradation that invites violence, even while it is also desired and expropriated. Based on the intimacy of Ina speciesism and human racism, we might understand *Fledgling*'s deployment of the former as a means of critiquing the latter. After all, the vampiric relationship between Ina and humans, in its juxtaposition of attraction and repulsion, intimacy and hierarchy, appreciation and expropriation, resembles racism's contradictory

---

22. Consider the fact that Black fashion and hairstyles are often discriminated against until they are adopted by white people (Mejía Chaves and Bacharach 335).

23. Even Shori's supporters, who oppose discriminating against transgenic Ina because doing so would emulate human forms of racism, obscure the history of prejudice among Ina and against other species and thus reiterate the speciesism they claim to deny (274).

24. Similar dynamics, in which vampires adopt human racial biases, can be found in Tananarive Due's *African Immortal* series (M. Allen 100) and in the 1974 film *Vampira* (Gateward).

operations. As I discuss in chapter 6, speciesism can certainly underwrite racism; when human beings are designated as "subhuman" or "nonhuman" in a society that subjugates animals, it is easier to justify their exploitation, exclusion, or eradication. At the same time, *Fledgling* does not use speciesism among the Ina simply to illuminate racism among humans; here, speciesism and racism are presented as modes of othering that overlap, diverge, and borrow from each other.[25] The novel is less interested in speciesism per se than in how regimes of othering operate through deeply ingrained ways of reading bodies and moving through the world. These learned reflexes operate even in the absence of their (original) objects or contexts, such that ways of reading the flesh that arose with slavery, for example, continue to be practiced after the end of the slave era.

Despite the fact that she has become marginal in a narrative that, paradoxically, could not exist without her, Jessica is not an anonymous human from whom a DNA sample was surreptitiously extracted and used. She is a member of the family, with all of the physical, emotional, personal, and ethical complications this status implies. To take note of her—to remember her in the flesh—is to see this complicated picture, rather than simply the skin color she has passed along to her Ina daughter. Shori has more power within the Ina kinship system than her mother—or her own symbionts, but, like them, her flesh is also subject to expropriation for the benefit of others: her very existence is a response to a physical need in the Ina community that her (reproductive) body is meant to answer. Together, Shori and her human partners are engaged in the work of negotiating agency and redefining kinship and subjectivity within this complex situation. Although *Fledgling* does not present this work as utopian, the novel does illustrate the possibility of what Sylvia Wynter calls new "genres of being human" ("Unsettling" 281)—not through the literal transformation of the (human or Ina) body through genetic engineering, but through "enfleshed" forms of dialogue, self-reflection, negotiation, and, as it happens, reading.

Reading Flesh and Fleshy Reading

"Reading" DNA, stereotypically understood, depends on a process of abstraction by which a tissue sample is transformed into code, severed from both somatic and social context. This sloughing off of pesky "flesh" could explain the marginalization of Shori's human mother in *Fledgling*. Her

---

25. My thinking here is informed by Weheliye's critique of posthumanist scholarship that analogizes speciesism and racism (9–11).

tissue—collected, distilled, sequenced, edited—serves its narrative purpose and is then discarded. Her DNA is the text that matters, making possible the enhancements that both promise survival and inspire violence. But, in addition to enabling the rearticulation of racism in new forms, losing sight of the flesh—whether by distilling DNA to code or, its literary corollary, reducing reading to disembodied cognition—also means losing sight of the human as an always-emerging "languaging" species who can take part in meaningful rearticulations of self, community, and environment, the very effort that Shori is engaged in (Wynter, "1492" 7).[26]

The work of Black feminist theorists is foundational for understanding the contradictory operations of racism on the flesh and for rethinking species and kinship in response to these operations. In her classic essay "Mama's Baby, Papa's Maybe: An American Grammar Book" (1987), Hortense Spillers peels back the layers of meaning that have been "assigned" to the figure of the Black woman in the New World, a process of resignification that begins with the extreme violence of the Middle Passage (65). On slave ships, Spillers explains, African men and women were suspended in a (literal and Freudian) "oceanic" state initiated by the violent separation from homeland, name, family, and even gender identity; in other words, human beings were transformed into undifferentiated flesh (72). This flesh was then subject to the various (and contradictory) misreadings of Blackness used to justify enslavement: "These undecipherable markings on the captive body," Spillers writes, "render a kind of hieroglyphics of the flesh whose severe disjunctures come to be hidden to the cultural seeing by skin color." Raising the specter of intergenerational trauma repeatedly enacted on bodies racialized as Black, she goes on: "We might well ask if this phenomenon of marking and branding actually 'transfers' from one generation to another, finding its various *symbolic substitutions* in an efficacy of meanings that repeat the initiating moments?" (67).

Despite the extraordinary trauma of these "initiating moments" and their ongoing repetitions, Black people are uniquely positioned, Spillers argues, to reorganize the flesh into bodily, familial, and social forms that challenge hegemonic racial and gender hierarchies and make possible a new subject, one version of which is "the monstrosity (of a female with the potential to 'name')"—a formulation that takes on special meaning in relation to Jessica's assertion of the right to name Shori (80). Such a subject would be an alternative to what Sylvia Wynter calls "Man" ("Unsettling" 281), a figure, grounded in European colonialism, that is the dominant "genre of being human"—a phrase that, merging aesthetic and species categorization,

---

26. Wynter borrows the term "languaging" from Maturana and Varela.

reflects the integration of biology and culture that Wynter posits as central to human identity (269).[27] "Unsettling" the "coloniality of power" that underwrites this figure requires more than the banal assertion of genetic similarity (i.e., the repeated claim that human beings are 99.9 percent genetically identical).[28] What is needed is a fundamental "redescription of the human," undertaken in our capacity as a *languaging species*—both word and flesh (268). Wynter, deeply informed by systems biology, challenges "biocentric" definitions of the human, which present human biology as separate from and prior to human creativity; she argues, as Katherine McKittrick explains, "that we must notice the ways in which we, as humans, are simultaneously biological *and* cultural and alterable beings—skin *and* masks, bios *and* mythoi" (McKittrick 137).[29]

Black feminist theories of the flesh have the potential, in Alexander Weheliye's terms, to enable "new formations of humanity" (4) derived from the "lines of flight, freedom dreams, practices of liberation, and possibilities of other worlds" present in the lived experience of "extreme subjection." These are not modes of "resistance" or "agency," terms that obfuscate "occurrences of freedom" other than open opposition performed by a fully agential subject. They are, rather, the movements and imaginings by which constrained humans maneuver within the interstices of power. *Fledgling* does not describe the extreme violence against the flesh that Spillers, Wynter, and Weheliye consider in their work; however, it does explore power structures that foreclose "the full agency of the oppressed" (2) and yet in which "alternative modes of life" can be imagined (1). Shori is faced with the challenge of rearticulating (in Stuart Hall's "doubl[ed]" sense of the term [Clarke 277–78]) kinship and selfhood in ways that account for complicated relations of authority and intimacy. Her negotiation of this context involves practices of reading her environment, herself, and the bodies of others—as well as literal texts. As she takes this interpretive journey, the novel also highlights the inextricable relationship between flesh and text, body and book.

---

27. For Wynter, culture, like (and in relation with) biology, is in a continual process of becoming, and the human is "a set of practices" that shapes our world and ourselves, rather than the expression of unmediated genetic code (Erasmus 56).

28. "Coloniality of power" is a phrase Wynter borrows from Aníbal Quijano and aligns with Walter Mignolo's "colonial difference" and Howard Winant's "racial longue durée" (Wynter, "Unsettling" 263).

29. Wynter draws upon Humberto Maturana and Francisco Varela's concept of "autopoiesis" (which describes the ability of life to regenerate itself) and Frantz Fanon's concept of "sociogeny" (which describes the development of social phenomena) in order to posit the human as a hybrid species—biological *and* cultural—that emerges in different "genres" in different environments (Erasmus 47–48).

In so doing, *Fledgling* illustrates the insights developed by scholars of "embodied cognition," who approach thinking as "embodied action," rather than representation or computation (Varela et al. xx). For these scholars, a human being is not "a brain in a body, but an embodied brain . . . and a brainified body" (Gee and Zhang 237), and the body is both "a lived, experiential structure" and "a milieu of cognitive mechanisms," which include the body's "sensorimotor capacities" (Varela et al. xvi).[30] Perception and action are "co-evolved," and "perceptually guided action" (173), through repetition, shapes the physical structures of the brain, resulting in "sensorimotor intelligence": the neurological and physical operations involved in thinking and acting within a specific environment (176).[31] Bodily sensations not only influence cognition and action in any given moment; they also are ingrained, physically, in the neuronal connections that constitute memory, "the ability to retain, inside the creature's body, a record of past inner and outer sensations and the ability to reactivate them as a source of anticipation of and reaction to new challenges" (Gee and Zhang 234). The "automatic association[s]" created through experiential learning are "crucial for survival," as is the capacity for "simulation"—the ability to "imagine seeing and doing things in different ways and trying new responses," which assists in "undoing habitual responses" and "changing our worldviews" (240).

Embodied cognition has significant implications for how we understand language and reading. Linguists George Lakoff and Mark Johnson have shown that metaphor—though often dismissed as "rhetorical flourish" (3)—is, in fact, grounded in the material experience of our bodies. Whether "conventional" (as in everyday speech) or "new" (as in literary language), metaphors are informed by and structure our physical experience (139).[32] For Lakoff and Johnson, metaphor is akin to a sensorimotor function: "It is as though the ability to comprehend experience through metaphor were a sense, like seeing or touching or hearing" (239). Literature is a form of language that introduces novel metaphors, which can reshape reality by reshaping human perception and action, and that enables simulation, by allowing readers to play out different scenarios in their imaginations. Furthermore, although reading is sometimes characterized as an undertaking that enables temporary dissociation from one's material circumstances, it is,

---

30. In making this point, the authors, like many proponents of embodied cognition, draw from the work of philosopher Maurice Merleau-Ponty.

31. For specific examples of sensorimotor intelligence, see Shapiro 4, 63. Also see Stacy Alaimo's concept of "trans-corporeality," which I discuss in chapter 5 (*Bodily* 20).

32. The type of physical body we have and the physical and cultural environment we live in are the grounds from which metaphors emerge; metaphors, in turn, influence our behavior, which, then, leaves its mark on our environment (Lakoff and Johnson 14).

in fact, a physical activity that engages multiple bodily systems, including specialized neuronal structures, within a complex material context.

Indeed, reading is both inextricable from and integral to that context. Many proponents of embodied cognition emphasize the idea that human beings are in complex relation with other organisms and their environments, with which they have "co-evolv[ed]" (Sumara 92).[33] From this perspective, reading, like any human activity, is inseparable from, and in mutual relation with, the physical world. As Dennis Sumara explains, "There is fundamentally no fixed boundary between the literary fiction and anything else in our environment" (112), and reading shapes both us and the world we live in: "The experience of reading has not only altered us phenomenologically, it has altered us biologically.... Fictional readings become an inextricable part of our daily embodied action in the world and, therefore, fundamentally change all relations we have in the world" (108). In keeping with the way systems biology understands evolution, Sumara views the literary meanings produced in "reader-text interactions" not in terms of "optimization" (i.e., measured against a *best* or *final* interpretation) but, rather, in terms of evolutionary co-emergence and "drift": "the infinite contingencies that are part [of] the act of reading are continually in the process of evolving" (113).[34]

Sumara introduces the concept of "unskinning" (107–15) to describe this complex relationship among readers, texts, and contexts. This deliberately slippery term, which contains a base word—"skinning"—that is arguably both synonym and antonym to "unskinning," alludes at once to embodiment and the porous boundary between body and environment. Though the association is inadvertent, "unskinning" draws our attention back to the literal stripping of the flesh that, Spillers explains, sets in motion the resignification of African people as "Black" via the metonym of skin color. The uncomfortable adjacency of these metaphors—"unskinning" and "the flesh"—should alert us to the crucial distinction between porousness as a condition of human being and porousness enacted upon the body through violence. For Spillers, and other Black feminist thinkers, the emergence of alternative subjectivities is a process inseparable from, if also in excess of, colonial and racist violence, carrying with it both pain and possibility.

---

33. Also see Lakoff and Johnson 217.

34. Systems biology is focused on "understanding the larger picture—be it at the level of the organism, tissue, or cell—by putting its pieces together. It's in stark contrast to decades of reductionist biology, which involves taking the pieces apart" (Wanjek). A systems approach to evolution counters the view that "individual genes" were "both the underlying cause of biological variation/innovation and ... the best measure of change over time in the history of life on Earth," proposing instead that "genes have evolved in the service of living organisms" (Corning). Genetic drift is "the random fluctuation of gene frequencies in populations" (Cavalli-Sforza, *Genes* 42).

Returning to the flesh via embodied cognition—and embodied reading—also invites us to consider how racializing ways of reading the flesh are themselves forms of embodied cognition, deeply ingrained habits of orienting oneself to other people and the world. Sara Ahmed, drawing from phenomenology (which has also influenced theorists of embodied cognition) and, specifically, the phenomenology of race (with sustained attention to the work of Frantz Fanon), describes whiteness as an "ongoing and unfinished history, which orientates bodies in specific directions, affecting how they 'take up' space" and "shap[ing] what it is that bodies 'can do'" (150). Colonialism shapes the material world, producing racialized bodies and an environment that directs the movement of these bodies in materially different ways: "Colonialism makes the world 'white,' which is of course a world 'ready' for certain kinds of bodies, as a world that puts certain objects within their reach" (153–54). In other words, the environment that co-evolves with the species who exist within it (and are part of it) is shaped by racism. Racism also molds the learning that goes on in that environment and that leaves its mark on the neuronal connections, reflexes, and physical forms of the body: "Bodies remember such histories, even when we forget them. Such histories, we might say, surface on the body, or even shape how bodies surface." Our physical inheritance, "the conditions in which we live," is not a simple matter of biological reproduction ("blood" and "genes") but, rather, is handed down "through the work or labour of generations" (154). And our "place" within those conditions is maintained through "habits," the repeated actions of bodies within an environment that orients them toward or away from certain objects and actions, and that is itself oriented toward some bodies and away from others (156). Interestingly, Ahmed locates "skin" not just on the bodies habituated to their environments but also in the environments themselves, explaining that "spaces acquire the 'skin' of the bodies that inhabit them. . . . When we describe institutions as 'being' white . . . , we are pointing to how institutional spaces are shaped by the proximity of some bodies and not others: white bodies gather, and cohere to form the edges of such spaces" (157). "White" (or "Black") skin is not a natural or self-evident attribute; it is produced in and through spatial/racial orientations and disorientations. If whiteness is the inheritance of an environment that is oriented for one's comfort and convenience, and the habitual reinscription of that orientation in the body, then Blackness is, in part, the inheritance of an environment that is not oriented for one's comfort and convenience; it is the inheritance of "disorientation," of "the failure of things to be habitual" (163).

In *Fledgling*, Shori is twice disoriented. She has inherited an environment that is not oriented toward her (whether she is moving within Ina or human spaces), and she has awakened within that environment carrying its inscriptions in her body but not in her conscious memory. As she works to reorient herself, habituated Ina norms bump up against Shori's discomfort with those norms, and it is from this position of discomfort that we can glimpse the possibility of reshaping the self and its mutually constitutive environments. As Ahmed writes, "Every experience I have had of pleasure and excitement about a world opening up has begun with such ordinary feelings of discomfort, of not quite fitting in a chair, of becoming unseated, of being left holding onto the ground" (163). In other words, Shori is uniquely poised to transform Ina cultural norms and, indirectly, to encourage reflection on norms in the world outside the text.

Through a reading of scenes of "reading" in *Fledgling*, and drawing from the meditations on flesh, the body, thinking, and reading described above, I offer the term "fleshy reading" to describe critical and narrative approaches that emphasize reading as material, embodied, and experiential. Fleshy reading acknowledges that narratives shape and are shaped by our lived experience in measurable, material ways, and it is attentive to how narratives can both reinforce and interrupt norms that affect our embodied experience and inform our interpretation and treatment of each other's bodies. Fleshy reading is alert to narrative elisions of the flesh (as in the near erasure of Jessica from *Fledgling*) and to the possibilities alive in enfleshment, which include novel rearrangements of self, family, race, and species that do not rely on the total subjection of others or demand total liberation but, rather, are grounded in ongoing renegotiations of power and intimacy. I attempt to trace the possibilities in fleshy reading through Shori's experiences reading the world, other people, and texts, considering how the novel theorizes reading as a matter of the body, how it intervenes in habitual ways of reading race, and how it invites a fleshy reading from its audience, one that might also fill in the blank at its center.

•

Over the course of Shori's journey to learn about and define herself and her family, *Fledgling* illustrates several core concepts of embodied cognition and "fleshy reading." "Experiential" learning and "sensorimotor intelligence" are frequently on display, as Shori—a quintessential Wynterian cultural/biological subject—makes use of physical senses, embodied knowledge, and ethical inquiry to navigate a social and material environment with which she has co-evolved but about which her conscious knowledge is incomplete. We see Shori exhibit the "automatic associations" that stem from neuronal connections forged through experience, and we see how encounters with novel metaphors work to undo habitual responses and set the groundwork for new ways of being. After all, Shori is not just relearning Ina norms; she is also working out new ways of being in the world and relating to others. As she heals physically and emotionally, novel arrangements of self and kinship become possible.

When Shori awakens after the devastating attack that has destroyed her maternal family, she is blind with hunger and pain and consumes several nearby animals (one of whom, she later learns, was a human man—one of her brother's symbionts). At this point in the novel, Shori is not Wynter's languaging species but a being driven exclusively by instinct and the need to survive. However, as she regains her health, language returns to her. It is sensorimotor experience that prompts her linguistic memory: moving through the landscape, she remembers individual words ("I had to look at these things, let the sight of them remind me what they were called—the hillside, the rock face, the trees—pine?" [3]), and hearing Wright's voice, language rushes back ("I heard the words, but at first, they meant nothing at all. . . . After a moment, though, they seemed to click into place as language" [7]). Talking with Wright, she also begins to remember both her status as a genetic experiment and the contradictory meanings of "Blackness": when he calls her "black," she begins to "protest that [she] was brown, not black," but then a memory is "triggered" and, along with it, recollection of the (artificial) language of race: "I think I'm an experiment. . . . I don't know who the experimenters are, though, the ones who made me black" (31).

With language comes higher order thinking, as Shori undergoes a sensorimotor learning process that involves sensation, observation, inquiry, and reasoning.[35] Take this representative passage, which appears soon after she emerges from the cave:

> It occurred to me that I had come to this place hoping to kill an animal and eat it. Somehow, I had expected to find food here. And yet I remembered nothing about this place. . . . So why would I expect to find food here? How had I known to come here? Either I had visited here before or this place had been my home. If it was my home, why didn't I recognize it as home? Had my injuries come from the fire that destroyed this place? I had an endless stream of questions and no answers. (5)

---

35. On the connection between vampires and surveillance, see Erman 595–96.

Here, Shori has developed the cognitive capacity to observe the instinctual drives that initially governed her behavior, and she employs reasoning to generate interpretations and new questions. From this point on, Shori uses her senses to investigate scenes of violence, identify potential mates and symbionts, read the emotional states of others, and determine whether someone is telling the truth. Although Shori cannot remember the facts of Ina-human symbiosis, she begins to reason them out based on what she observes and feels. "You have amnesia, and yet you know that?" one of her symbionts asks, referring to Shori's observation that an Ina can only "go after" another Ina's symbionts when they are not fully bonded. "I'm alive, Celia. My senses work. I can't help but know," Shori responds (111). The fact that sensation is crucial to cognition is evident also in Shori's habit of describing scents as "interesting."[36] The first appearance of this adjective (to describe Wright's scent) is especially telling: "I realized he smelled . . . really interesting. Also, I didn't want to stop talking to him. I felt almost as hungry for conversation as I was for food" (9, original ellipsis). Shori's attraction to Wright is both physical and intellectual; language and scent together draw her to him.

Pramod Nayar argues that "Butler calls attention to biology as technë, the tools Shori uses are her own biological states—hunger, smell, mobility, strength—and not culturally acquired ones" (799). I would revise Nayar's observation slightly: Shori's senses are adapted not only to her biological needs but also to the cultural norms in which she was raised, and which are intertwined with biology. Even though she cannot remember them, these norms have left their mark on her, influencing her behavior through the brain's well-worn reward paths. Associating physical pleasure and well-being with ethical rightness, Shori often "feels" her way through situations, including morally complex ones. For example, she is attracted to humans who "smell lonely" and senses that she should not feed too heavily from any single person; these feelings lead to actions that reduce harm against humans. Similarly, before she understands Ina family structure, she *feels* that it is right for her symbionts to have intimate relationships with each other: "They were both mine. And yet there was something deeply right about seeing them together" (126). Such moments, which Nayar describes as evidence of "the remnants of Ina morality that Shori carries as a species

---

36. Shori uses the term "interesting" to describe the scent of potential Ina mates (181), wonders if her own scent is "interesting" (210), and speculates about whether she would have found the scent of certain symbionts "interesting" before they were bonded to other Ina (211). On the novel's treatment of olfaction, see Jue 18.

memory," could also be the remnants of disorientation and discomfort, given Shori's complicated position within Ina society (806). In either case, these moments suggest that ethical decisions involve the physical senses as much as thought, and that prosocial behavior is ingrained through sensory experience.

Although Shori often acts with tremendous confidence, she also recognizes her weaknesses (due to amnesia) and worries incessantly about harming others. Seeking to supplement instinct and sensorimotor learning with reading and research, Shori regularly browses the internet and reads books, absorbing what she can about vampire mythology as well as Ina religion, biology, history, language, and law. Ina writings stretch back thousands of years, and, perusing these materials, Shori learns a great deal about feuds among Ina families, cruel treatment of humans by Ina—and of Ina by humans—and competing Ina origin stories. As she does so, the novel consistently presents reading as an embodied experience and books as physical objects that exist in intimate relation with physical bodies. Even the well-loved smell of books (which confirms reading as a sensory experience) is, for the sensitive Ina, wrapped up with the smell of the people who read them, as when Shori notes of another Ina, "I had found her looking through a book she'd borrowed from Hayden. I hadn't seen her borrow it, but the book smelled deeply of him and only a little of her" (288). This observation is a reminder not only of the embodiment of readers (including the reader with *Fledgling* in hand) but also of the porousness between flesh and the material world, as reading leaves a physical residue on the text.

Shori's interaction with Theodora, a poet and librarian who becomes one of her symbionts, exemplifies the novel's approach to fleshy reading. Shori is drawn to Theodora in part because she senses, in this middle-aged white woman, a longing for connection and physical touch: "You have a particularly good scent," she tells her, "open, wanting, alone"—a description that a voracious reader might find applicable to the scent of books (92). Theodora confirms that she is, indeed, lonely. Since her husband's death, "all [she's] really cared about—all [she's] been able to care about—is [her] poetry" (93). Their conversation takes place in Theodora's office, where she and Shori are literally surrounded by books:

> She took my hand and led me up the stairs into a room whose walls were covered with books. There was a sofa and two chairs also piled high with books and papers. In the middle of the room was a large, messy desk covered with open books, papers, a computer and monitor, a radio, a telephone,

a box of pencils and pens, a stack of notebooks and crossword puzzle magazines, a long decorative wooden box of compact discs, bottles of aspirin, hand lotion, antacid, correction fluid, and who knew what else.

. . . It was the most disorderly mass of stuff I had run across, and yet it all looked—felt—familiar. (89)

In Theodora's room, we see clearly that "the life of the mind" is also the life of the body, as books and papers share space with aspirin, hand lotion, and antacid—reminders of the physical self and its vulnerabilities. Even the items related to reading and writing (pens, pencils, paper, a computer, open books) draw attention to the materiality of these practices and to the way the space is oriented around Theodora's body and its needs. Although Theodora has not been touched in a long while, it is evident that her books are touched regularly—and that this touching is coincident with other senses: hearing (the telephone, radio, and compact discs), taste (the antacid), smell (the hand lotion). Theodora's room shows that one does not recede into the literary life and leave the body behind. At the same time, reading and writing cannot, on their own, satisfy the body, hence Shori's promise to attend to Theodora's neglected flesh.

This scene also begins to address how the contents of books shape our material interactions with one another, including how we read each other's bodies. At one point during their conversation, Theodora asks Shori who and what she is. Instead of answering her directly, Shori responds by biting her, saying, "You told me I was a vampire." Theodora responds, "You are a vampire. . . . Although, according to what I've read, you're supposed to be a tall, handsome, fully grown white man" (91). Indeed, when Theodora first looks at Shori, her face betrays "a kind of horror," and Shori asks, "Is it my skin color or my apparent age that's upsetting you so?" (89). The well-read Theodora has absorbed the most common vampire tropes and, it is implied, tropes about Blackness as well; her "habitual responses" to both bump up against the reality of Shori's body, which combines traits that Theodora does not expect to be combined. In other words, vampire lore and racial ideology together contest the material facts of Shori's experience. Shori, addressing vampire fictions, muses that "some [vampires] could hypnotize people by staring at them. Some read and controlled people's thoughts. It would be handy to be able to do things like that. Easier than biting them and waiting for the chemicals in my saliva to do their work" (37). Although they aspire to objectivity, scientific explanations for vampire folklore do not hew any closer to Shori's lived experience than works of pure fantasy. Through extensive reading, Shori learns, for example, that "there were diseases that people might once have mistaken for vampirism"; such explanations erase vampires entirely, alerting Shori to a massive gap in the literature (parallel to the literary gap Butler's own writing has worked to fill): "Whoever and whatever I was," Shori reflects, "no one seemed to be writing about my kind" (33).

Shori generally responds to the misapprehensions propagated by vampire lore with wry amusement. She even occasionally amuses herself by performing "a bit of vampire theater," as when she commands Theodora to invite her in (alluding to the belief that a vampire must be invited into a home by its owner; 88). But she also knows that the literary imagination can have a real impact on the world, both benign (e.g., the humans she reads about who cosplay as vampires) and dangerous (e.g., the humans who, she also learns about through reading, have persecuted Ina over the centuries). Despite their absurdity, vampire stories can even have an emotional and physical effect on Shori. For example, when she reads, with incredulity, that vampires kill their prey, Shori is suddenly reminded that she, too, is guilty of such an act: "I killed and fed as viciously as any fictional vampire," she reflects with horror (37). This upsetting recollection also stimulates a sense memory, as scents from the ruins of her family home return to her, and she begins to sort through them in search of clues, demonstrating the intimacy of reading, sensation, emotion, and cognition.

Although Shori openly and repeatedly contemplates the distance between vampire narratives and her lived experience—and the ways that vampire lore shapes the (human) world into a dangerous space for her and other Ina—she does not spend an equivalent amount of energy considering the racial narratives that make her body unsettling to Theodora and render the world (both human and Ina) inhospitable for her and others who look like her. The horror on Theodora's face when she looks at Shori for the first time recalls the pivotal incident Fanon recounts in *Black Skin, White Masks* (1952)—and which Ahmed, too, calls up—when a white child points at him and announces, "Look! A Negro!" causing Fanon's bodily integrity to "collapse" into "an epidermal racial schema" (Fanon 91). Notably, the parallel moment in *Fledgling* is followed by Theodora taking refuge in her office, a space explicitly oriented toward her, rather than Shori's, body: *her* books, *her* papers, *her* poems, *her* medications, *her* chair, *her* desk—*her* home territory. That this space is a writer's office is a suggestive coincidence, in that Ahmed elaborates the "spatiality of situation" through discussions of desks and chairs, with special attention to the metaphor of *losing a chair at the table*, which describes the experience of being a person of color in a white space (156). Shori recognizes that her skin color—and, behind it, narratives about Blackness—might be one cause of Theodora's horrified expression. However, not well habituated to racism, she subsumes the issue of race within the more salient (for her) issue of vampirism (i.e., her Blackness matters to the extent that whiteness is a vampire cliché). Shori does not read Theodora's space as oriented toward whiteness, instead interpreting the clutter as "familiar." But we might read the trace of something sinister in this space: a room organized around Theodora's body, stacked high with books and papers that represent the role narrative plays in the orientations of whiteness, in which there is practically no room for Shori.

To build interracial and interspecies intimacy within this fraught context, to make room within co-evolved narratives and spaces, requires reading against the grain of dominant narratives *and* reading new narratives entirely, which is to say rerouting neuronal connections formed, in part, through reading. When Shori says to Theodora that she wants them to exchange stories ("I need to talk to you, tell you my story, hear yours"), she acknowledges the fact that embodied, lived experience differs from narrative clichés and the "knowledge" they ingrain in us, even if she hasn't yet developed a sophisticated form of racial literacy (90). In her departure from the typical literary vampire, Shori also constitutes, for Theodora and Butler's readers, something akin to a novel metaphor, in Lakoff and Johnson's sense. Her Blackness and her youth, her ethical quandaries, her methodical thinking—all of these prompt a reconsideration of vampires that also has the potential to prompt a reconsideration of the race and gender norms within which vampires are themselves constructed, and of the constitutive gaps, the "ornate absences," within vampire literature and perhaps beyond.

In addition to acting as a novel metaphor, Shori also offers a novel metaphor that works to undermine the racial investments that underwrite the vampire genre. Shori's Ina father, Iosif, is a vehement critic of vampire lore: "We have very little in common with the vampire creatures Bram Stoker described in *Dracula*," he explains, proceeding to provide a scientific explanation of the Ina species that cites "mutualistic symbiosis" (63), "growth stages" (64), reproduction, genetic relatedness, and evolution—anything but mythology and fiction. "I think we evolved right here on Earth alongside humanity as a cousin species," he explains (67).[37] However, despite his effort to distance the Ina from Dracula and his innumerable literary and cinematic progeny, Iosif fully embodies the quintessential literary vampire. He *is* the "tall, handsome, fully grown white man" Theodora expects to see before she takes Shori up to her office, as if he has stepped out of the pages of a book. Shori simultaneously underlines and undermines this resemblance with a remarkable statement, describing Iosif as "a tall, spidery man, empty-handed, and visibly my kind except that he was blond and very

---

37. Humans are not the only "languaging" species in *Fledgling*; Ina also invent stories to explain their existence and relations with one another and the world.

pale-skinned—not just light-skinned like Wright, but *as white as the pages of Wright's books*" (61; emphasis added). Iosif is, in fact, as white as Dracula himself, but Shori compares him instead to the physical pages of the books in which figures like Dracula appear.

This novel metaphor avoids lending credence to fictional vampire lore and its race and gender norms, instead presenting whiteness as a literally superficial physical trait—meaningful in a human context but not core to what it means to be Ina. In fact, Shori identifies the Ina species as *"my* kind" and her father as the exception to the norm (*"except* that he was blond and very pale-skinned"), reversing the typical orientation that places her on the side of the exceptions and Iosif squarely in the narrative center. This subtle move clears space for the introduction of Black Ina into Ina families, communities, and history—and, outside the world of the text, into the vampire genre. Describing Iosif as "white as the pages of Wright's books," Shori might even be dismissing the whiteness asserted by vampire narratives altogether: to be as white as the pages of the books isn't to be white at all, or is to be white only in fiction. But given the attention the novel pays to the intimacy between text and body, page and skin, it seems more apt to read this figure in precisely the opposite way, as an acknowledgment of the role narrative plays in creating and sustaining racial categories, in training readers to interpret the markings on both skin and paper (the "hieroglyphics of the flesh") in racially meaningful ways (Spillers 67). In so doing, narrative has a material impact on the world, even though the meanings of a book or a body are always in excess of the markings themselves. Whiteness, in this case, is the "skin" of the text; produced through repeated readings and passed down through habit, it reflects and reinforces the whiteness of the spaces it also helps to shape.

The fact that Shori refers to *Wright's* books in this moment, rather than Theodora's, is notable, since it's Theodora who is a great reader, while Wright only checks out books about vampires from the library for Shori to read. But while Theodora's racial investments stay relatively muted, Wright openly expresses racial resentment when, upset by Shori's decision to take on another male symbiont, he expresses his gender-based jealousy through the language of race: "I met [Joel, the new symbiont] in the upstairs hall. He had the nerve to ask me which bedrooms were empty. You know [Shori] never even told me he was black," he complains to Brook, another (white) symbiont. Wright recounts here a moment of shock parallel to Theodora's; expecting Joel to be white (because his race has not been named), Wright encounters him in the hallway and presumably thinks something along the lines of "Look! A Negro!" Wright's perceived loss of masculine authority is articulated to a perceived loss of racial authority; on the basis of both, he "deserved" to know Joel's racial status and to maintain control over the intimate spaces of the home—even though he is actually a guest in this space. Joel's free movement through the hallway and intention to take possession of a bedroom is the material and mobile expression of a man who, from Wright's perspective, does not know his "place." The reference to Wright's books is a subtle reminder that his way of reading Joel's body is forged through the circulation of narratives about race and Blackness. "They're not human, Wright," Brook replies. "They don't care about white or black," a statement meant to cordon off human racism from the world of the Ina (162). Of course, this claim is belied throughout the novel, as Ina are themselves habituated, in varying degrees, to human racial norms.

Another elder Ina, Hayden Gordon, prompts a second opportunity to contemplate the connection between bodies and books in a way that challenges biosocial hierarchies. Hayden explains to Shori that, according to Ina tradition, Ina writing emerged during a period when an epidemic illness threatened the survival of the species: "I think some of us were writing to leave behind some sign that we had lived, because it seemed we would all die." In fact, both the species and the writings survive, meaning that a record of the trauma is kept in written texts and, it would seem, in the bodies of survivors and their descendants: "Perhaps we had simply undergone a kind of microbial winnowing. The illness killed most of us. Those left were resistant to it, as were their children" (189). Presumably, this event is legible in both the Ina written tradition (specifically, the Ina "bible") and the Ina genome, whether in the form of genetic traits that predisposed some Ina to survival or in epigenetic notations effected by disease and its attendant horrors. The parallel between scripture, which the Ina are prompted to write because of the threat of annihilation, and genetic script, which accounts for their survival, casts light on the outsize reaction of some Ina to the genetic experiments that have produced Shori. If the Ina view the genome as akin to scripture, they cannot countenance its revision. But the analogy can also run in the other direction: if the scriptures are just records produced by bodies—in this case, bodies under extreme duress—then, rather than elevating the genome to the status of holy writ, both are brought down to earth. The idea that the Ina who survived the epidemic are superior because of superior DNA (or, for that matter, the idea that the Ina are superior to humans for the same reason) is tainted with metaphysical thinking that sees survival as superiority, evolution as perfection, and DNA as destiny.[38]

---

38. Wald offers a concrete example of the racist implications of genetic "winnowing" theories in her discussion of journalistic accounts of research on the bubonic plague and AIDS that "manifest[ed] a common mischaracterization of Darwinian analysis" and served claims to white racial superiority ("Future Perfect" 689).

When Iosif explains to Shori that Ina and humans are co-evolved species, he offers an addendum in the form of casual speciesism: "Perhaps we're the more gifted cousin" (67). If all of the reading Shori does in *Fledgling* is an effort to relearn what has been forgotten, then that would include those aspects of Ina society that are, perhaps, most in need of change—including the persistent speciesism that, at a minimum, complicates Ina-human relationships and is regularly intertwined with racism. While a great deal of Ina thinking is ingrained in her, Shori is also open to new ways of thinking—to forging new neuronal connections, as evidenced by the dialogical (if still hierarchical) relationships she builds with her symbionts. Shori will never be able to recapture what was lost (including the person she once was); in rebuilding her family, she is necessarily building something new. The violence of the attack against her flesh is an unforgivable trauma, but the possibility of novel ways of living in a world structured by violence and hierarchy endures.

Navigating such possibilities is a messy process, one that conjoins instinct and reason, science and ethics. In an interesting parallel to Gerald Vizenor's *The Heirs of Columbus*, the subject of chapter 3, *Fledgling* devotes a significant portion of the narrative—in this case, the final third—to a courtroom drama. Here, however, it is not the question of vampirism (e.g., the expropriation of blood or DNA) that is on trial; this is, rather, a murder trial, the accused being the Silk family, who have killed Shori's maternal relatives in an attempt to halt their genetic experiments. After much testimony—which is evaluated through both intellectual and sensory means, as the Ina use their sense of smell to separate truth from lies—the Ina Council finds in Shori's favor, punishing her attackers through bodily and family dismembering. Although Shori can countenance the former (in fact, she preferred the death penalty for certain of the defendants), she is made uncomfortable by the latter: "It still seemed wrong to me that [the children of the perpetrators] should be the ones to bear the worst of the punishment. . . . They were the only ones truly not responsible" (302). On the one hand, the judgment is perhaps less about punishment than it is about creating the conditions necessary for reform: the Silk children will live with other Ina families who will, theoretically, raise them in more equitable ways of being. Meanwhile, Shori will undergo a similar process, as she and her symbionts plan to live with Ina relatives in order to learn social and kinship norms before setting out on their own. On the other hand, Shori's discomfort with the judgment is a reminder that Shori's awkward position in Ina society, her navigation of spaces that were not set up for her, positions her to notice what has been normalized for her Ina peers and what might be ripe for change. The breaking up of families *feels* wrong to her, and this is a feeling that draws upon personal and intergenerational experience, including experience she doesn't remember. Her discomfort in response to this judgment might be a sensory experience worth tracing to its ethical conclusions.

Like Shori, Butler's readers must also try to make sense of a world that is familiar but not remembered. As we follow her journey, we are prompted, however subtly, to reconsider our own habitual responses in ways that might make possible new ways of understanding, shaping, and being shaped by our world. Through Shori, the novel offers a model for navigating postgenomic discourses of race and kinship—for addressing thorny issues of consent, bodily autonomy, and belonging rearticulated (not raised) by postgenomic discourse. *Fledgling* argues that there is no easy way to address the ethical issues attending genetic engineering, there is no guiltless approach to kinship, and there is no way to fully abstract stories from the living, breathing bodies that write and read them. There are only embodied and reasoning agents who must do the ongoing work required to create and sustain livable communities. *Fledgling* asks us to keep our eyes on the flesh, paying attention to those who, like Jessica, are elided, reduced to serviceable bodies, or transmuted to symbol or code in the narratives that circulate around and through us. And it prompts us to recognize the complicated and compromised environments within which humans work to make meaningful connections. The possibility of intimacy within such structures does not negate their violence, nor the imperative to reevaluate and revise when possible. There is no end to this process, no utopia to achieve, just ongoing negotiations, within which the stories we share play a significant role. This role isn't abstract; the responses our bodies have to the stories we read, including chemical reactions and neuronal restructurings akin to those illustrated in this novel, are crucial to the process of reorienting ourselves and our world toward more just coordinates. The book we hold in our hands, and the hands holding that book, are in intimate, dynamic relation, and it is through repeated encounters with stories that interrupt habitual ways of thinking about—and moving through—the world that our thinking and our moving and our world might change. As another Butler heroine famously says, "All that you touch you change. All that you Change Changes you. The only lasting truth is Change. God is Change."[39]

---

39. This phrase is repeated throughout *Parable of the Sower* (1993) by protagonist Lauren Olamina and becomes a central tenet of the religion she creates and leads.

PART 3

Usable Futures

CHAPTER 5

Usable Futures and Trans-Corporeal Reading in Alina Troyano's *Chicas 2000*

In the closing scene of the futuristic farce *Chicas 2000* (1997), a play by queer Cuban American performance artist Alina Troyano,[1] Troyano's alter ego, Carmelita Tropicana, performs "This Is My Life," a song first made famous by Welsh singer Shirley Bassey and later recorded by Cuban recording artist La Lupe.[2] Accompanying Carmelita in this impromptu performance are Clana and Cluna, clones of Carmelita made by the mad scientist Dr. Igor. All three women are fugitives from state discipline, Clana and Cluna for being "illegal" clones and Carmelita for possessing the "chusma" gene—a genetic variation that supposedly predisposes her to "loud, gross, tacky and excessive behavior" (72).[3] Just moments before the song, Troyano's genetic

---

1. Troyano publishes most of her work under the name "Carmelita Tropicana" and rarely appears out of character. Román observes that Carmelita "is not just a stage persona" and that many of Troyano's friends refer to her by this name (87). Troyano describes Carmelita as a constructed persona while also, at times, referring to "Alina" in the third person (Román 92). I use "Troyano" throughout this chapter because the primary work I cite is published under that name. However, assigning authorship to only part of Troyano/Tropicana's plural identity is necessarily inadequate.

2. Ruiz calls La Lupe Latin America's "first performance artist" (99).

3. *Chicas 2000* was inspired by the cloning of Dolly the sheep and a message on Troyano's answering machine from scholar José Esteban Muñoz that began "Oye, chusma" (Troyano, Author's Introduction xxiii).

refugees are pitted against one another in a battle royal for legal papers at Dr. Igor's "Chusmatic Casino," where "chusmas" and "nonchusmas" alike gawk at such spectacles (113).[4] However, upon realizing their connection, Carmelita, Clana, and Cluna embrace one another as "family," defying the system that marks them as genetic inferiors while exploiting them as exotic entertainment. It is in a spirit of resistance that they sing La Lupe's rousing anthem to the right to a life full of love and meaning, a life that matters.

This closing scene, like much of the rest of the play, challenges definitions of a "life" that depend upon the singularity of genetic code or the discreteness of individual bodies or species. Troyano's joyous, messy vision of lives intertwined eschews taxonomy and individuation, reveling in recontextualization and repetition with a difference, whether biological or linguistic.[5] Indeed, Troyano rejects the opposition of embodiment and speech through a performance in which both flesh and words are multiplied in imperfect unison. That neither La Lupe's recording of the song, which plays in the background, nor Clana and Cluna's genetic code is an "original" text underscores the point. The lyrics of "This Is My Life" emphasize identity grounded in a larger whole—in "this great big thing" that is both "part of me and my life" (120) and equivalent to a single life ("this great thing, *it's me, it's my life*"; 121; emphasis added). When the women sing "This is me, this is me," while pointing to one another, they insist that the self is more than the individual subject, that their lives are intimately bound up with the lives of others. And when the lyrics turn from "this is my life," to "let me live," this claim is extended to the audience, who are exhorted to see that their actions can limit or liberate the lives of others and their own.

This message is distinct from the vision of individual rights stripped away by genetic discipline offered by some genomic-era dystopian narratives. As Jenny Reardon writes, "There are no shortages of articles and books that tell us of the great ends and great troubles that might result from human genomics, but there are scant few that help us to think about what we are doing along the way, and how to respond" (*Postgenomic* 21). Instead of presenting genetic technology as the catalyst for new forms of oppression extended to previously free subjects, Troyano presents genetic technology as merely a tool—a potential means of extending (or disrupting) current systems of exploitation and oppression but not their source. Troyano thus rejects both genetic determinism and "genetic dismissivism,"

---

4. Troyano's Chusmatic Casino, like Vizenor's Genome Pavilion, emphasizes play and chance as central features of genetic inheritance.

5. This vision aligns with Choksey's description of the inability of genomics to fully discipline the "messiness" of life (5).

instead turning her attention to the systems in which genetic science is being developed (Hamner 16). When Carmelita sings "This is my life *today*," we would do well to place emphasis on that final word. We are responsible not for preventing the arrival of a racist medico-police state, suggests Troyano, but for dismantling the one we already live in.[6]

Chicas 2000, a work of near-future speculation from the height of the genome era, thus fulfills the call for texts that represent apocalypse as incremental, ongoing—as happening *now*. In so doing, it draws upon what I am calling *the usable future*. If *the usable past* refers to the excavation and reclamation of histories and traditions—often suppressed—for the purposes of surviving the present and making possible a more just future, then *the usable future* strategically posits a future vision in service of the same ends. Although set in a dystopian tomorrow in which genetic engineering looms large in everyday life, *Chicas* presents genomics not as the handmaiden of coming catastrophe but as an occasion for examining crises in the racist and capitalist regimes that organize life at the turn of the millennium. Like Margaret Atwood, whose *MaddAddam* trilogy I discuss in the next chapter, Troyano offers a critique aimed not at transgenics, per se; instead, she illuminates present structures of inequity, within which genetic testing and engineering are merely the newest in a long line of technologies adopted to maintain or exacerbate the status quo.[7]

Evading the horror tropes that traditionally accompany transgression across species lines, Troyano also makes room for new modes of intra- and interspecies kinship and illuminates racist, sexist, speciesist, and classist boundaries as illusory but powerful mechanisms of subordination and destruction. Through strategies that recall Ruth Ozeki's and Gerald Vizenor's recombinative language games (discussed in the introduction and chapter 3, respectively), she literally stages embodied linguistic resistance to the surveillance of race, sex, and species and to the phantasmagorical severing of DNA from the body through the rhetoric of data and codes. Returning our attention to bodies in relation to other bodies, a strategy heightened by the physicality of theater and performance art, *Chicas 2000* ultimately articulates an ethics of trans-corporeality that challenges the boundary between audience and play and posits mutual permeability as a state of possibility and promise, rather than fear and dread. A text about the future that isn't

---

6. Troyano's temporal vision is also a rejection of what Choksey calls "genomic futurism" (4), "health futures" (7), and "Silicon Valley transhumanism," utopian visions poised to reinforce existing inequities (10).

7. As Troyano has said, technology is "a tool that can be used for good or bad" (qtd. in McHugh).

really about the future, and a text about genomics that isn't really about genomics, *Chicas 2000* is a strategically slippery, deceptively silly work that posits alternative modes of being—and reading—in a world already defined by technological innovation and biopolitical discipline.

Usable Futures and Genome Time

The 1997 film *Gattaca*, written and directed by Andrew Niccol, is perhaps the quintessential film of the genome era. *Gattaca* follows the story of Vincent, a child conceived naturally (i.e., an "in-valid") in a near-future dominated by genetic engineering. In Vincent's world, reproductive discipline is enacted through a eugenics program, whereby parents select traits for their children with the knowledge that educational and professional opportunities will be distributed based on probabilistic projections of physical capability, intelligence, disease, and even criminality. Subject to explicit discrimination throughout his youth, Vincent eventually passes as a "valid" using fraudulent DNA samples; nevertheless, he is kept running throughout the film, as he attempts to prove that DNA does not tell the whole story of his life. *Gattaca* challenges the gene fetishism on the rise in the 1990s, as the Human Genome Project accelerated and "gene talk" permeated popular culture, and offers a vivid illustration of the assaults on privacy, freedom, and opportunity that could be enacted by a genetic state. When it comes to genetic engineering, the film contends, good intentions (security, health, happiness) can result in bad outcomes (unfreedom, discrimination, disillusionment); we must wake up from our collective genetic dream, before we find ourselves in a nightmare.[8] *Gattaca* thus joins the longstanding science fictional tradition of imagining a future in which technological advances promise utopia but lead to dystopia.[9] (Indeed, such narratives almost always reveal that *utopia* and *dystopia* are intimately intertwined, not least because utopia for some tends to require dystopia for others.) The effectiveness of such cautionary tales depends on the idea that audiences have something to lose. Freedom, individuality, mobility, privacy—these are all at risk, we are warned, if we do not take steps to prevent their erosion.

---

8. Hamner points out that *Gattaca* "glosses over" the technical difficulty of "meaningfully interpreting the immense quantities of information" produced by genomic analysis (32); nevertheless, "the *feelings* [*Gattaca* and similar films] evoke remain relevant" because "human beings have always worried that our destinies might be predetermined" (33).

9. "Science fiction expresses a technophobic fear of losing our human identity, our freedom, our emotions, our values, and our lives to machines" (Dinello 2).

However, as *Chicas 2000* prods us to remember, scores of people already live without access to these vaunted principles, often in the name of racial difference. For them, dystopia is not a future to be avoided but a present to be survived. New biotechnologies are to be feared not for the world they might bring about but for the way they might exacerbate the "preexisting conditions" of colonialism, racism, sexism, and ableism. This point has been articulated by several postgenomic-era scholars and writers. For example, at the end of her history of cell biology, *Culturing Life* (2007), Hannah Landecker critiques the tendency of social scientists and humanists to concern themselves with biotechnology only to the degree that it portends a dystopian future, arguing that we should be attentive to how biotechnology informs our understanding of "life itself" in ways that matter *now* (225). And Priscilla Wald makes a similar claim in "American Studies and the Politics of Life" (2012), insisting that narratives that engage transgenics, cloning, genetic surveillance, and environmental catastrophe should illuminate *present* structures of biopolitical exploitation and inequity, including health disparities, human trafficking, housing and employment discrimination, and the disproportionate incarceration of Black and brown people, rather than projecting such structures into an imagined future. Landecker and Wald suggest that critiques of genetic engineering that focus on avoiding future threats misunderstand the chronology of apocalypse and risk ignoring historical and ongoing assaults on human (and more-than-human) lives, thus serving the interests of privileged observers who worry that the centuries-old practice of commodifying human beings might soon affect them, rather than "situat[ing] the danger of scientific innovation in the *business* of scientific medicine, which treats bodies as commodities *now*, not in some abstract, science fictional future" (Wald, "American" 202).

To be clear, science fiction has a long record of articulating critical perspectives on the here and now. As writer and theorist Samuel Delany explains,

> Science fiction is not "about the future." Science fiction *is in dialogue with the present*. We SF writers often say that science fiction prepares readers to think about the real future—but that's because it relates to the real present in the particular way it does; and that relation is neither one of prediction nor one of prophecy. It is one of dialogic, contestatory, agonistic creativity. In science fiction the future is only a writerly convention that allows the SF writer to indulge in a significant distortion of the present that sets up a rich and complex dialogue with the reader's here and now. (165)

Many Indigenous writers and writers of color see science fictional techniques as especially incisive tools for laying bare the pathologies of the present. As Paula M. L. Moya and I have written elsewhere, ethnospeculative writers[10] regularly disrupt the expected timeline of apocalypse, pointing out that the task at hand is not to evade imminent cataclysm but to seek renewal in cataclysm's wake.[11] Many such writers invoke elements of a disavowed past to survive a present trauma and/or chart an alternative future; in other words, they draw upon a *usable past*—cultural resources, especially those erased or marginalized by the dominant culture, reclaimed and refashioned for today.[12] Simultaneously looking forward, many ethnofuturist writers also enact what I call the *usable future*: future-tense imaginings that draw attention to the reverberating *presence* of apocalypse and that enable visions of liberation in the contemporary moment. If the *usable past* names strategies for managing intergenerational trauma, the *usable future* names complementary strategies that work not to "keep the future at bay" but to reorient readers toward the now, offering tools of survival for some, illuminating structures of injustice for others.[13] Rather than only counseling us to change course so as to avoid the *coming* dystopia (what Margaret Atwood has referred to as the work of "antiprediction"), usable futures also disrupt the normalization of the *current* dystopia, refusing to center the anticipatory fear of privileged perspectives and drawing upon culturally specific notions of time, history, and story to rewrite the present.[14] My notion of the *usable future* is aligned with what Alys Eve Weinbaum describes as a *"conjunctural*

---

10. "Ethnospeculative fiction is genre fiction . . . written by and/or about people of color that seeks to . . . facilitate the development of more racially just and life-affirming selves and ways of living" (Moya and Larkin 228).

11. See, for example, Junot Díaz's articulation of the contemporary dystopia he describes as a "zombie stage of capitalism," Nalo Hopkinson's discussion of the speculative as a necessary mode for critiques of colonialism and its aftermath in her interview with Alondra Nelson (A. Nelson, "Making" 101), and Mark Dery's discussion of Afrofuturism as a genre that addresses the catastrophes of colonialism and slavery as instances of alien invasion and abduction (180).

12. The term "usable past" first appears in Van Wyck Brooks's 1918 essay "On Creating a Usable Past," in which he calls for literary critics to construct a selective version of American history that would enable the nation to move into the future: "What, out of all the multifarious achievements and impulses and desires of the American literary mind, ought we to elect to remember?" (340). More recently, the term has been applied to texts that reimagine suppressed or disavowed histories and traditions. See A. Nelson's discussion of the "usable past" as an Afrofuturist technique ("Future Texts" 7) and Scott's use of the term in relation to Black revolutionary writing (54).

13. With the phrase "keep the future at bay," I invoke a linked phrase, "keeping the past at bay," repeated throughout Morrison's neo-slave narrative *Beloved* (51). As that novel powerfully illustrates, to keep the past at bay is also to keep the future at bay, in that it stalls forward motion.

14. Atwood has described *The Handmaid's Tale* as "an antiprediction: If this future can be described in detail, maybe it won't happen" ("What").

intervention": the "timely and time-sensitive refusal of clear-cut divisions between old and new dystopias" and the "capacity to constellate past and present realities in the interest of imagining the future that lies in the balance" (*Afterlife* 112).

The *usable future* is related to a wide variety of temporal interventions staged by writers of color, Indigenous writers, and queer writers, from the Anishinaabe concept of "biskaabiiyang," or "returning to ourselves," which emphasizes personal and collective practices of decolonization in a postapocalyptic world (Dillon 10), to "Chicanafuturism," which critiques idealized versions of technological advancement that erase Chicanes and other people of color, and which enable complex rethinking of past and present (Ramírez).[15] As Catherine Ramírez poignantly explains, "Already, people of color have been erased from the future, just as many of us were excised from narratives of the past and remain hidden from view in the barrios, ghettoes, reservations, and prisons of the present" (188). The purpose of Chicanafuturism (Ramírez's concept) and other complex temporal interventions staged by writers of color is to reclaim agency across this multilateral timescape, to interrupt violent and ongoing erasure from past, present, and future. Jose Esteban Muñoz's project of "queer futurity," elaborated in *Cruising Utopia* (2009), also fits into rubric, in its illumination of queerness as future-oriented and optimistic. Muñoz imagines an alternative tomorrow, but this imagining first requires active engagement of the present; as Sandra Ruiz explains, "To be transported to a *there*, as . . . Muñoz indicates . . . , we must part ways with the world we thought we lived in and envisage another one. But, even in this adieu, he invites us to play our part in *this here*, for in doing so, we release ourselves from the grips of immobility, melancholia, complacency in that search for the 'not yet here'" (95).[16] One of the best-known temporal interventions in this diverse archive is Toni Morrison's "rememory," which, elaborated in the novel *Beloved* (1987), describes the material repetitions of the past in the present. The kind of strategic remembering—and forgetting—enacted in the novel's present is at once past- and future-oriented, as the formerly enslaved characters figure out how to move forward despite the weight of the past. As Paul D says to Sethe, "me and you, we got more yesterday than anybody. We need some

---

15. Another important instance of the "usable past" among Latine writers is the resignification of religious, folk, and historical subjects (O'Neill 590–94). On Troyano's queer reimagining of Cuban history, see Caballero 131; Cespedes 147; Sugg 164–93; and Yarbro-Bejarano 201, 207–8.

16. Also see Clayton's discussion of these trends in queer temporality (*Literature* 154–55).

kind of tomorrow" (273). Scholar and novelist Viet Thanh Nguyen's concept of "just memory," directly influenced by Morrison's work, further clarifies how remembering—and disremembering—have significant present and future implications. "Just memory" exceeds both "remembering one's own" (the mnemonic glue of in-groups) and "remembering others" (a corrective to the former) by accounting for the full humanity of selves and others and evading mnemonic loops that reinforce claims to innocence or guilt (Nguyen 4–19). Just memory recognizes, in all of us, the potential for a vast array of moral actions and therefore keeps the future open: "The impossible might yet be possible at some point in the future" (286). In their complex engagement of past, present, and future, temporal interventions like these reorient the future timeline to, in William Calvo-Quirós's words, "propos[e] (and produc[e]) a new world": "our current world, the one *in* the present, is only a phantom; the real world is the one in which we were meant to live as full humans" (155–56).[17] Calvo-Quirós's vision hijacks the teleological language of progress in service of justice in the present, where the fictions of racism and colonialism govern our lives.

In the postgenomic age, thinking differently about past, present, and future also means resisting specious narratives of evolutionary progress, which are projected onto DNA and have been employed to erase people of color from future visions. The usable future, in this context, is thus aligned with an understanding of "genome time" as a temporal mode that is open-ended, rather than definitive, and whose central feature is possibility, rather than determination.[18] In his influential essay "Genome Time," Jay Clayton explains how evolution and, later, genomics have altered temporal perception. Evolution, Clayton argues, vastly expanded a linear sense of time to include the "deep time" of evolution and a future end of time:

> Evolution . . . linked the individual not just to familial ancestors but to generations back before the dawn of history, to the animal kingdom, and before that, to the protozoa. The future was changed as well. Posterity came to signify . . . an impersonal futurity, a time beyond the individual, a time beyond even the species, a time that entailed the prospect of extinction. (58)

In contrast, genomics, Clayton argues, encourages a cyclical, rather than linear, sense of time by "fusing" the diachronic time of a human lifespan and

---

17. Calvo-Quirós is writing specifically about "Chican@ Speculative Productions."
18. Also see Choksey's discussion of how genomics has disrupted liberal humanism's representation of time as the chronological context in which the individual develops (12–13).

the synchronic time of the genome. Each human life is both unique in its genetic code and connected to the diverse "organism" that is humanity and to the "life cycle" of the entire species, via infinite recombinative possibilities. Clayton explains:

> On the one hand, your genetic code is unique, a personal inheritance from your parents that defines key aspects of your identity and influences your singular destiny. From this perspective genetic inheritance occurs in linear time. Your genetic code is the species's *parole*, a speech act that can never be repeated. On the other hand, the genome has a synchronic dimension. It is a four-letter *langue* that runs through and beyond the individual, reaching back to the first primordial cell and forward to whatever future humanity may encounter. As a self-contained sign system, the relationship between past, present, and future seems arbitrary, a game of chance and necessity that challenges ordinary notions of time. Although actual variations occur in linear time, the set of possible evolutionary variations are always already "there," in potentia. The past and future appear inscribed as theoretical possibilities within the virtual space of the code. (58–59)

Genomics, in Clayton's analysis, disrupts our sense of time as linear, upending causality and determinism in favor of simultaneity, potentiality, and chance. Yes, apocalypse is one potential variation, but so is renewal, as we live out our (diachronic) lives as expressions of the (synchronic) variability of the species. Notably, the metaphor Clayton uses to explain genome time is linguistic: we are, each of us, a *speech act*, a singular instance of expression drawn from a deep and evolving well of language. This play on genomic discourse's textual metaphors emphasizes potentiality and intertextuality as a properties not only of human genomes but of all texts, properties expressed by the various "outcomes" achieved through multiple readings. Literary works, as instances of language (*parole*), also contain tremendous variability in their relation to "the set of possible [linguistic] variations" (*langue*), to paraphrase Clayton. Genomics and literature alike are discourses of possibility, not fate.[19]

By giving us a glimpse of both the diachronic and the synchronic, genome time also alerts us to our intersubjective relatedness, to horizontal and vertical relations among living beings, to the past, present, and future

---

19. Clayton has written that "changing conceptions of time" link biology and literature: "The innovative temporal structures found in . . . novels about evolution, genetics, and genomics from the nineteenth century to today indicate a deeper affinity between literature and the life sciences" (*Literature* xiii).

impacts of these relationships, and to myriad present and future potentialities. As Everett Hamner writes, "Genome time untethers easy assumptions about linear causality and straightforward determinism, pulling material existence into a simultaneous awareness of circularity and simultaneity, the interdependence of all things" (209). These insights align genome time with bionarrativity, systems biology, embodied cognition, and the "new materialisms," a corrective to the "linguistic turn" in literary and cultural studies that returns attention to materiality, not as a self-evident reality prior to language but an "agential" substance in complex relation with language and subjectivity (Barad, *Meeting* 132–85).[20] In the words of theoretical physicist Karen Barad, "Matter is not a linguistic construction but a discursive production in the posthumanist sense that discursive practices are themselves material (re)configurings of the world" (151). Matter is discursive and discourse is material—and both are "mutually implicated in the dynamics of intra-activity" (140). The notion of "intra-activity" also decenters human subjects, undermining the opposition between "human" and "nature" that has underwritten historical and ongoing regimes of exclusion, oppression, and exploitation. Stacy Alaimo's concept of "trans-corporeality" similarly captures how "the substance of one's self" is "interconnected with the wider environment" and with "networks that are simultaneously economic, political, cultural, scientific, and substantial" (Alaimo, *Bodily* 20).[21] The "posthuman environmental ethics" that follows this insight "denies the human the sense of separation from the interconnected, mutually constitutive actions of material reality" (157) and "focuses on interfaces, interchanges, and transformative material/discursive practices" (142). In other words, it turns our attention to "this great big thing" that is both part and whole of our lives.

Drawing from the various temporal theories described above, as well as material ecocritics and theorists like Barad and Alaimo, I would propose that the usable future is a literary technique that emphasizes open-endedness over teleology and adaptation over progress, engages both diachronic and synchronic temporal registers, and recognizes memory as a practice that draws from both past and future in its critical engagement of the present. Usable-future narratives draw attention to current inequities as continuous with past traumas and dystopian future imaginings, offering (to paraphrase Atwood) "a whole new take" on the hackneyed phrase *the future is*

---

20. Indigenous theorizations of material agency have influenced the new materialisms, though these connections have not always been acknowledged. See Hamilton 13–17; Rosiek et al.

21. See my discussion of "embodied cognition" in chapter 4. Also see Choksey 2; Hanson 145.

now (*Oryx* 97).[22] Much has been made, rightly, of the *presence* of the past in the form of intergenerational trauma that extends from European imperialism, colonialism, and enslavement. The concept of the *usable future* draws our attention, in complementary fashion, to the *presence* of the future, to the concrete, material ways that future thinking shapes our present world. Ideas about the future can draw our attention to present structures of inequity or obscure them; they can justify oppression—or revolution—by signaling who "belongs" to the future and who belongs to the past; they can offer maps of destruction and liberation. Usable-future texts illuminate how future narratives shape our present world and, in so doing, they depict the present more clearly, highlighting the material bonds that connect us to one another. By remembering the future, they turn our attention to the imaginative work necessary to create a more just world today.

The Usable Future in *Chicas 2000*

That Troyano wishes her audience to focus on the present is obvious enough in her emphasis on the very near future. First performed in 1997, *Chicas 2000* is set between the years 1999 and 2014. The millennial anxieties that frame the play—cloning and genetic engineering, Y2K, "welfare mothers," and "illegal" immigration—are anxieties that belong largely to white and privileged citizens.[23] While such subjects worry about "the browning of America," the play's heroine, Carmelita, is trying to survive a dystopian regime that uses technologies both old and new to enact its racist and heterosexist agenda.[24] At the beginning of the play, Carmelita is swept up in a police raid targeting Latine people, who are said to possess the so-called chusma gene. Dr. Igor, the scientist who "discovered" the gene, bails her out only to take her captive; when she won't submit to his sexual advances, he hacks off part of her buttocks and uses the tissue to create the clones, Clana and Cluna. Carmelita is arrested for shooting Dr. Igor and sent to a Behavioral Modification Unit, where she fails at being "recoded," falls in love with an "oso-woman" (a human/bear hybrid), and finally escapes. The play ends with Carmelita's plan—in direct opposition to the family values set—to create a same-sex, mixed-species clan with her clone daughters and transhuman lover.

---

22. See my discussion of Atwood's use of the phrase "a whole new take on *indigenous*" in chapter 6.

23. On anxieties related to cloning, see Hanson 122–23.

24. The April 9, 1990, *Time* cover story, "Beyond the Melting Pot," uses the phrase "browning of America" to describe the nation's changing demography (Henry).

With its outrageous plot, *Chicas 2000* lampoons not just gene fetishism—the idea that genetic explanations can be provided for complex somatic, psychological, behavioral, and social phenomena—but, specifically, the reinscription of racist thinking in the genome. Three years before the Human Genome Project completed its initial genome draft, Troyano anticipates the use of genome analysis to link specific DNA sequences to geographical ancestry (and, implicitly, race) and to link geographical ancestry to disease profiles. She also responds to the racial reinscriptions already under way in the 1990s, despite the antiracist claims of many genome researchers. The criminalizing and pathologizing of "chusmería" alludes to the role DNA analysis has played in devastatingly unequal—and intertwined—medical and criminal justice systems, abetting modes of surveillance enacted disproportionately on racialized subjects.

The most creative speculative leaps—human/bear hybrids, DNA "remodeling" camps, coerced cloning—in *Chicas 2000* are not, then, the direct subject of its critique. Indeed, Troyano mocks the apoplexy—apo(calypse) plexy?—that sometimes accompanies discussions of transgenics. Rather than signaling a world gone mad with the godlike power of molecular biology, the biotechnological transgressions in *Chicas 2000* highlight the continuities in racial, ethnic, and sexual oppression that characterize the postgenomic age. Rather than imagining a future that must be avoided at all costs, Troyano offers a usable future that illuminates already existing abuses: medical, reproductive, and labor exploitation; disproportionate imprisonment; the criminalization of immigration; and the use of education as a tool of oppression. And rather than centering the fear that white people will soon be subject to the kinds of surveillance and exploitation experienced by people of color, Troyano centers marginalized perspectives on present oppression and future possibility.

Troyano's usable future is rendered through the modes of camp, which Muñoz describes as a form of "artificial respiration" that "breathes new life into old situations" (*Disidentifications* 128), and *choteo*, a Cuban "form of play that acts as a way to filter serious or distressing experiences in a nonserious, often irreverent, relaxed manner," while still articulating a pointed critique (Laguna 516).[25] Troyano's hilarious rendering of new genetic technologies taken to their most outrageous conclusions draws attention to an old and ongoing situation—the exploitation and oppression of queer Latinas—that has long since been naturalized. Troyano's comic techniques are a

---

25. "*Choteo* is like camp in that it *can be* a fierce send-up of dominant cultural formations" and "a style of colonial mimicry that is simultaneously a form of resemblance *and* menace" (Muñoz, *Disidentifications* 135–36).

"strategic" and "measured response to the forced evacuation from dominant culture that the minority subject experiences," a critique that passes as entertainment and yet is resistant to commercialization or instrumentalization (Muñoz, *Disidentifications* 128). Camp and choteo allow Troyano to send up cautionary dystopian narratives that privilege white fears about the future—specifically, fears about the erosion of the white supremacy.[26]

In the opening scene of the play, Carmelita—in her capacity as host of a TV variety show called "Chicas 2000"—makes a prediction that had become quite familiar in the 1990s: "Latinos will be the majority in the U.S.A." by the year 2000, she declares, the specter of Y2K threatening a disruption of America's literal and metaphorical power grid (75).[27] The racialized fear that America is descending into primitivity and chaos is quickly linked to an American exceptionalism that extends from the Puritan vision of America as a "city upon a hill" to the late twentieth-century declaration of the United States as the "indispensable nation."[28] This link is forged by Pingalito Betancourt, a "typical" Cuban American man (also played by Troyano) who appears on Carmelita's program as the winner of the "Hoi Polloi" contest, which gives him the opportunity to dilate on a topic of his choosing.[29] Pingalito takes "Puritanism" as his theme and begins in charming absurdity:

> I started investigating Puritanism last Thanksgiving when I was eating turkey and watching *Pocahontas*. I know you look at me and see a very Puritan kind of guy, a regular John Smith. Well that is correct. I have many of the components of Puritanism: self-reliance, industry, and frugality. (73)

---

26. Although its context and intention are very different, television host Conan O'Brien's long-running bit "In the Year 2000" comes to mind for its mockery of facile future thinking. The sketch, in which O'Brien waxes comical about mind-boggling innovations to come, was performed well into the 2000s, drawing attention to the way the millennial turn evokes a sense of the future even after it is in the rearview mirror.

27. The fear was that digital date-keeping protocols were not prepared to accommodate the numerical shift from 1999 to 2000, potentially leading to power outages, software meltdowns, and other unforeseen catastrophes.

28. In 1998, US Secretary of State Madeleine Albright stated, "We are the indispensable nation. We stand tall and we see further than other countries into the future" (Albright).

29. Troyano has said that "Pingalito is a compilation of a lot of different men in the Latino community," while also being "a stereotype that perhaps is more universal than we think" (qtd. in Horowitz 104). Muñoz highlights the critical effect of the character: "Carmelita's drag does not wink at the jingoistic Cuban nationalist and reassure him that everything is satisfactory; rather, it renders visible the mechanisms of privilege that such subjectivities attempt to occlude" (*Disidentifications* 135).

The joke is that Pingalito—"dressed in a typical Cuban guayabera shirt, chomping on a cigar," and in possession of a decidedly non-Anglo name (that means "little penis" and thus undercuts his cartoonish machismo)—can't possibly be mistaken for a Puritan. Pingalito provides more evidence of his "impure" status by sprinkling Spanish into his speech, misusing English idioms, and misunderstanding Puritan values (e.g., "Industry. Yes, America should have many many factories"; 73). However, Pingalito is, in fact, quite typically "American," in that his knowledge of the Puritans is superficial and cartoonish (literally—see: *Pocahontas*). Furthermore, he exposes the discontinuity between his audience and their supposed Puritan heritage by emphasizing their sexual hypocrisy: Pingalito "part[s] company with Puritanism" when it comes to sex and asks his viewers to raise their hands if they have never masturbated (73). Paraphrasing President George H. W. Bush, he then calls for a "gentler, kinder Puritanism" (74).[30]

That a "gentler, kinder" America is not imminent goes without saying. The demographic threat posed by Latine people to the fantasy of national purity is instead met with a draconian solution that is both genetic and carceral. Not long after Carmelita's pronouncement, the FBI's DNA Remodeling Agency storms the set of "Chicas 2000" and arrests everyone with Carmelita's allelic variation, a group that is suspiciously ethnically homogeneous. Although some of the more famous figures afflicted with "chusmería" are not Latine (e.g., Dennis Rodman, Tonya Harding, Martha Stewart), the "chusma gene" is understood to predominate among Latine and Caribbean people. In other words, the genetic variation stands in for an ethnic identity (along the lines of a haplotype) and is used to discipline members of a specific group while providing an alibi in the face of accusations of racism.[31] Given the shift, in the 1980s and 1990s, toward a "color-blind" ideology, which required the use of racial "codes" as political cover for racist policies, DNA is as an especially promising code for signaling race.[32] Purified of external markers like skin color, accent, or other ethnocultural "features" (all misleading synecdoches for "race"), genetic markers promise an

---

30. Bush called for a "kinder" and "gentler" nation in his 1989 inaugural address (Bush).

31. A haplotype "is a physical grouping of genomic variants (or polymorphisms) that tend to be inherited together. A specific haplotype typically reflects a unique combination of variants that reside near each other on a chromosome" (Biesecker). Haplotypes are used in genetic ancestry and medical research; see my discussion in chapter 3.

32. On the shift to racially coded language in the 1980s and 1990s, see Omi and Winant.

objective means of defining out-groups.³³ In *Chicas 2000*, chusmería—which just happens to have a high frequency in a particular population—launders anti-Latine sentiment: funneled through the DNA database, the purported "tacky" behavior of Latine people emerges as a discrete and objective fact of inheritance.

Belying this assertion of genetic determinism is the fact that "gene remodeling," in the world of *Chicas 2000*, actually involves *training*, rather than medical intervention. Troyano places in her near-future world the same old effort to use education as a tool of cultural imperialism and genocide (as in the system of residential schools for Indigenous children and punitive English-only policies in majority Latine schools). As Carmelita and her cellmates take classes in elocution, table manners, heterosexuality, and housekeeping, they are trained to be docile racial subjects. Such "remodeling"—a kind of postgenetic editing—resembles colonial mimicry, the demand that colonized subjects attempt, but always fail, to imitate the cultural norms of the dominant class, thereby affirming the superiority of those norms and the inferiority of colonial subjects.³⁴ Although the "problem" identified by the powers that be in *Chicas 2000* is genetic, the "solution" is ideological and, when necessary, explicitly repressive. In other words, Troyano's dystopian future looks a lot like the twentieth century.

Having mockingly dismissed white concerns about becoming a minority group—and, more to the point, about being treated like one—Troyano centers the concerns of queer Latinas directly through Carmelita and indirectly signals them through the clones and oso-women who are also the targets of state discipline. These characters shine a light on the intersectional oppression experienced by queer women of color, while also affording Troyano the opportunity to imagine a freer world not limited by heteronormative racial patriarchy.³⁵ In so doing, she engages in "queer futurity," inviting her audience to imagine different ways of being in the world and, perhaps, a different world altogether.

The alternative family values Carmelita announces at the end of the play have a humorous antecedent in the opening scene, when Pingalito turns to the logic of transspecies genetic relation to elaborate his vision of a more

33. See Gill's discussion of the shift from external racial markers to interior racial markers (8) and of the way color-blind ideology "enabled genomicists to position their research as beyond the influence of race and racism" (14).

34. "The success of colonial appropriation depends on a proliferation of inappropriate objects that ensure its strategic failure, so that mimicry is at once resemblance and menace" (Bhabha 127).

35. Hanson explains that part of the threat of cloning was its implicit transcendence of heteronormative kinship (119).

humane social order. Pingalito claims that humans should behave more like one of our closest primate relatives, the bonobo, with whom, he tells us, "We share ninety-eight percent of the same genes." The bonobo, Pingalito explains, have sex for pleasure and enjoy a gender-equitable social structure that we should emulate: "I say, Let us invigorate America by creating a real banana bonobo republic," he exhorts his audience. To be clear, Pingalito is not an exemplar of gender equity or social justice. After all, by calling his dream society a "banana bonobo republic," he alludes uncritically to US imperialism in Latin America and inadvertently implies that the result of his experiment might not be just. Furthermore, his primary goal is to create a world in which he has greater sexual access to women. (Following his speech, Pingalito "scratches his crotch" [like a bonobo?] and a commercial for "Piagra," a sexual stimulant in the form of a pie, plays [74].) But the possibility of reorganizing society along the lines of free sexual expression, gender egalitarianism, and the rejection of speciesism is something other than absurd. Notably, Pingalito does not describe bonobos as the "ancestors" of humans, as popular evolutionary thinking might encourage, but as cousins, articulating a synchronic, horizontal family relationship, rather than a diachronic, vertical one. Pingalito is not asking his audience to return to a more primitive state but to acknowledge those elements of their genetic "nature" that have been repressed. In other words, he is making a claim about the "set of possible evolutionary variations" that are "always already 'there,' in potentia"—a claim about the present genetic potential of human beings (Clayton, "Genome" 59). Pingalito, despite himself, raises the possibility of fashioning a more just world on the basis of our relatedness to other living beings.

Positing shared genetic inheritance as a foundation for just social arrangements has a fraught history. Pingalito emphasizes commonality and, in so doing, anticipates the doomed claim that the discovery that humans share 99.9 percent of their DNA would strike a death blow against racism. The claim that all humans are very closely related genetically has not resulted in a more equitable world, nor has the discovery of genetic similarity between humans and other primates led to the expansion of (nonhuman) animal rights: "Notwithstanding the fact that humans are 98% genetically identical to chimps, much of the discourse of *the* Human Genome Project resonates with the old-fashioned humanist sensibility of distinctiveness," explains Alaimo (*Bodily* 155). Pingalito's speech calls into question whether shared genetic code is even a meaningful way of identifying relationships within and between species. As biological anthropologist Jonathan Marks notes, living beings can be no more than 75% different from one another and claims to genetic similarity do not have obvious political meanings (4). After all, do we need to know how much DNA humans share with bonobos to treat nonhuman animals more "humanely"? Do we need to know how much DNA humans share with one another to build a more just society? Troyano's contemplation of such questions, hinted at in Pingalito's riff on our primate cousins, leads her to a vision of relatedness that does not depend on genetic similarity but, rather, on the intimacy and interconnection of living beings and the matter that makes up our shared world.

Performing Trans-Corporeality

The usable future, as it is deployed in *Chicas 2000*, ultimately directs its audience toward the recognition of what Alaimo calls "trans-corporeality," the "interconnected, mutually constitutive actions of material reality" (Alaimo, *Bodily* 157). Mutual permeability and interactive, enmeshed agency are everywhere in the play, as the characters seek new ways of living with one another in a still-imperfect world, challenging systems of heteronormativity, racism, classism, and speciesism. Moreover, and perhaps more importantly, the play ultimately enjoins audiences to recognize how they, too, are part of "this great big thing" that Carmelita and her clones sing about at the end of the play. Troyano makes clear that audiences are not "outside" the play, a fact that the material practices of performance art help to underscore. However, this claim to "intra-action" between play and audience obtains even for readers of the play, as Troyano's material/discursive deconstruction of hegemonic binaries extends beyond the scene of performance to supposedly private scenes of reading.

The spatial organization of *Chicas 2000* vividly illustrates the mutual permeability that Alaimo and others attribute to our shared world—and that bely efforts to enforce rigid hierarchies through borders, ghettoes, and prisons. The ironically named "Free Zone," which anticipates the "pleeblands" in Atwood's *MaddAddam* trilogy (discussed in the next chapter), is a dystopian nightmare of pollution, radiation, and plastic where "chusmas" and other castoffs are consigned to live, while those residing in pockets of wealth and security pretend they are untouched by material and cultural contaminants. Officially, the borders between legitimate and illegitimate spaces are impermeable; a plastic curtain and warning signs are meant to isolate the Free Zone, and Carmelita and her clones need legal papers to escape it. In reality, these boundaries are phantasmagorical, as pollution (including acid rain and nuclear waste) and living beings (human, transhuman, more-than-human) find their way across and around them. In the world of *Chicas 2000*, "what is outside is always already inside," whether we are talking about environmental or genetic exchange (Alaimo, *Exposed* 21).

Chicas 2000 also challenges the various dualisms (human/animal, human/nature, human/machine, human/thing) that deny "intra-action" and "trans-corporeality" and that underwrite systems of subordination made visible, if not impenetrable, through regimes of spatial segregation. This challenge is clearest in the treatment of the "humani," or human-animal hybrids, who constitute a transspecies subclass even more abject, in the world of the play, than queer women of color. "A woman can be with another woman and that's okay," laments Rodesia, Carmelita's oso-woman lover, "but a chusma woman like you and a woman-oso humani like me, we couldn't hold hands together or kiss in public. You know how many humani epithets we'd get" (97). In *Chicas 2000*, lesbians have gained a measure of acceptance, but newly produced abject subjectivities, like "chusma woman" and "woman-oso," are seen as discontinuous with the category "woman," on which "acceptable" lesbian subjectivities are based. While "chusma woman" seems to disqualify Carmelita from womanhood on the basis of ethnicity, and "woman-oso" seems to disqualify Rodesia on the basis of species, ethnicity and species are, in fact, at work in both terms: "oso," the Spanish word for "bear," signals Rodesia's ethnic otherness alongside her species otherness, and the parallel between "chusma woman" and "woman-oso" (more commonly presented as "oso-woman," in the play) implies that the logic of species difference is also levied against Carmelita. Troyano thus illustrates how the human/animal dualism underwrites a perpetual expansion of the category of "human" through the continuous production of new "others." As Troyano has said, "Maybe in the future, Latinos won't be the ones discriminated against; maybe that concept won't exist. However, there will be other concepts, classifications like transspecies, who may be subject to discrimination" (qtd. in McHugh). Transgenic technology does not manufacture abject subjectivities; it is a tool levied in this ongoing process of violence.

Although terms like "oso-woman" and "chusma" are intertwined with the systems that oppress Rodesia and Carmelita, they are also vulnerable to resignification, suggesting the possibility that the social structures they are part of could be reimagined too. Rodesia's inversion of the term "oso-woman" (to "woman-oso") illustrates both possibilities by suggesting several contradictory meanings at once: (1) that "woman" is an adjective modifying "oso," making "oso"—the nonhuman part of her subjectivity—the operative term, thus drawing attention to her species difference; (2) that "oso" is a modifier for "woman," using Spanish grammar rules that place the adjective after the noun, suggesting that Rodesia is, in fact, resisting her exclusion from the category "woman"; (3) that both "halves" of the term are of equal importance, if we see the hyphen as a fulcrum for nouns of equal weight; and, most intriguingly, (4) that the hyphen makes "woman-oso" a two-word adjective for an unnamed noun—a subjectivity not yet uttered. Rodesia's linguistic *inversion* (a term that itself recalls older regimes of sexual oppression that are partly continuous with the play's present) draws attention to the potential flexibility of exclusionary language—to "discursive practices" as "material (re)configurations of the world," to borrow Barad's language, that can be both oppressive and liberatory.

Ultimately, Carmelita articulates a material reconfiguration of the family, inviting Clana, Cluna, and Rodesia into (nonheteronormative, transhuman) kinship: "With me you'll inherit the wind," she says, "but we can be family" (120). Carmelita's use of the phrase "inherit the wind" does double duty here. The biblical source is Proverbs 11 ("He that troubles his own house shall inherit the wind"), and Carmelita is most certainly troubling her own house, if we take that phrase to allude to patriarchal structures of inheritance and the categories of race, gender, nationality, and species they imply. Many audience members may be more familiar with *Inherit the Wind* as the title of a 1955 play by Jerome Lawrence and Robert E. Lee (and its 1960 film adaptation) based on the 1925 Scopes "Monkey" case, in which a public school teacher was tried for teaching evolution. Recalling the dramatic upending of traditional notions of family, inheritance, and time effected by the advent of the theory of evolution, Troyano's doubled allusion makes clear the radical intervention her claim to transspecies queer kinship makes.

If Carmelita's kinship connection to Rodesia serves to remind audiences of the tenuousness of human species exceptionalism, Troyano's challenge to the human/object (person/thing) binary emerges most clearly in the play's treatment of clones.[36] The ongoing debate between Carmelita and Dr. Igor over "possession" of Clana and Cluna is characterized by a thoroughgoing slippage among humanness, livingness, and thingness. Dr. Igor asserts his claim to the clones through the language of patrilineage, inheritance,

---

36. Cluna and Clana also recall the monstrous images of cells living outside their proper somatic boundaries that haunt genetic discourse. One need only think of the "immortal" HeLa cells that "contaminated" laboratories around the world; French biologist Alexis Carrel's so-called "immortal" chicken heart cells, which drew significant public attention in the first half of the twentieth century (Landecker 16); or the genetically engineered "chickie nobs" produced for human consumption in Atwood's *MaddAddam* trilogy (*Oryx* 202).

citizenship, and imperialism: "I am your papa, the man who cloned you," he asserts; "I built this casino for you. You will have papers, and more. My empire is yours" (119). Conflating paternity and genetic replication, Dr. Igor claims the authority to confer (or withhold) subjectivity for all things (living or otherwise) within his realm. Although he has contributed neither genetic material nor parental care to Cluna and Clana, he declares himself *father* and erases Carmelita from the reproductive equation. In so doing, he replicates the claim made by biotech companies that scientific innovation, rather than biological origin, confers ownership of biological material and evokes conflicts over parentage that have emerged when women of color serve as surrogates for white families.

Initially, Carmelita challenges Dr. Igor by asserting the living status of the clones and, thereby, their autonomy. "Babies are not possessions, like objects, they're alive," exclaims Carmelita, implying that living status countermands claims of ownership. Her statement, however, does not hold up to scrutiny, given the status of pets and plants and (even) children—not to mention the history of enslavement. Aliveness does not protect one against ownership, nor does object status necessitate possession. Complicating her argument further, Carmelita upholds the clones' thingness when she insists that "they belong to me" (81). That the clones are sometimes represented by human actors and, at other times, by Barbie dolls underscores the permeable border between subject and object that women of color, in particular, have found themselves on the wrong side of for centuries. Troyano invites us, specifically, to see debates over the legal status of the clones as analogous to debates over the legal status of immigrants. Not sanctioned by the state, Clana and Cluna evoke the illicit status of undocumented immigrants and are similarly branded "illegals," a grammatical mutation that, transforming an adjective into a noun, literalizes their abject/object status.[37]

At the same time, symbols of objecthood are deployed, in *Chicas 2000*, to suggest changeability, flexibility, possibility. This subversion of expectations is clearest in the motif of plastic, which is both a ubiquitous presence in the Free Zone ("Nothing but styrofoam and plastic" [105]) and the substance used to cordon off this abject space, in the form of a "curtain made of neon-orange plastic mesh" (100). Those consigned to the Free Zone are also compared to plastic, thrown away like so much "sandwich wrap" (105). Despite all this, the meaning of plastic is never simple abjection/objectification in the play. The permeability of the Free Zone's plastic border suggests unfixed meaning, and the dress that Carmelita fashions out of discarded plastic is

---

37. *Chicas 2000* aligns with Clayton's observation that literary treatment of clones is often "sympathetic," drawing analogies to "marginalized groups in current society" (*Literature* 184).

evidence that detritus can be recycled and, even, transformed into art. In other words, plastic in *Chicas 2000* is *plastic*—malleable and full of potential. Perhaps this is why Carmelita "loves plastic," at least according to Dr. Igor, who brings her "plastic roses" (75) and is drawn to what he views, through a stereotyping lens, as her "world full of color, plastic, grease" (79). Dr. Igor loves plastic too, because he wishes to mold it into objects for his personal pleasure; however, like grease, plastic is slippery and evades his grasp—literally, in fact, when the Barbie-doll clones fly out of his hands, just before Carmelita shoots him (82). "We like to pick terms with multiple meanings," Troyano has said of "plastic," in particular; in this case, the properties of the term's referent underscore its semantic multiplicity (qtd. in McHugh).[38]

Resignifying the markers of object status also implies a challenge to objectivity itself, to the clean line drawn between research subject and scientific process. Although Clana and Cluna are produced in a laboratory and viewed as artificial (and thus as objects, rather than subjects), their *plasticity* overrides this limiting origin story. Indeed, the play consistently contaminates the sterile laboratory space with the earthiness of the body. For example, Carmelita and her clones repeat the phrase "like staring at my reflection in a toilet bowl full of clean water" to describe the uncanny experience of seeing themselves in one another's faces (102, 118). While DNA tests are often performed on samples taken from human mouths, a site that evokes communication (a privileged term in genetic discourse), this phrase reminds audiences that the source material for the clones is Carmelita's buttocks, a body part that connotes waste, taboo sexuality, and sexual objectification. The mouth, too, remains stubbornly resistant to disembodiment in the play. The repeated figure of the "tongue," referring to both language and body, is a subtle reminder that DNA is physical; efforts to abstract it to bloodless, fleshless code or transform it into fungible tissue are interrupted by Troyano's resistant, impertinent, invasive tongue.[39] In several scenes, an untamed tongue interrupts the enactment of genetic and racial discipline (including moments marked "ad lib" in the stage directions), as when Carmelita's orgasmic scream hits the exact frequency needed to unlock the doors of the prison where she is being held. In *Chicas 2000*, Carmelita is, as she claims at the beginning of the film *Carmelita Tropicana: Your Kunst Is Your Waffen* (1994), "good with the tongue":

---

38. Troyano points out another meaning: "In Spanish when we say '*no seas plástica*,' we mean don't be vapid, don't be a surface person" (qtd. in McHugh).

39. The tongue thus becomes a figure that can "hold off living processes from complete subsumption into raw material, because [its] signification cannot be fully processed by capitalism's metaphorical and machine infrastructure" (Choksey 8–9).

> I am Carmelita Tropicana. I say Loisaida is the place to be. It is multicultural, multinational, multigenerational, mucho multi. And like myself, you've got to be multilingual. I am very good with the tongue. As a matter of fact the first language I pick up when I come to New York is Jewish. I learn from my girlfriend Charo, she's Jewish. She teach me and I write poem for her in Jewish. I recite for you today. Title of the poem is "Oy Vey Number One." "Oy vey, I schlep and shlep, I hurt my tuchus today, I feel—meshuggener, oy vey." (Troyano, *Carmelita* 137)

Tropicana's celebration of multiplicity ("mucho multi") crosses boundaries of culture, religion, sexuality, nation, generation, and language.[40] Although the performance includes "errors" (e.g., English grammar mistakes, misnaming Yiddish as "Jewish"), Carmelita is pleased to show off her linguistic flexibility, as she mixes English, Yiddish, and Spanglish ("Loisaida" for "Lower East Side") and engages in double entendre, using the phrase "good with the tongue" to suggest both linguistic and (queer) sexual virtuosity. The ability of the same word or phrase to mean two different things is also inverted, in the script, in an example of the same meaning being represented by two different spellings of a word: "schlep" and "shlep." This textual duality, reminiscent of Derrida's *différance*, subtly associates the undecidability of language with the body, suggesting, in Judith Butler's words, "the way in which a speaking body signifies in ways that are not reducible to what such a body 'says'" (Butler 10).[41] "S[c]hlep," referring to the act of hauling or carrying something heavy, and "tuchus," referring (once again) to the buttocks, draw our attention to the body—its burdens and its pleasures. It is a loving, laboring body that speaks; the same tongue forms words and kisses lips.[42]

Carmelita's claim that she is good with the tongue also evokes longstanding Latina resistance to what Gloria Anzaldúa calls "linguistic terrorism." Anzaldúa's aptly titled "How to Tame a Wild Tongue" recounts the multifaceted operations of this form of cultural violence, which ranges from overt discipline to internalized oppression. The elocution classes Carmelita is forced to attend in the Behavior Modification Unit are not an innovation; they constitute a mundane punitive technique that has been used against Latine people for generations.[43] Playfully turning the tables on her

---

40. "For Troyano, that 'multi' is language itself, but it is a language that is always imprecise, especially when working between national cultures, political frameworks, or sexual orientations" (Noriega ix).

41. Butler explains that the "the speech act, as the act of a speaking body, is always to some extent unknowing about what it performs" (10).

42. "Lips" is also intended to do double duty here.

43. "At Pan American University," Anzaldúa recalls, "I, and all Chicano students were required to take two speech classes. Their purpose: to get rid of our accents" (76).

linguistic oppressors, Carmelita uses her unbridled tongue to celebrate the Latine "penetration" of US culture: "There is penetration through the ear with the music, through the mouth with the food, through the tongue with the tongue. Una penetración total," she exclaims (75). The tongue-in-cheek tone of Carmelita's demographic forecast cleverly materializes in the repeated figure of the penetrating tongue; indeed, Carmelita's tongue is in *America's* cheek when it penetrates "the mouth"—that is, as Latine culture (food, music, language) enters various "American" orifices. Surprisingly, the Latine tongue can even penetrate another tongue ("penetration . . . through the tongue with the tongue"), a paradoxical act that leads to "total penetration." When Troyano shifts to Spanish ("Una penetración total"), the Spanish "tongue" literally enters the English "tongue" of the play. One cannot miss the carnal overtones of Carmelita's prophecy: the term "penetration" evokes sexual intercourse and, with it, white anxieties about the rate of Latine reproduction. The tongue that penetrates another tongue also subtly queers the feared loss of racial purity, activating nationalism in its homophobic register. Tropicana's penetrating tongue (a phrase that also suggests an ability to probe complex situations and reveal truths) illuminates connections among xenophobia, racism, and heterosexism in white anxieties about the future, while enunciating (annunciating, perhaps) an incarnate Latine presence in the US body politic.

One particularly inventive example of Carmelita's "untamed tongue" occurs when Dr. Igor tries to tell her about his cloning plan by alluding to Dolly the sheep, famously cloned in 1996. The scene begins with Dr. Igor making sexual advances toward Carmelita, whose attempts to rebuff him are unsuccessful. When she calls him "coño" ("cunt"), he resignifies the insult in terms of his own prurient obsession with chusmería: "Coño, what a sweet word, music to my ears. A real chusma" (78). In turn, when Dr. Igor responds to Carmelita's unambiguous rejection with "Oh poppycock!" it is her turn to turn his words around: "I say no cock, papi." Dr. Igor has technologies at his disposal that will allow him to "have [her] one way or another" (79), but Carmelita's untamed tongue disrupts his attempts at what she aptly describes as a "nonconsexual act" (an act—i.e., cloning—that lacks both consent and sex itself; 80):

DR. IGOR: I'll give you un clue. Hello Dolly.
CARMELITA: Hello, Dolly, it's so nice to have . . .
DR. IGOR: No. Dolly . . .
CARMELITA: Parton.
DR. IGOR: No. Dolly . . .
CARMELITA: Lama. (79–80; original ellipses)

In this exchange, Dr. Igor's faith in his ability to reproduce an exact copy of Carmelita is undercut not only by the tendency of a word to point to multiple referents but also by a speaking body that repeatedly resists his advances, sexual, genetic, and linguistic.[44] The specific alternative referents for *Dolly* (the sheep) are revealing: Dolly Parton and the Dalai Lama would seem to occupy opposite ends of a chusmería spectrum, suggesting that, despite his best efforts, Dr. Igor might not get exactly what he hopes to get out of his clones. The wordplay throughout this exchange deploys the instability of language against the reproducibility implied by cloning, and puns, specifically, operate as a code that jams Dr. Igor's genetic technologies.[45] These linguistic interventions are examples of "transformative material/discursive practices" that resist the reproduction of the current power structure and make space for new relational possibilities (Alaimo, *Bodily* 142).

Finally, *Chicas 2000* illuminates the fact that audiences, fully embedded in the trans-corporeal vision of the play, are themselves part of a network of "transformative material/discursive practices" that can intervene in existing discursive and material orders. After Carmelita invites Clana and Cluna to join her nonnormative family, the clones repeat their earlier pronouncements ("You're my bio" and "Our bio"), shifting to a collective sensibility that Carmelita articulates more fully in the monologue that follows: "Look at us, we are all in the soup together. All complicit in this Chusmatic Casino. You, Igor, for pitting chusma against chusma, we chusmas for fighting one another, and you ladies and gentlemen for coming here to watch chusmas degrade themselves before your very eyes" (120). Troyano articulates here an ethics of mutual responsibility that includes her audience, who are suddenly playing a role within the play. No longer just viewers of *Chicas 2000*, the audience is identified as viewers of, and even participants in, the battle royal taking place not only in the Chusmatic Casino but also, symbolically, in the larger social contexts in which they live. Carmelita's shifting pronouns ("we," "you [singular]" "we," "you [plural]") chart her movement past the logics of individualism and ownership toward a web of relatedness that extends to those watching the play.

Troyano's engagement of audience agency is supported by the practices and investments of performance art, which, as many scholars have argued, draw attention to the embodied, active presence of both performers and

---

44. On cloning and the failure to produce exact copies, see Hanson's analysis of Eva Hoffman's *The Secret* (2000) and Kazuo Ishiguro's *Never Let Me Go* (2005; 118–46), as well as Clayton's discussion of the film *The Boys from Brazil* (1978; *Literature* 182–83).

45. McHugh has described Troyano's use of puns as a kind of "verbal cloning."

audiences.[46] Performance "artists 'become'/em*body* their texts, circumventing—at least in part—the limitations of language" (Danielson 121), and performance art requires audience participation, making impossible the displacement of ethnicity, for example, to the "there" of stage or screen (Worthen 282).[47] It is in the "civic space" of performance art that new ways of relating to one another can be negotiated, an achievement that, in artist and writer Coco Fusco's view, "conventional aesthetic languages" simply cannot reproduce (10). As Troyano herself has said, "Performance art changes the way you look at the world. Your perceptions are changed; an object is no longer what it seems" ("Performance" 177). In other words, the themes of "intra-action" and "trans-corporeality" represented in the play also characterize the play in its material performance, in the dynamic relation between performers and audience.

It is almost certainly the case that performance draws direct attention to the embodiment of both performer and audience in ways that written texts simply do not, and that its explicit wedding of the material and the discursive is especially well suited to the kind of trans-corporeal intervention I am claiming for *Chicas 2000*. But just as explicitly metatextual works ultimately draw attention to the self-reflexivity of all texts, we might say that performance art draws our attention to the embodiment of all audiences, including readers. This is perhaps especially the case in works that, like *Chicas 2000*, emphasize language and body in equal measure—and challenge the distinction between them. Audiences are always engaged in "material-discursive practices," whether they are watching a performance in a theater, reading a script on the bus, or participating in any number of other configurations of text and audience. Part of what it means to read trans-corporeally is to acknowledge that scenes of reading are crucial "interfaces" and "interchanges" of "intra-active becoming," as readers and texts act in and through one another and come into being—and meaning—within broader material/discursive networks, including the channels (physical and ideological) through which texts are written, published, produced, disseminated, taught, and discussed.

Importantly, "material-semiotic agency" is distributed broadly (if unevenly) along these networks, concentrating in subjects and objects that

---

46. Troyano's work was developed in the queer, feminist, collaborative environment of New York's WOW Café Theater, where performers saw each other as their primary audience, rather than creating work for "collector[s]" (López-Craig 49), and where "anarchic" feminist expression was celebrated and "lesbianism [was] a *given*, rather than an issue to be addressed" (Davy 8).

47. Also see Hall 116.

might not be typically accorded the status of "author" or "reader." Alaimo notes, for example, that Donna Haraway's theorization of "companion species" includes a characterization of nonhuman primates as "authors"—as subjects with material-semiotic agency (Alaimo, *Bodily* 144). A trans-corporeal theory of reading recognizes material-semiotic agency in authors, readers, texts, textual subjects, and reading sites; it also asserts that reading is never singular and is always performed within contexts structured by privilege and exclusion. It both illuminates the intersubjective relations within which we read and has the potential to reorganize those relations, prompting multidirectional reverberations. This is so even when those reverberations are not immediately visible. Consider, for example, Alaimo's observation that humans are already affecting life in the deep sea, even though direct observation of these spaces is impossible (*Exposed* 161). To read trans-corporeally is to remain aware of such reverberations, even when one sits alone in a room, book in hand.

When, at the end of *Chicas 2000*, Carmelita crawls through Cluna and Clana's legs to sing "This is my life" once more, the audience is reminded of an earlier scene when Desiree, another prisoner at the Behavioral Modification Unit, lies on her back and imitates the hands of a clock with her legs. The stage directions explain:

> Desiree's back is on the table and when she lifts her legs a sign with the number 12 drops down on and hangs above them. Desiree's legs simulate the hands of a clock, her shoes have arrows painted on the soles. Her legs move clockwise as music comes on. Carmelita dances and tries to stop her legs from keeping time, making them go counterclockwise. (93)

"Reloj" ("Clock"), a Latin standard, plays, and Carmelita translates the song into English, while she tries to "stop time" by stopping Desiree's legs: "Oh, clock don't mark the hours, or I'll go crazy. She will leave me forever when the morning comes and we only have tonight to live our love" (94). These lyrics are nearly literal for Carmelita: her lover Rodesia will soon be transferred to "intensive rehab," having proven herself to be unmodifiable, leaving Carmelita alone in prison. Carmelita's desire to stop the clock, however, is in conflict with Desiree's desire to speed up time so she can reach the end of her sentence sooner. Desiree becomes the embodiment of time itself, her name underscoring the shared desire that has paradoxically placed her and Carmelita in temporal conflict.

One way to read Carmelita's desperate attempt to stop the "legs" of Desiree's clock is as an exhortation to stop time and look at what is happening *right now*. Indeed, Troyano has articulated the goal of *Chicas 2000* as explicitly presentist: "*Chicas* aims at a class and ethnic critique and what it means to be a person of color in 1997. . . . I was trying to make an Anglo audience reflect on the term [*chusma*] and their perception of Latinos. I was referencing race and class and what was happening in New York City's Lower East Side with gentrification" (qtd. in McHugh). This is precisely the remit of the usable future: to use the techniques of future speculation to intervene directly in the present moment. But there's a deeper layer to this work as well, a gesture toward queer, interspecies intersubjectivity—toward synchronic intimacy. One woman flat on her back, legs splayed in the air, the other clinging to those legs and sobbing, both wishing for liberation, both trapped in an oppressive timeline. With this affecting and absurd tableau, Troyano provides a vivid picture of the multiple temporalities working in us at once: here, time is linear and yet circular, propelling us forward and yet returning us again and again to the same moments, promising freedom as well as imprisonment. Desiree's open legs suggest childbirth and, thus, vertical relatedness and generational time, while Rodesia (asleep and snoring in a nearby chair) evokes the possibility of synchronic connection across species lines as well as the diachronic workings of evolution that have produced the very speciation Troyano disrupts and queers. Speaking, singing, sobbing, snoring, and splayed, the bodies on stage and page draw attention to the experience of time as complex, embodied, intimate, and interspecies. In other words, Troyano's deployment of the usable future points our attention not only to the present moment, and its continuation of longstanding social ills, but also to our experience of time itself. By asking us to look anew at our shared *now*, *Chicas 2000* also asks us to see our connections to one another, as well as to those who have come before us, those who are still to come, and the earth we share.

CHAPTER 6

The Humanities and the Inhumanities
Rereading Discipline and Species in Margaret Atwood's *MaddAddam* Trilogy

Margaret Atwood's popular *MaddAddam* trilogy, comprising *Oryx and Crake* (2003), *The Year of the Flood* (2009), and *MaddAddam* (2013), hinges on a familiar apocalyptic trope: in a future world, genome science has run amok, leading to myriad abominations—everything from genetically engineered chicken flesh to pigs with human neocortex tissue. In this world, the phrase "Scales and Tales," the name of a prostitution business where women wear semi-permanent animal costumes, serves as shorthand for increasingly blurry species boundaries.[1] More terrifying than transgenic experiments themselves are the actions of the companies that undertake them, including a devious business model that involves selling pharmaceutical products that both cause and cure disease. Eventually, a mad scientist called "Crake" exploits existing pharmaceutical disease vectors to cause a global pandemic, wiping out the vast majority of humans. Crake has also created a species to take their place; his "Crakers" resemble humans but are designed to lack several characteristics that Crake links to war and environmental destruction, including sexual competition, religious belief, artistic expression, carnivorousness, and, tellingly, literacy.

---

1. In the opening passage of *Oryx and Crake*, the main character's use of this phrase suggests a difficulty in maintaining human distinctiveness.

Crake's effort to supplant humans with a superior transhuman species is motivated, at least in part, by an accurate perception of the preapocalyptic world as already dystopian. Incidents of climate chaos are frequent, the political system is corrupted by corporate interests, and dramatic wealth differentials are the norm. In North America, where most of the series takes place, the "haves" live within corporate "Compounds" with top-tier education, health care, and other amenities—as well as militarized security, constant surveillance, and extreme restrictions on mobility. The reach of the private military/police force known as the Corporate Security Corps (the shorthand for which—"CorpSeCorps"—makes visible their necropolitical function) extends beyond Compound walls to the "pleeblands," which, recalling Troyano's "Free Zone," are suffused with violence and poverty.[2] Narrative glimpses outside North America reveal global systems of exploitation, including human trafficking, forced labor, and unsustainable agriculture. Although the series does not endorse his genocidal actions, Atwood makes clear that Crake is not wrong in assessing the status quo as apocalyptic in its own right.[3]

In other words, like Troyano's *Chicas 2000*, the subject of the previous chapter, the *MaddAddam* trilogy also articulates a "usable future" designed to draw attention to the dystopian elements of the present. The "preapocalyptic" segments of the *MaddAddam* trilogy actually take place *in medias apocalypsis*—in the midst of multiple and ongoing apocalypses, including the "slow violence"[4] of climate change and environmental destruction and the routine slaughter of populations based on race and religion. Despite these phenomena, regularly broadcast via the internet, the occupants of privileged spaces do not recognize their world as dystopian. Yes, "everyone's parents moaned on about" changes that have taken place in their lifetime: *"Remember when you could drive anywhere? Remember when everyone lived in the pleeblands? . . . Remember when voting mattered?"* (63). But this perspective obscures the fact that "before" was also characterized by restricted freedom, class- and race-based segregation, voter suppression, and environmental ruin. Taking "apocalypse" to mean "to uncover" is especially apt in relation to the *MaddAddam* trilogy, as Atwood works to reveal the widespread exploitation that underwrites the daily lives of the global elite. Apocalypse isn't apocalypse until it comes to your front door, Atwood tells us, and this

---

2. Appleton describes the government as a "Corp(Se)ocracy," a neologism that suggests corporate rule infused with necroeconomics (64).

3. Also see Canavan 141, 152; Ciobanu 153.

4. See Nixon.

myopia—a problem both within and outside the texts—is what her trilogy seeks to correct.[5]

Atwood's intervention is literary and, therefore, perhaps already doomed. In *Oryx and Crake,* the first novel in the series, one of the signs that the End Times precede Crake's engineered pandemic is the radical devaluation of the arts and humanities, a phenomenon already underway in the extradiegetic world.[6] From childhood, Jimmy, the novel's protagonist, is made to feel inferior for being a "word [person]" rather than a "numbers person" (25). He grows up in a biotech compound, surrounded by STEM geniuses—chief among them Crake (then known as Glenn), with whom he carries on a lifelong debate about the value of art. (Jimmy: "When any civilization is dust and ashes . . . art is all that's left over. Images, words, music. Imaginative structures. Meaning—human meaning, that is—is defined by them" [167]. Glenn: Art is "an empty drainpipe. An amplifier. A stab at getting laid" [168].) Jimmy attends a dilapidated, underfunded, and low-ranked arts college that emphasizes skills and employability. His subsequent advertising career culminates, ignominiously, in his naïve promotion of the drug that brings about the end of the world. Depicting a society in which the most grotesque forms of "entertainment" (public executions, child pornography, violent video games) have overtaken more refined and humane endeavors, Atwood dares us—her literate, literary readers—to thank Crake, just a little, for wiping us from the face of the earth. In other words, she draws to the surface what is buried within every reader: the cruel, the genocidal, the inhuman—what scholar and novelist Viet Thanh Nguyen calls "the heart of darkness [that] beats within" (19).

In *Nothing Ever Dies: Vietnam and the Memory of War* (2016), Nguyen argues that the term "inhumanities" is a more accurate and responsible name for the unwieldy field usually called the "humanities," drawing attention to its legacies of colonialism, racism, sexism, and speciesism. Nguyen writes,

---

5. Atwood has explained that *The Handmaid's Tale* is very much grounded in the real ("What"). An epigraph to *Oryx and Crake* taken from Jonathan Swift's *Gulliver's Travels* makes this same point for the *MaddAddam* trilogy: "I could perhaps like others have astonished you with strange improbable tales; but I rather chose to relate plain matter of fact in the simplest manner and style; because my principal design was to inform you, and not to amuse you." It is not just residents of the Compounds who need to wake up to the world around them, it is also Atwood's readers, who are prompted to recognize that her subject is "our mad world, gone even madder" (Canavan 140). Also see Clayton's discussion of how Atwood's trilogy informs contemporary ethical and policy debates (*Literature* 173–81).

6. Watkins identifies this theme as central to several works of apocalyptic fiction by contemporary women writers (131).

"Any project of the humanities . . . should . . . also be a project of the inhumanities, of how civilizations are built on forgotten barbarism toward others" (19). Nguyen zeroes in on the slippage between the "humanities" and "humanism" and rejects the perpetual expansion of the category "human" to gradually encompass the formerly "othered"—a process premised on the exclusion of still *other* others.[7] He calls for humanities scholars to recognize the negations and disavowals that define the "human" against its "others," to see the "inhuman" that is enclosed within the "human," despite having been erased orthographically.[8] Sensitive to the way that humanities scholarship can subtly, or overtly, shore up exclusionary and idealized definitions of the "human," Nguyen calls for "projects of the inhumanities" that acknowledge human beings in their full moral complexity, a stance he associates with an "ethics of recognition." Without such an ethics, he argues, we will continue to wage war in the name of "good" selves against "bad" others.

Although Nguyen does not address nonhuman animals or more-than-human life in his explication of the "inhuman," any discussion of the "human" and the "humanities" necessarily calls up these categories. After all, those "others" who have only recently (and often precariously) been welcomed under the human umbrella—women, racialized groups, people with disabilities, queer people, children—were previously defined as more animal than human. Maintaining the human/nonhuman binary justifies all manner of abuses against human *and* more-than-human life. "As long as it is institutionally taken for granted that it is all right to systematically exploit and kill nonhuman animals simply because of their species," writes Cary Wolfe, "then the humanist discourse of species will always be available for use by some humans against other humans as well" (*Animal* 8). Recent scientific research has challenged the justifications for human exceptionalism, including the claim that language sets humans apart from all other life (1–2). While such rationales for rethinking the human/nonhuman boundary rely on scientific authority, an ideological and ethical revolution requires awareness of the limits of human knowledge and what Wolfe describes as "our readiness to be vulnerable to other knowledges in our embodiment of our own, an embodiment that arrives at the site of the other before we do, as our scent reaches the dog's nose before we round the corner" (5). This vulnerability is not about flipping the script, rendering the human now other to the nonhuman animal. Rather, it is about what Donna Haraway describes as transspecies "encounters" (*When* 4): "the fleshly historical

---

7. Also see Wolfe, "Human" 568.
8. For a distinct discussion of the term "inhuman," see Wolfe, *Animal* 11, 54–62.

reality of face-to-face, body-to-body subject making across species" (66). Importantly, such critiques of the human/nonhuman divide—enunciated from the interdisciplinary fields of animal studies, environmental humanities, and science and technology studies—are also critiques of the humanities/science divide. They approach the relationship between these fields as a rich, mutual encounter that involves "thinking being," rather than reifying "human being." As Wolfe puts it, "the 'human' . . . is not now, and never was, itself" (*Animal* 9). Neither, it seems, were the humanities.

In this final chapter, I submit Atwood's *MaddAddam* trilogy as a "project of the inhumanities" for the postgenomic age, one that richly contributes to our understanding of both discipline and species. In this series, Atwood imagines a postanthropocentric world in which the extinction of humans and the extinction of the humanities go hand in hand. Given the role transgenic science plays in both fictional catastrophes, readers would be forgiven for reading the series as a straightforward denunciation of genetic engineering and lament for the humanities. Those familiar with Atwood's oeuvre, however, will not be surprised to find it is neither.[9] The primary object of Atwood's critique is not genetic engineering per se but global capitalism, which objectifies all life and transforms the sciences and the humanities alike into tools that serve its inhumane ends. Atwood's series is not a cautionary tale aimed at forestalling a transgenic dystopia via the healing powers of the humanities; rather, it is an illumination of the capitalist dystopia in which we already live, a dystopia that depends upon maintaining, rather than disrupting, the human/nonhuman boundary. Rather than reinforcing the naïve view that the arts and humanities, in contradistinction to technoscience, train us to be more human, the *MaddAddam* series draws our attention to the arts and humanities as crucial sites of both oppression and liberation. Foregrounding the "inhuman" within the human, as Nguyen advises, Atwood articulates an "ethics of recognition" that extends to the more-than-human world, challenging—rather than simply moving—the human/nonhuman boundary and complicating the science/humanities binary along the way.

Interdisciplinary Inquiry in the Postgenomic Age

The anticapitalist challenge to the false science/humanities binary that Atwood stages through the *MaddAddam* trilogy has deeply informed the

---

9. "The *MaddAddam* trilogy attends simultaneously to the genome's biological reality and its metaphorical significance, demonstrating why we can afford neither an overcautious Luddism nor an insufficiently suspicious technophilia" (Hamner 28).

interdisciplinary impulses of this book. In each of the previous chapters, I have explored how genomic and postgenomic narratives engage ethical concerns that straddle the sciences and the humanities, biology and literature. These are works that, in investigating the ethical implications of tissue sampling, genetic testing, and the commodification of genes and genetic technologies, cannot help but draw attention to questions of power and privilege in the field of literature itself. What I describe as the double resonance of genomic discourse winds contemporary biology and literature around each other in a double helical structure whose "base pairs" are linked metaphor. This discursive intimacy supports—perhaps even demands—attention to complementary ethical considerations, which the texts in question raise through a variety of narrative strategies and, sometimes, accidents. These works overlay questions of biomedical ethics with questions of narrative ethics, and in presenting these questions as necessarily intertwined, they also challenge the disciplinary line that separates science, medicine, and technology from the arts and humanities. While this critique is evident throughout the archive of postgenomic literature, it is perhaps most explicit in Atwood's work, which commits our current articulation of the science/humanities binary, and the economic and political forces undergirding it, directly to the page.

Like any good binary, science/humanities is also a hierarchy, although not a straightforward one. In the postgenomic age, as Atwood herself makes abundantly clear, science—molecular biology, in particular—retains a complicated authority to comment on a wide variety of cultural, social, and political phenomena, even if its reign in biology has been challenged by the postgenomic turn. This may seem odd in an era of widespread distrust of scientific expertise, a phenomenon blatantly on display in discussions of climate change, vaccines, and the COVID-19 pandemic.[10] The explanation for continuing faith in genetics is not so much that the general public trusts the expertise of molecular biologists but that condensed and oversimplified ideas about "genes" and "DNA"—at odds with scientific consensus—carry their own weight and authority. One need only look as far as their currency in the lexicon of contemporary business ("it's in our DNA!" is an advertising cliché) to see how far genomic discourse has strayed into general discourse.

Molecular biology has ascended not only in the popular imagination but also in the academy, where it has reigned in the life sciences since the middle of the last century. Its prominence has been enhanced more recently by the

---

10. On the political and historical forces that have contributed to widespread distrust of science, see Green.

dramatic migration of STEM fields to the center of the academic enterprise, both ideologically and structurally, while the arts and humanities—once considered the academy's heart and soul—have found themselves marginalized. Today's corporate university relies increasingly on tuition, private funding, and corporate partnerships (often for STEM research); funnels money into student services and amenities at the expense of academic instruction; and increases its share of both full-time administrators and vulnerable part-time faculty at the expense of full-time faculty positions. It's no accident that the main characters in two postgenomic novels discussed earlier in this book, Ruth Ozeki's *All Over Creation* and Richard Powers's *Generosity: An Enhancement*, are adjunct English instructors—exemplars of academic precarity. Furthermore, the economic recession that began in 2008 has contributed to a major change in the public understanding of higher education. Anxious, debt-ridden students who see a college degree primarily as a preprofessional qualification flock toward STEM majors, and universities—concerned with their own bottom line—adjust offerings accordingly.[11]

One response made by vulnerable humanities disciplines is to recast themselves as skills-based fields with real-world applications in corporate and STEM environments. Rather than defended as an end in themselves, or as a means of developing well-rounded citizens, the humanities are now frequently promoted for their cultivation of the "soft skills" that success in business requires.[12] More daringly, they are said to develop an ethical sensibility that is much needed in STEM enterprises, as well as business and finance. The field of narrative medicine specifically rests on the assumption that narrative "humanizes" a profession increasingly characterized by the objectification of patients (Peterkin 398). And, since the incorporation of the Ethical, Legal, and Social Implications (ELSI) program within the Human Genome Project in 1990, ethicists have been routinely hired to advise research teams, and social scientists have embedded themselves everywhere from biotech labs to informal genealogical communities.

These developments have been significant and salutary, if also uneven. (Notably, literary scholars rarely take part in interdisciplinary genomics research.)[13] Measurable effects of ELSI research include "novel approaches to community-based participatory research," new "policies related to the

---

11. On the economic and social forces underlying the decline of the humanities, see Schmidt. For data on which college majors are rising and falling, see "Most Popular Majors."

12. This refrain is repeated across the media (see Appelbaum; Deming; Gregoire; Harman; Matz; Waller) and on numerous English and humanities department websites.

13. See Wald and Clayton x.

use of genomic information in the clinic," and new legislation barring discrimination by health insurers on the basis of "genetic predisposition." ELSI scholars also acknowledge, however, the conflicts of interest that could result from embedding an ethics program within the very science funding organization it is meant to act as a check on (McEwen et al. 493); indeed, some critics have argued that ELSI has been a "handmaiden" to genome science, rather than a true ethical check (Zwart and Nelis 543). Expanding on these caveats, I would identify three risks in justifying the humanities through their potential contributions to STEM fields: (1) the suggestion that the arts and humanities are valuable to the degree that they can be instrumentalized for practical and commercial purposes, (2) the suggestion that the arts and humanities are naturally "ethical" or "humanizing," and (3) the suggestion that relations between the humanities and the sciences are unidirectional (i.e., the humanities are assumed to have something to offer the sciences, while the reverse is not acknowledged).

Recently, several scholars and writers have pushed back against what they see as the instrumentalization of the humanities in service of commercial goals. Philosopher Martha Nussbaum, for example, has argued that by minimizing and instrumentalizing the humanities, we endanger our ability to create and sustain democratic societies. And historian L. D. Burnett argues that we should stop defending the humanities on capitalist terms: "The value of the humanities . . . does not lie primarily in 'transferrable skills' nor in the 'critical thinking' that employers presumably want. Instead, a core education in the humanities gives students the intellectual space to grapple with questions of enduring importance" (119). These scholars rightly resist the subordination of the humanities to the "profit motive" of the modern corporate university (Nussbaum 7).

Other scholars have resisted the instrumentalization of the humanities within the fields of science and medicine, arguing that the opportunity for ethical or affective contemplation is diminished when humanities techniques are simply tacked on to scientific or medical research. Tod Chambers has argued, for example, that narrative is often presented as a "mere aid" to bioethics, rather than as a rich means of critiquing its "central philosophic features" (3), and Jeffrey Bishop claims that "medical humanism does not escape the Western metaphysics of efficiency" it is meant to challenge (16). Similarly, Susan Squier insists that narrative cannot humanize medicine if it is simply "applied" without disrupting traditional biomedical and literary "frames"; literary works should not be approached as "illustrations" of medical issues, she argues, but as sites of transformation for both fields (338). Miriam Solomon notes that medical narratives are often treated as "singular" and personal, thereby discouraging systemic political analysis (204); Rebecca Garden questions whether empathy, often cited as an effect of literary study, is a desirable or measurable outcome of narrative training; and Sayantani DasGupta has noted that the concept of "narrative competency" reinforces the drive to mastery that underwrites existing power dynamics in medical contexts.[14]

As these critiques make clear, mechanistic applications of the humanities to science or medicine buttress the sciences/humanities binary and ultimately mischaracterize both fields. Perhaps most surprising is the naïve characterization of the arts and humanities as naturally humanizing fields when scholars in these fields, for the last several decades at least, have critiqued the role the arts and literature—as well as humanist scholarship itself—have played in sustaining unjust social arrangements. Scholars working within the frameworks of postcolonial, poststructuralist, Marxist, feminist, antiracist, queer, and Indigenous studies have illuminated and critiqued literary, artistic, discursive, and intellectual traditions that support and reproduce systems of power.[15] It is no secret, within the humanities, that the systems of representation that are our bread and butter can be—often are—poisonous, laced with colonial, racist, heterosexist and neoliberal values. Humanities scholarship can both serve humanism's problematic ends *and* provide a means of critiquing it as an ideology of exclusion.

Instrumentalizing deployments of the humanities within science and medicine also risk implying that interdisciplinary exchange and transformation only flow in one direction: from the humanities to the sciences. As Bishop argues, when the humanities seek to demonstrate their value through empirical evidence (e.g., improved outcomes in patients whose doctors are trained in narrative competency), they implicitly support the hegemonic dominance of science and sidestep the actual promise of interdisciplinary exchange: a deeper understanding that both intellectual endeavors are intertwined ways of "thinking human being" (16). By "mechanical[ly]" introducing narrative into science or medicine as a supplement or remedy for the objectifying effects of clinical or research practices—by understanding "the narrative act" as a means of "invest[ing] the biological . . . with meaning"—we reinscribe the very body/soul divide that has enabled those

---

14. Also see my discussion of these concerns in chapter 2.
15. These scholars elicited a backlash evident in the "culture wars" of the 1980s and ongoing debates about the purpose of literary criticism. Recently, new practices, such as "surface reading," quantitative analysis, new formalisms, and new materialisms, have challenged reigning critical approaches, some taking aim at "symptomatic" or "committed" readings. See Menely and Taylor 10–12; Moya 1–6.

objectifying effects in the first place (Bishop 20). And we miss the potential for mutual illumination. Rita Charon argues, for example, that biological concepts, such as the cellular membrane, can be useful for reorienting us to reading and writing as embodied acts of "intersubjectivity" ("Novelization" 43). And Karen Barad's work has richly demonstrated how concepts from physics, such as entanglement, can prompt deep reconsideration of apparently straightforward concepts, such as "'humans' and 'nonhumans,' 'culture' and 'nature,' the 'social' and the 'scientific'" ("Posthumanist" 135). When the sciences and the humanities are presented as absolutely discrete (and, almost always, hierarchized), it impoverishes both fields, dismissing the "spirit of the humanities" in the sciences (Nussbaum 7), reducing the humanities to a supportive role, and obscuring the "inhuman" legacies of the humanities themselves.[16]

Indeed, our historical moment—the moment Atwood accelerates in her series, a moment defined by the legible and devastating impact of human beings on the earth—seems to require rich and mutual interdisciplinary exchange. Despite widespread debate about how to define the "Anthropocene," and where to draw its temporal boundary, there is agreement on this point: "Any definition of the Anthropocene identifies a point of entanglement between the Earth system and social systems," a point where human activity alters our climate and inscribes itself deep in rock and earth. The "implications" of this sociogeological fact "productively unsettle conventional disciplinary modes of inquiry," leading scholars in various disciplines to rethink received practices and norms (Menely and Taylor 3). Turning their attention to literary scholarship, Tobias Menely and Jesse Oak Taylor, the editors of the volume *Anthropocene Reading* (2017), articulate a project that is in some ways parallel to my own; like genomics and postgenomics, "The Anthropocene provides an opportunity for literary studies to test and transform its methods" (5). "Anthropocene reading," as Menely and Taylor imagine it, is not a stable methodology but a "multiplicity of approaches" that have one key commonality: "a shared commitment to the interpretation of human and natural history in their double internality." The concept of the Anthropocene "establishes the conditions under which *all* reading must henceforth proceed" (13–14).

The *MaddAddam* trilogy makes it easy to see how Anthropocene reading might overlap with postgenomic reading; indeed, Atwood addresses

---

16. I do not take the naïve position that the sciences and humanities are ultimately indistinguishable; indeed, the value of their distinct approaches must be protected. Rather, I emphasize the spirit of inquiry they share and challenge their overly rigid separation and asymmetrical valuation according to the capitalist "profit motive" (Nussbaum 7).

the ethics of commercial bioengineering (as well as fossil fuel consumption) within broader questions about the impact of homo sapiens on the earth. And figures of reading, as well as literal scenes of reading, sprawl across the series, subtly alluding to the textual practices and metaphors of both genomics and stratigraphy and inviting contemplation of the embeddedness and agency of narrative in material contexts. If the postgenomic literary works I foreground in this volume train readers to resist the temptations and distortions of "gene fetishism," Atwood's series contributes an additional lesson in resisting the temptation of species fetishism, a concept challenged by the ease with which her characters splice and dice DNA. And if the Anthropocene requires interdisciplinary inquiry, its end or, at least, its amelioration—as depicted by Atwood—requires interspecies literacy, a rethinking of the literary project that decenters the human in favor of a more complex narrative and material web.

"Pointless Repinings": In Defense of the Inhumanities

Jimmy, the main character in *Oryx and Crake,* whom Jennifer Lawn describes as "the future flotsam of the humanities," is Atwood's chief case study in how humanities study can fail to transcend its speciesist baggage (392). Jimmy's story foregrounds the marginalization and instrumentalization of the humanities as major factors in his failures as a reader: his inability to correctly perceive the dystopia in which he lives, his tendency to exoticize and appropriate stories of difference, his lapses in critical empathy. Positioned as a defender—before and after the pandemic—of the arts and humanities as bastions of "the human," Jimmy is unable to fully recognize the "inhuman" contained by this category. This failure, of course, is not Jimmy's alone; it is "structured," as he begins to understand, in economic, educational, and social systems (Atwood, *Oryx* 184). Importantly, this structuring is not only about the devaluation of the arts and humanities; it is also about the complicity of these fields with systems of slavery, colonialism, and capitalism. Atwood's series acknowledges the longstanding embeddedness of the arts and humanities in systems of exploitation, while—as the existence of the trilogy itself suggests—also recognizing that they can work against such systems.

As a child and teenager, Jimmy's exposure to art and literature is almost exclusively commercial. His first experience of Shakespeare, after all, is provided by a young woman whose profitable live-stream broadcasts involve reciting *Macbeth* from the toilet. Of course, Shakespeare was himself a commercial artist, and Atwood implies throughout the novel that the attempt to sever the arts from economic context is an obfuscating move. The historical embeddedness of art in economic and political systems is even more obvious in a computer game called "Blood and Roses," which involves valuing great works of art in the currency of human lives ("one *Mona Lisa* equalled Bergen-Belsen, one Armenian genocide equalled the *Ninth Symphony* plus three Great Pyramids"; 79). "Blood and Roses" suggests that humanity's artistic legacy is the result of a long history of obscene trade-offs. As Gerry Canavan writes, the game "suggests that the apparent 'failures' of civilization are, in fact, the true underpinning of all its supposed triumphs" and leads one to "wonder . . . if the human history that has been wiped out by the apocalypse is actually worthy of being mourned at all" (143–44). Through such examples, Atwood makes clear that the arts and humanities, at least as they are known in Western civilization, are inextricable from systems of exploitation.[17]

Upon graduating from high school, Jimmy is shipped off to the Martha Graham Academy, an arts and humanities school whose glory days are in the distant past: "A lot of what went on at Martha Graham," the narrator tells us, "was like studying Latin or book-binding: pleasant to contemplate in its way, but no longer central to anything" (187). The university's namesake, described as "some gory old dance goddess of the twentieth century," is memorialized in "a gruesome statue," suggesting that the arts persist only in zombie form. Dismissing the statue as "Retro feminist shit," defacing it, and claiming it as a "mascot" that "represented life, or art, or something," Jimmy and his peers express ambivalence about the artistic enterprise (186). The decay of the arts and humanities is not just cultural but also material—legible in the extreme disrepair of the campus and its proximity to "the tackiest kind of pleeblands" (185). All this in contrast to Watson Crick, an elite biotech university that offers its student body (which includes Glenn/Crake) posh accommodations.[18]

While Watson Crick keeps itself flush through corporate funding, Martha Graham stays (barely) afloat by presenting the arts and humanities as

---

17. W. J. T. Mitchell points out that "the old ethical conundrum about rescuing a Rembrandt or an infant from a burning building makes sense only in a culture that already believes some objects have a strong claim to human protection, care, and loving attention" (xi). The corollary to the attribution of rights and personhood to objects, of course, is the attribution of object status to persons.

18. The difference in the institutions' names is worth remarking on: an artist and feminist icon versus male scientists whose accomplishments depended on the contributions of a female scientist (Rosalind Franklin) who is often erased from the narrative of scientific discovery.

servants of corporate enterprise—"*Contemporary* arenas, they were called." Having appended to its original motto, "*Ars Longa Vita Brevis*" ("Art is Long, Life is Short"), a new slogan, "Our Students Graduate With Employable Skills," Martha Graham, like today's corporate university, justifies arts and humanities education through utilitarian appeals. Jimmy majors in "Problematics," what the students call "Spin and Grin," and prepares for a career in advertising. He is not enthusiastic about this path. Indeed, he sees "his future life stretched before him like a sentence; not a prison sentence, but a long-winded sentence with a lot of unnecessary subordinate clauses, as he was soon in the habit of quipping during Happy Hour pickup time at the local campus bars and pubs" (188). Jimmy implies that word work is a kind of imprisonment, and he makes this point through a sentence that turns upon linguistic ambivalence (the double meaning of "sentence"). However, the ingenuity of this play on words—itself richly suggestive of the limitations of language, both inherent and imposed—is immediately undercut by its reduction to a pickup line ("a stab at getting laid," to use Crake's phrase). In other words, this is a sentence that sentences itself to the same fate (devaluation, irrelevance, instrumentalism) that it implies is being imposed on the textual arts. This move is paralleled by Jimmy's frequent deployment of arcane words and phrases for social and, later, material capital.

Jimmy's life sentence does not unfold exactly as planned—in fact, its latter clauses are much worse than expected. But initially, his career is indeed that of corporate hack, writing ad copy so effective that he tricks himself into buying the questionable health products he promotes. (His success lies in his ability to create empty scientific-sounding terms, such as "fibracionous" and "pheromonimal" [248]).[19] Jimmy is saved from commercial drudgery by Crake who, now a top-ranking scientist at the biotech giant Rejoov, hires him to be his right-hand man. There, Jimmy contributes to the global promotion of BlyssPluss, a drug that promises sexual enhancement, STD prevention, and birth control but actually carries the hemorrhagic virus that wipes out most of the earth's human population and makes way for the Crakers, whom Crake has secretly developed in the Rejoov compound. In other words, Jimmy's humanist training, such as it is, is instrumentalized for a decidedly antihuman project.

After the pandemic, Jimmy recognizes that his prior life depended upon his own ignorance—that in many ways he was living in a bubble of privilege: "There had been something willed about . . . his ignorance. Or not

---

19. López Rúa explains that the neologisms in Atwood's prepandemic world are indicative of how, in Orwellian fashion, "the privileged group is trying to control behaviour by narrowing thought" (163). Also see Grimbeek.

willed, exactly: structured. He'd grown up in walled spaces, and then he had become one" (184). Jimmy is deeply ignorant about life outside Compound walls, and when he does venture into the pleeblands, he does so as a tourist—slumming and fucking his way through an "exotic" space. Like the readers to whom Atwood directs her project, he fails to see the dystopia he already lives in.

Jimmy's humanistic orientation also fails to insulate him from breathtaking lapses in empathy, most evident in his relationship to Oryx, a sex-worker-turned-teacher who instructs the Crakers about the natural world and is also Crake's assistant and lover. All we know of Oryx—including her vaguely "third world," racialized origins—is filtered, in the first novel, through Jimmy's exoticizing perspective. Jimmy believes that he first encounters Oryx on a child pornography website when a young girl turns and looks at the camera. This uncanny moment is Jimmy's first experience of the "other" looking back, even while it simultaneously suggests Jimmy's tendency to put himself at the center of every story. Jimmy saves the image of the child's gaze, carrying it with him as a kind of sacred object.[20] When he arrives at Rejoov, he is stunned to find what he believes is a three-dimensional, adult manifestation of the girl in the picture—a development that reveals his tendency to view women from impoverished and "foreign" backgrounds as interchangeable. Oryx, who begins an intimate relationship with Jimmy, confirms that she was indeed a child sex worker but equivocates on whether the picture Jimmy carries is of her—and whether she is one of the victims in a trafficking scandal involving girls locked in a California garage.

Jimmy's obsession with Oryx is not strictly sexual; it also has significant narrative dimensions. As Pilar Cuder Domínguez puts it, Oryx is the narrator and Jimmy her "demanding narratee" (63). Jimmy constantly hounds her for details about her life, demanding that she answer his questions and confirm that she is the girl in the picture, the girl in the garage—the perfect victim to his perfect hero. Their conversations take the form of interrogations, as Jimmy tries to dig up information: "In those days he'd wanted to know whatever it was possible to know, about Oryx, about anywhere she'd been." Perversely, Jimmy transforms himself into the interrogation's *real* victim: "He'd tortured himself with painful knowledge: every white-hot factoid he could collect he'd shove up under his fingernails" (135).

Jimmy enacts a problematic version of what Nguyen calls an ethics of "remembering others"; in his effort to acknowledge victims of injustice he

---

20. Crake also saved this image and uses it as a portal for hacking into a radical environmentalist website.

risks obscuring their full humanity. The impulse to remember others relies on empathy, sometimes in ways that keep the self at the center of the narrative: "remembering others can simply be a reversal, a mirror, of remembering one's own" (Nguyen 12). In Jimmy's enactment of this reversal, he plays the (would-be) hero, she the guileless victim. Tellingly, the narrator uses stage directions to describe Jimmy's memory of Oryx's entry into the drama of *his* life. "*Enter Oryx,*" Snowman repeats in reverie:

> Now he's come to . . . the place in the tragic play where it would say: *Enter Oryx.* Fatal moment. But which fatal moment? *Enter Oryx as a young girl on a kiddie-porn site* . . . ; or, *Enter Oryx as a teenage news item, sprung from a pervert's garage;* or, *Enter Oryx, stark naked and pedagogical in the Crakers' inner sanctum;* . . . or, *Enter Oryx, in a pewter-grey silk pantsuit* . . . , *the image of a professional Compound globewise saleswoman?* (307–8)

This framing retains Jimmy as the star of a tragic play while attempting (and failing) to impose coherent narrative structure on Oryx's complex life.

Oryx resists Jimmy's incessant questions and one-sided interpretations, insisting that "her own story about herself . . . was . . . not very romantic at all" and turning Jimmy's interrogations back on him: "You have a lot of pictures in your head, Jimmy. Where did you get them? Why do you think they are pictures of me?" (114). Oryx does not see herself as a tragic victim in need of protection and asserts her full humanity in the face of the two-dimensional version that Jimmy literally carries in his pocket. When Jimmy tells Oryx he'd "like to kill" the man who bought her from her family when she was a child, Oryx replies, "Oh Jimmy, you would like it better maybe if we all starved to death?" (119). And when he expresses rage at a man who sexually exploited her when she was a child, Oryx expresses her gratitude for the English lessons the man provided (142). What Jimmy "knows" about Oryx is based on confident ignorance: "Looking at her, *you knew* that a woman of such beauty, slightness, and one-time poverty must have led a difficult life," the narrator muses through Jimmy's point of view, Atwood's use of the second person also implicating readers in Jimmy's narrative presumption (115; emphasis added).

Despite the dismal outlook for humanities training suggested by Jimmy's story, Atwood reserves some space for resistance. Jimmy does not find Crake's better-world-through-bioengineering vision appealing. The sole "word person" in Crake's research lab, Jimmy poses several pointed questions about the implications of biotech innovations: "What if they get out?" (in response to wolf-dog hybrids; 205), "What if the fewer people are very greedy and wasteful?" (in response to plans for population control), and "Where do you get the subjects?" (in response to the clinical trials for Blyss-Pluss; 295–96). It is Jimmy who wonders, "How much is too much, how far is too far?" Although Crake rejects his friend's thinking as naïve and sentimental, he also values Jimmy's capacity for empathy, that rarefied trait attributed to the humanities. It is this capacity that leads Crake to pose to Jimmy ethical questions of his own ("Would you kill someone you loved to spare them pain?") and to put Jimmy in charge of the Crakers in the event of Crake's demise (320). Of course, the "word person" does *not* save the day in this story: Crake dies, and Jimmy is left in a world where "wolvogs" do "get out," where Crake has indeed gone "too far." Worst of all, Jimmy's skills with language have helped bring this world about.

After the pandemic, the issue is no longer the devaluation and instrumentalization of the arts and humanities but, rather, their literal destruction. In this new context, Jimmy, now called "Snowman," sees himself as the quixotic defender of language as a marker of human distinction in a context in which humans have all but disappeared. Snowman, fearing the loss of his own humanity, clings to words that are, like his species, at risk of extinction: "'Hang on to the words,' he tells himself. The odd words, the old words, the rare ones. *Valance. Norn. Serendipity. Pibroch. Lubricious.* When they're gone out of his head, these words, they'll be gone, everywhere, forever. As if they had never been" (68). Interestingly, the most apt citations in this register are drawn from scientific vocabularies: "From nowhere, a word appears: *Mesozoic*. He can see the word, he can hear the word, but he can't reach the word. He can't attach anything to it" (39). "Mesozoic," the name of a geological era demarcated by mass extinctions, is literally relevant to Snowman's perch on the brink of annihilation, as is "australopithecine," an extinct ancestor of humans and another entry in Snowman's verbal archive (194). Although the postpandemic context makes these terms germane in a way they haven't been, for Jimmy, before, the linguistic and intellectual situation in which "Mesozoic" and "australopithecine" are meaningful has disappeared, a paradoxical circumstance that renders these terms, like many on Jimmy's wordlists, uncanny. These are the "Rag ends of language," which Jimmy increasingly links by sound, rather than meaning: "*mephitic, metronome, mastitis, metatarsal, maudlin*" (148), "goon, buffoon, poltroon," and, in a series that suggests devolution, "humanoid, . . . hominid, . . . aberration, . . . abominable" (307). As Jimmy repeats these words, they start to resemble onomatopoeic exclamations from the horror films he watches during the first days of the pandemic: "He watched Alfred Hitchcock's *The Birds. Flap-flapflap, eek, screech. . . .* Or he watched *Night of the Living Dead. Lurch, aargh, gnaw, choke, gurgle*" (345). The difference between these sounds and words like "trull," "grutch," "woad" (327), and "frass," also found in Jimmy's arcane dictionary, is minimal (344). Within just a few lines of the "Mesozoic" passage, Snowman imagines himself using his tongue for a purpose quite distinct from speech: "He wishes he could cool himself by hanging out his tongue" (39).[21]

Importantly, the "burning scrapbook in [Jimmy's] head" is a project begun long before the pandemic (10). As a child, Jimmy develops an interest in "retro words" (such as "bogus" and "awesome") that he finds on old DVDs in the library (77, 83). At college, he continues to collect old words as part of his commitment to "the superfluous as an end in itself": "He compiled lists of old words . . . words of a precision and suggestiveness that no longer had a meaningful application in today's world, or *toady's world*, as Jimmy sometimes deliberately misspelled it." Jimmy, refusing to be a "toady" to the system of power, pursues the "obsolete" and forgotten as an end in itself, resisting the relentless commodification and instrumentalization of word work: "Part of what impelled him was stubbornness; resentment, even. The system had filed him among the rejects, and what he was studying was considered . . . an archaic waste of time." At the same time, Jimmy instrumentalizes his archive for his own ends. Despite the heroic dimensions of his pre- and postpandemic linguistic efforts, Jimmy's relationship to esoteric language has never been "pure." Throughout his youth Jimmy "tosse[s] left-handed into conversation" obscure words and quotations as a means of acquiring social approbation and romantic success (195). It's an easy shift to the linguistic manipulations required of him in corporate environments.

Furthermore, because they come from a hierarchical society deeply inscribed with a variety of oppressions and horrors (the very problems Crake sought to eradicate through genocide), the terms and quotations in Jimmy's library complicate his nostalgia and loneliness with shades of colonialism, sexism, racism, and speciesism. Over and over again, Jimmy's desire for human interlocutors and his yearning for the past are bound up with nostalgia for bygone systems of power whose residues adhere to his decontextualized quotations. One specific and seemingly innocuous phrase repeated throughout the trilogy, "pointless repinings," serves as both apt descriptor and important instance of recitation as an expression of longing for interpersonal connection as well as intra- and interspecies dominance.[22] This phrase

---

21. We might say that Jimmy sees language as separate from material reality, a problem akin to what Barad calls "representationalism" ("Posthumanist" 122–29).

22. Variations on this phrase also appear in *MaddAddam* (44, 138).

first appears early in *Oryx and Crake*, when Snowman is feeling particularly despondent and crying out for "someone, anyone, listen to me please!" A text lodged in his memory responds: "*It is important*, says the book in his head, *to ignore minor irritants, to avoid pointless repinings, and to turn one's mental energies to immediate realities and to the tasks at hand*" (45). This sound bite, which implores him to stop perseverating and turn to action, has precisely the opposite effect by shifting Jimmy's attention to language and, specifically, to the very act of repetition in which he is engaged:

> He must have read that somewhere. Surely his own mind would never have come up with *pointless repinings*, not all by itself.
> ... "Pointless repinings," he says out loud. As often, he feels he has a listener, someone unseen, hidden behind the screen of leaves, watching him slyly. (45–46)

On the one hand, this quotation, perhaps drawn from one of the self-help books that were the subject of Jimmy's undergraduate thesis, is truly "pointless," failing to speak to his immediate situation (which involves more than "minor irritants") and dismissing his longing for human connection. On the other hand, it links him to other human consciousnesses, as he recognizes that his mind is not strictly his own and imagines an audience and potential interlocutor. That we, the readers of Atwood's novel, are "someone unseen, hidden behind the screen of leaves," suggests that Jimmy's repinings are not entirely pointless.

Subsequent repetitions of the phrase, now lifted from his archive and into his idiolect, reinforce Jimmy's longing for human encounter. For example, after scolding himself for "pointless repinings," the next page brims with citations and recitations, culminating in an expressed desire for reading material and acknowledgment of words that have lost their meaning and context: "'I used to be erudite,' he says out loud. *Erudite*. A hopeless word. What are all those things he once thought he knew, and where have they gone?" (148).[23] Shortly after another appearance of the phrase, when he tells himself there is "no time for pointless repinings," he imagines encountering another person: "He can't rid himself of the notion that someone—someone like him—is lying in wait, around some corner, behind some half-opened door" (228–29). As he explores devastated Compound homes, he deliberately seeks himself there, looking at his reflection in a mirror, identifying

---

23. Snowman's citations are "painful because those words are no longer shared and therefore they are useless" (López Rúa 163).

one of the dead inhabitants as "a word person" and "spin doctor," as he was in his previous life, and feeling as if "it's his own house he's broken into" (233). In these examples, Snowman's "pointless repinings" both manage and name his longing for meaningful encounter while also pointing back to himself and his aggrieved sense of linguistic exceptionality. And, once again, Atwood's readers are positioned structurally "behind some half-opened door," watching and weighing whether we are more than just a "reflection" of Jimmy.

Snowman's difficulty in getting out of this cycle points to a fundamental self-centeredness related to larger problems of ethnocentrism and anthropocentrism—problems that also show up in his recitations. For example, the very first of these, found in the opening passage of the novel, is drawn from what appears to be an overtly colonial tome. Snowman has awakened in his beachside tree and is going through his postapocalyptic morning routine, when he speaks the following aloud: "It is the strict adherence to daily routine that tends towards the maintenance of good morale and the preservation of sanity." Snowman "has the feeling he's quoting from a book, some obsolete, ponderous directive written in aid of European colonials running plantations of one kind or another." Snowman elaborates on the quotation:

> They would have been told to wear solar topis, dress for dinner, refrain from raping the natives. It wouldn't have said *raping*. Refrain from fraternizing with the female inhabitants. . . .
> He bets they didn't refrain, though. Nine times out of ten. (4)

Snowman's acknowledgment of the function of euphemism in maintaining an unequal system of power suggests bitterness—toward colonialism and, perhaps, toward his previous career bending language to suit corporate purposes. However, this passage can also be taken as an expression of longing—for women, for a position of power, for the world as it used to be. We might read unspoken yearning in the pause that follows Snowman's failure to complete the half-remembered text: "In view of the mitigating," he begins, and then "finds himself standing with his mouth open" (5). Filling his mouth with a mango, eating rather than speaking, he inches subtly closer to animal status, a deeply unsettling demotion to the far end of a continuum that also includes colonized people and women in general.

The hierarchical power system that buoys human exceptionalism has sunk, and Snowman finds himself unmoored. Everyone is better suited to survival than he—particularly the Crakers. In this uncomfortable situation, scraps of colonial discourse express Snowman's fraught relationship to his transhuman companions. During one of many frustrating conversations with the Crakers, we find this passage:

> *When dealing with indigenous peoples,* says the book in his head . . . *you must attempt to respect their traditions and confine your explanations to simple concepts that can be understood within the contexts of their belief systems.* Some earnest aid worker in a khaki jungle outfit. . . . Condescending self-righteous cow, thinks she's got all the answers. . . . If she were here she'd need a whole new take on *indigenous.* (97)

An underlying connotation of the term *indigenous* is exposed here: it does not simply mean having a longstanding physical and cultural connection to a place; after all, neither Jimmy nor the Crakers can claim this kind of connection. "Indigenous" can also mean occupying a position of subordination such that one can be condescended to—admiringly or pityingly or violently.[24] When deployed in this fashion, the term "indigenous" is structurally other to "colonizer"; the autonyms for many Indigenous peoples, in contrast, require no such "opposite." Jimmy derides the condescending attitude of this passage. But his response seems to be at least partly derived from his sense that *he* now occupies an "indigenous" structural position—this is one interpretation of "the whole new take on *indigenous*" he demands. Notably, his resentful appropriation of this term is also imbued with gender resentment, as he codes the condescending recitation as female.

Snowman's resentment sometimes leads him to recapitulate colonial behaviors. For example, he extemporizes a belief system for the Crakers that is designed, in equal measure, to spite Crake, support his own survival, and maintain a shred of authority in relation to his transhuman companions. Not only does he cynically impose his invented religion; he also borrows freely from stories that are not his own to create his "sacred" teachings. For example, a detail from Oryx's story of being a childhood sex worker—a watch that the man who runs the business claims to use for surveillance—is reconstituted in the watch Jimmy claims to use to communicate with Crake, who, along with Oryx, is a godlike figure in Jimmy's ersatz cosmology. Such cartoonish acts of appropriation, fueled by his literary imagination, suggest again that Jimmy is having a hard time letting go of his belief in the "rightness" of a humanism defined by myriad "others," even while he rapidly falls into the category of "other" himself.

---

24. "Jimmy's is not a 'new take' on the colonialist perspective, however, but a reiteration of the assumption that indigenous peoples require the 'civilizing' influences of Western culture" (Jennings 22).

The "othered" status Snowman fears is shaded not only by colonialism and sexism but also by speciesism. Several of Snowman's postapocalyptic recitations are focused on maintaining exceptional human status despite the loss of station his species has experienced. For example, shortly after his second use of "pointless repinings," Snowman is watching "a great scrawl of birds" thriving in a world no longer dominated by humans:

> A mile or so to the south, a salt marsh is forming on a one-time landfill dotted with semi-flooded townhouses. That's where all the birds are going: minnow city. He watches them with resentment: everything is fine with them, not a care in the world. Eat, fuck, poop, screech, that's all they do. (148)

In this passage, which immediately precedes Jimmy's longing for reading material and despondency over his loss of "erudition," the use of the term "scrawl" to describe the flock of birds implies that the story of the Anthropocene and its archives, which Jimmy jealously protects, are being overwritten by the more-than-human world.[25] This overwriting encompasses not only words that have lost a meaningful social context but also the very terrain previously scarred by the devastating activities of human civilization. Tellingly, Jimmy can only read this instance of environmental renewal through a category of human geography ("minnow *city*"), and his dismissive description of the birds' activities ("that's all they do") works at once to reinforce his precarious sense of human superiority and to signal his growing perception that less distance exists between himself and other species than he wants to believe.

Snowman's dizzying turn of fortune prompts him to retrospectively imagine being in a position of superiority to birds, a position enacted through observation: "In a former life," he thinks, "he might have snuck up on them, studied them through binoculars, wondering at their grace." There would have been no need to envy birds in that previous life, or to feel threatened by them; they could safely remain objects of wonder or scientific inquiry, whereas now Snowman "yearns for a big slingshot" with which to assert dominance. However, Snowman was not, in fact, a birdwatcher before the pandemic: "No, he never would have [observed birds with wonder], it hadn't been his style. Some grade-school teacher, a nature snoop—Sally

---

25. Special status is not conferred equally to all humans, and individual humans are not equally responsible for climate disaster. Some scholars have offered alternative terms, such as "Capitalocene" and "Plantationocene," that foreground this fact (Menely and Taylor 8). Also see Jennings 18; Squire 14.

Whatshername?—herding them along on what she called field trips. . . . *Look! See the nice ducks? Those are called mallards!*" Jimmy's observation of the birds, and the recitation it elicits, suggests deep investment in species taxonomy and hierarchy, even—maybe especially—in those humans privileged enough to find nature "tedious" (148).[26]

Jimmy has not always held this cavalier attitude toward the more-than-human world; as a child he expresses concern for contaminated research animals burned on a bonfire and even toward the plastic ducks on his rain boots. But transspecies empathy is drummed out of him by academic, economic, and cultural systems that train him to see nonhuman animals (and some humans) as objects to be consumed. Indeed, the explanation he receives about the ducks on his rubber boots (they "were only like pictures, they weren't real and had no feelings") seems to be extended to most of the nonhuman—and much of the human—world (15). After all, Oryx, too, is "only like [a] picture[ ]." Jimmy's childhood sense that objectified others might not be just "pictures," that they might actually be sentient beings capable of looking back at him—and his corollary perception that he bears some responsibility for their condition of objectification ("In some way all of this . . . was his fault," he thinks at the bonfire, imagining that the animals are "looking at him reproachfully out of their burning eyes")—complicates his response to the girl who interrupts his smooth consumption of child pornography (18). After the pandemic, Jimmy's experience of being watched by other living beings, including predators, challenges his sense of species superiority and recalls these suppressed, incipient urges toward more complex encounters with human and more-than-human subjects.

Toward Interspecies Literacy

Although *Oryx and Crake* challenges the naïve view that art, literature, or humanities study is necessarily liberatory, the *MaddAddam* series also retains faith in the capacity for narrative to effect change in the world. The multivocal structure of the trilogy, which culminates in an act of collaborative, interspecies literacy, exemplifies one strategy through which narrative can challenge dominant ways of thinking and seeing. Across the series, Atwood's apocalyptic revelations are related through the perspectives of characters who survive the same catastrophic event but from distinctly different social

---

26. We might call this phenomenon, paraphrasing W. E. B. Du Bois, "the wages of humanness."

and economic positions. The first two books, *Oryx and Crake* and *The Year of the Flood*, encompass the same time period (before, during, and after the pandemic) and tell roughly the same story, but they do so through substantively different points of view. In *Oryx and Crake*, our focus is on Jimmy, while *The Year of the Flood* centers on Toby and Ren, young women who have spent much (or, in the case of Toby, all) of their lives in the pleeblands. Connected through the fringe environmentalist/religious group known as "God's Gardeners," and through economic and gender vulnerability, Toby and Ren offer a radically different perspective on the events related through Jimmy/Snowman's perspective in *Oryx and Crake*.[27] By doubling her narrative in this way, Atwood fills in some of the gaps and corrects some of the distortions caused by Jimmy's limited perspective. However, *The Year of the Flood* is not set up as authoritative over *Oryx and Crake*. Rather, in this second text, we meet characters who are structurally disenfranchised by the neoliberalism-on-steroids that reigns in Atwood's fictional world and who are also morally complex—no simple victims here.[28] It's the doubling of the narrative that matters, the demand that readers pay attention to multiple points of view—a practice at odds with Jimmy's problematic approach to "remembering others."

With *MaddAddam*, the narrative triples, and, as Everett Hamner points out, the third novel effects a radical rereading of the first two: *MaddAddam* implies that Adam One, the leader of the God's Gardeners, is actually the mastermind behind the pandemic, manipulating Crake into his genocidal actions in order to bring about the "waterless flood" he prophesies—and, in striking parallel to Crake's secret inoculation of his employees, subtly preparing his followers to survive it (Hamner 160). The multiplication of the pandemic story across the series accelerates in the final book, in which narration is provided primarily by Toby and her lover Zeb, a former God's Gardener and radical environmentalist. Toby and Zeb tell stories to each other, and Toby relates these stories to the Crakers. These dialogical exchanges are followed by a story read aloud by Blackbeard, a young Craker whom Toby has taught to read and write. The multivocality of the third volume underscores the possibility of interspecies literacy as a way forward after the Anthropocene: the book that Toby writes, and Blackbeard continues,

---

27. Ren and Toby "provide a feminine, comic reworking of the tragic masculine perspective or narrative of Jimmy in the first novel" (Watkins 132). Also see Ciobanu 154.

28. On Atwood's critique of neoliberalism, see Sullivan; Vials. Sullivan's definition of the "petro-text" parallels my definition of postgenomic literature: any modern text can be identified as a petro-text because of its contexts of creation and distribution, but there are also petro-texts that critically intervene in these contexts.

asserts a future in its expectation of future readers, despite Toby's personal doubts. Atwood's posthuman future is not a transgenic nightmare (despite the nightmare that precipitates it) but, rather, is a case study in forging intra- and interspecies bonds in complicated ethical contexts. In other words, in its articulation of a usable future, *MaddAddam*, to borrow Nguyen's phrasing, asks, "What is to be done in the present, with actual others, where the struggle over ethics and justice is often tied to people's deeply rooted sense of past recriminations, where any ethical achievement will be inevitably compromised, where any act of justice has a limit . . . ?" (Nguyen 79).[29]

In *The Year of the Flood*, the God's Gardeners follow a complex theology that places humans in a web of interconnected species defined by "interspecies empathy" (Atwood, *Year* 311). "Many recall the Covenant with Noah, but forget the Covenant with all other living Beings," explains Adam One; "the Animals are not senseless matter, not mere chunks of meat. No; they have living Souls" (91). Rather than viewing human beings as holding dominion over other species, the Gardeners believe in transspecies kinship: "To Name is—we hope—to greet; to draw another towards one's self. Let us imagine Adam calling out the Names of the Animals in fondness and joy, as if to say, *There you are, my dearest! Welcome!* Adam's first act towards the Animals was thus one of loving-kindness and kinship" (12–13). As the sermon snippet above suggests, language—the capacity to name—remains a defining feature of humanity, but it is wrested from the concept of dominion, instead serving as one means (among many) of pursuing what Donna Haraway calls, in her work on "companion species," interspecies "encounter." Indeed, Adam One seems to channel Haraway's concept of the "intersecting gaze" (*When* 21), when he describes "those gentle eyes [of nonhuman animals] that regard you with such trust—a trust that has not yet been violated by bloodshed and gluttony and pride and disdain" (Atwood, *Year* 13). At the same time, his perspective also recalls Jimmy's problematic enactment of "remembering others," as Adam One presents nonhuman animals as innocent and human beings as "fallen."

Notably, the Gardeners are wary of the power and agency of language—particularly written language. Early in *The Year of the Flood*, Ren recalls the admonition to "*Beware of words. Be careful what you write. Leave no trails*" (6). Although the novel is punctuated with sermons and songs that articulate the group's theology, these are, respectively, "spoken by Adam One"

---

29. Jennings puts this question in ecofeminist terms: "Atwood's posthumanist perspective requires readers to confront and engage with radical otherness, including our own annihilation, and without simply preparing for some inevitable catastrophic end" (32).

and drawn from *The God's Gardeners Oral Hymnbook*, their appearance in writing presumably the result of unofficial or retrospective transcription. There is a practical reason for this graphophobia: The Gardeners are a fringe group covertly involved in radical environmentalist activism; they have to "leave no trails." But as an ethic, the Gardeners' emphasis on orality, which both preserves language and allows it to change and adapt to circumstance, stands in stark contrast to Jimmy's effort to hang on to words at all costs.

The Gardeners associate written words with the Anthropocene, an era which, they believe, will naturally come to an end due to humanity's self-destruction: "This history [of violence and speciesism] will soon be swept away by the Waterless Flood," predicts (promises?) Adam One, at which time "all works of Man will be as words written on water" (312). The idea that words themselves might have a life cycle is graphically (double-meaning intended) represented in "The Living Word," a bioart series created by Amanda, who ends up at the Martha Graham Academy with Jimmy.[30] In one installation of the series, Amanda writes "kaputt [*sic*]" (57) with cow bones covered in syrup; when the bones are covered in insects, she takes videos of them from a helicopter: "She liked to watch things move and grow and then disappear." Amanda's work literalizes both its subject matter (the environmental devastation that has transformed the Midwest into a bone-littered desert) and its form (the word "kaputt" goes kaput). At the same time, "The Living Word" is embedded in the neoliberal structures of the prepandemic world. The latest in a long line of artists dependent on patronage (the House of Medici and the Catholic Church come to mind), "Amanda always got the money to do her art capers. She was kind of famous in the circles that went in for culture. They weren't big circles, but they were rich circles" (56). Amanda's art is happily consumed by those at the top of the very system it critiques, as Atwood again refuses to separate art from its economic and political contexts.

If Amanda works out her complicated feelings about Gardener teachings through spectacular art projects, Toby does so through private recollections that ironically recall Jimmy's citations. Indeed, the opening passage of *The Year of the Flood* closely echoes that of *Oryx and Crake*, only it is Toby we see undertaking her morning routine and being visited by a quotation from the past. In Jimmy's case, the quotation is from a colonial tome; in Toby's, it is from the oral teachings of the Gardeners, drawn from biblical and scientific sources: "*Vultures are our friends*, the Gardeners used to teach. *They purify the earth. They are God's necessary dark Angels of bodily dissolution*" (3). This initial

---

30. See Stock for examples of bioart that influenced Atwood.

citation differs from Jimmy's in two additional respects: (1) it remains relevant in the postpandemic context, and (2) it is followed by self-reflective questioning on Toby's part. While Jimmy bitterly criticizes his quote and then trails off into silence as he longs for a lost world, Toby asks herself, "Do I still believe this?" (4). Grappling with belief even before the "waterless flood," after the pandemic both Toby and Ren return to teachings that prompt new questions and ideas. For example, Ren recalls that "the Adams and Eves [Gardener leaders] used to say, *We are what we eat*, but I prefer to say, *We are what we wish*. Because if you can't wish, why bother?" (400).

Like Jimmy, Toby believes she could be the last human survivor of the pandemic and fixates on words, though their contemplations are distinct. Jimmy tends not to define the archaic words he recalls, instead "tossing them left-handed" into the void, leaning into their descent into sound. Toby, on the other hand, fingers their meaning, often in relation to the natural context in which they come to mind. For example, "It's daybreak. The break of day. Toby turns this word over: break, broke, broken. What breaks in daybreak? Is it the night? Is it the sun, cracked in two by the horizon like an egg, spilling out light?" (15). While Jimmy gets stuck on words like "erudite," which can only *mean* in a hierarchized human context, Toby meditates on a word that cannot fully capture the natural phenomenon it describes and yet enables a poetic proliferation that approaches its subject, however asymptotically. Not incidentally, "daybreak" returns at the very end of *MaddAddam*, appearing in a simile that describes Blackbeard's smile when he tells Toby he will help her write her book. On its surface, this moment suggests that the acquisition of writing makes possible a new future for the Crakers. But this is an interpretation that Toby herself is not sure of: "What comes next?" she wonders. "Rules, dogmas, laws? The Testament of Crake? How soon before there are ancient texts they feel they have to obey but have forgotten how to interpret? Have I ruined them?" (*MaddAddam* 204). "Daybreak" thus signals, at once, the emancipatory and oppressive potential of language.

Like Jimmy, Toby also contemplates the meaning of human language on the precipice of extinction, though again these contemplations lead her to somewhat different conclusions:

> Mourning dove, robin, crow, bluejay, bullfrog. Toby says their names, but these names mean nothing to them. Soon her own language will be gone out of her head and this will be all that's left in there. Ooodle-oodle-oo, hoom hoo. The ceaseless repetition, the song with no beginning and no end. No questions, no answers, not in so many words. Not in any words at all. Or is it all one huge Word?

> Where has this notion come from, out of nowhere and into her head?
> *Tobeee!*
> So much like someone calling her. But it's only birdsong. (*Year 350*)

When Jimmy observes the birds who are reclaiming their habitats, given new life by the devastations of the pandemic, he does so with bitterness, jealousy, and longing for species advantage. Toby, facing the same situation, remains open to the possibility that her language—and her life—are not distinct from those of other species ("is it all one huge Word?"). And while Jimmy persistently looks for an interlocutor with whom he can identify as closely as possible, Toby imagines—however fleetingly—the possibility of interspecies communication, when she hears her own name in the birdsong.

This possibility is explored most fully in the third novel, *MaddAddam*, which focuses on an interspecies community that includes humans, Crakers, and "pigoons," pigs with partly human brains who are now known, more respectfully, as "Pig Ones." (The possibility that the Crakers might also be renamed is raised when Toby recognizes that "Craker" is not an autonym and begins calling them "people"—a move that ironically actualizes the "whole new take on indigenous" Jimmy calls for in the first book.) These groups join forces against violent humans and learn to communicate through storytelling, writing, and—in the case of the Crakers and the Pig Ones—telepathy. By the end of the story, the humans have agreed to stop eating the Pig Ones' flesh, several hybrid children have been born to human and Craker parents, and Blackbeard has taken over Toby's storytelling role (previously held by Jimmy). We read about Blackbeard showing Toby's book to the Crakers and explaining writing to them, and then we read a segment of the book Blackbeard is reading to the Crakers. Along with visual art and religious belief, this new practice of reading and writing is another example of the survival of those problematic "human" elements that Crake tried to eliminate through genetic engineering. If the novel sympathizes with Crake's diagnosis of the prepandemic world as deeply ill, it takes a much more nuanced view of the human traits he singles out for gene editing.

In "*The Handmaid's Tale* and *Oryx and Crake* in Context," Atwood explains that literature is a means of making visible the human imagination, enabling critical contemplation of our thoughts and feelings—and their implications in the world:

> Literature is an uttering, or outering, of the human imagination. It puts the shadowy forms of thought and feeling—heaven, hell, monsters, angels, and all—out into the light, where we can take a good look at them and perhaps

come to a better understanding of who we are and what we want, and what our limits may be. Understanding the imagination is no longer a pastime or even a duty but a necessity, because increasingly, if we can imagine something, we'll be able to do it. (517)

For Atwood, narrative is both an extension of the human imagination and a means of understanding it. As such, it is crucial and not neutral; the work of readers and writers is necessary to *"perhaps* come to a better understanding" of ourselves—an outcome that is not predestined (emphasis added). Jimmy's narrative imagination—the literary structure he imposes on the lives of others—reveals his unreckoned investments in speciesist, ethnocentric, and gender hierarchies; he is so locked into those structures and the story forms that support them that he is blinded to other ways of understanding the world. Atwood's clever move is to narrativize the narrativization—to turn into story the very impulse to story, revealing that storytelling is not so much heroic as it is necessary but fraught: "There's the story, then there's the real story, then there's the story of how the story came to be told," explains Toby, in one of the third novel's most oft-quoted lines. "Then there's what you leave out of the story. Which is part of the story too" (*MaddAddam* 56).

Storytelling, like all artistic activity, is shaped by context. In a hypercapitalist world it can take on the characteristics of—and shore up the structures of—hypercapitalism. Like any technology (including, say, genetic engineering), writing's output is dependent upon its input.[31] This is not to suggest that Atwood presents science, technology, the arts, and the humanities as equivalent or even parallel endeavors, and it certainly is the case that Atwood expresses skepticism toward genetic engineering and naive faith in technology. But she expresses skepticism about art and writing too; as Jennifer Lawn argues, "Neither poetry nor art in general emerge from the narrative as an effectual or unqualified good" (394).[32]

Atwood appears to agree with Martha Nussbaum that the "spirit of the humanities" is present in scientific inquiry, such that it, too, is characterized by "searching critical thought, daring imagination, empathetic understanding of human experiences of many different kinds, and understanding of the complexity of the world we live in" (Nussbaum 7). The problem she diagnoses in the trilogy is not the eclipsing of the humanities by the sciences but,

---

31. On the trilogy as a literary technology that seeks to alter readers' brain functioning, see Winstead.

32. Lake and Gretzky read *Oryx* and the trilogy, respectively, as a straightforward defense of the arts and humanities, a position that underplays Atwood's association of art with human suffering. For more nuanced discussions, see Narkunas 2; Lawn 391–92.

rather, the suffusion and deformation of both by commercialism: Atwood contends, "Science isn't the bad thing; the bad thing is making all science completely commercial" (qtd. in Halliwell 261). Her true target is that which instrumentalizes "searching critical thought" and transforms everyone and everything into an object to be consumed. As Gerry Canavan writes, "The political content of both *Oryx and Crake* and *The Year of the Flood* is predicated on the increasingly desperate need to find some 'outside' to the closed, totalizing system called capitalism, which has swallowed the entire globe and remade all of human history, all the way down to the level of the gene, in its image" (154). While it may seem that there is a winner (science and technology) and a loser (the arts and humanities) in this system, Atwood insists that all of the above are warped by the monster of neoliberalism, just as they have been warped before by colonialism and capitalism.[33] Her hope, however, is that science, the arts, and the humanities can also be avenues of social critique and life affirmation—alone and in concert. Indeed, *MaddAddam* seems to suggest that it is impossible to separate these fields.

Whatever hope is present at the end of *MaddAddam* exists in the space between text and audience, as Blackbeard reads to his fellow Crakers. Trained in literacy by Toby and carrying on a narrative project begun by Jimmy, Blackbeard recapitulates the manipulations and elisions of his human models. He recites the phony cosmology, he acts out the spurious rituals, he tells his listeners—just as Jimmy and Toby used to—to please stop singing so he can get on with the story. Even the structural anthropocentrism of Toby and Jimmy's storytelling (we read their responses to the Crakers, but we do not read the Crakers' interruptions) is repeated in Blackbeard's orations. In other words, this "book" (both the trilogy and the book-within-a-book that ends it) is not a perfect story, and we ought to be concerned, as Toby is, that the human problems inscribed in Atwood's layered text will be carried forward in Blackbeard's world and our own. And yet the gaps in this hybrid narrative—epitomized by the moments in which the Crakers are speaking but we cannot read/hear them—open up space for dialogue and, even more importantly, for an interspecies imaginary. We are asked, by narrative omission, to imagine the voice of the Crakers, to take on their perspective and position while also recognizing the limits of such an attempt, just as the characters in this fictional interspecies community are forced again and again to try to understand each other's perspective and learn to communicate. The narrative project that becomes the centerpiece of *MaddAddam* is indeed a project of the inhumanities, in that it both depicts and invites

---

33. See Bouson, "We're" and "It's."

practices of remembering ourselves and remembering others that do not require fidelity to the "human" and its perpetual expansion. Rather, Atwood models for us the articulation of a "just memory," to use Nguyen's helpfully ambivalent term, that is also *just memory*, and thus open to error, revision, and debate—and, if we're lucky, that is usable in our mutual construction of a livable future.

•

As I near the end of these meditations on reading in the postgenomic age, so many of which have focused on genomics' textual metaphors and their many (often contradictory) meanings and effects, a metaphor offered in a different disciplinary context comes to mind for its ability to capture the material intermeshment and reverberations attending scenes of reading that Atwood (like the other authors in this study) illuminates: the cell membrane. Physician and narrative medicine scholar Rita Charon has argued that stories set off a chain of reactions that resound on multiple levels (interpersonal, narrative, social, political), just as when a receptor on a cell's surface connects to the molecule for which it is primed. "We accrue a bank of stories . . . that are then activated when some other story reminds us of them," Charon explains. "Hence we are 'primed' to hear, to attend, to make connections, to ask questions, to get the meaning of the new story. . . . We have the internal machinery to metabolize the new stories that dock on our membranes" ("Novelization" 46). When we, as readers, "metabolize" a story, we alter it and are altered by it. We also take some responsibility for the stories we absorb and digest and excrete: the waves set in motion by every act of reading demand that narrative participants become conscious of the material and ethical entanglements that structure an act so often mischaracterized as singular and discrete.

The cell membrane is an especially apt figure for reading against the "code" of genomic and postgenomic discourse. Despite a tremendous number of representations to the contrary, DNA does, in fact, have a material existence. It abides in cells—cells that affect its expression in proteins whose functions, in turn, are shaped by complex intra-actions within a body that is itself in complex intra-action with other agential matter. If the ascendance of DNA within the life sciences has drawn attention away from cells and seeds and bodies and environments, postgenomic literature returns these forms to view as figures for trans-corporeal reading and as part of the matter of reading itself. The cell is a reminder that reading is not an abstract decoding but, rather, a material and agential practice embedded in complex networks of dramatically varying scale and scope. We might say, then, that reading in the postgenomic age is a matter of reading cellularly, reading somatically, reading intersubjectively, reading ecologically. These are practices that have significant value within the field of literary criticism, encouraging approaches that engage ethical and environmental questions that structure the literary enterprise, questions that have not always taken center stage for literary scholars. But postgenomic reading's value is not exclusive to the study of literature, inasmuch as we are challenged with navigating social, political, and ecological crises that connect each of us, irrevocably and irresistibly, to life and matter as it exists around the globe. As in any other age, to read critically, productively, and ethically is to read with an eye toward the signal metaphors, narratives, and moral questions of the time, as they travel across discourses (literary and otherwise) and the interconnected contexts in which those discourses materialize. In the postgenomic age, the stakes of this imperative are significant indeed, extending well past questions of individual rights and agency and toward our mutual accountability to the living, breathing systems in which we live. The small archive of texts I have gathered in this volume points us in this direction, but, as always, the responsibility of reading is literally in our hands.

WORKS CITED

Abu El-Haj, Nadia. "Rethinking Genetic Genealogy: A Response to Stephan Palmié." *American Ethnologist*, vol. 34, no. 2, pp. 223–26.

Adamson, Joni. *American Indian Literature, Environmental Justice, and Ecocriticism: The Middle Place*. U of Arizona P, 2001.

Ahmed, Sara. "A Phenomenology of Whiteness." *Feminist Theory*, vol. 8, no. 2, 2007, pp. 149–68.

Alaimo, Stacy. *Bodily Natures: Science, Environment, and the Material Self*. Indiana UP, 2010.

———. *Exposed: Environmental Politics & Pleasures in Posthuman Times*. U of Minnesota P, 2016.

Al-Amrani, Safa, et al. "Proteomics: Concepts and Applications in Human Medicine." *World Journal of Biological Chemistry*, vol. 12, no. 5, 2021, pp. 57–69.

Albright, Madeleine K. Interview on NBC-TV "The Today Show" with Matt Lauer, 19 Feb. 1998. *U.S. Department of State Archive*. https://1997-2001.state.gov/statements/1998/980219a.html.

Allen, Chadwick. "Blood (and) Memory." *American Literature*, vol. 71, no. 1, 1999, pp. 93–116.

Allen, Marlene D. "Kindred Spirits: The Speculative Fictions of Pauline E. Hopkins, Octavia E. Butler, and Tananarive Due." *CLA Journal*, vol. 61, no. 1–2, 2017, pp. 95–108.

Anzaldúa, Gloria. "How to Tame a Wild Tongue." *Borderlands / La Frontera: The New Mestiza*, by Anzaldúa, Aunt Lute Books, 1999, pp. 75–86.

Appelbaum, Yoni. "Why America's Business Majors Are in Desperate Need of a Liberal-Arts Education." *The Atlantic*, 28 June 2016, https://www.theatlantic.com/business/archive/2016/06/why-americas-business-majors-are-in-desperate-need-of-a-liberal-arts-education/489209/.

Appleton, Sarah. "Corp(Se)ocracy: Marketing Death in Margaret Atwood's *Oryx and Crake* and *The Year of the Flood*." *LATCH*, vol. 4, 2011, pp. 63–73.

Arnold, Ellen. "Healing with Holograms: Science and Orality in Gerald Vizenor's *The Heirs of Columbus*." *Restoring the Mystery of the Rainbow: Literature's Refraction of Science*, edited by Valeria Tinkler-Villani and C. C. Barfoot, Rodopi, 2011, pp. 529–47.

Atwood, Margaret. "*The Handmaid's Tale* and *Oryx and Crake* in Context." *PMLA*, vol. 119, no. 3, 2004, pp. 513–17.

———. *MaddAddam*. Doubleday, 2013.

———. *Oryx and Crake*. Anchor Books, 2003.

———. "What 'The Handmaid's Tale' Means in the Age of Trump." *New York Times*, 10 Mar. 2017, https://www.nytimes.com/2017/03/10/books/review/margaret-atwood-handmaids-tale-age-of-trump.html.

———. *The Year of the Flood*. Anchor Books, 2009.

Austin, J. L. "Performative Utterances." *Philosophical Papers*, Oxford UP, 1979, pp. 233–52.

Avise, John C. "Evolving Genomic Metaphors: A New Look at the Language of DNA." *Science*, vol. 294, no. 5540, 2001, pp. 86–87.

Avrahami, Einat. *The Invading Body: Reading Illness Autobiographies*. U of Virginia P, 2007.

Barad, Karen. *Meeting the Universe Halfway: Quantum Physics and the Entanglement of Matter and Meaning*. Duke UP, 2007.

———. "Posthumanist Performativity: Toward an Understanding of How Matter Comes to Matter." *Material Feminisms*, edited by Stacy Alaimo and Susan Hekman, Indiana UP, 2008, pp. 120–54.

Barthes, Roland. "The Death of the Author." *Image-Music-Text*, by Barthes, Hill and Wang, 1978, pp. 142–48.

Bast, Florian. "'I Won't Always Ask': Complicating Agency in Octavia Butler's *Fledgling*." *Current Objectives of Postgraduate American Studies*, vol. 11, 2010. https://copas.uni-regensburg.de/index.php/copas/article/view/128/152.

Beckerman, Michael. "Dvořák's 'New World' Largo and *The Song of Hiawatha*." *19th Century Music*, vol. 16, no. 1, 1992, pp. 35–48.

———. "Henry Krehbiel, Antonín Dvořák, and the Symphony 'From the New World.'" *Notes*, vol. 49, no. 2, 1992, pp. 447–73.

Benjamin, Ruha. "The Emperor's New Genes: Science, Public Policy, and the Allure of Objectivity." *The Annals of the American Academy of Political and Social Science*, vol. 661, 2015, pp. 130–42.

Bergethon, Peter R. "Landscapes of Change: Science, Science Fiction, and Advances in Biology." *New Boundaries in Political Science Fiction*, edited by Donald M. Hassler and Clyde Wilcox, U of South Carolina P, 2008, pp. 3–16.

Beverley, John. *Testimonio: On the Politics of Truth*. U of Minnesota P, 2004.

Bhabha, Homi. "Of Mimicry and Man: The Ambivalence of Colonial Discourse." *October*, vol. 28, 1984, pp. 125–33.

Bianchi, Diana W., et al. "Male Fetal Progenitor Cells Persist in Maternal Blood for as Long as 27 Years." *Proceedings of the National Academy of Sciences of the United States of America*, vol. 93, no. 2, 1996, pp. 705–8.

Biesecker, Leslie G. "Haplotype." *Talking Glossary of Genomic and Genetic Terms*. National Human Genome Research Institute, https://www.genome.gov/genetics-glossary/haplotype. Accessed 12 July 2024.

Bishop, Jeffrey. "Rejecting Medical Humanism: Medical Humanities and the Metaphysics of Medicine." *Journal of Medical Humanities*, vol. 29, 2008, pp. 15–25.

Blaeser, Kimberly M. "The New 'Frontier' of Native American Literature: Dis-Arming History with Tribal Humor." *Native American Perspectives on Literature and History*, edited by Alan R. Velie, U of Oklahoma P, pp. 37–50.

Bliss, Catherine. "Defining Health Justice in the Postgenomic Era." Richardson and Stevens, pp. 174–91.

———. "The Marketization of Identity Politics." *Sociology*, vol. 47, no. 5, 2013, pp. 1011–25.

———. "Racial Taxonomy in Genomics." *Social Science and Medicine*, vol. 73, no. 7, 2011, pp. 1019–27.

Bolnick, Deborah A. "Individual Ancestry Inference and the Reification of Race as a Biological Phenomenon." Koenig et al., pp. 70–85.

Borges, Jorge Luis. "Kafka and His Precursors." *Labyrinths*, by Borges, New Directions, 1962, pp. 199–201.

Bould, Mark. "Come Alive by Saying No: An Introduction to Black Power SF." *Science Fiction Studies*, vol. 34, no. 2, 2007, pp. 220–40.

Bouson, J. Brooks. "'It's Game Over Forever': Atwood's Satiric Vision of a Bioengineered Posthuman Future in *Oryx and Crake*." *Commonwealth Literature*, vol. 39, no. 3, 2004, pp. 139–56.

———. "'We're Using Up the Earth. It's Almost Gone': A Return to the Post-Apocalyptic Future in Margaret Atwood's *The Year of the Flood*." *Journal of Commonwealth Literature*, vol. 46, no. 1, 2011, pp. 9–26.

Brody, Howard. "'My Story Is Broken; Can You Help Me Fix It?' Medical Ethics and the Joint Construction of Narrative." *Literature and Medicine*, vol. 13, no. 1, 1994, pp. 79–92.

Brooks, Van Wyck. "On Creating a Usable Past." *The Dial*, vol. 64, no. 764, 1918, p. 337.

Brown, Lois. "Death-Defying Testimony: Women's Private Lives and the Politics of Public Documents." *Legacy*, vol. 27, no. 1, 2010, pp. 130–39.

Brox, Ali. "'Every Age Has the Vampire It Needs': Octavia Butler's Vampiric Vision in *Fledgling*." *Utopian Studies*, vol. 19, no. 3, 2008, pp. 391–409.

Burgess, Benjamin V. "Elaboration Therapy in the Midewiwin and Gerald Vizenor's *The Heirs of Columbus*." *Studies in American Indian Literatures*, vol. 18, no. 1, 2006, pp. 22–36.

Burn, Stephen J. "An Interview with Richard Powers." *Contemporary Literature*, vol. 49, no. 2, 2008, pp. 163–79.

Burnett, L. D. "Holding on to What Makes Us Human: Defending the Humanities in a Skills-Obsessed University." *Chronicle of Higher Education*, 7 Aug. 2016, https://www.chronicle.com/article/holding-on-to-what-makes-us-human/.

Bush, George H. W. Inaugural Address. *The Avalon Project: Documents in Law, History, and Diplomacy,* Yale Law School, Lillian Goldman Law Library. https://avalon.law.yale.edu/20th_century/bush.asp.

Butalia, Urvashi. *The Other Side of Silence: Voices from the Partition of India.* Duke UP, 2000.

Butler, Judith. *Excitable Speech: A Politics of the Performative.* Routledge, 1997.

Butler, Octavia. *Bloodchild and Other Stories.* Seven Stories Press, 1996.

———. *Fledgling.* Grand Central Publishing, 2007.

———. *Parable of the Sower.* Grand Central Publishing, 2023.

Caballero, Carolina. "The Queering of Cuban History: Carmelita Tropicana and *Memories of the Revolution.*" *Latin American Theatre Review,* vol. 37, no. 2, 2004, pp. 127–40.

Calvo-Quirós, William A. "The Emancipatory Power of the Imaginary: Defining Chican@ Speculative Productions." *Aztlán: A Journal of Chicano Studies,* vol. 41, no. 1, 2016, pp. 155–70.

Canavan, Gerry. "Hope, But Not for Us: Ecological Science Fiction and the End of the World in Margaret Atwood's *Oryx and Crake* and *The Year of the Flood.*" *LIT: Literature Interpretation Theory,* vol. 23, no. 2, 2012, pp. 138–59.

Casteel, Sarah Phillips. "Sephardism and Marranism in Native American Fiction of the Quincentenary." *MELUS,* vol. 37, no. 2, 2012, pp. 59–81.

Cavalier, Christine R. "Jane Johnston Schoolcraft's Sentimental Lessons: Native Literary Collaboration and Resistance." *MELUS,* vol. 38, no. 1, 2013, pp. 98–118.

Cavalli-Sforza, Luigi. *Genes, Peoples, and Languages.* Translated by Mark Seielstad, North Point Press, 2000.

———. "The Human Genome Diversity Project." Presentation Transcript, UNESCO, Paris, 12 Sept. 1994, *U.S. Department of Energy Office of Scientific and Technical Information,* https://www.osti.gov/servlets/purl/505327.

Cespedes, Karina Lissette. "*Bomberas* on Stage: Carmelita Tropicana Speaking in Tongues against History, Madness, Fate, and the State." *Tortilleras: Hispanic and U.S. Latina Lesbian Expression,* edited by Lourdes Torres and Inmaculada Pertusa, Temple UP, 2003, pp. 147–58.

Chambers, Tod. *The Fiction of Bioethics: Cases as Literary Texts.* Routledge, 1999.

Charon, Rita. "Narrative Medicine: A Model for Empathy, Reflection, Profession, and Trust." *JAMA,* vol. 286, no. 15, 2001, pp. 1897–902.

———. "The Novelization of the Body, or, How Medicine and Stories Need One Another." *Narrative,* vol. 19, no. 1, 2011, pp. 33–50.

Choksey, Lara. *Narrative in the Age of the Genome: Genetic Worlds.* Bloomsbury Academic, 2022.

Christie, Stuart. "Trickster Gone Golfing: Vizenor's 'Heirs of Columbus' and the Chelhten-em Development Controversy," *American Indian Quarterly,* vol. 21, no. 3, 1997, pp. 359–83.

Chu, Seo-Young. *Do Metaphors Dream of Literal Sleep? A Science-Fictional Theory of Representation.* Harvard UP, 2010.

Ciobanu, Calina. "Rewriting the Human at the End of the Anthropocene in Margaret Atwood's *MaddAddam* Trilogy." *Minnesota Review,* vol. 83, 2014, pp. 153–62.

Clapham, John. "Dvořák and the American Indian." *Musical Times,* vol. 107, no. 1484, 1966, pp. 863–67.

———. "The Evolution of Dvořák's Symphony 'From the New World.'" *Musical Quarterly*, vol. 44, no. 2, 1958, pp. 167–83.

Clarke, John. "Stuart Hall and the Theory and Practice of Articulation." *Discourse*, vol. 36, no. 2, 2015, pp. 275–86.

Clayton, Jay. "Genome Time: Post-Darwinism Then and Now." *Critical Quarterly*, vol. 55, no. 1, 2013, pp. 57–74.

———. *Literature, Science, and Public Policy: From Darwin to Genomics*. Cambridge UP, 2023.

Clayton, Jay, and Claire Sisco King. "How Can Literary and Film Studies Contribute to Science Policy? The Case of Henrietta Lacks." *The Palgrave Handbook of Twentieth and Twenty-First Century Literature and Science*, edited by Neel Ahuja et al., Palgrave Macmillan, 2020, pp. 201–19.

Coltelli, Laura. *Winged Words: American Indian Writers Speak*. U of Nebraska P, 1990.

Comfort, Nathaniel. *The Science of Human Perfection: How Genes Became the Heart of American Medicine*. Yale UP, 2012.

Condit, Celeste Michelle et al. "Recipes or Blueprints for Our Genes? How Contexts Selectively Activate the Multiple Meanings of Metaphors." *Quarterly Journal of Speech*, vol. 88, no. 3, 2002, pp. 303–25.

Contreras, Jorge L. *The Genome Defense: Inside the Epic Legal Battle to Determine Who Owns Your DNA*. Algonquin Books, 2021.

Conway, Kathlyn. *Beyond Words: Illness and the Limits of Expression*. U of New Mexico P, 2013.

Corning, Peter A. "A Systems Theory of Biological Evolution." *Biosystems*, vol. 214, 2022, https://www.sciencedirect.com/science/article/abs/pii/S0303264722000235.

Couser, G. Thomas. *Vulnerable Subjects: Ethics and Life Writing*. Cornell UP, 2003.

Cuder Domínguez, Pilar. "Margaret Atwood's Metafictional Acts: Collaborative Storytelling in *The Blind Assassin* and *Oryx and Crake*." *Revista Canaria de Estudios Ingleses*, vol. 56, 2008, pp. 57–68.

Danielson, Marivel T. *Homecoming Queers: Desire and Difference in Chicana Latina Cultural Production*. Rutgers UP, 2009.

DasGupta, Sayantani. "The Art of Medicine: Narrative Humility." *The Lancet*, vol. 371, no. 9617, 2008, p. 980.

Davy, Kate. *Lady Dicks and Lesbian Brothers: Staging the Unimaginable at the WOW Café Theatre*. U of Michigan P, 2013.

Delany, Samuel. "*Dichtung und* Science Fiction." *Starboard Wine: More Notes on the Language of Science Fiction*, by Delany, Wesleyan UP, pp. 153–84.

Deloria, Vine, Jr. *Custer Died for Your Sins*. U of Oklahoma P, 1988.

Deming, David. "In the Salary Race, Engineers Sprint but English Majors Endure." *New York Times*, 20 Sept. 2019, https://www.nytimes.com/2019/09/20/business/liberal-arts-stem-salaries.html.

Derrida, Jacques. "Différance." *Speech and Phenomena and Other Essays on Husserl's Theory of Signs*, by Derrida, translated by David B. Allison, Northwestern UP, 1973, pp. 129–60.

Dery, Mark. "Black to the Future: Interviews with Samuel R. Delany, Greg Tate, and Tricia Rose." *Flame Wars: The Discourse of Cyberculture*, by Dery, Duke UP, 1994, pp. 179–222.

Díaz, Junot. "Apocalypse." *Boston Review*, 1 May 2011, https://www.bostonreview.net/articles/junot-diaz-apocalypse-haiti-earthquake/.

Dillon, Grace. "Imagining Indigenous Futurisms." *Walking the Clouds: An Anthology of Indigenous Science Fiction*, edited by Dillon, U of Arizona P, 2012, pp. 1–10.

Dinello, Daniel. *Technophobia! Science Fiction Visions of Posthuman Technology*. U of Texas P, 2005.

Doctorow, Cory. "Consent Theater: Some of Privacy's Thorniest Questions." *OneZero*, 20 May 2021, https://medium.com/one-zero/consent-theater-a32b98cd8d96.

Doerfler, Jill. *Those Who Belong: Identity, Family, Blood, and Citizenship among the White Earth Anishinaabeg*. Michigan State UP, 2015.

Dore, Bhavya. "Despite Mixed Results, South Asian Adoptees Turn to DNA Tests." *Quartz*, 20 Oct. 2020, https://qz.com/1919511/despite-mixed-results-south-asian-adoptees-turn-to-dna-tests.

Du Bois, W. E. B. *Black Reconstruction in America, 1860–1880*. Free Press, 1998.

Dupré, John. "The Polygenomic Organism." Richardson and Stevens, pp. 56–72.

Duster, Troy. *Backdoor to Eugenics*. Routledge, 2003.

Engel, John D., et al. *Narrative in Health Care: Healing Patients, Practitioners, Profession, and Community*. Radcliffe Publishing, 2008.

Erasmus, Zimitri. "Sylvia Wynter's Theory of the Human: Counter-, Not Post-Humanist." *Theory, Culture & Society*, vol. 37, no. 6, 2020, pp. 47–65.

Erman, Irina M. "Sympathetic Vampires and Zombies with Brains: The Modern Monster as a Master of Self-Control." *Journal of Popular Culture*, vol. 54, no. 3, 2021, pp. 594–612.

Esteve, Mary. "The Idea of Happiness: Back to the Postwar Future." *Postmodern/Postwar and After: Rethinking American Literature*, edited by Jason Gladstone et al., U of Iowa P, 2016, pp. 127–40.

Fanon, Frantz. *Black Skin, White Masks*. Grove Press, 2008.

Feldman, Marcus W. and Richard C. Lewontin. "Race, Ancestry, and Medicine." Koenig et al., pp. 89–101.

Fields, Barbara J. "Ideology and Race in American History." *Region, Race, and Reconstruction: Essays in Honor of C. Vann Woodward*, edited by J. Morgan Kousser and James M. McPherson, Oxford UP, 1982, pp. 143–77.

Fink, Marty. "AIDS Vampires: Reimagining Illness in Octavia Butler's *Fledgling*." *Science Fiction Studies*, vol. 37, no. 3, 2010, pp. 416–32.

Foucault, Michel. *The History of Sexuality, Volume 1*. Vintage, 1980.

Frank, Arthur W. *The Wounded Storyteller: Body, Illness & Ethics*. U of Chicago P, 1995.

Frye, Mitch. "Circulatory Systems: Vitality and Rhetoric in Richard Powers's *The Gold Bug Variations*." *Critique*, vol. 49, no. 1, 2007, pp. 96–112.

Fusco, Coco. "Introduction: Latin American Performance and the *Reconquista* of Civil Space." *Corpus Delecti: Performance Art of the Americas*, edited by Fusco, Routledge, 2000, pp. 1–22.

Gannett, Lisa. "Questions Asked and Unasked: How by Worrying Less about the 'Really Real,' Philosophers of Science Might Better Contribute to Debates about Genetics and Race." *Synthese*, vol. 177, no. 3, 2010, pp. 363–85.

Garden, Rebecca. "Expanding Clinical Empathy: An Activist Perspective." *Journal of General Internal Medicine*, vol. 24, no. 1, 2008, pp. 122–25.

———. "Telling Stories about Illness and Disability: The Limits and Lessons of Narrative." *Perspectives in Biology and Medicine*, vol. 53, no. 1, 2010, pp. 121–35.

———. "Who Speaks for Whom? Health Humanities and the Ethics of Representation." *Medical Humanities*, vol. 41, no. 2, 2015, pp. 77–80.

Gateward, Frances. "Daywalkin' Night Stalkin' Bloodsuckas: Black Vampires in Contemporary Film." *Genders*, vol. 40, 2004, https://web.archive.org/web/20141022142156/http://www.genders.org/g40/g40_gateward.html.

Gattaca. Directed by Andrew Niccol, Columbia Pictures, 1997.

Gay, Roxane. "The Solace of Preparing Fried Foods and Other Quaint Remembrances from 1960s Mississippi: Thoughts on *The Help*." *The Rumpus*, 17 Aug. 2011. https://therumpus.net/2011/08/17/the-solace-of-preparing-fried-foods-and-other-quaint-remembrances-from-1960s-mississippi-thoughts-on-the-help/.

Gee, James Paul, and Qing Archer Zhang. "A Sensational View of Human Learning, Thinking, and Language." *Literacy Research: Theory, Method, and Practice*, vol. 71, no. 1, 2022, pp. 233–48.

Ghorayshi, Azeen. "Trans Swimmer Revives an Old Debate in Elite Sports: What Defines a Woman?" *New York Times*, 16 Feb. 2022, https://www.nytimes.com/2022/02/16/science/lia-thomas-testosterone-womens-sports.html.

Gill, Josie. *Biofictions: Race, Genetics, and the Contemporary Novel*. Bloomsbury, 2020.

Gillan, Jennifer. "Restoring the Flow: Comic Circulation in Gerald Vizenor's Fiction." *North Dakota Quarterly*, vol. 67, no. 3–4, 2000, pp. 242–55.

Gilmore, Leigh. "Autobiographics." Smith and Watson, *Women*, pp. 183–89.

Grady, Constance. "The Controversy over the New Immigration Novel *American Dirt* Explained." *Vox*, 30 Jan. 2020, www.vox.com/culture/2020/1/22/21075629/american-dirt-controversy-explained-jeanine-cummins-oprah-flatiron.

Green, Ronald M. "From *Arrowsmith* to Atwood: How Did We Come to Disrespect Science?" *After the Genome: A Language for Our Biotechnological Future*, edited by Michael J. Hyde and James A. Herrick, Baylor UP, 2013, pp. 41–53.

Gregoire, Carolyn. "In Defense of the 'Impractical' English Major." *Huffington Post*, 14 Mar. 2014, https://www.huffpost.com/entry/how-english-majors-are-ch_n_4943792.

Gretzky, Madison. "After the Fall: Humanity Narrated in Margaret Atwood's *MaddAddam* Trilogy." *Margaret Atwood Studies*, vol. 11, 2017, pp. 41–54.

Grgas, Stipe. "Reading Richard Powers at the Turn of the Century." *Mapping the World of Anglo-American Studies at the Turn of the Century*, edited by Aleksandra Nikčević-Batrićević and Marija Krivokapić, Cambridge Scholars Publishing, 2015, pp. 3–20.

Grimbeek, Marinette. "Wholesale Apocalypse: Brand Names in Margaret Atwood's *Oryx and Crake*." *Names*, vol. 64, no. 2, 2016, pp. 88–98.

Gross, Lawrence W. "The Comic Vision of Anishinaabe Culture and Religion." *American Indian Quarterly*, vol. 26, no. 3, 2002, pp. 436–59.

Hall, Lynda. "Lorde, Anzaldúa, and Tropicana Performatively Embody the Written." *Auto/biography Studies: a/b*, vol. 15, no. 1, 2000, pp. 96–122.

Halliwell, Martin. "Awaiting the Perfect Storm." *Waltzing Again: New and Selected Conversations with Margaret Atwood*, edited by Earl G. Ingersoll, Ontario Review Press, 2016, pp. 253–64.

Hamann-Rose, Paul. "New Poetics of Postcolonial Relations: Global Genetic Kinship in Zadie Smith's *White Teeth* and Amitav Ghosh's *The Calcutta Chromosome*." *Medical Humanities*, vol. 47, no. 2, 2021, pp. 167–76.

Hamilton, Amy. *Peregrinations: Walking in American Literature*. U of Nevada P, 2018.

Hamner, Everett. *Editing the Soul: Science and Fiction in the Genome Age*. Penn State UP, 2017.

Hanson, Clare. *Genetics and the Literary Imagination*. Oxford UP, 2020.

Hapiuk, William J., Jr. "Of Kitsch and Kachinas: A Critical Analysis of the 'Indian Arts and Crafts Act of 1990.'" *Stanford Law Review*, vol. 53, no. 4, 2001, pp. 1009–75.

Haraway, Donna. *Modest_Witness@Second_Millennium.FemaleMan_Meets_OncoMouse: Feminism and Technoscience*. Routledge, 1997.

———. *When Species Meet*. U of Minnesota P, 2008.

Harman, Mark. "Creative and Arts Graduates Have the Soft Skills Needed to Make Them 'Work Ready.'" *Independent*, 22 June 2016, https://www.independent.co.uk/student/career-planning/creative-arts-graduates-soft-skills-graduate-employment-university-subjects-work-ready-a7095311.html.

Harry, Debra. "The Human Genome Diversity Project and Its Implications for Indigenous Peoples." *Information about Intellectual Property Rights*, no. 6, 1995, http://www.ipcb.org/publications/briefing_papers/files/hgdp.html.

Hartman, Saidiya. *Lose Your Mother: A Journey along the Atlantic Slave Route*. Farrar, Strauss and Giroux, 2008.

Hendrix, Steve. "On the Eve of an Oprah Movie about Henrietta Lacks, an Ugly Feud Consumes the Family." *Washington Post*, 29 Mar. 2017, https://www.washingtonpost.com/local/on-the-eve-of-an-oprah-movie-about-henrietta-lacks-an-ugly-feud-consumes-the-family/2017/03/28/d33d3418-1248-11e7-ada0-1489b735b3a3_story.html.

Henry, William A. "Beyond the Melting Pot." *Time*, 9 Apr. 1990, https://content.time.com/time/subscriber/article/0,33009,969770,00.html.

Herman, Luc, and Geert Lenout. "Genetic Coding and Aesthetic Clues: Richard Powers's *Gold Bug Variations*." *Mosaic*, vol. 31, no. 4, 1998, pp. 151–64.

Herrington, Emily, and Eva Jablonka. "Creating a 'Gestalt Shift' in Evolutionary Science: Roles for Metaphor in the Conceptual Landscape of the Extended Evolutionary Synthesis (EES)." *Interdisciplinary Science Reviews*, vol. 45, no. 3, 2020, pp. 360–79.

Hogue, W. Lawrence. *Postmodern American Literature and Its Other*. U of Illinois P, 2008.

Holpuch, Amanda. "Family of Henrietta Lacks Settles with Biotech Company that Used Her Cells." *New York Times*, 1 Aug. 2023, https://www.nytimes.com/2023/08/01/science/henrietta-lacks-cells-lawsuit-settlement.html.

Höpker, Karin. "Happiness in Distress: Richard Powers's *Generosity* and Narratives of the Biomedical Self." *Ideas of Order: Narrative Patterns in the Novels of Richard Powers*, edited by Antje Kley and Jan D. Kucharzewski, Heidelberg, 2012, pp. 285–312.

Horowitz, Adam S. "Global Voices: Performers in Conversation." *Transformations*, vol. 20, no. 1, 2009, pp. 97–105.

Howe, LeAnne. "Embodied Tribalography: Mound Building, Ball Games, and Native Endurance in the Southeast." *Studies in American Indian Literatures*, vol. 26, no. 2, 2014, pp. 75–93.

———. "Tribalography: The Power of Native Stories." *Journal of Dramatic Theory and Criticism*, vol. 14, no. 1, 1999, pp. 117–25.

"The Human Genome Project." *National Human Genome Research Institute*. https://www.genome.gov/about-genomics/educational-resources/fact-sheets/human-genome-project. Accessed 13 July 2024.

Hurston, Zora Neale. "High John de Conquer." *The Complete Stories*, by Hurston, HarperPerennial, 1995, pp. 139–48.

Ibrahim, Habiba. *Black Age: Oceanic Lifespans and the Time of Black Life*. New York UP, 2021.

"Introducing AncestryDNA." *YouTube*, 13 June 2016, https://www.youtube.com/watch?v=8_IpBsmnGeQ.

Iovino, Serenella, and Serpil Opperman. "Introduction: Stories Come to Matter." *Material Ecocriticism*, edited by Iovino and Opperman, Indiana UP, 2014, pp. 1–18.

Irmscher, Christoph. "Crossblood Columbus: Gerald Vizenor's Narrative 'Discoveries.'" *Amerikastudien*, vol. 40, no. 1, 1995, pp. 83–98.

"It's in Our Genes." *Discipleship Ministries*, the United Methodist Church, 4 Dec. 2006, https://www.umcdiscipleship.org/resources/its-in-our-genes.

Jennings, Hope. "Anthropocene Feminism, Companion Species, and the *MaddAddam* Trilogy." *Contemporary Women's Writing*, vol. 13, no. 1, 2019, pp. 16–33.

Jones, Louis B. "Bach Would've Liked This Molecule." *New York Times*, 25 Aug. 1991, https://www.nytimes.com/1991/08/25/books/bach-wouldve-liked-this-molecule.html.

Jue, Melody. "Scenting Community: Microbial Symbionts in Octavia Butler's *Fledgling*." *Journal of Science Fiction*, vol. 4, no. 1, 2020, pp. 17–19.

Kaur, Harjyot, and Pooja Jaggi. "Intergenerational Trauma in the Context of the 1947 India Pakistan Partition." *Psychological Studies*, vol. 68, 2023, pp. 374–87.

Kay, Lily. *Who Wrote the Book of Life? A History of the Genetic Code*. Stanford UP, 2000.

Keller, Evelyn Fox. *The Century of the Gene*. Harvard UP, 2000.

———. "The Postgenomic Genome." Richardson and Stevens, pp. 9–31.

———. *Refiguring Life: Metaphors of Twentieth-Century Biology*. Columbia UP, 1996.

———. "Thinking about Biology and Culture: Can the Natural and Human Sciences Be Integrated?" *Sociological Review*, vol. 64, no. 1, 2017, pp. 26–41.

Khan, Yasmin Cordery. *The Great Partition: The Making of India and Pakistan*. Yale UP, 2017.

Koenig, Barbara A., et al., eds. *Revisiting Race in a Genomic Age*. Rutgers UP, 2008.

Koepke, Yvette, and Christopher Nelson. "Genetic Crossing: Imagining Tribal Identity and Nation in Gerald Vizenor's *The Heirs of Columbus*." *Studies in American Indian Literature*, vol. 23, no. 3, 2011, pp. 1–33.

Kroeber, Karl. "Why It's a Good Thing Gerald Vizenor Is Not an Indian." Vizenor, *Survivance*, pp. 25–38.

Kruger, Steven F. *AIDS Narratives: Gender and Sexuality, Fiction and Science*. Garland Publishing, 1996.

Krupat, Arnold. "'Stories in the Blood': *Ratio-* and *Natio-* in Gerald Vizenor's *The Heirs of Columbus*." Lee, *Loosening*, pp. 166–77.

———. *The Voice in the Margin: Native American Literature and the Canon*. U of California P, 1989.

Lacey, Lauren J. "Octavia E. Butler on Coping with Power in *Parable of the Sower, Parable of the Talents*, and *Fledgling*." *Critique*, vol. 49, no. 4, 2008, pp. 379–430.

Lacks, David. "An Evening with the Lacks Family." Public Presentation. Northern Michigan University. Marquette, Michigan. 15 Apr. 2013.

Laguna, Albert Sergio. "*Aquí Está Alvarez Guedes*: Cuban *Choteo* and the Politics of Play." *Latino Studies*, vol. 8, no. 4, 2010, pp. 509–31.

Lake, Christina Bieber. *Prophets of the Posthuman: American Fiction, Biotechnology, and the Ethics of Personhood*. U of Notre Dame P, 2013.

Lakoff, George, and Mark Johnson. *Metaphors We Live By*. The U of Chicago P, 1980.

Landecker, Hannah. *Culturing Life: How Cells Became Technologies*. Harvard UP, 2007.

Larkin, Lesley. *Race and the Literary Encounter: Black Literature from James Weldon Johnson to Percival Everett*. Indiana UP, 2015.

Lawn, Jennifer. "The Word as Remnant: Margaret Atwood and Janet Frame." *New Windows on a Woman's World: A Festschrift for Jocelyn Harris*, edited by Colin Gibson and Lisa Marr, U of Otago Department of English, 2005, pp. 385–401.

Lee, A. Robert. Introduction. Lee, *Loosening*, pp. 1–19.

———, ed. *Loosening the Seams: Interpretations of Gerald Vizenor*. Bowling Green State U Popular P, 2000.

Leitch, Vincent. *Deconstructive Criticism*. Columbia UP, 1983.

Liatsos, Yianna. "Rereading Literary Affordances in Narrative Medicine Pedagogy." *Storyworlds*, vol. 11, no. 2, 2019, pp. 1–25.

Liddicoat, Johnathon, et al. "Continental Drift? Do European Clinical Genetic Testing Laboratories Have a Patent Problem?" *European Journal of Human Genetics*, vol. 27, 2019, pp. 997–1007.

Lock, Margaret. "Alienation of Body Parts and the Biopolitics of Immortalized Cell Lines." *Beyond the Body Proper: Reading the Anthropology of Material Life*, edited by Lock and Judith Farquhar, Duke UP, 2007, pp. 567–83.

———. "Comprehending the Body in the Era of the Epigenome." *Current Anthropology*, vol. 56, no. 2, 2015, pp. 151–77.

Lockard, Joe. "Facing the Wiindigoo." Vizenor, *Survivance*, pp. 209–19.

Lonetree, Amy. *Decolonizing Museums: Representing Native America in National and Tribal Museums*. The U of North Carolina P, 2012.

López, José Julián. "Notes on Metaphors, Notes as Metaphors: The Genome as Musical Spectacle." *Science Communication*, vol. 29, no. 1, pp. 7–34.

López Rúa, Paula. "The Manipulative Power of Word-Formation Devices in Margaret Atwood's *Oryx and Crake*." *Revista Alicantina de Estudios Ingleses*, vol. 18, 2005, pp. 149–65.

López-Craig, Tonya. "The Role of Carmelita Tropicana in the Performance Art of Alina Troyano." *Journal of Lesbian Studies*, vol. 7, no. 3, 2003, pp. 47–56.

Lundberg, Elizabeth. "'Let Me Bite You Again': Vampiric Agency in Octavia Butler's *Fledgling*." *GLQ: A Journal of Lesbian and Gay Studies*, vol. 21, no. 4, 2015, pp. 561–84.

Lush, Rebecca M. "Turning Tricks: Sexuality and Language in Vizenor's *The Heirs of Columbus*." *Studies in American Indian Literatures*, vol. 24, no. 2, 2012, pp. 1–16.

MacNaughton, Jane. "The Dangerous Practice of Empathy." *The Lancet*, vol. 373, no. 9679, 2009, pp. 1940–41.

Madsen, Deborah. "On Subjectivity and Survivance: Rereading Trauma through *The Heirs of Columbus* and *The Crown of Columbus*." Vizenor, *Survivance*, pp. 61–87.

———. "The Sovereignty of Transmotion in a State of Exception: Lessons from the Internment of 'Praying Indians' on Deer Island, Massachusetts Bay Colony, 1675–1676." *Transmotion*, vol. 1, no. 1, 2015, pp. 23–47.

Marks, Jonathan. *What It Means to Be 98% Chimpanzee: Apes, People, and Their Genes*. U of California P, 2002.

Mataatua Declaration on Cultural and Intellectual Property Rights of Indigenous Peoples, prepared by the Commission on Human Rights, the Sub-Commission of Prevention of Discrimination and Protection of Minorities, and the Working Group on Indigenous Populations for the First International Conference on the Cultural & Indigenous Populations, Whakatane, Aotearoa (New Zealand), June 1993, https://www.wipo.int/export/sites/www/tk/en/databases/creative_heritage/docs/mataatua.pdf. Accessed 12 July 2024.

Matz, Robert. "The Myth of the English Major Barista." *Inside Higher Ed*, 6 July 2016, https://www.insidehighered.com/views/2016/07/06/cultural-implications-myth-english-majors-end-working-permanently-starbucks-essay.

McDevitt, Kelly. "Childhood Sexuality as Posthuman Subjectivity in Octavia E. Butler's *Fledgling*." *Science Fiction Studies*, vol. 47, no. 2, 2020, pp. 219–40.

McEwen, Jean, et al. "The Ethical, Legal, and Social Implications Program of the National Human Genome Research Institute: Reflections on an Ongoing Experiment." *Annual Review of Genomics and Human Genetics*, vol. 15, 2014, pp. 481–505.

McGlennen, Molly. "'By My Heart': Gerald Vizenor's *Almost Ashore* and *Bear Island: The War at Sugar Point*." *Transmotion*, vol. 1, no. 2, 2015, pp. 1–25.

McHugh, Kathleen. "Bio-Performatives, Cross-Species, and Continents of Plastic in *Chicas 2000* and *Post Plastica*: An Interview with Carmelita Tropicana and Ela Troyano." *S&F Online*, vol. 11, no. 3, 2013, https://sfonline.barnard.edu/bio-performatives-cross-species-and-continents-of-plastic-in-chicas-2000-and-post-plastica-an-interview-with-carmelita-tropicana-and-ela-troyano/.

McKittrick, Katherine. *Dear Science and Other Stories*. Duke UP, 2021.

Mehaffy, Marilyn, and AnaLouise Keating. "'Radio Imagination': Octavia Butler on the Poetics of Narrative Embodiment." *MELUS*, vol. 26, no. 1, 2001, pp. 45–76.

Meisenhelder, Susan. *Hitting a Straight Lick with a Crooked Stick: Race and Gender in the Work of Zora Neale Hurston*. U of Alabama P, 2001.

Mejía Chaves, Andrea, and Sondra Bacharach. "Hair Oppression and Appropriation." *British Journal of Aesthetics*, vol. 61, no. 3, 2021, pp. 335–52.

Meloni, Maurizio, et al. "The Biosocial: Sociological Themes and Issues." *Sociological Review Monographs*, vol. 64, no. 1, 2016, pp. 7–25.

Menely, Tobias, and Jesse Oak Taylor. Introduction. *Anthropocene Reading: Literary History in Geologic Times*, edited by Menely and Taylor, Pennsylvania State UP, 2017, pp. 1–24.

Mitchell, Robert. "Sacrifice, Individuation, and the Economics of Genomics." *Literature and Medicine*, vol. 26, no. 1, 2007, pp. 126–58.

Mitchell, W. J. T. "The Rights of Things." Foreword to Wolfe, *Animal*, pp. ix–xiv.

Monani, Salma, and Joni Adamson, eds. *Ecocriticism and Indigenous Studies: Conversations from Earth to Cosmos*. Routledge, 2017.

Morning, Ann. "Reconstructing Race in Science and Society: Biology Textbooks, 1952–2002." *American Journal of Sociology*, vol. 114, no. S1, 2008, pp. S106–S137.

Morrison, Toni. *Beloved*. Vintage, 1987.

———. Nobel Lecture. 7 Dec. 1993. *The Nobel Prize*, https://www.nobelprize.org/prizes/literature/1993/morrison/lecture/. Accessed 12 July 2024.

———. *Playing in the Dark: Whiteness and the Literary Imagination*. Vintage, 1993.

———. "The Site of Memory." *The Source of Self-Regard: Selected Essays, Speeches, and Meditations*, by Morrison, Alfred A. Knopf, 2019, pp. 233–45.

———. "Unspeakable Things Unspoken." *Michigan Quarterly Review*, vol. 28, no. 1, pp. 1–34.

"Most Popular Majors." *National Center for Education Statistics*, https://nces.ed.gov/fastfacts/display.asp?id=37.

Moya, Paula M. L. *The Social Imperative: Race, Close Reading, and Contemporary Literary Criticism*. Stanford UP, 2015.

Moya, Paula M. L., and Lesley Larkin. "The Decolonial Virtues of Ethnospeculative Fiction." *Cultivating Virtue in the University*, edited by Jonathan Brant et al., Oxford UP, 2022, pp. 226–49.

Mukherjee, Siddhartha. *The Gene: An Intimate History*. Scribner, 2016.

Muñoz, José Esteban. *Cruising Utopia: The Then and There of Queer Futurity*. NYU Press, 2019.

———. *Disidentifications: Queers of Color and the Performance of Politics*. U of Minnesota P, 1999.

Narkunas, J. Paul. "Between Words, Numbers, and Things: Transgenics and Other Objects of Life in Margaret Atwood's MaddAddams." *Critique: Studies in Contemporary Fiction*, vol. 56, no. 1, 2015, pp. 1–25.

Nash, Stephen E., and Chip Colwell. "NAGPRA at 30: The Effects of Repatriation." *Annual Review of Anthropology*, vol. 49, no. 1, 2020, pp. 225–39.

Nayar, Pramod K. "A New Biological Citizenship: Posthumanism in Octavia Butler's *Fledgling*." *Modern Fiction Studies*, vol. 58, no. 4, 2012, pp. 796–817.

Nelkin, Dorothy. "Molecular Metaphors: The Gene in Popular Discourse." *Nature Reviews Genetics*, vol. 2, no. 7, 2001, pp. 555–59.

Nelson, Alondra. "Bio Science: Genetic Genealogy Testing and the Pursuit of African Ancestry." *Social Studies of Science*, vol. 38, no. 5, 2008, pp. 759–83.

———. "Future Texts." *Social Text*, vol. 71, no. 2, 2002, pp. 1–15.

———. "Making the Impossible Possible: An Interview with Nalo Hopkinson." *Social Text*, vol. 20, no. 2, 2002, pp. 97–113.

———. *The Social Life of DNA: Race, Reparations, and Reconciliation after the Genome*. Beacon Press, 2016.

Nelson, Chris. "State(s) and Statements: Reflections on Native American Literary Criticism." *Great Plains Quarterly*, vol. 35, no. 4, 2015, pp. 377–89.

Nguyen, Viet Thanh. *Nothing Ever Dies: Vietnam and the Memory of War*. Harvard UP, 2017.

"NIH, Lacks Family Reach Understanding to Share Genomic Data of HeLa Cells." *National Institutes of Health,* 7 Aug. 2013, https://www.nih.gov/news-events/news-releases/nih-lacks-family-reach-understanding-share-genomic-data-hela-cells.

Nixon, Rob. *Slow Violence and the Environmentalism of the Poor.* Harvard UP, 2013.

Noble, Denis. *The Music of Life: Biology Beyond Genes.* Oxford UP, 2008.

Noori, Margaret. *Bawaajimo: A Dialect of Dreams in Anishinaabe Language and Literature.* Michigan State UP, 2014.

Noriega, Chon. "Editor's Introduction: Very Good with the Tongue." Troyano, *I, Carmelita,* pp. ix–xii.

Nussbaum, Martha. *Not for Profit: Why Democracy Needs the Humanities.* Princeton UP, 2010.

Omi, Michael, and Howard Winant. *Racial Formation in the United States.* 2nd ed., Routledge, 1994.

O'Neill, Kimberly. "Latina Writers and the Usable Past." *The Cambridge History of American Women's Literature,* edited by Dale M. Bauer, Cambridge UP, 2012, pp. 590–607.

Ostrander, Elaine A. "Central Dogma." *Talking Glossary of Genomic and Genetic Terms,* National Human Genome Research Institute, https://www.genome.gov/genetics-glossary/Central-Dogma. Accessed 12 July 2024.

Ozeki, Ruth. *All Over Creation.* Penguin, 2003.

Parker, Robert Dale. "The World and Writing of Jane Johnston Schoolcraft." *The Sound the Stars Make Rushing through the Sky: The Writings of Jane Johnston Schoolcraft,* edited by Parker, U of Pennsylvania P, 2007, pp. 1–84.

"Passion, Innovation, Courage: It's in Our Genes; The Celgene Story." *Celgene.com.* https://media2.celgene.com/content/uploads/the-celgene-story.pdf. Accessed 13 July 2024.

Peterkin, Allan. "*Primum Non Nocere*: On Accountability in Narrative-Based Medicine." *Literature and Medicine,* vol. 11, no. 2, 2011, pp. 396–411.

Phelan, Jo C., et al. "The Genomic Revolution and Beliefs about Essential Racial Differences: A Backdoor to Eugenics?" *American Sociological Review,* vol. 78, no. 2, 2013, pp. 167–91.

Porta, Miquel. "The Genome Sequence is a Jazz Score." *International Journal of Epidemiology,* vol. 32, 2003, pp. 29–31.

Portin, Petter, and Adam Wilkins. "The Evolving Definition of the Term 'Gene.'" *Genetics,* vol. 205, 2017, pp. 1353–64.

Powers, Richard. "The Book of Me." *GQ,* 30 Sept. 2008, https://www.gq.com/story/richard-powers-genome-sequence.

———. *Generosity: An Enhancement.* Farrar, Strauss and Giroux, 2009.

———. *The Gold Bug Variations.* William Morrow, 1991.

———. *Orfeo.* W. W. Norton, 2014.

Queremel Milani, Daniel A., and Pradip R. Chauhan. "Genetics, Mosaicism." *National Library of Medicine,* 1 May 2023, https://www.ncbi.nlm.nih.gov/books/NBK559193/.

Rajan, Kaushik Sunder. *Biocapital: The Constitution of Postgenomic Life.* Duke UP, 2006.

Ramírez, Catherine. "Afrofuturism/Chicanafuturism: Fictive Kin." *Aztlán*, vol. 33, no. 1, 2008, pp. 185–94.

Reardon, Jenny. "On the Emergence of Science and Justice." *Science, Technology, & Human Values*, vol. 38, no. 2, 2013, pp. 176–200.

———. *The Postgenomic Condition: Ethics, Justice & Knowledge after the Genome*. U of Chicago P, 2017.

———. *Race to the Finish: Identity and Governance in an Age of Genomics*. Princeton UP, 2005.

"Remarks by the President, Prime Minister Tony Blair of England (via Satellite), Dr. Francis Collins, Director of the National Human Genome Research Institute, and Dr. Craig Venter, President and Chief Scientific Officer, Celera Genomics Corporation, of the Completion of the First Survey of the Entire Human Genome Project." *National Archives*, 26 June 2000, https://www.genome.gov/10001356/june-2000-white-house-event. Accessed 12 July 2024.

Richardson, Sarah S. *Sex Itself: The Search for Male and Female in the Human Genome*. The U of Chicago P, 2013.

Richardson, Sarah S., and Hallam Stevens. "Beyond the Genome." Richardson and Stevens, pp. 1–8.

———, eds. *Postgenomics: Perspectives on Biology after the Genome*. Duke UP, 2015.

Riding In, James. "Decolonizing NAGPRA." *For Indigenous Eyes Only: A Decolonization Handbook*, edited by Waziyatawin Angela Wilson and Michael Yellow Bird, School of American Research Press, 2005, pp. 53–66.

Roberts, Dorothy. "Can Research on the Genetics of Intelligence Be 'Socially Neutral'?" *Hastings Center Report*, vol. 45, no. 5, 2015, pp. S50–S53.

———. *Fatal Invention: How Science, Politics, and Big Business Re-Create Race in the Twenty-first Century*. New Press, 2011.

———. *Killing the Black Body: Race, Reproduction, and the Meaning of Liberty*. Vintage, 2014.

Rodríguez, Juana María. "Vizenorian Jurisprudence: Legal Interventions, Narrative Strategies, and the Interpretative Possibilities of Shadows." Lee, *Loosening*, pp. 246–62.

Román, David. "Carmelita Tropicana Unplugged." *TDR*, vol. 39, no. 3, 1995, pp. 83–93.

Roof, Judith. *The Poetics of DNA*. U of Minnesota P, 2007.

Rose, Hilary, and Steven Rose. *Genes, Cells and Brains: The Promethean Promises of the New Biology*. Verso, 2012.

Rose, Nikolas, and Carlos Novas. "Biological Citizenship." *Global Assemblages: Technology, Politics, and Ethics as Anthropological Problems*, edited by Aihwa Wong and Stephen J. Collier, Blackwell, 2005, pp. 439–64.

Rosiek, Jerry Lee, et al. "The New Materialisms and Indigenous Theories of Non-Human Agency: Making the Case for Respectful Anti-Colonial Engagement." *Qualitative Inquiry*, vol. 26, no. 3–4, 2019, pp. 331–46.

Rosner, Mary, and T. R. Johnson. "Telling Stories: Metaphors of the Human Genome Project." *Hypatia*, vol. 10, no. 4, 1995, pp. 104–29.

Rotimi, Charles. "Genetic Drift." *Talking Glossary of Genomic and Genetic Terms*, National Human Genome Research Institute, https://www.genome.gov/genetics-glossary/Genetic-Drift#:~:text=Genetic%20drift%20is%20the%20change,D. Accessed 12 July 2024.

Roxburgh, Natalie, and Jay Clayton. "Science and Society in Recent Fiction." *Under the Literary Microscope: Science and Society in the Contemporary Novel*, edited by Sina Farzin et al., Pennsylvania State UP, 2021, pp. 21–36.

Ruiz, Sandra. "El Caribe on the Horizon: José Esteban Muñoz and the Commitment to Futurity." *Small Axe*, vol. 19, no. 2, 2015, pp. 94–103.

Said, Khalid. "The Grammar of Folklorization: An Integrated Critical Discourse Analysis of the Linguistic Depiction of Amazigh Social Actors in Selected Moroccan ESL Textbooks (1980s–Present)." *Cogent Education*, vol. 10, no. 2, 2023, pp. 1–23.

Sarkowsky, Katja. "'Out of the Belly of Christopher's Ship': Mapping the 'Red Atlantic' and Indigenous Modernity." *Comparative Indigenous Studies*, edited by Mita Banerjee, Universitätsverlag Winter, 2016, pp. 353–81.

Schiff, Sarah Eden. "Power Literature and the Myth of Racial Memory." *Modern Fiction Studies*, vol. 57, no. 1, 2011, pp. 96–122.

Schmidt, Benjamin. "The Humanities Are in Crisis." *The Atlantic*, 23 Aug. 2018, https://www.theatlantic.com/ideas/archive/2018/08/the-humanities-face-a-crisisof-confidence/567565/.

Schubert, Charlotte. "Straight Talk with . . . Charles Rotimi." *Nature Medicine*, vol. 14, no. 7, 2008, pp. 704–5.

Scott, Darieck. *Extravagant Abjection*. New York UP, 2010.

Segre, Julie. "Methylation." *Talking Glossary of Genomic and Genetic Terms*, National Human Genome Research Institute, https://www.genome.gov/genetics-glossary/Methylation. Accessed 12 July 2024.

Shapiro, Lawrence. *Embodied Cognition*. Routledge, 2011.

Sheffield, Gail K. *The Arbitrary Indian: The Indian Arts and Crafts Act of 1990*. U of Oklahoma P, 1997.

Shim, Janet K. "Cultural Health Capital: A Theoretical Approach to Understanding Health Care Interactions and the Dynamics of Unequal Treatment." *Journal of Health and Social Behavior*, vol. 51, no. 1, 2010, pp. 1–15.

Sinclair, Niigonwedom James. "A Sovereignty of Transmotion: Imagination and the 'Real,' Gerald Vizenor, and Native Literary Nationalism." *Stories through Theories / Theories through Stories*, edited by Gordon D. Henry Jr., et al., Michigan State UP, 2009, pp. 123–58.

Skloot, Rebecca. *The Immortal Life of Henrietta Lacks*. Crown, 2010.

Smith, Jeremy. "Outside and against the Quincentenary: Modern Indigenous Representations at the Time of the Colombian Celebrations." *Atlantic Studies*, vol. 6, 2009, pp. 63–80.

Smith, Linda Tuhiwai. *Decolonizing Methodologies: Research and Indigenous Peoples*. 2nd ed., Zed Books, 2012.

Smith, Sidonie. "Presidential Address 2011: Narrating Lives and Contemporary Imaginings." *PMLA*, vol. 126, no. 3, 2011, pp. 564–74.

Smith, Sidonie, and Julia Watson. Introduction. Smith and Watson, *Women*, pp. 3–56.

———. *Reading Autobiography: A Guide for Interpreting Life Narratives*. U of Minnesota P, 2001.

———, eds. *Women, Autobiography, Theory: A Reader*. U of Wisconsin P, 1998.

Smith, Valerie. "Black Women's Memories and *The Help*." *Southern Cultures*, vol. 20, no. 1, 2014, pp. 26–37.

———. *Self-Discovery and Authority in Afro-American Narrative.* Harvard UP, 1991.

Snow, C. P. *The Two Cultures and the Scientific Revolution.* Martino Fine Books, 2013.

Solomon, Miriam. *Making Medical Knowledge.* Oxford UP, 2015.

Sommer, Doris. *Proceed with Caution When Engaged by Minority Writing in the Americas.* Harvard UP, 1999.

Spillers, Hortense. "Mama's Baby, Papa's Maybe: An American Grammar Book." *Diacritics,* vol. 17, no. 2, 1987, pp. 64–81.

Squier, Susan Merrill. "Beyond Nescience: The Intersectional Insights of Health Humanities." *Perspectives in Biology and Medicine,* vol. 50, no. 3, 2007, pp. 334–47.

Squire, Louise. "'I Am Not Afraid to Die': Contemporary Environmental Crisis Fiction and the Post-Theory Era." *Extending Ecocriticism: Crisis, Collaboration, and Challenges in the Environmental Humanities,* edited by Peter Barry and William Welstead, U of Iowa P, 2017, pp. 14–29.

Stanciu, Cristina. "Gerald Vizenor." *The Encyclopedia of Contemporary American Fiction 1980–2020,* edited by Patrick O'Donnell et al., Wiley, 2022, pp. 1366–71.

Stearns, Frank W. "One Hundred Years of Pleiotropy: A Retrospective." *Genetics,* vol. 186, 2010, pp. 767–73.

Stevens, Hallam. "Networks: Representations and Tools in Postgenomics." Richardson and Stevens, pp. 103–25.

Stevens, Wallace. "On the Road Home." *The Collected Poems of Wallace Stevens,* Vintage Books, 1990, pp. 203–4.

Stock, Adam. "Making Art in Dystopia." *Alluvium: 21st Century Writing,* vol. 1, no. 3, 2012, https://alluvium.bacls.org/2012/08/01/making-art-in-dystopia/.

Stotz, Karola, and Paul E. Griffiths. "Biohumanities: Rethinking the Relationship between Biosciences, Philosophy and History of Science, and Society." *Quarterly Review of Biology,* vol. 83, no. 1, 2008, pp. 37–45.

Sugg, Katherine. *Gender and Allegory in Transamerican Fiction and Performance.* Palgrave Macmillan, 2008.

Sullivan, Heather I. "Material Ecocriticism and the Petro-Text." *The Routledge Companion to the Environmental Humanities,* edited by Ursula K. Heise et al., Routledge, 2017, pp. 414–23.

Sumara, Dennis J. *Private Readings in Public: Schooling the Literary Imagination.* Peter Lang, 1996.

TallBear, Kim. *Native American DNA: Tribal Belonging and the False Promise of Genetic Science.* U of Minnesota P, 2013.

Tate, Sarah K., and David B. Goldstein. "Will Tomorrow's Medicines Work for Everyone?" *Nature Genetics Supplement,* vol. 36, no. 11, 2004, pp. S34–S42.

Timmermans, Stefan, and Mara Buchbinder. "Patients-in-Waiting: Living between Sickness and Health in the Genomics Era." *Journal of Health and Social Behavior,* vol. 51, no. 4, 2010, pp. 408–23.

Tinker, George "Tink." "The Stones Shall Cry Out: Consciousness, Rocks, and Indians." *Wicazo Sa Review,* vol. 19, no. 2, 2004, pp. 105–25.

Troyano, Alina. Author's Introduction. Troyano, *I, Carmelita,* pp. xiii–xxv.

———. *Carmelita Tropicana: Your Kunst Is Your Waffen.* Troyano, *I, Carmelita,* pp. 137–70.

———. *Chicas 2000.* Troyano, *I, Carmelita,* pp. 72–122.

———. *I, Carmelita Tropicana: Performing Between Cultures.* Beacon Press, 2000.

———. "Performance Art Manifesto." Troyano, *I, Carmelita*, pp. 177–78.

Valentine, Rand. "Noun Gender: Animate and Inanimate." *Anishinaabemowin.* U of Wisconsin. https://ojibwegrammar.langsci.wisc.edu/Grammar/InflMorphology/nouns001.htm. Accessed 12 July 2024.

"The 'Vampire Project.'" Podcast. *Innate: How Science Invented the Myth of Race*, 28 Feb. 2023, https://www.sciencehistory.org/stories/distillations-pod/the-vampire-project/.

Van der Weele, Cor. "Roads towards a *Lingua Democratica* on Genomics: How Can Metaphors Guide Us?" *Genomics, Society, and Policy*, vol. 5, no. 3, 2009, pp. ii–vii.

Van Dijck, José. *Imagenation: Popular Images of Genetics.* New York UP, 1998.

Varela, Francisco J., et al. *The Embodied Mind: Cognitive Science and Human Experience.* The MIT P, 1991.

Vials, Chris. "Margaret Atwood's Dystopic Fiction and the Contradictions of Neoliberal Freedom." *Textual Practice*, vol. 29, no. 2, 2015, pp. 235–54.

Vizenor, Gerald. "Aesthetics of Survivance: Literary Theory and Practice." Vizenor, *Survivance*, pp. 1–24.

———. *Bear Island: The War at Sugar Point.* U of Minnesota P, 2006.

———. "Bone Courts: The Rights and Narrative Representation of Tribal Bones." *American Indian Quarterly*, vol. 10, no. 4, 1986, pp. 319–31.

———. *Fugitive Poses: Native American Indian Scenes of Absence and Presence.* U of Nebraska P, 1998.

———. "Genome Survivance." *Biomapping Indigenous Peoples: Towards an Understanding of the Issues*, edited by Susanne Berthier-Foglar et al., Rodopi, 2012, pp. 221–31.

———. *The Heirs of Columbus.* Wesleyan UP, 1991.

———. *Manifest Manners: Narratives on Postindian Survivance.* U of Nebraska P, 1994.

———, ed. *Narrative Chance: Postmodern Discourse on Native American Indian Literatures.* U of Oklahoma P, 1993.

———. "A Postmodern Introduction." Vizenor, *Narrative*, pp. 3–15.

———. Preface. Vizenor, *Narrative*, pp. ix–xiii.

———. "Socioacupuncture." *Out There: Marginalization and Contemporary Cultures*, edited by Russell Ferguson et al., New Museum of Contemporary Art, 1990, pp. 411–19.

———, ed. *Survivance: Narratives of Native Presence.* U of Nebraska P, 2008.

———. "Trickster Discourse: Comic Holotropes and Language Games." Vizenor, *Narrative*, pp. 187–211.

Wade, Nicholas. *A Troublesome Inheritance: Genes, Race, and Human History.* Penguin, 2014.

Wade, Peter, et al. "Genomics, Race Mixture, and Nation in Latin America." *Mestizo Genomics: Race, Mixture, Nation, and Science in Latin America*, edited by P. Wade et al., Duke UP, 2014, pp. 1–32.

Wailoo, Keith. "Who Am I? Genes and the Problem of Historical Identity." *Genetics and the Unsettled Past: The Collision of DNA, Race, and History*, edited by Wailoo et al., Rutgers UP, 2012, pp. 13–19.

Wald, Priscilla. "American Studies and the Politics of Life." *American Quarterly*, vol. 64, no. 2, 2012, pp. 185–204.

———. "Future Perfect: Grammar, Genes, and Geography." *New Literary History*, vol. 31, 2000, pp. 681–708.

Wald, Priscilla, and Jay Clayton. "Editors' Preface: Genomics in Literature, Visual Art, and Culture." *Literature and Medicine*, vol. 26, no. 1, 2007, vi–xvi.

Waller, Nikki. "Hunting for Soft Skills: Companies Scoop Up English Majors." *Wall Street Journal*, 25 Oct. 2016, https://www.wsj.com/articles/hunting-for-soft-skills-companies-scoop-up-english-majors-1477404061.

Wanjek, Christopher. "Systems Biology as Defined by NIH: An Intellectual Resource for Integrative Biology." *NIH Catalyst*, vol. 19, no. 6, 2011, https://irp.nih.gov/catalyst/19/6/systems-biology-as-defined-by-nih.

Washington, Harriet. *Medical Apartheid: The Dark History of Medical Experimentation on Black Americans from Colonial Times to the Present*. Anchor, 2008.

Wasserloos, Arnd. "Whose Genes? Whose Ethics? Culture, Representation, and Controversy in the Debates Surrounding the Human Genome Diversity Project." *Jahrbuch für Recht und Ethik / Annual Review of Law and Ethics*, vol. 9, 2001, pp. 65–86.

Watkins, Susan. "Future Shock: Rewriting the Apocalypse in Contemporary Women's Fiction." *LIT: Literature Interpretation Theory*, vol. 23, no. 2, 2012, pp. 119–37.

Weheliye, Alexander. *Habeas Viscus: Racializing Assemblages, Biopolitics, and Black Feminist Thought*. Duke UP, 2014.

Weinbaum, Alys Eve. *The Afterlife of Reproductive Slavery*. Duke UP, 2019.

———. "Racial Aura: Walter Benjamin and the Work of Art in a Biotechnological Age." *Literature and Medicine*, vol. 26, no. 1, 2007, pp. 207–39.

Wexler, Alice. *Mapping Fate: A Memoir of Family, Risk, and Genetic Research*. Random House, 1995.

———. "Mapping Lives: 'Truth,' Life Writing, and DNA." *The Ethics of Life Writing*, edited by Paul John Eakin, Cornell UP, 2004, pp. 163–73.

"What Makes Starbucks One of the World's Top 5 Most Admired Employers?" *Starbucks Stories and News*, 23 Jan. 2018, https://stories.starbucks.com/stories/2018/starbucks-one-of-the-worlds-top-5-most-admired/.

Wheeler, Ryan, et al. "Beyond NAGPRA/Not NAGPRA." *Collections: A Journal for Museum and Archive Professionals*, vol. 18, no. 1, 2022, pp. 8–17.

Winstead, Ashley. "Beyond Persuasion: Margaret Atwood's Speculative Politics." *Studies in the Novel*, vol. 49, no. 2, 2017, pp. 228–49.

Wolfe, Cary. *Animal Rites: American Culture, the Discourse of Species, and Posthumanist Theory*. U of Chicago P, 2003.

———. "Human, All Too Human: 'Animal Studies' and the Humanities." *PMLA*, vol. 124, no. 2, 2009, pp. 564–75.

Worthen, W. B. "Bordering Space." *Land/scape/theater*, edited by Elinor Fuchs and Una Chaudhuri, U of Michigan P, 2002, pp. 280–300.

Wynter, Sylvia. "1492: A New World View." *Race, Discourse, and the Origin of the Americas*, edited by Vera Lawrence Hyatt and Rex Nettleford, Smithsonian Institution Press, 1995, pp. 5–57.

———. "Unsettling the Coloniality of Being/Power/Truth/Freedom: Towards the Human, after Man, Its Overrepresentation—An Argument." *CR: The New Centennial Review*, vol. 3, no. 3, 2003, pp. 257–337.

Yarbro-Bejarano, Yvonne. "Traveling Transgressions: Cubanidad in Performances by Carmelita Tropicana and Marga Gómez." *Reading and Writing the Ambiente: Queer Sexualities in Latino, Latin American, and Spanish Culture*, edited by Susana Chávez-Silverman and Librada Hernández, U of Wisconsin P, 2000, pp. 200–217.

Zwart, Hub, and Annemiek Nelis. "What Is ELSA Genomics?" *EMBO Reports*, vol. 10, no. 6, 2009, pp. 540–44.

INDEX

ableism, 169. *See also* disability
abolitionist texts, 79
adaptation, 6, 124–31, 174
African Americans: ancestry testing, 15–16, 144; medical exploitation of, 16–17; signifying, 82. *See also* Blackness; Black women; race
Age of Exploration, 102–3
agency, 19–20, 40, 85–86, 134, 138, 146, 181, 188–90, 215–16, 222; bionarrative, 104–5 (*see also* bionarrativity)
Ahmed, Sara, 151–52, 157
Alaimo, Stacy, 33, 174, 180–81, 190
Algeria, 86, 91, 93, 96
Amazigh people, 86n27
American exceptionalism, 177
ancestry testing, 6, 10, 15–16, 57n22, 62, 72–73, 75, 104, 110, 111, 113, 122, 144. *See also* genetic ancestry
Anishinaabe, 104n7, 115n30, 118–20, 123, 171
Anishinaabemowin, 118, 127n45
Anthropocene, 24, 201–2, 214, 216
anthropocentrism, 210, 220
anthropomorphism, 115n30

Anzaldúa, Gloria, 186
apocalypse, 33, 167, 169–73, 192–94, 196–97, 201–21
Appleton, Sarah, 193n2
appropriation, 8, 20, 78, 105, 119–22, 129, 211
Armstrong, Jeannette, 102n3
arts. *See* humanities and arts scholarship
Asimov, Isaac, 27
assimilation, 110
Association for Molecular Pathology v. Myriad (2013), 17, 109n17
associations, literary and genetic, 105, 117, 121, 125, 127
Atwood, Margaret, 28, 170, 174; *The Handmaid's Tale*, 138n8, 170n14, 194n5; *MaddAddam*, 192, 208n22, 218–21; *MaddAddam* trilogy, 28, 33–34, 137, 167, 181, 183n36, 192–94, 196–97, 201–21; *Oryx and Crake*, 192, 194, 202–14, 220; *The Year of the Flood*, 192, 214–18, 220
authenticity, 71–72, 75, 76, 80, 83, 102, 105, 112–13, 127
authorship, 20, 41, 89, 95
autobiography, 71. *See also* life writing

autonomy, 184; bodily, 16–17, 40, 109, 134, 139
Avise, John C., 41n6
Avrahami, Einat, 76

Bacigalupi, Paolo, 28
Bamewawagezhikaquay. See Schoolcraft, Jane Johnston
Barad, Karen, 29, 174, 183, 201, 208n21
Barthes, Roland, 50
Bast, Florian, 138, 138n7, 139n9
Bateson, William, 58
Bell Curve, The (Herrnstein and Murray), 54
Benjamin, Ruha, 62, 75n12
Bergethon, Peter R., 27–29
Bérubé, Michael, 30
Bhabha, Homi, 179n34
biocolonialism, 19, 29, 103, 107. See also colonialism
biography, 27, 39, 67, 69. See also life writing
biology: developmental, 13n15. See also molecular biology; systems biology
bionarrativity, 25, 32, 33, 114–32; agency and, 104–5; appropriation and, 105, 119–22; genome time and, 174; therapeutic bionarrative signatures, 105–6, 122–32. See also fleshy reading
biopower, 20
bioprospecting, 7, 16–17, 103, 104, 107, 109, 119
Bishop, Jeffrey, 199, 200
Black feminist theories, 32, 78, 134–36, 135n2, 147–48, 150
Black futurism, 27. See also ethnofuturism
Black women, 19; erasures of, 134–36; medical exploitation of, 16–17, 77, 136, 139–40, 143–46; mothers, 136; reading and writing by, 83–86
Blackness, 79, 135, 147, 150–51, 153, 156–60. See also race
Bliss, Catherine, 14
blood: quantum, 110–11, 124; in vampire fiction, 132, 142–43
bodily autonomy. See autonomy
bonobos, 180–81
Book of Life metaphor, 4–6, 10, 29–31, 38–41, 47–48, 76, 115
Borges, Jorge Luis, 49–50

Brody, Howard, 21
Brooks, Van Wyck, 170n12
Brown, Lois, 83
Burnett, L. D., 199
Butalia, Urvashi, 59, 61n24
Butler, Judith, 186
Butler, Octavia, 25, 28, 67; "Bloodchild," 135n2, 138; Fledgling, 28, 32, 132–62; Parable of the Sower, 162n39; Xenogenesis trilogy, 28, 138

Cajete, Gregory, 25
Calvo-Quirós, William, 172
camp, 176–77
Camus, Albert, 93–94
Canavan, Gerry, 203, 220
cannibalistic reading, 79–83
capitalism, 7–8, 167, 196–97, 202, 219–20
Capitalocene, 212n25
Carmelita Tropicana: Your Kunst Is Your Waffen (1994), 185
Carrel, Alexis, 183n36
Cavalli-Sforza, Luigi Luca, 106, 108
Celera, 62
cells, 68n1; cell membranes, 201, 221–22. See also HeLa cells
Chambers, Tod, 199
chance, 6n5, 26, 49, 106, 111, 113, 115, 123–25, 131, 166n4, 173
change, 34, 53, 71, 105, 113, 124, 150, 161–62, 170, 184, 213, 216
Charon, Rita, 21, 201, 221
Chicanafuturism, 171. See also ethnofuturism
Choksey, Lara, 18n27, 25n37, 27–28, 28n41, 29, 45n10, 82n21, 85n25, 135n2, 166n5, 167n6, 172n18, 185n39
choteo, 176–77
Christie, Stuart, 111n21
Chu, Seo-Young, 29
class hierarchy, 86, 191
Clayton, Jay, 21, 28n41, 30, 33, 172–73, 184n37, 194n5
climate change, 193, 197
Clinton, Bill, 13, 55
cloning, 165n3, 169, 175–76, 179, 181, 183–85, 187–88
close reading, 31, 90, 95
"code" metaphors, 4, 10, 40, 45, 115, 162

Collins, Francis, 62
colonialism, 34, 91, 208, 210–12, 220; as bionarrative consumption, 120; discovery and, 102–3, 128–30; genetics and, 54, 56–58, 62–64, 169; healing from wounds of, 102, 104, 113–15, 122–31; humanities scholarship and, 194–95, 200, 202; intergenerational trauma of, 175; material exploitations of, 103–4; racialized bodies and, 147, 151; violence of, 112, 122, 123. *See also* biocolonialism; imperialism; neocolonialism
color-blind ideology, 178
Columbo, Realdo, 127n44
Columbus, Christopher, 32, 101–5, 116, 118, 119, 122–31
Colville, 109
commodification, 8, 20, 112, 135, 139, 208
computer-assisted analysis, 14, 105, 131
Conrad, Joseph, 23n35
consent, 71, 134, 136–46, 187; informed, 7, 16, 108, 140
constructivism, genomic, 41
context, 26, 95–96; genes as indivisible from, 31, 39–40, 54–55, 64–66; historical, 31, 39–40, 53–66, 104, 107n9, 109–10; textual metaphors and, 42–44, 66–67
contingency, genetic and linguistic, 2, 6, 26, 44, 150
Cook-Deegan, Robert, 106
Corner, Peter, 47
corporate monoculture, 2, 6–8
corporate university, 199, 204; adjunct faculty, 1, 8, 23, 198
corporations: advertising, 10, 194, 197, 204; profits from medical exploitation, 78, 81
Couser, G. Thomas, 22, 72, 73, 78
creative nonfiction, 70, 86–87, 91–94
critical life reading, 75–76
critical race theory, 22n34
Cuder Domínguez, Pilar, 205
Curtis, Edward, 121

DasGupta, Sayantani, 21, 75, 200
Dawkins, Richard, 26n39
deconstruction, 26, 41, 44, 51. *See also* poststructuralism

Delany, Samuel, 169
Derrida, Jacques, 41, 51n15, 186
Dery, Mark, 170n11
Diamond v. Chakrabarty (1980), 17
Díaz, Junot, 170n11
disability, 30, 73, 195. *See also* ableism
discovery: colonialism and, 102–3, 128–30; computer-assisted analysis and, 105, 131; narrative, 83n24; scientific, 11, 14–15, 42, 50, 54, 63–65, 69, 102, 106–14
disease. *See* heritable disease
DNA: discourse on, 10, 40–44, 88, 116, 146–47, 160, 178–79, 197 (*see also* textual metaphors); expropriation of, 142–46; interpretation of, 53; as language, 3–4, 51–52; material existence of, 185, 221; meanings of, 20; morphology and, 97; noncoding, 11–12. *See also* genes; genomics
Doerfler, Jill, 110n18
Dolly the sheep, cloning of, 165n3, 187–88
Dorris, Michael, 102n3
Dracula, 158–59
drift, 6; genetic, 150
Du Bois, W. E. B., 213n26
Due, Tananarive, 145n24
Dupré, John, 12
Duster, Troy, 13
Dvořák, Antonín, 128–30
dyslexia, 55
dystopia, 28, 33–34, 181; capitalist, 196; genetic engineering and, 28, 167–81, 192–94, 205–7, 219; present inequities and, 169–75; in science fiction, 168

ecocriticism, 25, 33, 174
ecofeminism, 215n29
Ellison, Ralph, 82
embodied cognition, 136, 149–56, 174
empathy, 74, 200, 205–7, 213, 215
English language, 5, 50–52, 56–57, 179, 186–87
enslavement, 16, 76–77, 128, 135n2, 139–41, 143–47, 171–72, 175, 184, 202; slave narratives, 79
entanglement, 74n10, 201
environmental destruction, 169, 193, 197, 216

environmental stimuli, 12, 97
epigenetics, 11, 49–50, 61, 117, 145, 160
Erdrich, Louise, 28, 102n3
ethics: in biology and literature, 5, 6–7, 19–20, 24, 29, 31–32, 69–71, 73–76, 79, 97, 197, 222; expropriation and, 142–46; humanities scholarship and, 195; justice and, 215; kinship and, 137–46; life writing and, 19, 70–72, 80, 96–97 (*see also* critical life reading); physical senses and, 154–55; of recognition, 195–96. *See also* medical ethics; narrative ethics; scientific ethics
ethnocentrism, 7–8, 210
ethnofuturism, 27, 33, 169–71
eugenics, 7, 13, 64n28, 108, 168
Eugenides, Jeffrey, 28
evolution, 42, 107, 150, 160, 172, 183
exploitation, 8, 17; global systems of, 193; humanities scholarship and, 194–96, 202–13; present structures of, 166–68, 176; reading practices and, 20. *See also* medical exploitation; narrative exploitation
exploration, 63, 102–3
expropriation, 63, 142–46, 161
"Extended Evolutionary Synthesis" (EES), 42
extinction, 172, 196, 207, 217

families, 132–34, 135n2, 136–46, 161–62, 166, 179–80, 183, 188. *See also* kinship
Fanon, Frantz, 148n29, 151, 157
feminism. *See* Black feminist theories
fiction/nonfiction divide, 88–92. *See also* creative nonfiction
Fields, Barbara, 16
figurative language, 42, 51, 61, 89. *See also* metaphor
fixity, genetic and linguistic, 66, 106, 116, 131
fleshy reading, 25, 32, 136, 152–62
flexibility, 183, 184, 186
Foucault, Michel, 20n29, 41
freedom, 141n12, 148, 168, 191, 193
Fusco, Coco, 189

Garden, Rebecca, 74, 200
Gattaca (1997), 168

gender: egalitarianism, 180; essentialism, 4, 10, 20, 72–73; stereotypes, 77–78; vampire fiction and, 156–59
gender hierarchies, 86, 138, 147. *See also* heterosexism; sexism
gene fetishism, 4, 6, 10, 26, 65, 104, 168, 176, 202
gene therapy, 101, 105, 114, 122, 131
genes: complexity of, 44–47, 50–51; as indivisible, 31, 39–40, 43, 45–46, 53–65; mapping of, 61–63, 95; regulation of, 48–49. *See also* DNA; genomics
genetic ancestry, 50, 54, 111, 124, 133–34, 176. *See also* ancestry testing
genetic determinism, 4, 22, 42–43, 179; rejection of, 106, 115, 166
genetic discrimination, 16
genetic dismissivism, 22, 166
genetic engineering, 1–4, 7–8, 32, 45, 47, 133–34, 139, 162; anxieties about, 137; dystopia and, 28, 167–81, 192–94, 205–7, 219; fiction and, 88; kinship and, 137–46. *See also* transgenic species
genetic realism, 28–29
genetic recombination, 2, 124
genetic research, 5, 10–17, 19–20, 38–39, 41, 72–73; Indigenous criticism of, 32, 103–4; racial categories and, 55 (*see also* race). *See also* genomics
genetic sequencing, 51, 87, 105, 117; Indigenous people and, 17, 32, 106–11; as reading practice, 125; whole-genome, 9–11, 17, 32, 89. *See also* genomics
genetic similarity, 13, 148, 180
genetic surveillance, 169, 176. *See also* surveillance
genetic testing, 68n1, 72–73, 117–18. *See also* ancestry testing
genome time, 172–74
genomics, 5; as creative nonfiction, 92; oppressive politics and, 54; "splitting and lumping," 53; whole-genome sequencing, 9–11, 17, 32, 89. *See also* Human Genome Diversity Project (HGDP); Human Genome Project (HGP); postgenomic age; postgenomic literature
genre boundaries, 27–30, 48–49, 90. *See also* fiction/nonfiction divide

geology, 24, 201, 207
Gill, Josie, 13, 15n22, 16, 22, 22n34, 30, 179n33
Gilmore, Leigh, 75, 85n26
Gobert, Judy, 107n9
Gretzky, Madison, 219n32
Gross, Lawrence W., 123
Guaymi General Congress, 107n10, 109n16
Gyasi, Yaa, 135n2

Hall, Stuart, 148
Hamann-Rose, Paul, 60n23
Hamner, Everett, 21n30, 22, 26, 27n40, 88n30, 108n11, 168n8, 174, 196n9, 214
Hanson, Clare, 26n39, 30, 94n36, 179n35
haplotypes, 111, 113, 122–23, 178
HapMap project, 15n20
Haraway, Donna, 23, 190, 195–96, 215
Harjo, Joy, 102n3
Harris, Taylor, 30
Harry, Debra, 107
Hartman, Saidiya, 16, 135n2
health, 4, 13n17, 14, 17, 18, 72–73, 77, 84, 125, 137, 153, 168, 169, 204. *See also* heritable disease
health care, 8, 34, 73, 80–81, 193, 199. *See also* medical ethics; medical exploitation; medical racism
health humanities, 9, 19, 21
HeLa cells, 17, 18–19, 68n1, 69–70, 76–86, 97, 140, 183n36
Hemings, Sally, 19
heritable disease, 10, 12, 31, 37–38, 53–54, 59–60, 63–66, 73
Herman, Luc, 88n29
Herrington, Emily, 42
Herrnstein, Richard, 54
heterosexism, 175, 187, 200. *See also* sexism
hierarchy: in science/humanities binary, 197. *See also* gender hierarchies; racial hierarchies
historical context. *See* context
homophobia, 33, 187
Höpker, Karin, 88n28, 93, 95n37, 96n38
Hopkinson, Nalo, 170n11
Howe, LeAnne, 118, 119n36

human beings: categories of difference, 59; exceptionalism, 195, 210–13; human/nonhuman binary, 195–96. *See also* genes; identity; subjectivities
Human Genome Diversity Project (HGDP), 15n20, 17; critiqued as "vampire project," 32, 103, 106–11, 114, 119
Human Genome Project (HGP), 5, 13, 42, 62, 102, 106, 168, 176, 180; Ethical, Legal, and Social Implications (ELSI), 21, 198–99
humanities and arts scholarship: devaluation of, 194, 198, 202; ethical and social contexts, 8, 22–24, 33–34, 97; instrumentalization of, 198–200, 204, 208; systems of exploitation and, 194–96, 202–13. *See also* interdisciplinarity; science/humanities binary
humor, 113, 122–31
Huntington's disease, 63–65
Hurston, Zora Neale, 19, 83

Ibrahim, Habiba, 143
identity, 15, 66; authenticity and, 102; blood quantum, 110–11, 124; collective, 134 (*see also* race); connection and, 166; genetics and, 86, 104, 110, 113, 123. *See also* ancestry testing
illocutionary language, 53
imperialism, 7–8, 62–64, 119, 175, 179, 180. *See also* colonialism
India. *See* Partition of India and Pakistan
Indian Arts and Crafts Act (IACA), 102, 119
Indigenous futurism, 27. *See also* ethnofuturism
Indigenous people, 14, 211; ancestry testing, 15, 110, 113; authenticity and, 105, 112–13, 127; criticism of genetic research, 32, 103–4; ecocriticism and, 25; genealogies, 109–10; genetic sequencing and, 17, 32, 106–11; healing and genome survivance, 102, 104, 113–15, 122–31; residential schools, 179; scientific ethics and, 139; sovereignty, 104, 107, 111, 126; stereotypes of, 103–4, 112, 120; tribal membership, 110; victimization of, 123. *See also* Native storytelling
Indigenous People's Council on Biocolonialism, 107
individualism, 41, 166

inequity, 30, 33, 74, 167, 169, 174. *See also* colonialism; exploitation; heterosexism; racism; sexism
informatics, 40
informed consent, 7, 16, 108, 140. *See also* consent
inheritance, 38. *See also* genetic ancestry; heritable disease
Inherit the Wind (1955), 183
"inhumanities," 23–24, 34, 194–96, 220–21
instability, genetic and linguistic, 2–3, 39–40, 116; textual, 95
interdisciplinarity, 20–24, 34, 200–202
International Human Genome Sequencing Consortium, 9
intersectional oppression, 33, 139, 179
interspecies literacy, 213–21
intersubjectivity, 183, 191, 201
intertextuality, 50, 173
irony, 122–23
Ishiguro, Kazuo, 28

Jablonka, Eva, 42
Jakobson, Roman, 40
Jasanoff, Sheila, 75n12
Jennings, Hope, 211n24, 215n29
Jewish ancestry, 101, 186; Sephardism, 120n38, 127
Johannsen, Wilhelm, 52
Johnson, Mark, 149, 158
Johnson, T. R., 41n5, 61–62

Kay, Lily, 4–5, 20, 26, 40–41
Keller, Evelyn Fox, 11, 40; *Refiguring Life*, 42–43
Khan, Yasmin, 57
Kimmerer, Robin Wall, 25
King, Mary-Claire, 106
King, Thomas, 102n3
kinship, 134–48, 153, 161–62, 183, 191, 215. *See also* families
Korn, David, 81
Krupat, Arnold, 115, 117

Lacks, David, 19, 80
Lacks, Henrietta, 16–19, 68–70, 76–86, 94, 140, 143
Lacks-Pullum, Deborah, 68–69, 80, 82–86
Lake, Christina Bieber, 219n32
Lakoff, George, 149, 158
Landecker, Hannah, 77, 169
language: ambivalence in, 39–40, 204; context and, 66–67; distinction between writing and, 51–52; DNA compared to, 3–4, 51–52; figurative, 42, 51, 61, 89; humans as "languaging" species, 147, 148, 153, 158n37; illocutionary, 53; instability of, 2–3, 39–40, 95, 116; as marker of human distinction, 207–13, 217–18; performativity of, 52–53; perlocutionary, 53; power and agency of, 215–16; recombinative games, 2–3, 38, 105, 118, 122–31, 167; scientific, 27, 42, 52–53, 58; words in, 207–10, 217. *See also* English language; narrative play; "splitting and lumping"; textual metaphors
Laquer, Thomas, 127n44
Latine futurism, 27, 33. *See also* ethnofuturism
Latine people, 175–79, 182, 186–87, 191
Lawn, Jennifer, 202, 219
Le Plongeon, Augustus, 114n27
Lenout, Geert, 88n29
lesbians, 182, 189n46
liberation, 43, 148, 152, 170, 175, 191, 196
life writing, 29–32, 70–76; collaborative, 19, 71, 79, 81–86; ethical issues in, 19, 70–72, 80, 96–97 (*see also* critical life reading); kinds of, 39; metafiction and, 92. *See also* autobiography; biography
linguistic turn, 25, 174
literacy, 84, 213–21
literary allusions, 39, 44–47, 49–50, 53, 55, 66–67
literary criticism, 21
literature: linguistic turn, 25, 174; material turn, 25–27, 174; power and privilege in, 197 (*see also* ethics). *See also* humanities and arts scholarship
Lock, Margaret, 68n1, 109
Longfellow, Henry Wadsworth, 112–13, 129
López Rúa, Paula, 204n19
Lummi, 111n21
Lyon, Jeff, 47

Maori Congress Indigenous Peoples Roundtable, 107n10
mapping, 61–63
Marks, Jonathan, 180–81
mastery, 75, 76, 80, 200
material turn, 25–27, 174
material-semiotic agency, 189–90
matter, narrative dimensions of, 5, 8–9, 25–27, 105. *See also* bionarrativity; fleshy reading
Maturana, Humberto, 148n29
Maya, 101, 114
McDevitt, Kelly, 142n15
McHugh, Kathleen, 188n45
McKittrick, Katherine, 43, 148
medical ethics, 70, 73–74, 84, 139, 197–99. *See also* consent; ethics
medical exploitation, 16–17, 31–32, 34, 77–81, 86, 136, 139–40, 143–46
medical racism, 78, 80–81, 139–40
memoir, 27, 31. *See also* life writing
memory, 171–72, 174, 205–6, 221; "racial memory," 115
Mendel, Gregor, 1n1, 50, 58
Menely, Tobias, 24, 201
Merleau-Ponty, Maurice, 149n30
metafictional reading, 26, 31, 70, 90–97
metaphor: novel, 149–50, 153, 158–59. *See also* figurative language; textual metaphors
metatextuality, 3, 9, 31–32, 38, 50–52, 55, 65, 67; in life writing, 70; self-reflexivity and, 189; textual metaphors and, 27, 30, 89–90
Mignolo, Walter, 148n28
migration, 6, 15, 50, 59, 110
millennial anxieties, 175–77
Mitchell, David, 28
Mitchell, W. J. T., 203n17
Mitochondrial Eve, 142
modernist fiction, 49–50
molecular biology, 9–17, 19–20, 26–28, 38, 40, 197–98; authority of, 197. *See also* genetic research; genomics
Momaday, N. Scott, 25, 115, 117
Morrison, Toni, 23, 134–35; *Beloved*, 170n13, 171–72
Moya, Paula M. L., 29, 170

Mukherjee, Siddhartha, *The Gene*, 30–31, 37–41, 43, 45–46, 53–66
multiplicity, 116, 125
Muñoz, José Esteban, 165n3, 171, 176, 177n29
Murray, Charles, 54
mutation, 1n1, 2–3, 6, 44, 116, 184

narrative: appropriation, 105, 119–22; doubling of, 214; human imagination and, 218–19; intimacy in, 80; material dimensions of, 5, 8–9, 25–27, 105 (*see also* bionarrativity; fleshy reading); misdirection and double-voicedness, 82
narrative desire, 94, 96
narrative ethics, 70–71, 73, 96–97, 197. *See also* ethics
narrative exploitation, 31–32, 78–79, 86–97
narrative humility, 75–76, 79, 81, 83, 97
narrative medicine, 73–74, 198–200
narrative play, 106, 111n21, 113, 117–18, 122, 124–28, 130–31
narrative theory, 21
National Institutes of Health, 108
Native American Graves Protection and Repatriation Act (NAGPRA), 102, 109, 119, 121
Native American Renaissance, 116
Native BioData Consortium (NBDC), 17
Native storytelling: academic misreadings of, 105–6, 112–13; "stories in the blood," 115–18; trickster discourse and, 113, 123, 127–28. *See also* Indigenous people
nativism, 2, 7
Nayar, Pramod, 154
necropolitics, 193
Nelkin, Dorothy, 61
Nelson, Alondra, 15–16, 68n1, 144
neocolonialism, 17, 63, 103–4, 119, 125
neoliberalism, 135n2, 200, 214, 216, 220
new materialisms, 174, 200n15
New World Symphony (Dvořák), 128–30
Nguyen, Viet Thanh, 23–24, 34, 172, 194–95, 205, 215, 221
"noble savage" stereotype, 120
nonfiction genres, 29–30
Noriega, Chon, 186n40

novel metaphors, 149–50, 153, 158–59
Nowacyk, Margaret, 30
Nussbaum, Martha, 23, 199, 219

objectification, 2, 104n7, 184–85, 198, 213
objectivism, genomic, 41
objectivity, 42, 75n12, 112–13, 156, 185. *See also* truth
Ojibwe, 120
open-endedness, narrative and genetic, 53, 75, 96n38, 125, 131, 174
oppression: humanities scholarship and, 196; intersectional, 33, 139, 179. *See also* colonialism; exploitation; heterosexism; racism; sexism
origin, 6, 38, 51, 62, 65, 110, 134, 155, 184–85
Osage, 118n34
othering, 22, 146
Ozeki, Ruth, 167; *All Over Creation*, 1–9, 28, 198

Partition of India and Pakistan, 31, 53–54, 57–62
Patchett, Ann, 28
patents, 7, 16–17, 29, 62, 78n17, 84, 92, 107, 109
performance art, 27, 167, 181, 188–89, 189n46
perlocutionary language, 53
permeability, 167, 181, 184
personality, 10, 94
Peterkin, Allan, 74n11
phenomenology, 151
phrenology, 111
Plantationocene, 212n25
plastic, 184–85
Pocahontas, 119–21, 127, 130, 177–78
polygenesis, 111
polysemy, 117
possibility and potentiality, linguistic and genetic, 150, 152, 161, 167, 172–73, 176, 180–84, 218
postgenomic age, 9–17
postgenomic literature, 3–9, 18–30; definition of, 18
posthumanism, 174, 215
postmodernism, 125

poststructuralism, 26, 41, 76. *See also* deconstruction
power: asymmetrical relations of, 140–43, 148; hierarchical systems of, 210 (*see also* gender hierarchies; racial hierarchies); humanities scholarship and, 20, 112, 197, 200; negotiations of, 152, 162; systems of, 97
Powers, Richard, 27–29, 67; "The Book of Me," 88–89; *Generosity: An Enhancement*, 28, 31–32, 70, 86–97, 198; *The Gold Bug Variations*, 28–29, 88; *Orfeo*, 28, 88
privacy, 7, 16, 81, 139, 168; life writing and, 19, 71, 80
privilege, 34, 104n7, 169, 193, 197
progress, 172, 174
property rights (ownership of genetic material), 16–17, 41, 69–70, 81, 109, 184
Proust, Marcel, 49–50

queer futurity, 171, 179
queer women of color, 179
Quijano, Aníbal, 148n28

race, 55–56, 132; and color-blind ideology, 178; essentialism, 4, 12–16, 20, 115, 117; genetics and, 85–86; interracial relations, 158; social constructionist approach to, 16; stereotypes, 77–78, 83, 103–4, 112, 120; vampire fiction and, 155–62. *See also* Blackness; Indigenous people; whiteness
racial hierarchies, 86, 111, 137, 147, 159–60; white anxieties about, 175, 177, 187
racialized bodies, 147, 151
racism, 7–8, 10, 13, 33–34, 145–47, 208; genetics and, 54, 107–8, 169, 176, 180; humanities scholarship and, 23–24, 194–95, 200; present structures of, 167, 169, 175–76, 187; scientific, 108; speciesism and, 161. *See also* medical racism
Ramírez, Catherine, 171
reading practices: adaptation and, 124–31, 174; association, 125; cannibalistic, 79–83; close reading, 31, 90, 95; context and, 90, 97; counternarratives and insurgent voices, 81–86; critical life reading, 75–76;

disembodied, 135, 147; ethical issues in, 6–7, 19–20, 24, 97; fleshy reading, 25, 32, 136, 152–62; against the grain, 105–6; material, embodied, and experiential, 40, 149–62, 189, 221–22; metatextual aspects and, 40; narrative humility, 75–76, 79, 81, 83, 97; self-fulfilling, 94, 96; sequencing, 125; trans-corporeal, 25, 33, 181, 221–22; trickster, 113, 123, 127–28

realist fiction, 27, 28–29
Reardon, Jenny, 14, 16, 29, 95, 107, 166
recombinations, 2, 3, 38, 44, 50, 105, 123–24, 167, 173
Reich, David, 13n17
remembering. *See* memory
reproductive practices, 41, 135n2, 138. *See also* cloning; genetic engineering; sterilization; surrogacy
revision, 94–95
Richardson, Sarah S., 11–12, 13n15
Roberts, Dorothy, 14, 78, 139
Rodríguez, Juana María, 118n33
Román, David, 165n1
Roof, Judith, 39, 41, 42
Roosevelt, Theodore, 121
Rose, Hilary, 46n11
Rose, Steven, 46n11
Rosenberg, Noah, 14, 108n14
Rosner, Mary, 41n5, 61–62
Rotimi, Charles, 14n18
Ruiz, Sandra, 171
Rural Advancement Foundation International (RAFI), 107n10

Said, Edward, 23
Schiff, Sarah Eden, 115
Schoolcraft, Henry Rowe, 112–13, 119–20
Schoolcraft, Jane Johnston, 120
science fiction, 27–28, 168–70
science/humanities binary, 5, 16, 21, 33–34, 88, 92–94, 97, 103–4, 194–97. *See also* interdisciplinarity
scientific ethics, 21, 87–88, 139, 197–99. *See also* ethics
scientific language, 27, 42, 52–53, 58
seeds, 1–2, 6–9, 17, 221
self-reflexivity, 27, 75, 81, 90, 94, 95, 189
sensorimotor intelligence, 149, 152, 153–55

"sentence" metaphors, 38, 44, 46, 48, 50–53, 56–57, 66, 115
sexism, 7–8, 33–34, 169, 175–76, 208, 212; humanities scholarship and, 194–95, 200. *See also* heterosexism
sexuality, 2, 29, 72, 140, 175, 178, 180, 185–88, 192, 204–6
signatures, bionarrative, 105–6, 117, 118, 122–32
Silko, Leslie Marmon, 102n3
Sims, Marion, 16, 140
single-nucleotide polymorphisms (SNPs), 14, 109, 145
Skloot, Rebecca, 39, 67; *The Immortal Life of Henrietta Lacks*, 18–19, 30, 31–32, 68–70, 76–86, 94, 97, 143
slave narratives, 79. *See also* enslavement
slipstream, 27
Smith, Linda Tuhiwai, 112n23
Smith, Zadie, 28
Solomon, Miriam, 199–200
Sommer, Doris, 79–80, 82
species, 134; distinctions between, 137; relations within and between, 138–41, 158, 167, 180–81, 183, 191, 195–96, 213, 215
speciesism, 146, 161, 202, 208, 212; humanities scholarship and, 194–95
speculative fiction, 27–28, 33
speech, 51
Spillers, Hortense, 76–77, 77n16, 136, 147–48, 150
Spivak, Gayatri, 23
"splitting and lumping," 31, 39–40, 46, 53
Squier, Susan, 22, 199
STEM fields, 23, 194, 198–99
sterilization, 139, 143
Stevens, Hallam, 11–12
Stevens, Wallace, "On the Road Home," 46–47, 65–66
Stockett, Kathryn, 55
Stoker, Bram, 158
Stone, Christopher, 121
"stories in the blood," 115–18
structuralism, 42; in linguistics, 40
subjectivities: abject, 182; queer interspecies intersubjectivity, 183, 191
Sullivan, Heather I., 214n28
Sumara, Dennis, 150

surrogacy, 135n2, 139, 184
surveillance, 33, 72, 167, 169, 176, 193, 211
survivance, 104, 111, 114, 116–18, 122–24, 130; genome, 104, 111, 114, 122, 124
Swift, Jonathan, 61, 194n5
systems biology, 12, 150, 174

TallBear, Kim, 15, 110, 111
Tamazight women, 86
Taylor, Jesse Oak, 24, 201
teleology, 174
textual metaphors, 3–6, 26–27, 30–31, 40–44; in Atwood, 202; cell membranes, 221–22; context and, 42–44, 66–67; DNA as "Book of Life," 4–6, 10, 29–31, 38–41, 47–48, 76, 115; DNA as code, 4, 10, 40, 45, 115, 162; DNA as sentence, 38, 44, 46, 48, 50–53, 56–57, 66, 115; material status of language and, 43; metatextuality and, 27, 30, 89–90; in Mukherjee, 38–41, 44–53; postmodern treatment of, 50–52; potentiality and, 173; in Powers, 89; in Vizenor, 114–15
Thacker, Eugene, 25n37
Third World Network, 107n10
time, 190–91. *See also* genome time; usable futures
Tinker, George "Tink," 118n34
trans-corporeal reading, 25, 33, 181, 221–22
trans-corporeality, 167–68, 174, 181–91
transgender athletes, 10n8, 73
transgenic species, 2, 33, 137, 167, 169, 175–76, 182–83, 192, 196, 206–7, 215
transhumanism, 211
trauma, 54, 86–87, 91, 93, 120, 160–61; intergenerational, 170, 175; of Partition of India and Pakistan, 59–61
trickster discourse, 111n21, 113, 117, 123, 127–28
Tropicana, Carmelita. *See* Troyano, Alina
Troyano, Alina, 25; *Chicas 2000*, 33, 137, 165–69, 175–91, 193

truth: construction of, 87–88; demand for, 90–91. *See also* objectivity

Ukupseni Declaration on the HGDP, 107n10
Umatilla, 109
usable futures, 33, 167–91, 193, 215
usable past, 15, 33, 167, 170, 171n15
utopia, 168

Vampira (1974), 145n24
vampire fiction, 27, 32, 93n34, 132, 142–43, 155–62
"vampire projects," 32, 103, 106–11, 114, 119, 132
Varela, Francisco, 148n29
Venter, Craig, 62
Vizenor, Gerald, 23, 25, 67, 108, 166n4, 167; "Bone Courts," 121–22; "Genome Survivance," 111; *The Heirs of Columbus*, 32, 101–6, 113–32, 161; "Trickster Discourse," 113; White Earth Constitution, 110n18, 111–12

Wade, Nicholas, 13n17
Wald, Priscilla, 81, 160n38, 169
Washington, Harriet, 16, 77, 78, 139
Watkins, Susan, 194n6
Weheliye, Alexander, 146, 148
Weinbaum, Alys Eve, 135n2, 170
Wexler, Alice, 30; *Mapping Fate*, 64–65, 73
Wexler, Nancy, 63–64
white supremacy, 175, 177, 187. *See also* racial hierarchies
whiteness, 79–81, 151, 158–59; "white savior" narrative, 84
Whyte, Kyle, 25
Winant, Howard, 148n28
Wolfe, Cary, 23, 195–96
World Congress of Indigenous Peoples, 107
WOW Café Theater, 189n46
Wynter, Sylvia, 136, 146, 147–48, 152, 153

NEW SUNS: RACE, GENDER, AND SEXUALITY IN THE SPECULATIVE
Susana M. Morris and Kinitra D. Brooks, Series Editors

Scholarly examinations of speculative fiction have been a burgeoning academic field for more than twenty-five years, but there has been a distinct lack of attention to how attending to nonhegemonic positionalities transforms our understanding of the speculative. New Suns: Race, Gender, and Sexuality in the Speculative addresses this oversight and promotes scholarship at the intersections of race, gender, sexuality, and the speculative, engaging interdisciplinary fields of research across literary, film, and cultural studies that examine multiple pasts, presents, and futures. Of particular interest are studies that offer new avenues into thinking about popular genre fictions and fan communities, including but not limited to the study of Afrofuturism, comics, ethnogothicism, ethnosurrealism, fantasy, film, futurity studies, gaming, horror, literature, science fiction, and visual studies. New Suns particularly encourages submissions that are written in a clear, accessible style that will be read both by scholars in the field as well as by nonspecialists.

Reading in the Postgenomic Age: Race, Discipline, and Bionarrativity in Contemporary North American Literature
LESLEY LARKIN

Black Speculative Feminisms: Memory and Liberated Futures in Black Women's Fiction
CASSANDRA L. JONES

Anti-Blackness and Human Monstrosity in Black American Horror Fiction
JERRY RAFIKI JENKINS

Gendered Defenders: Marvel's Heroines in Transmedia Spaces
EDITED BY BRYAN J. CARR AND META G. CARSTARPHEN

The Dreamer and the Dream: Afrofuturism and Black Religious Thought
ROGER A. SNEED

Diverse Futures: Science Fiction and Authors of Color
JOY SANCHEZ-TAYLOR

Impossible Stories: On the Space and Time of Black Destructive Creation
JOHN MURILLO III

Literary Afrofuturism in the Twenty-First Century
EDITED BY ISIAH LAVENDER III AND LISA YASZEK

Jordan Peele's Get Out: *Political Horror*
EDITED BY DAWN KEETLEY

Unstable Masks: Whiteness and American Superhero Comics
EDITED BY SEAN GUYNES AND MARTIN LUND

Afrofuturism Rising: The Literary Prehistory of a Movement
ISIAH LAVENDER III

The Paradox of Blackness in African American Vampire Fiction
JERRY RAFIKI JENKINS

www.ingramcontent.com/pod-product-compliance
Lightning Source LLC
Chambersburg PA
CBHW020122240426
43673CB00038B/563